Lecture Notes in Computer Scie

T0238109

Commenced Publication in 1973
Founding and Former Series Editors:
Gerhard Goos, Juris Hartmanis, and Jan van Leeuwen

Jean-Pierre Banâtre   Pascal Fradet
Jean-Louis Giavitto   Olivier Michel (Eds.)

Unconventional Programming Paradigms

International Workshop UPP 2004
Le Mont Saint Michel, France, September 15-17, 2004
Revised Selected and Invited Papers

 Springer

Volume Editors

Jean-Pierre Banâtre
Université de Rennes I and INRIA/IRISA
Campus de Beaulieu, 35042 Rennes Cedex, France
E-mail: jpbanatre@inria.fr

Pascal Fradet
INRIA Rhône-Alpes
655 av. de l'Europe, 38330 Montbonnot, France
E-mail: Pascal.Fradet@inria.fr

Jean-Louis Giavitto
LaMI/Université d'Évry Val d'Essonne
Tour Evry 2, GENOPOLE, 523 Place des terrasses de l'agora, 91000 Évry, France
E-mail: giavitto@lami.univ-evry.fr

Olivier Michel
LaMI/Université d'Évry Val d'Essonne
Cours Monseigneur Romero, 91025 Evry Cedex, France
E-mail: michel@lami.univ-evry.fr

Library of Congress Control Number: 2005928846

CR Subject Classification (1998): F.1, D.1, D.3, F.3, F.4

ISSN   0302-9743
ISBN-10   3-540-27884-2 Springer Berlin Heidelberg New York
ISBN-13   978-3-540-27884-9 Springer Berlin Heidelberg New York

Springer is a part of Springer Science+Business Media

springeronline.com

© Springer-Verlag Berlin Heidelberg 2005
Printed in Germany

Typesetting: Camera-ready by author, data conversion by Scientific Publishing Services, Chennai, India
Printed on acid-free paper   SPIN: 11527800   06/3142   5 4 3 2 1 0

Preface

Nowadays, developers have to face the proliferation of hardware and software environments, the increasing demands of the users, the multiplication of programs and the sharing of information, competences and services thanks to the generalization of data bases and communication networks. A program is no more a monolithic entity conceived, produced and finalized before being used. A program is now seen as an open and adaptive frame, which, for example, can dynamically incorporate services not foreseen by the initial designer. These new needs call for new control structures and program interactions.

Unconventional approaches to programming have long been developed in various niches and constitute a reservoir of alternative ways to face the programming languages crisis. New models of programming (e.g., bio-inspired computing, artificial chemistry, amorphous computing, ...) are also currently experiencing a renewed period of growth as they face specific needs and new application domains. These approaches provide new abstractions and notations or develop new ways of interacting with programs. They are implemented by embedding new sophisticated data structures in a classical programming model (API), by extending an existing language with new constructs (to handle concurrency, exceptions, open environments, ...), by conceiving new software life cycles and program executions (aspect weaving, run-time compilation) or by relying on an entire new paradigm to specify a computation. They are inspired by theoretical considerations (e.g., topological, algebraic or logical foundations), driven by the domain at hand (domain-specific languages like PostScript, musical notation, animation, signal processing, etc.) or by metaphors taken from various areas (quantum computing, computing with molecules, information processing in biological tissues, problem solving from nature, ethological and social modeling). The practical applications of these new programming paradigms and languages prompt research into the expressivity, semantics and implementation of programming languages and systems architectures, as well as into the algorithmic complexity and optimization of programs.

The purpose of the workshop was to bring together researchers from the various communities working on wild and crazy ideas in programming languages to present their results, to foster fertilization between theory and practice, and to favor the dissemination and growth of new programming paradigms.

The contributions were split up into five tracks:

- Chemical Computing
- Amorphous Computing
- Bio-inspired Computing
- Autonomic Computing
- Generative Programming

This workshop kept the same informal style of a previous successful meeting held in 1991 in Le Mont Saint Michel under the title *New Directions in High-Level Parallel Programming Languages*. Each track was handled by a well-known researcher in the concerned area. Each track leader was in charge of inviting other researchers on his topic and organizing his session. These track leaders plus the four promoters of this initiative constituted the Program Committee of the workshop (see below). This volume gathers extended and revised versions of most of the papers presented at the workshop, including the invited presentation given by Philippe Jorrand on quantum computing.

On the practical side, several persons contributed to the success of the workshop. We offer our sincere thanks to all of them. We are particularly grateful to Edith Corre and Elisabeth Lebret of IRISA and to Rémi Ronchaud from ERCIM who were very efficient and professional in the organization. Finally, we address our sincere acknowledgments to all the participants who, beside the high quality of their scientific contribution, made the workshop a friendly and unique event.

April 2005

Jean-Pierre Banâtre
Pascal Fradet
Jean-Louis Giavitto
Olivier Michel

Organization

The workshop was jointly supported by the European Commission's Information Society Technologies Programme, Future and Emerging Technologies Activity, and the US National Science Foundation, Directorate for Computer and Information Science and Engineering. This workshop is part of a series of strategic workshops that identify key research challenges and opportunities in information technology. It was organized by ERCIM (European Research Consortium for Informatics and Mathematics) and received additional support from INRIA, Université d'Evry Val d'Essonne, Université de Rennes 1, and Microsoft Research.

Program Committee

Organizing Committee

Jean-Pierre Banâtre	Université de Rennes 1, and INRIA/IRISA, France
Pascal Fradet	INRIA Rhône-Alpes, France
Jean-Louis Giavitto	LaMI/Université d'Evry Val d'Essonne, France
Olivier Michel	LaMI/Université d'Evry Val d'Essonne, France

Track Leaders

Pierre Cointe	Ecole des Mines de Nantes, France *Generative Programming*
Daniel Coore	University of West Indies, Jamaica *Amorphous Computing*
Peter Dittrich	Friedrich Schiller University Jena, Germany *Chemical Computing*
Manish Parashar	Rutgers, The State University of New Jersey, USA *Autonomic Computing*
Gheorghe Păun	Institute of Mathematics of the Romanian Academy, Romania *Bio-inspired Computing*

Table of Contents

Bio-inspired Computing

Autonomic Computing

Generative Programming

Invited Talk

From Quantum Physics to Programming Languages: A Process Algebraic Approach

Philippe Jorrand and Marie Lalire

Leibniz Laboratory, 46 avenue Felix Viallet,
38000 Grenoble, France
{Philippe.Jorrand, Marie.Lalire}@imag.fr

Abstract. Research in quantum computation is looking for the consequences of having information encoding, processing and communication exploit the laws of quantum physics, i.e. the laws of the ultimate knowledge that we have, today, of the foreign world of elementary particles, as described by quantum mechanics. After an introduction to the principles of quantum information processing and a brief survey of the major breakthroughs brought by the first ten years of research in this domain, this paper concentrates on a typically "computer science" way to reach a deeper understanding of what it means to compute with quantum resources, namely on the design of programming languages for quantum algorithms and protocols, and on the questions raised by the semantics of such languages. Special attention is devoted to the process algebraic approach to such languages, through a presentation of QPAlg, the Quantum Process Algebra which is being designed by the authors.

1 From Quantum Physics to Computation

Information is physical: the laws which govern its encoding, processing and communication are bound by those of its unavoidably physical incarnation. In today's informatics, information obeys the laws of Newton's and Maxwell's classical physics: this statement holds all the way from commercial computers down to (up to?) Turing machines and lambda-calculus. Today's computation is classical.

Quantum information processing and communication was born some ten years ago, as a child of two major scientific achievements of the 20th century, namely quantum physics and information sciences. The driving force of research in quantum computation is that of looking for the consequences of having information encoding, processing and communication based upon the laws of quantum physics, i.e. the ultimate knowledge that we have, today, of the foreign world of elementary particles, as described by quantum mechanics. The principles of quantum information processing are very briefly introduced in this section. For a more detailed, but still concise and gentle introduction, see [24]. A pedagogical and rather thorough textbook on quantum computing is [21]. For a dense and theoretically profound presentation, the reader is referred to [16].

J.-P. Banâtre et al. (Eds.): UPP 2004, LNCS 3566, pp. 1–16, 2005.

1.1 Four Postulates for Computing

Quantum mechanics, which is the mathematical formulation of the laws of quantum physics, relies on four postulates: (*i*) the state of a quantum system (i.e. a particle, or a collection of particles) is a unit element of a Hilbert space, that is a vector of norm 1 in a *d*-dimensional complex vector space; (*ii*) the evolution of the state of a closed quantum system (i.e. not interacting with its -classical- environment) is deterministic, linear, reversible and characterized by a unitary operator, that is by a *d*x*d* unitary matrix applied to the state vector; (*iii*) the measurement of a quantum system (i.e. the observation of a quantum system by its -classical- environment) irreversibly modifies the state of the system by performing a projection of the state vector onto a probabilistically chosen subspace of the Hilbert space, with renormalization of the resulting vector, and returns a value (e.g. an integer) to the classical world, which just tells which subspace was chosen; and (*iv*) the state space of a quantum system composed of several quantum subsystems is the tensor product of the state spaces of its components (given two vector spaces P and Q of dimensions p and q respectively, their tensor product is a vector space of dimension pxq).

The question is then: how to take advantage of these postulates to the benefits of computation? The most widely developed approach to quantum computation exploits all four postulates in a rather straightforward manner. The elementary physical carrier of information is a qubit (quantum bit), i.e. a quantum system (electron, photon, ion, ...) with a 2-dimensional state space (postulate *i*); the state of a *n*-qubit register lives in a 2^n-dimensional Hilbert space, the tensor product of n 2-dimensional Hilbert spaces (postulate *iv*). Then, by imitating in the quantum world the most traditional organization of classical computation, quantum computations are considered as comprising three steps in sequence: first, preparation of the initial state of a quantum register (postulate *iii* can be used for that, possibly with postulate *ii*); second, computation, by means of deterministic unitary transformations of the register state (postulate *ii*); and third, output of a result by probabilistic measurement of all or part of the register (postulate *iii*).

1.2 Quantum Ingredients for Information Processing

These postulates and their consequences can be interpreted from a more informational and computational point of view, thus providing the elementary quantum ingredients which are at the basis of quantum algorithm design:

Superposition. At any given moment, the state of quantum register of n qubits is a vector in a 2^n-dimensional complex vector space, i.e. a vector with at most 2^n non zero complex components, one for each of the 2^n different values on n bits: the basis of this vector space comprises the 2^n vectors $|i>$, for i in $\{0,1\}^n$ ($|i>$ is Dirac's notation for vectors denoting quantum states). This fact is exploited computationally by considering that this register can actually contain a superposition of all the 2^n different values on n bits, whereas a classical register of n bits may contain only one of these values at any given moment.

Quantum Parallelism and Deterministic Computation. Let f be a function from $\{0,1\}^n$ to $\{0,1\}^m$ and x be a quantum register of n qubits initialized in a superposition of all values in $\{0,1\}^n$ (this initialization can be done by one very simple step). Then, computing $f(x)$ is achieved by a deterministic, linear and unitary operation on the state of x: because of linearity, a single application of this operation produces all 2^n values of f in a single computation step. Performing this operation for any, possibly non linear f while obeying the linearity and unitarity laws of the quantum world, requires a register of $n+m$ qubits formed of the register x, augmented with a register y of m qubits. Initialy, y is in any arbitray state $|s>$ on m qubits: before the computation of f, the larger register of $n+m$ qubits contains a superposition of all pairs $|i,s>$ for i in $\{0,1\}^n$. After the computation of f, it contains a superposition of all pairs $|i, s\oplus f(i)>$ for i in $\{0,1\}^n$, where $\oplus$ is bitwise addition modulo 2. It is easy to verify that, for any f, this operation on a register of $n+m$ qubits is unitary (it is its own inverse). In many cases, it will be applied with $s=0$, which results in a superposition of all simpler pairs $|i, f(i)>$ for i in $\{0,1\}^n$.

Probabilistic Measurement and Output of a Result. After f has been computed, all its values $f(i)$, for i in $\{0,1\}^n$, are superposed in the y part (m qubits) of the register of $n+m$ qubits, each of these values facing (in the pair $|i,f(i)>$) their corresponding i which is still stored in the unchanged superposition contained in the x part (n qubits) of that register. Observing the contents of y will return only one value, j, among the possible values of f. This value is chosen with a probability which depends on f since, e.g. if $f(i)=j$ for more than one values of i, the probability of obtaining j as a result will be higher than that of obtaining k if $f(i)=k$ for only one value of I (and the probability of obtaining l if there is no i such that $f(i)=l$ will of course be 0). This measurement also causes the superposition in y to be projected onto the 1-dimensional subspace corresponding to the basis state $|j>$, i.e. the state of the y part collapses to $|j>$, which implies that all other values of f which were previously superposed in y are irreversibly lost.

Interference. Using appropriate unitary operations, the results of the 2^n parallel computations of f over its domain of definition can be made to interfere with each other. Substractive interference will lower the probability of observing some of these value in y, whereas additive interference will increase the probability of observing other values and bring it closer to 1. Because of probabilistic measurement, a major aim of the organization and principles of quantum algorithms will be to assemble the unitary operations for a given computation in such a way that, when a final measurement is applied, a relevant result has a high probability to be obtained.

Entangled States. Measuring y after the computation of f is in fact measuring only m qubits (the y part) among the $n+m$ qubits of a register. The state of this larger register is a superposition of all pairs $|i,f(i)>$ for i in $\{0,1\}^n$ (e.g., in this superposition, there is no pair like $|2,f(3)>$): this superposition is not a free cross-product of the domain $\{0,1\}^n$ of f by its image in $\{0,1\}^m$, i.e. there is a strong correlation between the contents of the x and y parts of the register. As a consequence, if measuring the y part returns a value j, with the state of that part collapsing to the basis state $|j>$, the state of the larger register will itself collapse to a superposition of all remaining pairs $|i,j>$

such that $f(i)=j$. This means that, in addition to producing a value j, the measurement of the y part also causes the state of the x part to collapse to a superposition of all elements of the $f^{-1}(j)$ subset of the domain of f. This correlation between the x and y parts of the register is called entanglement: in quantum physics, the state of a system composed of n sub-systems is not, in general, simply reducible to an n-tuple of the states of the components of that system. Entanglement has no equivalent in classical physics and it constitutes the most powerful resource for quantum information processing and communication.

No-Cloning. A direct consequence of the linearity of all operations that can be applied to quantum states (a two line trivial proof shows it) is that the state of a qubit a (this state is in general an arbitrary superposition, i.e. a vector made of a linear combination of the two basis state vectors |0> and |1>), cannot be duplicated and made the state of another qubit b, unless the state of a is simply either |0> or |1> (i.e. not an arbitrary superposition). This is true of the state of all quantum systems, including of course registers of n qubits used during a quantum computation. In programming terms, this means that the "value" (the state) of a quantum variable cannot be copied into another quantum variable.

These basic quantum ingredients and their peculiarities will of course have far reaching consequences, as soon as algorithm, programming languages and semantic frameworks incorporate and make use of quantum resources.

2   Quantum Algorithms

Richard Feynman launched in 1982 [10] the idea that computation based upon quantum physics would be exponentially more efficient than based upon classical physics. Then, after the pioneering insight of David Deutsch in the mid eighties [8], who showed, by means of a quantum Turing machine, that quantum computing could indeed not, in general, be simulated in polynomial time by classical computing, it was ten years before the potential power of quantum computing was demonstrated on actual computational problems.

2.1   Major Breakthroughs: Quantum Speedups and Teleportation

The first major breakthrough was by Peter Shor [27]: in 1994, he published a quantum algorithm operating in polynomial time ($O(\log^3 N)$) for factoring an integer N, whereas the best classical algorithm is exponential. Two years later, Lov Grover [13] published a quantum algorithm for searching an unordered database of size N, which achieves a quadratic acceleration (it operates in $O(N^{1/2})$) when compared with classical algorithms for the same problem (in $O(N)$). Shor's algorithm relies on a known reduction of the problem of factoring to that of finding the order of a group, or the period of a function: then, since order finding can be achieved by a Fourier Transform, the key of Shor's algorithm is a Quantum Fourier Transform, which is indeed exponentially more efficient than FFT, thanks to quantum parallelism, entanglement and tensor product. Grover's algorithm relies upon a very subtle use of interference, now known as amplitude amplification, which performs a stepwise increase of the probability of measuring a relevant item in the database, and which brings this probability very close to one after $N^{1/2}$ steps.

Another major result, by Charles Bennet and others in 1993 [3], was the design of theoretical principles leading to a quantum teleportation protocol, which takes advantage of entanglement and of probabilistic measurement: the state of a quantum system a (e.g. a qubit) localized at A's place can be assigned, after having been measured, thus destroyed, to another quantum system b (e.g. another qubit), localized at B's place, without the state of a being known neither by A nor by B, and without neither a, b nor any other quantum system being moved along a trajectory between A and B. It is important to notice that this is not in contradiction with no-cloning: there is still only one instance of the teleported state, whereas cloning would mean that there coexist one original and one copy.

Since then, these results have been generalized and extended to related classes of problems. Shor's algorithm solves an instance of the hidden subgroup problem [19] for abelian groups and a few extensions to non-abelian cases have been designed. In addition to Fourier Transform, order finding and amplitude amplification, other candidates to the status of higher level building blocks for quantum algorithmics have emerged, such as quantum random walks on graphs [15]. Principles for distributed quantum computing have also been studied and successfully applied to a few classes of problems. Very recently, on the basis of amplitude amplification, quadratic and other quantum speedups have been found for several problems on graphs, such as connectivity, minimum spanning tree and single source shortest paths [9].

Teleportation also has been generalized. The measurement used in its original formulation was such that the state eventually obtained for b was the same as the state initially held by a (up to a correcting operation which still had to be applied, depending on the probabilistic outcome of that measurement). By changing the way the measurement is done (in fact, by appropriately rotating the basis upon which the measurement of a will project the state of a), it has been found that the state teleported to b could be not the state initially held by a, but that state to which a rotation, i.e. a unitary operation has been applied. In other words, entanglement and measurement, i.e. the resources needed by teleportation, can be used to simulate computations by unitary tranformations. This has given rise to a whole new direction of research in quantum computation, namely measurement-based quantum computation [14,18,23].

2.2 No Quantum Computation Without Classical Control

There is an implicit, but obvious and ever present invariant in all these different ways of organizing quantum computations and quantum algorithms. Quantum computations operate in the quantum world, which is a foreign and unknowable world. No one in the classical world will ever know what the superposition state of an arbitrary qubit is, the only information one can get is 0 or 1, through measurement, i.e. the classical outcome of a probabilistic projection of the qubit state vector onto |0> or |1>: if one gets |0>, the only actual information which is provided about the state before measurement is that it was not |1>, because |0> and |1> are orthogonal vectors. Then, for the results of quantum computations to be useful in any way, there is an intrinsic necessity of cooperation and communication controlled by the classical world. All quantum algorithms, either based upon unitary transformations or upon measurements, if they are of any relevance, eventually end up in a final quantum state which hides, among its superposed basic states, a desired result. Such a result is asked for upon request by the classical world, which decides at that point to perform a measurement on part or all of the quantum register used by the computation. But measurement is probabilistic: its outcome may be a desired result, but it may well be something else. For example, Grover's algorithm ends up in a state where desired results have a probability close to 1 to be obtained, but other, unwanted results may also come out from the final measurement, although with a much lower probability.

The whole game of quantum algorithmics is thus to massage the state of the quantum register so that, in the end, desired results have a high probability to be obtained, while doing that at the minimum possible cost, i.e. minimal number of operations applied (time) and of qubits used (space). This is achieved through interferences (by means of appropriate unitary operations), through the establishment of entangled states and through measurements in appropriate bases. But this is not the end: once a measurement outcome is obtained by the classical world, it must be checked, by the classical world, for its validity. If the result satisfies the required conditions to be correct, termination is decided by the classical world. If it does not, the classical world decides to start the quantum part of the computation all over. For example, in the case of Grover's algorithm, if the element of the database produced by the measurement is not correct, the whole quantum search by amplitude amplification is started again by the classical world.

In general, algorithms will not contain one, but several quantum parts embedded within classical control structures like conditions, iterations, recursions. Measurement is not the only channel through which the classical and quantum worlds interact, there is also the initialization of quantum registers to a state chosen by the classical world (notice that such initializations can only be to one among the basis states, since they are the only quantum states which correspond, one to one, to values expressible by the classical world). A quantum part of an algorithm may also, under the control of the classical world, send one of its qubits to another quantum part. Notice that the physical carrier of the qubit must be sent, not its state, because of no-cloning. This quantum to quantum communication is especially useful for quantum secure communication protocols, a family of distributed quantum algorithms of high relevance, in a not too far future, among the practical applications of quantum information processing.

This means that not only the peculiarities of the basic quantum ingredients for computing have to be taken into account in the design of languages for the formal description of quantum algorithms and quantum protocols, but also the necessity of embedding quantum computations within classical computations, of having both worlds communicate and cooperate, of having classical and quantum parts be arbitrarily intermixed, under the control of the classical side, within the same program.

3 Quantum Programming

While quantum computing is in its infancy, quantum programming is still in embryonic state. Quantum computing is on its way to becoming an established discipline within computer science, much like, in a symmetric and very promising manner, quantum information theory is becoming a part of quantum physics. Since the recent birth of quantum computing, the most important efforts have been invested in the search for new quantum algorithms that would show evidence of significant drops in complexity compared with classical algorithms. Obtaining new and convincing results in this area is clearly a crucial issue for making progress in quantum computing. This research has been, as could be expected, largely focusing on complexity related questions, and relying on approaches and techniques provided by complexity theory.

However, the much longer experience from classical computer science tells that the study of complexity issues is not the only source of inspiration toward the creation, design and analysis of new algorithms. There are other roads, which run across the lands of language design and semantics. A few projects in this area have recently started, following these roads. Three quantum programming language styles are under study: imperative, parallel and distributed, and functional. This naturally opens new and challenging research issues in the domain of semantic frameworks (operational, denotational, axiomatic), where the peculiarities of quantum resources have to be dealt with in a formal, mathematical and consistent fashion. This research, in turn, is expected to provide fresh insights into the properties of the quantum world itself.

The sequential and imperative programming paradigm, upon which all major quantum algorithmic breakthroughs have relied, is still widely accepted as "the" way in which quantum + classical computations are organized and should be designed. However, before any language following that style was designed, and even today, the quantum parts of algorithms are mostly described by drawing quantum gate arrays, which are to quantum computing what logical gate circuits are to classical computing. This is of course very cumbersome and far from useful for understanding and proving properties of programs. This is why some imperative languages for quantum + classical programming have been design first.

The most representative quantum imperative programming language is QCL (Quantum Computing Language), a C flavoured language designed by B. Ömer at the University of Vienna [22]. Another one, qGCL (Quantum Guarded Command Language) was due to P. Zuliani at Oxford University [30], with the interesting design guideline of allowing the construction by refinement of proved correct programs.

Functional programming offers a higher level of abstraction than most other classical programming paradigms, especially than the imperative paradigm. Furthermore, it is certainly one of the most fruitful means of expression for inventing and studying algorithms, which is of prime importance in the case of quantum computing. A natural way to try and understand precisely how this programming style can be transposed to quantum computing is to study a quantum version of lambda-calculus.

This is done by A. Van Tonder at Brown University [28]. His approach puts forward the fact that there is a need for new semantic bases in order to accommodate disturbing peculiarities of the quantum world. A striking example are the consequences of no-cloning. In quantum programs, there are quantum variables, i.e. variables storing quantum states. However, since it is impossible to duplicate the state of a qubit, it is impossible to copy the value of a quantum variable. This has far reaching consequences, e.g., in lambda-calculus, an impossibility to stay with classical beta-reduction. Van Tonder [29] and J.Y. Girard [12] are suggesting that linear logic may be the way out of this specifically quantum issue.

On the functional side, there is also QPL (a Quantum Programming Language), designed by P. Selinger at the University of Ottawa [26]. QPL is a simple quantum programming language with high-level features such as loops, recursive procedures, and structured data types. The language is functional in nature, statically typed, and it has an interesting denotational semantics in terms of complete partial orders of superoperators (superoperators are a generalization of quantum operations). All of them are still fighting toward a satisfactory consistent integration of all quantum peculiarities, i.e. not only no-cloning, which naturally comes as their first major concern, but also probabilistic measurement, the necessary presence of both quantum and classical data and operations, etc.

The third style, process calculi, are an abstraction of communicating and cooperating computations which take place during the execution of parallel and distributed programs. They form a natural basis for rigorous and high level expression of several key aspects of quantum information processing: measurement, cooperation between quantum and classical parts of a computation, multi-party quantum computation, description and use of teleportation and of its generalization, description and analysis of quantum communication and cryptographic protocols.

CQP (Communicating Quantum Processes) is being designed by S. Gay and R. Nagarayan at the University of Warwick [11]. It combines the communication primitives of the pi-calculus with primitives for measurement and transformation of quantum states. A strong point of CQP is its static type system which classifies channels, distinguishes between quantum and classical data, and controls the use of quantum states: this type system guarantees that each qubit is owned by a unique process within a system.

QPAlg (Quantum Process Algebra) is being designed by M. Lalire and Ph. Jorrand at the University of Grenoble [17]. It does not have yet any elaborate typing system like that of CQP. But, in addition to modelling systems which combine quantum and classical communication and computation, the distinctive features of QPAlg are the explicit representation of qubit initialization through classical to quantum communication, and of measurement through quantum to classical communication, which are systematic and faithful abstractions of physical reality. Similarly, quantum to quantum communication actually models the sending of qubits (not of qubit states) and guarantees that the no-cloning law is enforced.

Both CQP and QPAlg have formally defined operational semantics, in the Plotkin's inference rules style, which include a treatment of probabilistic transitions due to the measurement postulate of quantum mechanics. The next section is devoted to a summary of the main quantum features of QPAlg.

4 Quantum Aspects of QPAlg, a Quantum Process Algebra

Since quantum computations operate in the unknowable quantum world, there is an intrinsic necessity of cooperation and communication controlled by the classical world, without which these computations would be purposeless. As a consequence, full formal and executable descriptions of algorithms and protocols making use of quantum resources must take into account both quantum and classical computing components and assemble them so that they communicate and cooperate. Moreover, to model concurrent and distributed quantum computations, as well as quantum communication protocols, quantum to quantum communications which move qubits physically from one place to another must also be taken into account. Inspired by classical process algebras [20], which provide a framework for modelling cooperating computations, a process algebraic notation is defined, named QPAlg for Quantum Process Algebra, which provides a homogeneous style to formal descriptions of concurrent and distributed computations comprising both quantum and classical parts.

"Quantumizing" a CCS-like process algebra means introducing quantum variables, operations on quantum variables (unitary operators and measurement observables), as well as new forms of communications in addition to the classical to classical communication of CCS, while making sure in the semantics that these quantum objects, operations and communications behave according to the postulates of quantum mechanics. The syntax of process terms in QPAlg is straightforward:

$$P := nil \mid a.P \mid P \parallel Q \mid P;Q \mid [\{c \rightarrow P\}] \mid [\{v : t\}. \ P \ ] \mid end \mid id$$
$$a := U[\{v\}] \mid M[\{v\}] \mid g ? v \mid g!e \mid g!M[\{v\}]$$

where P and Q are process terms, a an action, c a condition (on classical variables only), v a variable name, t a type (either a classical type, e.g. *Nat*, or a quantum type, e.g. *Qubit*), *id* is a declared process name, U is a unitary operator, M a measurement observable (both U and M are internal actions, i.e. instances of the traditional silent τ of process algebras, and they may be applied to quantum variables only), g is a communication gate used for input (?) or for output (!) and e is either an expression using classical variables only, or a quantum variable. The notation $\{x\}$ stands for one or more instances of x separated by commas. The idle process is *nil* and the successfully terminated process is *end* (necessary for the semantics of sequential composition). Variables are typed and are declared local to the scope of a process term.

A detailed presentation of the operational semantics of QPAlg, given in Plotkin's SOS style, can be found in [17]. The rest of this section is devoted to a survey of some of the interesting features, from a quantum point of view, of that semantics.

4.1 Entanglement and the Management of Variables

At declaration time, variables names are appended to a current context and remain there until exit of their scope of definition. This implies that the operational semantics take care not only of process terms, like in classical process algebras, but also of contexts, i.e. live variables names with their current bindings to (classical) values or to (quantum) states. The SOS rules thus deal with process states P/C where P is a process term and C a context of the form $<s, l=\rho, f>$: s is a stack containing the live variable names, l is the list of currently bound quantum variables with ρ their current state, and f maps classical variable names to their current values. For the purpose of generality and simplicity of the SOS rules, the state of quantum variables is not represented by a vector $|\psi>$ (a "pure state", in quantum mechanics), but by a more general "mixed state" ρ, i.e. a distribution of probabilities over pure states. In quantum mechanics (see the introduction to quantum mechanics in [21]), this is done by means of density matrices. In short, the density matrix corresponding to the pure state of a register of n qubits is the projector (a $2^n \times 2^n$ matrix) onto the vector representing this pure state, whereas the density matrix corresponding to a distribution of probabilities over several states is the weighted sum (by the respective probabilities) of the projectors onto these states.

At scope exit time, all local variable names are simply removed from the top of stack s in the current context $<s, l=\rho, f>$, while the domain of f is restricted accordingly to the remaining classical variables. The names of local quantum variables are also removed from the list l and the dimension of ρ must be reduced accordingly in order to represent the states of the remaining variables. But it may be the case that some remaining variables have had their states entangled with the states of local variables about to be removed from the context. This implies that the state of the remaining quantum variables is indeed a mixed state, i.e. a distribution of probabilities over the states of these variables (the reason is that an hypothetical measurement of the removed variables would indeed result, because of entanglement, into such a distribution of probabilities over the states of the remaining variables). The reduction of the dimension of ρ together with the appropriate update of the probabilities is achieved in linear algebra by the "trace out" operation on matrices, and is denoted by $Tr_r(\rho)$, where r denotes the removed subsystem (for more details on the linear algebra bases of quantum mechanics, see [21]). The corresponding rule in the semantics is the following, where δ is the event produced upon successful termination of a process:

$$\frac{P/C \xrightarrow{\delta} end \ /< r.s, l = \rho, f >}{[P]/C \xrightarrow{\delta} nil \ /< s, l \setminus r = Tr_{r\sim}(\rho), f \setminus r >}$$

4.2 Unitary Operations

According to the postulates of quantum mechanics, quantum states can obey two forms of evolutions: deterministic unitary evolution, and probabilistic measurement. A unitary evolution is determined by a unitary operator: if the state is represented by a density matrix ρ and the operator by a unitary matrix U, the state after applying this operator is $U\rho U^*$, where U^* is the adjoint of U (the adjoint U^* of U is the conjugate of the transpose of U: when U is unitary, $U^* = U^{-1}$, i.e. unitary matrices are always invertible). In QPAlg, applying U to a collection of disctinct quantum variables $x_1, x_2, \ldots, x_n$, is denoted by $U[x_1, x_2, \ldots, x_n]$. This is an internal action τ, and the corresponding rule in the semantics is:

$$\frac{}{U[x_1, \ldots, x_n].P/< s, l = \rho, f > \xrightarrow{\tau} P/< s, l = \rho', f >}$$

where $\rho'=\mathcal{T}_U(\rho)$. The operator $\mathcal{T}_U$ describes the evolution of ρ due to the application of U to the quantum variables $x_1, x_2, \ldots, x_n$. In general, $\mathcal{T}_A$ it is defined as follows, with A any $2^n \times 2^n$ matrix:

$$T_A : \rho \mapsto \Pi^*.\left(A \otimes I^{\otimes k}\right)\Pi.\rho.\Pi^*.\left(A^* \otimes I^{\otimes k}\right)\Pi$$

where

- Π is the permutation matrix which places the x_i's at the head of l
- $k =$ (number of variable names in l) $- n$
- $I^{\otimes k} =$ the k-fold tensor product of I, the 2×2 identity matrix

Since the unitary operation U may be applied to qubits which are anywhere within the list l, a permutation must be applied first, which moves the x_i's at the head of l in the order specified by $x_1, x_2, \ldots, x_n$. Then U can be applied to the first n elements and I to the remainder. Finally, the inverse of Π is applied, so that the elements in l and in ρ are placed back in the same order.

4.3 Measurement and Probabilistic Processes

A quantum measurement is determined by an observable, which is usually represented by a Hermitian matrix M, i.e. such that $M=M^*$. This requires some explanation. As briefly presented in section 1, quantum measurement performs a probabilistic projection of the quantum state onto one of the vectors of an orthonormal basis (in order to regain a valid quantum state, this projection is followed by renormalization). This can be done with respect to the standard basis $\{|i\rangle\}_{i=1..n}$, but it can also be done with respect to any other orthonormal basis. This is why quantum measurement, in general, can be characterized by a Hermitian matrix: if M is Hermitian, its eigenvectors constitute indeed an orthonormal basis. A measurement specified by an observable M thus results in a probabilistic projection onto one of the eigenspaces of M (followed by renormalization). By convention, the classical value sent back to the classical world is the eigenvalue of M associated with the chosen eigenspace.

A measurement M can be performed either for the sole purpose of modifying the quantum state, or for getting a classical value out of the current quantum state, while of course also modifying that state. In the first case, the outcoming classical value is simply discarded: this is denoted by $M[x_1, x_2, \ldots, x_n]$ in the syntax of QPAlg, where $x_1, x_2, \ldots, x_n$ are n distinct quantum variables. In the second case, this is denoted by $g!$ $M[x_1, x_2, \ldots, x_n]$, where g is a gate through which the classical outcome will be sent out to the classical world, i.e. to a process able to receive such a value and to perform some classical processing with it. The semantics of each case is reflected by a specific rule.

In the case of measurement without communication of a classical result, only the quantum state is modified probabilistically by the measurement, so the distribution of probabilities over the possibly resulting states can be reflected in a new density matrix. The semantic rule is:

$$\frac{}{M[x_1,...,x_n].P/<s,l=\rho,f> \xrightarrow{\tau} P/<s,l=\rho',f>}$$

with $\rho'=\sum_i \mathcal{T}_{P_i}(\rho)$, where P_i is the projector onto the ith eigenspace of M.

In the case of measurement with communication of a classical result, several such results are possible, each with some probability. This requires the introduction of a probabilistic composition operator on contexts, denoted $\oplus_p$: the state $P/C_1 \oplus_p P/C_2$ is P/C_1 with probability p, or P/C_2 with probability $1 - p$. Thus, in general, a context is either of the form $<s, l=\rho, f>$, or of the form $\oplus_{pi}<s_i, l_i=\rho_i, f_i>$, where the p_i's are probabilities adding to 1.

Earlier studies of probabilistic and nondeterministic processes [6] have shown that, if a process can perform a probabilistic choice and a nondeterministic choice, the probabilistic choice must always be made first. In QPAlg, nondeterminism appears with the semantics of parallel composition and with conditional choice. So as to guarantee that the probabilistic choice is always made first, a notion of probabilistic stability is introduced: a context C is probabilistically stable if it is of the form $<s, l=\rho, f>$. Whenever the context of a process state is not stable, a probabilistic transition must be performed first:

$$\frac{}{P/\oplus_{p_i} C_i \longrightarrow_{p_i} P/C_i} \quad \text{with} \sum_j p_j = 1$$

where $S_1 \longrightarrow_p S_2$ means that state S_1 becomes S_2 with probability p.

Finally, when the value coming out of the measurement is sent out, the rule is:

$$\frac{}{g!M[x_1,...,x_n].P/C \xrightarrow{\tau} [g!y.end]; P/\oplus_{p_i} C_i}$$

where M is an observable with spectral decomposition $M = \sum_i \lambda_i P_i$, and:

- $C =< s, l = \rho, f >$, which implies that C is probabilistically stable

- y is a fresh variable name, implicitly declared as $y:Nat$

- $C_i =< \{(y, Nat)\}.s, l = \rho_i, f \cup \{y \mapsto \lambda_i\}>$

- $p_i = Tr(T_{P_i}(\rho))$

- $\rho_i = \frac{1}{p_i} T_{P_i}(\rho)$

In both cases (i.e. with or without sending out a classical value), the computation of the new quantum state stems directly from the measurement postulate of quantum mechanics.

4.4 Communication and Physical Transportation of Qubits

Communication can take place from process P to process Q if these processes are together in a parallel composition $P\|Q$, if P is ready to perform an output action (!) and if Q is ready to perform an input action (?), both through the same gate name g. Classical to classical communication is no problem (i.e. $g!e$ by P where e is a classical expression, and $g?v$ by Q where v is a classical variable). In the three other cases, the quantum world is involved.

Classical to Quantum. Actions performed by processes P and Q: $g!e$ by P where e is a classical expression, and $g?v$ by Q where v is a quantum variable. This is initial state preparation of a quantum variable. If v is a qubit, and assuming a preparation in the standard basis $\{|0>,|1>\}$, e may only evaluate to 0 or to 1, preparing v accordingly in state $|0>$ or $|1>$. Once prepared, a quantum variable enters the binding list $l=\rho$ of quantum variables in the context.

Quantum to Classical. Actions performed by processes P and Q: $g!M[\{v\}]$ by P where M is an observable and $\{v\}$ is a list of quantum variables, and $g?w$ by Q where w is a classical variable. This is measurement of the quantum state of the variables listed in $\{v\}$, with the classical outcome received by w. This situation has been described in the previous paragraph.

Quantum to Quantum. Actions performed by processes P and Q: $g!v$ by P and $g?w$ by Q, where v and w are quantum variables. In this case, v must have been bound previously, i.e. there is a quantum state attached to it in the context by $l=\rho$, and w must not have been bound, i.e. w is a mere name with no quantum contents attached to it yet. As viewed by P, the semantics removes v (its name from s and its binding from $l=\rho$) while, as viewed by Q, w is bound in $l=\rho$ to the quantum state previously accessed through v by P. This semantics actually mimics the physical transfer of qubits from one place to another place (from P to Q), while making sure that no quantum state is ever cloned.

This view of the relations among the classaical and quantum parts of a computation, where communications among processes play a key unifying role, is a distinctive feature of QPAlg. This also shows that the communicating process algebra approach is indeed adequate for the description of quantum algorithms and protocols, together with their unavoidable classical control environment. Examples of various quantum algorithms, teleportation and secure quantum communication protocols described with QPAlg can be found in [17].

5 Quantum Semantics: Open Issues

All the language designs for quantum programming are still at the stage of promising work in progress. The core issues clearly remain at the semantics level, because of the many non-classical properties of the quantum world. No-cloning, entanglement, probabilistic measurement, mixed states (a more abstract view of quantum states, for representing probabilistic distributions over pure states), together with the necessary presence of both worlds, classical and quantum, within a same program, call for further in depth studies toward new bases for adequate semantic frameworks.

Operational semantics (i.e. a formal description of how a quantum + classical program operates) is the easiest part, although probabilities, no-cloning and entanglement already require a definitely quantumized treatment. The above brief presentation og QPAlg has shown, for example, that leaving the scope of a quantum variable is not as easy as leaving the scope of a classical variable, since the state of the former may be entangled with the state of more global variables. Both CQP [11] and QPAlg [17] have their semantics defined in the operational style. But, even in this rather naïve approach to semantics, much remains to be done like, for example, the definition of an equivalence among processes. This would not only provide a more satisfying and abstract semantics, but also allow a rigorous and formal approach to a number challenging questions in quantum computing. For example, it is known that quantum computations described by unitary transformations can be simulated by using measurements only [14,18,23], and that quantum computation by measurements is a way to get around decoherence, which is the major obstacle on the way to the physical implementation of a quantum computer. Then, it would be very useful to make sure, upon well founded formal bases, that a computation specified by means of unitary transformations is indeed correctly implemented by means of measurements.

Axiomatic semantics (what does a program do? How to reason about it? How to analyze its properties, its behaviour?) is a very tricky part. Defining quantum versions of Hoare's logic or Dijkstra's weakest precondition would indeed provide logical means for reasoning on quantum + classical programs and protocols and constitute formal bases for developing and analyzing such systems. Some attempts toward a dynamic quantum logic, based on the logical study of quantum mechanics initiated in the thirties by Birkhoff and von Neumann [4] have already been made, for example by Brunet and Jorrand [5], but such approaches rely upon the use of orthomodular logic, which is extremely uneasy to manipulate. Of much relevance, and in the same direction, is the recent work of D'Hondt and Panangaden on quantum weakest preconditions [7], which establishes a semantic universe where programs written in QPL [26] can be interpreted in a very elegant manner.

Another long-term goal is the definition of a compositional denotational semantics which would accommodate quantum as well as classical data and operations, and provide an answer to the question: what is a quantum + classical program, which mathematical object does it stand for? Working toward this objective has been rather successfully attempted by P. Selinger with QPL. Recent results on categorical semantics for quantum information processing by Abramsky and Coecke [1,2], and other different approaches like the the work of van Tonder [29] and the interesting manuscript of J. Y. Girard [12] on the relations between quantum computing and linear logic, are also worth considering for further research in those directions.

In fact, there are still a great number of wide open issues in the domain of languages for quantum programming and of their semantics. Two seemingly elementary examples show that there still is a lot to accomplish. First example: classical variables take classical values, quantum variables take quantum states. What would a type system look like for languages allowing both, and which quantum specific properties can be taken care of by such a type system? Second example: it would be very useful to know in advance whether the states of quantum variables will or will not be entangled during execution. Abstract interpretation would be the natural approach to answer such a question, but is there an adequate abstraction of quantum states for representing entanglement structures? At the current stage of research in quantum information processing and communication, these and many other similarly stimulating questions remain to be solved.

For a compilation of recent results and an overview of significant ongoing research on all these topics, the interested reader is referred to [25].

References

1. Abramsky, S., Coecke, B.: Physical traces: Quantum vs. Classical Information Processing. In: Blute, R., Selinger, P. (eds.): Category Therory and Computer Science (CTCS'02). Electronic Notes in Theoretical Computer Science 69, Elsevier (2003)
2. Abramsky, S., Coecke, B.: A Categorical Semantics of Quantum Protocols. In: Ganzinger, H. (ed.): Logic in Computer Science (LICS 2004). IEEE Proceedings 415-425 (2004)
3. Bennet, C., Brassard, G., Crepeau, C., Jozsa, R., Peres, A., Wootters: Teleporting an Unknown Quantum State via Dual Classical and EPR Channels. Physical Review Letters, 70:1895-1899 (1993)
4. Birkhoff, G., von Neumann, J.: Annals of Mathematics 37, 823 (1936)
5. Brunet, O., Jorrand, P.: Dynamic Logic for Quantum Programs. International Journal of Quantum Information (IJQI). World Scientific, 2(1):45-54 (2004)
6. Carloza, D., Cuartero, F., Valero, V., Pelayo, F.L., Pardo, J.: Algebraic Theory of Probabilistic and Nondeterministic Processes. The Journal of Logic and Algebraic Programming 55(1-2):57-103 (2003)
7. D'Hondt, E., Panangaden, P.:Quantum Weakest Preconditions. In [25]
8. Deutsch, D.: Quantum Theory, the Church-Turing Principle and the Universal Quantum Computer. In: Proceedings Royal Society London A, 400:97 (1985)
9. Durr, C., Heiligman, M., Hoyer, P., Mhalla, M.: Quantum Query Complexity of some Graph Problems. In: Diaz, J. (ed): International Colloquium on Automata, Languages and Programming (ICALP'04), Lecture Notes in Computer Science, Vol. 3142, Springer-Verlag, 481-493 (2004)
10. Feynmann, R.P.: Simulating Physics with Computers. International Journal of Theoretical Physics 21:467 (1982)
11. Gay, S.J., Nagarajan, R.: Communicating Quantum Processes. In [25]
12. Girard, J.Y.: Between Logic and Quantic: a Tract. Unpublished manuscript (2004)
13. Grover, L.K.: A Fast Quantum Mechanical Algorithm for Database Search. In: Proceedings 28th ACM Symposium on Theory of Computing (STOC'96) 212-219 (1996)
14. Jorrand, P., Perdrix, S.: Unifying Quantum Computation with Projective Measurements only and One-Way Quantum Computation. Los Alamos e-print arXiv, http://arxiv.org/abs/quant-ph/0404125 (2004)
15. Kempe, J.: Quantum Random Walks - An Introductory Overview. Los Alamos e-print arXiv, http://arxiv.org/abs/quant-ph/0303081 (2003)
16. Kitaev, A.Y., Shen, A.H., Vyalyi, M.N.: Classical and Quantum Computation. American Mathematical Society, Graduate Studies in Mathematics, 47 (2002)
17. Lalire, M., Jorrand, P.: A Process Algebraic Approach to Concurrent and Distributed Quantum Computation: Operational Semantics. In [25]
18. Leung, D.W.: Quantum Computation by Measurements. Los Alamos e-print arXiv, http://arxiv.org/abs/quant-ph/0310189 (2003)
19. Lomont, C.: The Hidden Subgroup Problem – Review and Open Problems. Los Alamos e-print arXiv, http://arxiv.org/abs/quant-ph/0411037 (2004)
20. Milner, R.: Communication and Concurrency. Prentice-Hall (1999)
21. Nielsen, M.A., Chuang, I.L.: Quantum Computation and Quantum Information. Cambridge University Press (2000)
22. Ömer, B.: Quantum Programming in QCL. Master's Thesis, Institute of Information Systems, Technical University of Vienna (2000)

23. Raussendorf, R., Browne, D.E., Briegel, H.J.: Measurement-based Quantum Computation with Cluster States. Los Alamos e-print arXiv, http://arxiv.org/abs/quant-ph/0301052 (2003)
24. Rieffel, E.G., Polak, W.: An Introduction to Quantum Computing for Non-Physicists. Los Alamos e-print arXiv, http://arxiv.org/abs/quant-ph/9809016 (1998)
25. Selinger, P. (ed.): Proceedings of 2nd International Workshop on Quantum Programming Languages. http://quasar.mathstat.uottawa.ca/~selinger/qpl2004/proceedings.html (2004)
26. Selinger, P.: Towards a Quantum Programming Language. Mathematical Structures in Computer Science. Cambridge University Press, 14(4):525-586 (2004)
27. Shor, P.W.: Algorithms for Quantum Computation: Discrete Logarithms and Factoring. In: Proceedings 35th Annual Symposium on Foundations of Computer Science, IEEE Proceedings (1994)
28. Van Tonder, A.: A Lambda Calculus for Quantum Computation. Los Alamos e-print arXiv, http://arxiv.org/abs/quant-ph/0307150 (2003)
29. Van Tonder, A.: Quantum Computation, Categorical Semantics and Linear Logic. Los Alamos e-print arXiv, http://arxiv.org/abs/quant-ph/0312174 (2003)
30. Zuliani, P.: Quantum Programming. PhD Thesis, St. Cross College, Oxford University (2001)

Chemical Computing

Chemical Computing

Peter Dittrich

Bio Systems Analysis Group,
Jena Centre for Bioinformatics (JCB) and
Department of Mathematics and Computer Science,
Friedrich-Schiller-University Jena,
D-07743 Jena, Germany
http://www.minet.uni-jena.de/csb/

Abstract. All information processing systems found in living organisms are based on chemical processes. Harnessing the power of chemistry for computing might lead to a new unifying paradigm coping with the rapidly increasing complexity and autonomy of computational systems. Chemical computing refers to computing with real molecules as well as to programming electronic devices using principles taken from chemistry. The paper focuses on the latter, called artificial chemical computing, and discusses several aspects of how the metaphor of chemistry can be employed to build technical information processing systems. In these systems, computation emerges out of an interplay of many decentralized relatively simple components analogized to molecules. Chemical programming encompassed then the definition of molecules, reaction rules, and the topology and dynamics of the reaction space. Due to the self-organizing nature of chemical dynamics, new programming methods are required. Potential approaches for chemical programming are discussed and a road map for developing chemical computing into a unifying and well grounded approach is sketched.

1 Introduction

All known life forms process information on a molecular level. Examples are: signal processing in bacteria (e.g., chemotaxis), gene expression and morphogenesis, defense coordination and adaptation in the immune system, and information broadcasting by the endocrine system. Chemical processes play also an important role, when an ant colony seeks a suitable route to a food source. This kind of chemical information processing is known to be robust, self-organizing, adaptive, decentralized, asynchronous, fault-tolerant, and evolvable. Computation emerges out of an orchestrated interplay of many decentralized relatively simple components (molecules).

How can chemistry be employed for computing? First, it should be noted that chemistry is used for the fabrication of electronic devices. However, here we are interested in approaches where chemistry stimulates the development of new computational paradigms. These approaches can be distinguished according to the following two dimensions: First, *real chemical computing* where real

J.-P. Banâtre et al. (Eds.): UPP 2004, LNCS 3566, pp. 19–32, 2005.

molecules and real chemical processes are employed to compute. Second, *artificial chemical computing* where the chemical metaphor is utilized to program or to build computational systems. The former aims at harnessing new substrates for computation. The latter takes the chemical metaphor as a design principle for new software or hardware architectures built on conventional silicon devices. So, artificial chemical computing includes constructing chemical-like formal system in order to model and master concurrent processes, e.g., Gamma [1], CHAM [2]; using the chemical metaphor as a new way to program conventional computers including distributed systems, e.g., smart dust; and taking the chemical metaphor as an inspiration for new architectures, e.g., reaction-diffusion processors [3].

1.1   The Chemical Metaphor

Chemistry is a science of experiment and observation, which provides a particular view on our world. Like physics, chemistry deals with matter and energy, but focuses on substances composed of molecules and how the composition of these substances is changed by "chemical" reactions. Compared with chemistry, physics is more concerned with energy, forces, and motion, ie. the physical change of a system.

Chemistry looks at the macro and micro level: On the macro level emergent properties and the emergent behavior of substances are studied, e.g., color or smell. On the microscopic level, molecular structures and reaction mechanisms are postulated, which are taken to explain macroscopic observations. Ideally, microscopic models allow to formally derive macroscopic observations. However, this is possible only in limited cases, e.g., no algorithm that computes the melting temperature of a molecule given its structure is known. In general, chemistry explains a chemical observation using a mixture of microscopic and macroscopic explanations.

The difficulty to predict the macroscopic behavior from microscopic details has its root in the nature of emergence. The time-evolution of a chemical system is a highly parallel self-organization process where many relatively simple components interact in a nonlinear fashion. And it is a central aim of chemical computing to harness the power inherent in these self-organization processes.

From a computer science perspective it would be quite appealing to achieve computation as an emergent process, where only microscopic rules have to be specified and information processing appears as global behavior. From knowing the biological archetype, we can expect a series of interesting properties, such as, fine grained parallelism without central control, fault tolerance, and evolvability. There is a wide application range, especially where the characteristics of chemical processes fit naturally to the desired task, as for example in highly distributed and dynamic "organic" processor networks or within one computing node to implement particular systems like artificial emotional [4], endocrine [5], or immune systems more naturally. It should be mentioned that chemical processes themselves can be seen as a natural media for information processing either in vitro or in vivo [6, 7, 8]; for a recent discussion of molecular computing see ref. [9]. Here we concentrate on how technical electronic systems can utilize the chemical metaphor.

1.2   The Organization of Chemical Explanations

When we study chemistry [10], first we learn how substances look like. We describe macroscopic properties of the substances, such as color, and how substances are composed from elementary objects, the atoms. Second, we learn how substances interact, in particular, we describe the outcome that results from their union. Reactive interactions among molecules require that these molecules come into contact, which can be the result of a collision. Third, we learn the detailed dynamical process of a chemical transformation of substances. All these steps of description can be done on a microscopic and macroscopic level. The steps are also not independent: The properties of substances are often described in terms of how a substance reacts with other substances, e.g., when we say "fluorine is not healthy in large quantities" we describe the property of fluorine by how it interacts with molecules in an organism. In fact, in times when nothing was known about the molecule's structure substances where classified according to their macroscopic appearance and reactive behavior.

Today, classification of substance usually refers to the structure of the molecules, e.g., alcohols are characterized by a functional OH-group. Sometimes only the composition of atoms is taken for classification, e.g., hydrocarbons. Interestingly and importantly for the success of the discipline Chemistry is the fact that structural classification coincide with classifications based on behavior and appearance. This phenomenon is not sufficiently explained by the fact that the function (ie. physical and reactive properties) of a molecule depends on its structure, which is a form of causality. Moreover, similarity in structure tends to coincide with similarity in function, which is a form of *strong* causality between structure and function.

Another important observation should be noted: When we combine some substance in a reaction vessel and wait while these substances react; as a result only a small subset of molecular species will appear, which is usually much smaller than the set of molecular species that could be build from the atoms present in the reaction vessel. So there is also a certain (strong) causality in the dynamics and a dependency on initial conditions. Not everything that is possible does appear, though there is also nondeterminism. So, we can say that a chemical system evolves over time in a contingent way that depends on its history.

1.3   Information Processing and Computing in Natural System

When we intend to take inspiration from chemistry, we have first to investigate where chemical information processing appears in natural systems. Obviously, living systems are prime candidates, since information processing is identified as a fundamental property of life [11].

Information processing in living systems can be observed on at least two different levels: the chemical and the neural level. Where the neural level is responsible for cognitive tasks and fast coherent control, such as vision, planing, and muscle control; chemical information processing is used for regulating and controlling fundamental processes like growth, ontogeny, gene expression, and immune system response. Neurons themselves are based on (electro-)chemical processes, and more often than not, chemical processes are combined with neuronal processes resulting in a large-scale computational result.

Real chemical computing utilizes a series of "chemical principles", which are also relevant for artificial chemical computing, such as: pattern recognition[12], change of conformation[13], chemical kinetics [14], formation of (spatial) structures, energy minimization, and optical activity [15]. Pattern recognition is a central mechanism for explaining reactions among complex biomolecules (e.g., transcription factors binding to DNA). It is also used in real as well as artificial chemical computing approaches, such as DNA computing [12] and rewriting systems [1, 16, 17], respectively.

1.4   Application of the Chemical Metaphor in Computing

There are already a series of approaches in computer science that have been inspired by chemistry: An early example are the *artificial molecular machines* suggested by Laing [18]. These machines consists of molecules (strings of symbols). Each molecule can appear in two forms: data or machine. During a reaction, two molecules come into contact at a particular position. One of the molecules is considered as the active machine, which is able to manipulate the passive data molecule. The primary motivation for developing these molecular machines was to construct artificial organisms in order to develop a general theory for living systems (cf. [19] for a comparing discussion of more recent approaches in that direction).

A fundamentally different motivation has been the starting point for the development of Gamma by Banâtre and Le Métayer, namely to introduce a new programming formalism that allows to automatize reasoning about programs, such as automatic semantic analysis [20, 1]. Gamma is defined by rewriting operations on multisets, which mimics chemical reactions in a well-stirred reaction vessel. Gamma inspired a series of other chemical rewriting systems: Berry and Boudol [2] introduced the *chemical abstract machine* (CHAM) as a tool to model concurrent processes. Păun's P-Systems [16] stress the importance of membranes. Suzuki and Tanaka [21] introduced a rewriting system on multisets in order to study chemical systems, e.g., to investigate the properties of chemical cycles [22], and to model chemical-like systems including economic processes.

Within biological organisms, the endocrine system is a control system, which transmits information by chemical messengers called hormones via a broadcast strategy. The humanoid robot torso COG [5] is an example where the endocrine system has inspired engineering. Artificial hormones are used to achieve a coherent behavior among COG's large number of independent processing elements [5]. In general, chemical-like systems can control the behavior and particularly emotions in artificial agents, e.g., the computer game Creatures [23] and the psychological model PSI by Dörner [4]. Further application areas of chemical computing are: the control of morpho-genetic systems, i.e. the control of morphogenesis by artificial gene expression; in particular, the control of growth of an artificial neural networks (cf. Astor and Adami [24]); and the control of amorphous computers [25]. Finally, Husbands et al. [26] introduced diffusing chemical substances in artificial neural networks (cf. GasNet).

2   Facets of Chemical Computing

As exemplified by the previous section, the world of chemical computing enjoys already a wide spectrum of approaches. This section discusses a set of important aspects, which allow to characterize chemical computing in more detail.

2.1   Microscopic vs. Macroscopic Computing

Chemical information processing can be characterized according to the level on which it appears: In approaches like chemical boolean circuits [27], the chemical neuron [14], or the hypercyclic memory (Sec. 4), information is represented by the concentration of substances and computation is carried out by an increase and decrease of concentration levels, which can be regarded as a form of *macroscopic chemical computing*. Alternatively, in *microscopic chemical computing*, the intermediately stored information and computational results are represented by single molecules. Examples are DNA computing [12] and the prime number chemistry (Sec. 4). The dynamics is usually stochastic, in contrast to macroscopic computation, which can be more readily described with ordinary differential equations. Nevertheless, microscopic computing also can deliver results virtually deterministically, as shown by the prime number chemistry example in Sec. 4.

2.2   Deterministic vs. Stochastic Processes

On the molecular level, chemical processes are stochastic in nature. However, in technical applications deterministic behavior is often required. There are various ways how this can be achieved:

(1) The problem can be stated such that the order of the sequence of collisions does not play a role[1]. An example is the prime number chemistry where we start with a population that contains all numbers between 2 and n. The outcome will be a reactor containing all and only prime numbers less or equal n, independently of the sequence of updates.

(2) Increasing the reactor size would reduce the effect of randomness. If the reactor size and together with it the number of molecules of each molecular type tends to infinity, the molecules' concentrations tend to a deterministic dynamics. In this case, the dynamics of the concentrations can be represented by a differential equation and simulated by numerical integration of this equation.

---

[1] For a theory that considers the effect of the order of update see "sequential dynamical systems" [28, 29].

(3) A well-defined deterministic update scheme can be used. For example we can check one reaction rule after another in a fixed predefined sequence, e.g., early ARMS [21] and MGS [17][2] Doing this, we gain determinism and might gain efficiency, but we loose aspects of the chemical metaphor and may introduce artifacts by the update scheme, e.g., when the rule order plays a significant role. This might be reasonable from a computing point of view, but is unnatural from a chemical point of view.

2.3   Closed vs. Open Systems

In thermodynamics, a system that can exchange mass and energy with its environment is called open.When mass is not exchanged the system is called closed If the system cannot exchange anything, it is called isolated. In chemical computing we also encounter closed and open systems, whose characteristics are quite different. In a *closed system*, molecules do not leave the reaction vessel. There is no dilution flow. Reaction rules must be balanced, which means that the mass on the left hand side must be equal to the mass on the right hand side. So, a molecule can only disappear by transforming it via a reaction into other molecules. In an isolated system, stable dissipative structures can not appear; they can only appear as transient phenomena locally. The prime number chemistry is an example for a closed and isolated system. There is no dilution flow and molecules are transformed by the mass-conserving rule: $a + b \rightarrow a + b/a$ for b being a multiple of a.

The hypercyclic memory is an example for an open system. Molecules constantly vanish and are regenerated from an implicitly assumed substrate, which is available at a constant concentration from the environment. Before the query, the system is in a quasi-stationary state, which is a dissipative structure that requires a constant regeneration of all of its components.

The hypercyclic memory is also an example where there is a so called *non-selective dilution flow*, where the rate of decay is proportional to the concentration of a molecule, or more precisely, the concentration of molecules in the dilution flow is the same as in the reaction vessel. Systems with selective dilution flows are not discussed here, but it should be noted that by introducing a selective dilution flow, we can move gradually from an open to a closed system and can capture aspects from both.

Does it make sense to consider open systems with a non-selective dilution flow, where we have to regenerate constantly molecules we wish to have in the reactor? From a formal point of view, both might be equivalent: In an open system, a stable solution is a self-regenerating set of molecules; while in a closed system, a stable solution is just a set of molecules, which do not react further to form other molecules (nevertheless there might be a reversible dynamics). So from this point of view, taking a closed systems approach appears more reasonable, because the solution is more stable. We do not have to fear that informa-

---

[2] Note that both mentioned systems (ARMS, MGS) allow also a randomized "natural" update scheme.

tion gets lost by the dilution flow and we do not have to care for regenerating molecules.

However, when using an open system approach we arrive at more robust and flexible organic systems. Open reaction systems are especially suitable, where the substrate is unreliable and highly dynamic. Consider for example a computational substrate that is under constant change, where nodes are added and removed at a relatively high rate, e.g., the network of activated cellular phones. In such a system, there is no place that exists for long. When a cellular phone is switched off, the molecules residing in that places vanish, too, which causes from a chemical point of view a general, non-selective dilution flow. Thus stable structures must consists of molecules that constantly reproduce themselves as a whole; according to the theory of chemical organization [30], they must encompass a self-maintaining set of molecules.

2.4   Computing with Invisible Networks

What is the difference between chemical computing and an artificial neural network (ANN)? In both approaches, a network is specified by a set of components (molecules/neurons), a set of interactions (reactions/connections), and a description of the behavior (dynamics/firing rule). In contrast to chemical computing, an ANN is usually accompanied by a learning procedure. However, learning can be added to chemical computing by means of evolutionary computation [31, 32] or by transferring learning techniques from computational intelligence, e.g., Hebbian learning. In particular, this should be straight forward for explicitly defined chemical systems operating macroscopically, which are quite similar to dynamical neural networks (see Sec. 4 or ref. [14]).

But there are some remarkable differences: When we consider a reaction system with implicitly defined molecules and rules like the prime number chemistry in Sec. 4, we can easily obtain giant networks that are "invisible". When we look inside a reaction vessel, no component that represents a connection can be seen. Even the nodes of the chemical network cannot be easily identified because they are not spatially differentiated from each other, since a chemical node may be represented by a collection of molecules that are instances of one molecular species. The prime number chemistry is an example where a couple of simple rules imply a giant network, much larger than a human brain, e.g., for $n = 10^{30}$.

Another important difference to ANNs should be mentioned: When executing a chemical computation, only a subnetwork is active at a certain point in time, which is illustrated by Fig. 1. Since the size of a reaction vessel is limited, it can only contain a fraction of molecules from the set of all possible molecules. These present molecules together with all reactions that can occur among them can be regarded as the active reaction network. Due to internal or external dynamics, the set of molecular species in the reaction vessel can change, and thus the active network evolves over time, too (Fig. 1). This phenomenon is captured theoretically by a movement through the set of chemical organizations [33, 30].

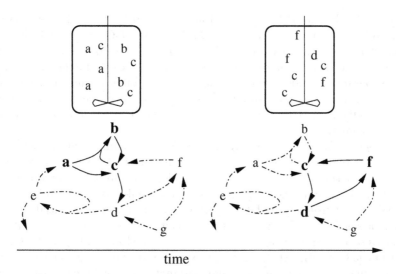

Fig. 1. Illustration of the invisible network, whose active part changes over time. A bold character denotes a molecular species that is present in the reactor. These species imply the currently active network highlighted by solid arrows. Note that a character in the reaction network denotes a molecular species, whereas the same character in the sketched reaction vessel denotes a concrete molecule (or instance) of that species

3   Chemical Programming

Programming a chemical computer means to define a chemical system, which is often also referred to as a *reaction system* or an *artificial chemistry* [34]. There are two fundamentally different approaches to chemical programming: (1) automatic programming by optimization, e.g. by means of evolutionary computation [31, 32], and (2) engineering by a human programmer, e.g. [1, 25]. Both approaches require specifying the following three aspects of the target chemistry:

(1) *Molecules*: In the first step, we have to specify how the molecules should look like. Should they be symbols or should they posses a structure, e.g., a sequence of characters [35], a hierarchical expression [36], or a graph like structure [37]. If molecules posses a structure, the definition of the reaction rules and the dynamics can refer to this structure, which allows to define large (even infinite) reaction systems, as exemplified by the prime number chemistry in Sec. 4. If the molecules are symbols, we have to specify the set of possible molecules *explicitly* by enumeration of all possible molecules, e.g., $\mathcal{M} = \{a, b, c, d\}$. If molecules posses a structure, we can define the set of all possible molecules implicitly, e.g., $\mathcal{M} = \{1, 2, \ldots, 10000\}$.

(2) *Reactions*: In the next step, we have to specify what happens when molecules collide. Real molecules can collide elastically or they can collide causing a reaction, which transforms the molecules. In a simple abstraction, a reaction rule is just a pair of two multisets of molecules, which specifies what

kind of molecules can be transformed and replaced by what kind of molecules, e.g., a well known reaction rules is $(\{H_2, H_2, O_2\}, \{H_2O, H_2O\})$, which is written in chemical notation equivalently as $2H_2 + O_2 \rightarrow 2H_2O$. In general, reaction rules can become more complicated and can carry further information, such as parameters specifying kinetic constants or environmental conditions under which this reaction can occur. Analogously to molecules, reaction rules can be specified *explicitly* like $2H_2 + O_2 \rightarrow 2H_2O$, or *implicitly*, as in the prime number chemistry.

(3) *Dynamics*: Finally, we have to specify the dynamics, which includes the geometry of reaction vessel. Do we assume a well-stirred vessel or vessel with a spatial structure? How do molecules collide? How are the reaction rules applied, e.g., deterministically or stochastically? Well-stirred deterministic reaction systems are usually simulated by integrating ordinary differential equations. Stochastic systems can be simulated by explicit stochastic collisions of individual molecules or by more advanced discrete event based methods like the Gillespie algorithm [38]. Spatial structures are usually introduced by some sort of cellular automata (e.g., lattice molecular automata [39]) or by compartments like in amorphous computing [25], membranes in P-systems [16] or mobile process calculi [40], or topology in MGS [17].

3.1   Strategies for Chemical Programming

We distinguish different strategies of chemical programming according to the components a programmer can manipulate:

(1) *Define molecules and reactions explicitly*: The programmer has to specify the set of molecules as a set of symbols and the reaction rules as a set of explicit transformation rules. An example for this approach is the hypercyclic memory (Sec. 4), the metabolic robot [41], and evolved chemical systems like those reported by Ziegler and Banzhaf [31].

(2) *Define molecules and reactions implicitly*: The programmer specifies molecules and reaction rules implicitly like demonstrated by the prime number chemistry in Sec. 4. For defining reaction rules implicitly, the molecules can not be just a list of symbols, rather they must posses a structure to which the definition of the reaction rules can refer to (see Sec. 3(1)). This approach is quite general, but because of its generality additional principle for guiding the programmer are required.

(3) *Change-molecules-only principle*: Again, the reaction rules are implicitly defined but fixed (predefined) and cannot be changed by the programmer. The programmer or an evolutionary process has "just" to select the right molecules and the dynamics, including the topology of the reaction space. This resembles the way real chemical computers are programmed, e.g., selecting appropriate DNA strands for solving a Hamiltonian path problem as in the famous example by Adleman [12]. Although the programmer has limited choices (compared to the previous setting), the expressive power is the same, if a universal chemistry is used. A *universal chemistry* is defined as a chemistry that includes every possible (let's say, finite) reaction network topology. Such chemistry can, for

example, easily be defined based on lambda-calculus [36] or combinators [42]. However, these abstract formalisms stemming from theoretical computer science can not be easily and intuitively handled by programmers, other approaches are more feasible for practical application (see Banâtre, Fradet, and Radenac in this volume).

(4) *Multi-level chemical programming*: As before, the programmer selects appropriate molecules and dynamics. At the same time, the "physics" can be manipulated, too, but at a slower rate. For example, the calculus specifying implicitly the set of possible molecules and the set of possible reactions can be altered and extended. By this, the function (meaning) of molecules can become more transparent (syntactic sugar). On a higher level of abstraction, molecules may be assembled to higher clusters resembling macro molecules or modules, which can again serve as building blocks for implicit definitions of other molecules, reaction rules, and dynamics. Therefore, a programmer operates on different levels, such as: Level 0: manipulation of the physics, e.g., combinator rules. Level 1: selecting (defining) the right molecules and reaction rules, and dynamics in the context of the chosen physics, e.g., selecting appropriate combinators. Level 2: Specifying higher level clusters, modules, macro-molecular complexes, e.g., based on membrane computing concepts.

4   Conclusion and Challenges

This essay discussed several aspects of artificial chemical computing. It has been shown that chemical-like systems possess a number of interesting properties, which appear especially feasible in domains like distributed computing, ambient computing, or organic computing. Furthermore, a couple of application scenarios have been described, including a first successful commercial application [23]. Taking heed of these facts, the chemical metaphor appears as a paradigm, which will qualitatively enrich our repertoire of programming techniques.

The road map of chemical computing includes a series of challenges: (1) Efficiency: How to obtain runtime and memory efficient chemical programs and their execution on electronic hardware? (2) Scalability: How do chemical computing paradigms scale up? (3) Programmability: How to program a chemical computer? (4) Adaptability and robustness: How to achieve self-adapting, learning, and reliable chemical computing systems? (5) Theory: How to describe chemical computing processes theoretically? Here, chemical organization theory [30] appears as a promising approach, especially when dealing with constructive chemical systems. Other sources for a theoretical base are classical dynamical systems theory and approaches from computer science like rewriting calculi [1, 2, 16, 40] and temporal logic. Furthermore we may investigate fundamental question concerning the power and limits of chemical computing by questions like: Can the chemical metaphor lead to new computational systems with abilities superior to conventional approaches, or even to systems that can not be realized by conventional approaches?

It is evident that the future will witness further integration of concepts from the natural sciences and computer science, which will reduce the differences between the living and the technological world. Like living systems, computing systems in the future will consist of decentralized and highly distributed components that interact with increasing autonomy and flexibility. For harnessing their potential it will be crucial to obtain new, organic methods for their construction and control. Chemical computing, which has been employed by nature with great success, offers a promising paradigm.

Acknowledgment. I am grateful to F. Centler, N. Matsumaru, and K.-P. Zauner for helpful comments. This work was supported by the Federal Ministry of Education and Research (BMBF) Grant 0312704A to Friedrich Schiller University Jena.

References

1. Banâtre, J.P., Métayer, D.L.: The GAMMA model and its discipline of programming. Sci. Comput. Program. **15** (1990) 55–77
2. Berry, G., Boudol, G.: The chemical abstract machine. Theor. Comput. Sci. **96** (1992) 217–248
3. Adamatzky, A.: Universal dynamical computation in multidimensional excitable lattices. Int. J. Theor. Phys. **37** (1998) 3069–3108
4. Dörner, D.: Bauplan einer Seele. Rowohlt, Reinbeck (1999)
5. Brooks, R.A.: Coherent behavior from many adaptive processes. In Cliff, D., Husbands, P., Meyer, J.A., Wilson, S., eds.: From animals to animats 3, Cambridge, MA, MIT Press (1994) 22–29
6. Conrad, M.: Information processing in molecular systems. Currents in Modern Biology **5** (1972) 1–14
7. Liberman, E.A.: Cell as a molecular computer (MCC). Biofizika **17** (1972) 932–43
8. Liberman, E.A.: Analog-digital molecular cell. BioSytems **11** (1979) 111–24
9. Zauner, K.P.: Molecular information technology. Cr. Rev. Sol. State **30** (2005) 33–69
10. Tilden, W.A.: Introduction to the Study of Chemical Philosophy. 6 edn. Longmans, Green and Co., London (1888)
11. Küppers, B.O.: Information and the Origin of Life. MIT Press, Cambridge, MA (1990)
12. Adleman, L.M.: Molecular computation of solutions to combinatorical problems. Science **266** (1994) 1021
13. Conrad, M., Zauner, K.P.: Conformation-driven computing: A comparison of designs based on DNA, RNA, and protein. Supramol. Sci. **5** (1998) 787–790
14. Hjelmfelt, A., Weinberger, E.D., Ross, J.: Chemical implementation of neural networks and turing machines. Proc. Natl. Acad. Sci. USA **88** (1991) 10983–10987
15. Bazhenov, V.Y., Soskin, M.S., Taranenko, V.B., Vasnetsov, M.V.: Biopolymers for real-time optical processing. In Arsenault, H.H., ed.: Optical Processing and Computing, San Diego, Academic Press (1989) 103–44
16. Păun, G.: Computing with membranes. J. Comput. Syst. Sci. **61** (2000) 108–143
17. Giavitto, J.L., Michel, O.: MGS: a rule-based programming language for complex objects and collections. In van den Brand, M., Verma, R., eds.: Electronic Notes in Theoretical Computer Science. Volume 59., Elsevier Science Publishers (2001)

18. Laing, R.: Artificial organisms and autonomous cell rules. J. Cybernetics **2** (1972) 38–49
19. Suzuki, H., Ono, N., Yuta, K.: Several necessary conditions for the evolution of complex forms of life in an artificial environment. Artif. Life **9** (2003) 153–174
20. Banâtre, J.P., Métayer, D.L.: A new computational model and its discipline of programming. technical report RR-0566, INRIA (1986)
21. Suzuki, Y., Tanaka, H.: Symbolic chemical system based on abstract rewriting and its behavior pattern. Artif. Life and Robotics **1** (1997) 211–219
22. Suzuki, Y., Tsumoto, S., Tanaka, H.: Analysis of cycles in symbolic chemical system based on abstract rewriting system on multisets. In Langton, C.G., Shimohara, K., eds.: Artificial Life V, Cambridge, MA, MIT Press (1996) 521–528
23. Cliff, D., Grand, S.: The creatures global digital ecosystem. Artif. Life **5** (1999) 77–94
24. Astor, J.C., Adami, C.: A developmental model for the evolution of artificial neural networks. Artif. Life **6** (2000) 189–218
25. Abelson, H., Allen, D., Coore, D., Hanson, C., Homsy, G., Knight, T.F., Nagpal, R., Rauch, E., Sussman, G.J., Weiss, R., Homsy, G.: Amorphous computing. Commun. ACM **43** (2000) 74–82
26. Husbands, P., Smith, T., Jakobi, N., O'Shea, M.: Better living through chemistry: Evolving gasnets for robot control. Connect. Sci. **10** (1998) 185–210
27. Seelig, L.A., Rössler, O.E.: A chemical reaction flip-flop with one unique switching input. Zeitschrift für Naturforschung **27b** (1972) 1441–1444
28. Barrett, C.L., Mortveit, H.S., Reidys, C.M.: Elements of a theory of simulation II: sequential dynamical systems. Appl. Math. Comput. **107** (2000) 121–136
29. Reidys, C.M.: On acyclic orientations and sequential dynamical systems. Adv. Appl. Math. **27** (2001) 790–804
30. Dittrich, P., di Fenizio, P.S.: Chemical organization theory: Towards a theory of constructive dynamical systems. (submitted), preprint arXiv:q-bio.MN/0501016 **x** (2005) 1–7
31. Ziegler, J., Banzhaf, W.: Evolving control metabolisms for a robot. Artif. Life **7** (2001) 171 – 190
32. Bedau, M.A., Buchanan, A., Gazzola, G., Hanczyc, M., Maeke, T., McCaskill, J., Poli, I., Packard, N.H.: Evolutionary design of a DDPD model of ligation. In: 7th Int. Conf. on Artificial Evolution. LNCS, Springer, Berlin (2005) (in press)
33. Speroni Di Fenizio, P., Dittrich, P.: Artificial chemistry's global dynamics. movement in the lattice of organisation. The Journal of Three Dimensional Images **16** (2002) 160–163
34. Dittrich, P., Ziegler, J., Banzhaf, W.: Artificial chemistries - a review. Artif. Life **7** (2001) 225–275
35. Banzhaf, W.: Self-replicating sequences of binary numbers – foundations I and II: General and strings of length n = 4. Biol. Cybern. **69** (1993) 269–281
36. Fontana, W., Buss, L.W.: 'The arrival of the fittest': Toward a theory of biological organization. Bull. Math. Biol. **56** (1994) 1–64
37. Benkö, G., Flamm, C., Stadler, P.F.: A graph-based toy model of chemistry. J. Chem. Inf. Comput. Sci. **43** (2003) 2759–2767
38. Gillespie, D.T.: Exact stochastic simulation of coupled chemical-reactions. J. Phys. Chem. **81** (1977) 2340–2361
39. Mayer, B., Rasmussen, S.: Dynamics and simulation of micellar self-reproduction. Int. J. Mod. Phys. C **11** (2000) 809–826

40. Cardelli, L.: Brane calculi. In Danos, V., Schachter, V., eds.: Computational Methods in Systems Biology (CMSB 2004). Volume 3082 of LNCS., Berlin, Springer (2005) 257–278

41. Dittrich, P.: Selbstorganisation in einem System von Binärstrings mit algorithmischen Sekundärstrukturen. Diploma thesis, Dept. of Computer Science, University of Dortmund (1995)

42. Speroni di Fenizio, P.: A less abstract artficial chemistry. In Bedau, M.A., McCaskill, J.S., Packard, N.H., Rasmussen, S., eds.: Artificial Life VII, Cambridge, MA, MIT Press (2000) 49–53

43. Banzhaf, W., Dittrich, P., Rauhe, H.: Emergent computation by catalytic reactions. Nanotechnology **7** (1996) 307–314

44. Eigen, M., Schuster, P.: The hypercycle: a principle of natural self-organisation, part A. Naturwissenschaften **64** (1977) 541–565

45. Fontana, W., Wagner, G., Buss, L.W.: Beyond digital naturalism. Artif. Life **1/2** (1994) 211–227

46. Dittrich, P., Banzhaf, W.: Self-evolution in a constructive binary string system. Artif. Life **4** (1998) 203–220

A   Appendix: Examples

A.1   Prime Number Chemistry

Banâtre and Le Metayer [1] suggested the numerical devision operator as an implicit reaction mechanism, which results in a prime number generating chemistry defined as follows (see ref. [41, 43] for details): the set of all possible molecules are all integers greater one and smaller $n + 1$: $\mathcal{M} = \{2, 3, 4, \ldots, n\}$. The reaction rules are defined by a devision operation: $\mathcal{R} = \{a + b \rightarrow a + c \mid a, b, c \in \mathcal{M}, c = a/b, a \mod b = 0\} = \{4 + 2 \rightarrow 2 + 2, 6 + 2 \rightarrow 3 + 2, 6 + 3 \rightarrow 2 + 3, \ldots\}$. So, two molecules a and b can react, if a is a multiple of b. For the dynamics, we assume a well-stirred reaction vessel. The state of the reaction vessel of size M is represented by a vector (or equivalently by a multi-set) $P = (p_1, p_2, \ldots, p_M)$ where $p_i \in \mathcal{M}$. The dynamics is simulated by the following stochastic algorithm: (1) chose two integers $i, j \in \{1, \ldots, M\}, i \neq j$ randomly. (2) if there is a rule in $\mathcal{R}$ where $p_i + p_j$ matches the left hand side, replace p_i and p_j by the right hand side. (3) goto 1.

Assume that we initialize the reaction vessel P such that every molecule from $\mathcal{M}$ is contained in P, then we will surely reach a stationary state where all molecules from P are prime numbers and every prime number greater one and less or equal n is contained in P. The outcome (prime numbers present in P) is deterministic and in particular independent from the sequence of reactions, where the actual concentration of each prime number can vary and depends on the sequence of reactions. Now assume that P is smaller than $\mathcal{M}$, e.g., $M = 100$ and $n = 10000$. The outcome (molecular species present in P) is not deterministic. It depends on the sequence of updates, e.g., $P = (20, 24, 600)$ can result in the stable solutions $P = (20, 24, 30)$ or $P = (20, 24, 25)$. Note that the behavior (ability to produce prime numbers) depends critically on the reactor size M [41, 43].

A.2   Hypercyclic Associative Memory

Assume that we have an unreliable media, where all molecules decay sooner or later. In order to store data over a longer period, molecules have to be reproduced. Simple self-replicating molecules are not sufficient, since, as discussed by Eigen and Schuster [44], in a limited volume, self-replicating molecules compete for resources and can not coexist stably (exponential growth and no interaction assumed).

In the following example [41], three "units" of data $\{d_1, d_2, d_3\}$ are stored in three different molecules $\{w_1, w_2, w_3\}$. In order to query the memory, there are three input molecules $\{q_1, q_2, q_3\}$. Our demanded specifications are: the chemical system should store the data for a long period of time, under constant dilution of the molecules. The system should produce d_i provided q_i as input. We assume the following reactions: $\mathcal{R} = \{w_1 + w_2 \rightarrow w_1 + w_2 + w_2, w_2 + w_3 \rightarrow w_2 + w_3 + w_3, w_3 + w_1 \rightarrow w_1 + w_2 + w_1, w_1 + q_1 \rightarrow w_1 + q_1 + d_1, w_2 + q_2 \rightarrow w_1 + q_2 + d_2, w_3 + q_3 \rightarrow w_1 + q_3 + d_3\}$. For the dynamics, we assume a well-stirred reaction vessel that contains a constant number of M molecules. The state of the vessel is represented by a vector (or equivalently by a multi-set) $P = (p_1, p_2, \ldots, p_M)$ where $p_i \in \mathcal{M}$. The dynamics is simulated by the following stochastic algorithm: (1) chose three integers $i, j, k \in \{1, \ldots, M\}, i \neq j$ randomly. (2) if there is a rule $p_i + p_j \rightarrow p_i + p_j + x$ in $\mathcal{R}$, replace molecule p_k by x. (3) goto 1. This kind of stochastic algorithm is equivalent to the deterministic replicator equation and catalytic network equation. It is also used in several other works [45, 35, 46].

Figure 2 shows an example of a simulation where 400 molecules of type q_1 are inserted into a reactor that contains approximately the same amount of each information molecule $\{w_1, w_2, w_3\}$. Interaction of q_1 with w_1 results in the production of d_1. Since all molecules are subject to a dilution flow and q_1 is not produced, q_1 and d_1 are washed out while the concentrations of $\{w_1, w_2, w_3\}$ stabilize again.

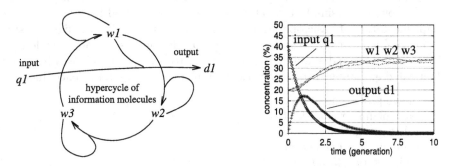

Fig. 2. Hypercyclic associative memory. **Left:** Illustration of the reaction network. An arrow represents a catalytic interaction where both reactants act as catalysts and are not used up. Only the active network is shown. **Right:** Example of a stochastic simulation of a query. 400 molecules of type q_1 are inserted. Reactor size $M = 1000$

Programming Reaction-Diffusion Processors

Andrew Adamatzky

Faculty of Computing, Engineering and Mathematics,
University of the West of England, UK
andrew.adamatzky@uwe.ac.uk
http://www.cems.uwe.ac.uk/~aadamatz

Abstract. In reaction-diffusion (RD) processors, both the data and the results of the computation are encoded as concentration profiles of the reagents. The computation is performed via the spreading and interaction of wave fronts. Most prototypes of RD computers are specialized to solve certain problems, they can not be, in general, re-programmed. In the paper, we try to show possible means of overcoming this drawback. We envisage an architecture and interface of programmable RD media capable of solving a wide range of problems.

1   Reaction-Diffusion Computers

Reaction-diffusion (RD) chemical systems are well known for their unique ability to efficiently solve combinatorial problems with natural parallelism [2].

In RD processors, both the data and the results of the computation are encoded as concentration profiles of the reagents. The computation *per se* is performed via the spreading and interaction of wave fronts.

The RD computers are parallel because the chemical medium's micro-volumes update their states simultaneously, and molecules diffuse and react in parallel (see overviews in [1, 2, 8]). RD information processing in chemical media became a hot topic of not simply theoretical but also experimental investigations since implementation of basic operations of image processing using the light-sensitive Belousov-Zhabotinsky (BZ) reaction [28]. During the last decade a wide range of experimental and simulated prototypes of RD computing devices have been fabricated and applied to solve various problems of computer science, including

- image processing [35, 3],
- path planning [43, 12, 34, 6],
- robot navigation [7, 10],
- computational geometry [5],
- logical gates [45, 39, 4],
- counting [24],
- memory units [30].

Despite promising preliminary results in RD computing, the field still remains art rather then science, most RD processors are produced on an *ad hoc* basis without structured top-down approaches, mathematical verification, rigorous

J.-P. Banâtre et al. (Eds.): UPP 2004, LNCS 3566, pp. 33–46, 2005.

methodology, relevance to other domains of advanced computing. There is a need to develop a coherent theoretical foundation of RD computing in chemical media. Particular attention should be paid to issues of programmability, because by making RD processors programmable we will transform them from marginal outcasts and curious freaks to enabled competitors of conventional architectures and devices.

2   How to Program Reaction-Diffusion Computers?

Controllability is inherent constituent of programmability. How do real chemical media respond to changes in physical conditions? Are they controllable? If yes then what properties of the media can be used most effectively to program these chemical systems? Despite the fact that the problem of controlling RD media did not receive proper attention until recently some preliminary although rather mosaic results have become accessible in the last decade. There is no coherent view on the subject and this will be a major future task to build a theoretical and experimental framework of chemical medium controllability. Below we provide an overview of the findings related to the external control of chemical media. They demonstrate viability of our ideas and show that the present state-of-the-art laboratory methods allow for the precise tuning of these chemical systems, and thus offer an opportunity to program RD processors.

2.1   Electric Field

The majority of the literature, related to theoretical and experimental studies concerning the controllability of RD medium, deals with application of an electric field. In a thin-layer BZ reactor stimulated by an electric field the following phenomena are observed:

- the velocity of excitation waves is increased by a negative and decreased by a positive electric field;
- a wave is split into two waves that move in opposite directions if a very high electric field is applied across the evolving medium [40];
- crescent waves are formed not commonly observed in the field absent evolution of the BZ reaction [23];
- stabilisation and destabilisation of wave fronts [26];
- an alternating electric field generates a spiral wave core that travels within the medium; the trajectory of the core depends on the field frequency and amplitude [38].

Computer simulations with the BZ medium confirm that

- waves do not exist in a field-free medium but emerge when a negative field is applied [33];
- an electric field causes the formation of waves that change their sign with a change in concentration, and applied constant field induces drift of vortices [32];
- externally applied currents cause the drift of spiral excitation patterns [42].

It is also demonstrated that by applying stationary two-dimensional fields to a RD system one can obtain induced heterogeneity in a RD system and thus increase the morphological diversity of the generated patterns (see e.g. [18]). These findings seem to be universal and valid for all RD systems: applying a negative field accelerates wave fronts; increasing the applied positive field causes wave deceleration, wave front retardation, and eventually wave front annihilation. Also a recurrent application of an electric field leads to formation of complex spatial patterns [41]. A system of methylene blue, sulfide, sulfite and oxygen in a polyacrylamide gel matrix gives us a brilliant example of electric-field controlled medium. Typically hexagon and strip patterns are observed in the medium. Application of an electric field makes striped patterns dominate in the medium, even orientation of the stripes is determined by the intensity of the electric field [31].

2.2   Temperature

Temperature is a key factor in the parameterisation of the space-time dynamics of RD media. It is shown that temperature is a bifurcation parameter in a closed non-stirred BZ reactor [29]. By increasing the temperature of the reactor one can drive the space-time dynamic of the reactor from periodic oscillations $(0 - 3^oC)$ to quasi-periodic oscillations $(4 - 6^oC)$ to chaotic oscillations $(7 - 8^oC)$. Similar findings are reported in simulation experiments on discrete media [2], where a lattice node's sensitivity can be considered as an analogue of temperature.

2.3   Substrate's Structure

Modifications of reagent concentrations and structure of physical substrate may indeed contribute to shaping space-time dynamics of RD media. Thus, by varying the concentration of malonic acid in a BZ medium one can achieve

- the formation of target waves;
- the annihilation of wave fronts;
- the generation of stable propagating reduction fronts [26].

By changing substrate we can achieve transitions between various types of patterns formed, see e.g. [22] on transitions between hexagons and stripes. This however could not be accomplished 'on-line', during the execution of a computational process, or even between two tasks, the whole computing device should be 're-fabricated', so we do not consider this option prospective. Convection is yet another useful factor governing space-time dynamics of RD media. Thus, e.g., convection 2nd order waves, generated in collisions of excitation waves in BZ medium, may travel across the medium and affect, e.g. annihilate, existing sources of the wave generation [36].

2.4   Illumination

Light was the first [27] and still remains the best, see overview in [35], way of controlling spatio-temporal dynamics of RD media (this clearly applies mostly to light-sensitive species as BZ reaction). Thus, applying light of varying intensity we can control medium's excitability [19] and excitation dynamic in

BZ-medium [17, 25], wave velocity [37], and patter formation [46]. Of particular interest to implementation of programmable logical circuits are experimental evidences of light-induced back propagating waves, wave-front splitting and phase shifting [47].

3   Three Examples of Programming RD Processors

In this section we briefly demonstrate a concept of control-based programmability in models of RD processors. Firstly, we show how to adjust reaction rates in RD medium to make it perform computation of Voronoi diagram over a set of given points. Secondly, we provide a toy model of tunable three-valued logical gates, and show how to re-program a simple excitable gate to implement several logical operations by simply changing excitability of the medium's sites. Thirdly, we indicate how to implement logical circuits in architecture-less RD excitable medium.

3.1   Programming with Reaction Rates

Consider a cellular automaton model of an abstract RD excitable medium. Let a cell x of two-dimensional lattice takes four states: resting $\circ$, excited $(+)$, refractory $(-)$ and precipitated $\star$, and update their states in discrete time t depending on a number $\sigma^t(x)$ of excited neighbors in its eight-cell neighborhood as follows (Fig. 1):

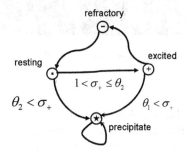

Fig. 1. Cell state transition graph for cellular-automaton model of precipitating RD medium

- Resting cell x becomes excited if $0 < \sigma^t(x) \leq \theta_2$ and precipitated if $\theta_2 < \sigma^t(x)$.
- Excited cell 'precipitates' if $\theta_1 < \sigma^t(x)$ and becomes refractory otherwise.
- Refractory cell recovers to resting state unconditionally, and precipitate cell does not change its state.

Initially we perturb the medium, excite it in several sites, thus inputting data. Waves of excitation are generated, they grow, collide with each other and

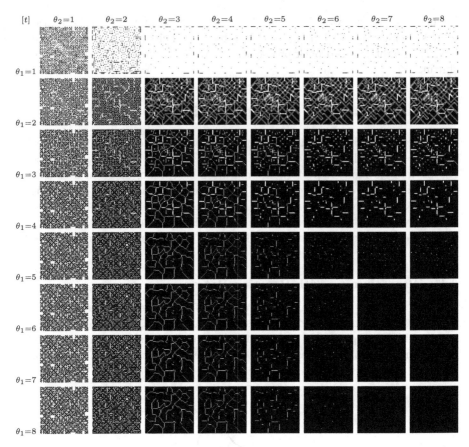

Fig. 2. Final configurations of RD medium for $1 \leq \theta_1 \leq \theta_2 \leq 2$. Resting sites are black, precipitate is white

annihilate in result of the collision. They may form a stationary inactive concentration profile of a precipitate, which represents result of the computation. Thus, we can only be concerned with reactions of precipitation:

$$+ \rightarrow^{k_1} \star$$

and

$$\circ \boxplus + \rightarrow^{k_2} \star,$$

where k_1 and k_2 are inversely proportional to θ_1 and θ_2, respectively. Varying θ_1 and θ_2 from 1 to 8, and thus changing precipitation rates from maximum possible to a minimum one, we obtain various kinds of precipitate patterns, as shown in Fig. 2.

Most of the patterns produced, see enlarged examples at Fig. 3abc, are relatively useless (at least there no sensible interpretations of them) Precipitate patterns developed for relatively high ranges of reactions rates: $3 \leq \theta_1, \theta_2 \leq 4$

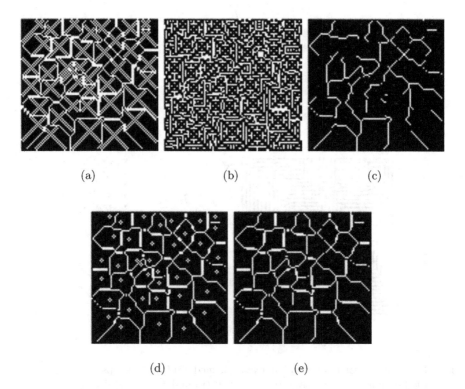

(a)   (b)   (c)

(d)   (e)

Fig. 3. Exemplar configurations of RD medium for (a) $\theta_1 = 2$ and $\theta_2 = 3$, (b) $\theta_1 = 4$ and $\theta_2 = 2$, (c) $\theta_1 = 7$ and $\theta_2 = 3$, (d) $\theta_1 = 3$ and $\theta_2 = 3$, (e) $\theta_1 = 4$ and $\theta_2 = 3$. Resting sites are black, precipitate is white

represent discrete Voronoi diagrams (given 'planar' set, represented by sites of initial excitation, is visible in pattern $\theta_1 = \theta_2 = 3$ as white dots inside Voronoi cells) derived from the set of initially excited sites, see Fig. 3de. This example demonstrates that externally controlling precipitation rates we can force RD medium to compute Voronoi diagram.

3.2   Programming with Excitability

When dealing with excitable media excitability, as one can infer from the name, is the key parameter to tune spatio-temporal dynamics. In [2] we demonstrated that by varying excitability we can force the medium to exhibit almost all possible types of excitation dynamics. Let each cell of 2D automaton takes three states: resting ($\cdot$), exciting ($+$) and refractory ($-$), and updates its state depending on number σ_+ of excited neighbors in its 8-cell neighborhood (Fig. 4a). A cell goes from excited to refractory and from refractory to resting states unconditionally, and resting cell excites if $\sigma_+ \in [\theta_1, \theta_2]$, $1 \leq \theta_1 \leq \theta_2 \leq 8$. By changing θ_1 and θ_2 we can move the medium dynamics in a domain of 'conventional' excitation waves, useful for image processing and robot navigation [7], as well as

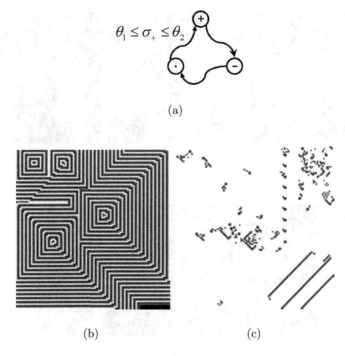

$$\theta_1 \leq \sigma_+ \leq \theta_2$$

(a)

(b)　　　　　　　　　　(c)

Fig. 4. Cell-state transition graph of excitable medium (a) and snapshots of space-time excitation dynamics for excitability $\sigma_+ \in [1,8]$ (b) and $\sigma_+ \in [2,2]$ (c)

to make it exhibits mobile localized excitations (quasi-particles, discrete analogs of dissipative solitons), employed in collision-based computing [2] (Fig. 4bc).

Let us discuss now a more advanced example on how we can program logical gates using excitability. Consider a T-shaped excitable RD medium built of three one-dimensional cellular arrays joined at one point (details are explained in [11]); two channels are considered as inputs, and third channel as an output. Every cell of this structure has two neighbors apart of end cells, which have one neighbor each, and a junction cell, which has three neighbors. Each cell takes three states: resting ($\circ$), excited ($+$) and refractory ($-$). A cell switches from excited state to refractory state, and from refractory to resting unconditionally. If resting cell excites when certain amount of its neighbors is excited then waves of excitation, in the form $+-$, travel along the channels of the gate. Waves generated in input channels, meet at a junction, and may pass or not pass to the output channel. We represent logical values as follows: no waves is FALSE, one wave $+-$ is NONSENSE and two waves $+ - \cdot + -$ represent TRUTH. Assume that sites of the excitable gate are highly excitable: every cell excites if at least one neighbor is excited. One or two waves generated at one of the inputs pass onto output channel; two single waves are merged in one single wave when collide at the junction; and, a single wave is 'absorbed' by train of two waves. Therefore, the gate with highly excitable sites implements Łukasiewicz disjunction (Fig. 5a).

$$
\begin{array}{c|ccc}
\vee_{\mathrm{L}} & T & F & \star \\
\hline
T & T & T & T \\
F & T & F & \star \\
\star & T & \star & \star
\end{array}
\qquad
\begin{array}{c|ccc}
\wedge_{\mathrm{L}} & T & F & \star \\
\hline
T & T & F & \star \\
F & F & F & F \\
\star & \star & F & \star
\end{array}
\qquad
\begin{array}{c|ccc}
\boxdot & T & F & \star \\
\hline
T & F & T & \star \\
F & T & F & \star \\
\star & \star & \star & F
\end{array}
$$

$$\quad\quad\text{(a)}\quad\quad\quad\quad\quad\text{(b)}\quad\quad\quad\quad\quad\text{(c)}$$

Fig. 5. Operations of Łukasiewics three-valued logic implemented in models of T-shaped excitable gate: (a) disjunction, $\sigma_+ \in \{\lfloor\frac{k}{2}\rfloor, \lceil\frac{k}{2}\rceil\}$ (b) conjunction, $\sigma_+ = \lceil\frac{k}{2}\rceil$, (c) NOT-Equivalence, $\sigma_+ = \lfloor\frac{k}{2}\rfloor$

Let us decrease sites sensitivity and make it depend on number k of cell neighbors: a cell excites if at least $\sigma_+ = \lceil\frac{k}{2}\rceil$ neighbors are excited. Then junction site can excite only when exactly two of its neighbors are excited, therefore, excitation spreads to output channels only when two waves meet at the junction. Therefore, when a single wave collide to a train of two waves the only single wave passes onto output channel. In such conditions of low excitability the gate implements Łukasiewicz conjunction (Fig. 5b). By further narrowing excitation interval: a cell is excited if exactly one neighbor is excited, we achieve situation when two colliding wave fronts annihilate, and thus output channel is excited only if either of input channels is excited, or if the input channels got different number of waves. Thus, we implement combination of Łukasiewicz NOT and Equivalence gates (Fig. 5c).

3.3   Dynamical Circuits

Logical circuits can be also fabricated in uniform, architecture-less, where not wires or channels are physically implemented, excitable RD medium, (e.g. sub-excitable BZ medium as numerically demonstrated in [9]) by generation, reflection and collision of traveling wave fragments. To study the medium we integrate two-variable Oregonator equation, adapted to a light-sensitive BZ reaction with applied illumination [17]

$$\frac{\partial u}{\partial t} = \frac{1}{\epsilon}(u - u^2 - (fv + \phi)\frac{u-q}{u+q}) + D_u\nabla^2 u$$

$$\frac{\partial v}{\partial t} = u - v$$

where variables u and v represent local concentrations of bromous acid and oxidized catalyst ruthenium, ϵ is a ratio of time scale of variables u and v, q is a scaling parameter depending on reaction rates, f is a stoichiometric coefficient, ϕ is a light-induced bromide production rate proportional to intensity of illumination. The system supports propagation of sustained wave fragments, which may be used as representations of logical variables (e.g. absence is False, presence is Truth). To program the medium we should design initial configuration of perturbations, that will cause excitation waves, and configurations of deflectors and prisms, to route these quasi-particle wave-fragments. While implementation

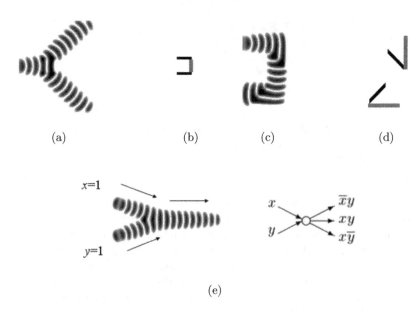

Fig. 6. Operating wave fragments. Overlay of images taken every 0.5 time units. Exciting domains of impurities are shown in black, inhibiting domains are gray. (a) Signal branching with impurity: wave fragment traveling west is split by impurity (b) into two waves traveling north-west and south-west. (c) Signal routing (U-turn) with impurities: wave fragment traveling east is routed north and then west by two impurities (d). A simple logical gate is shown in (e)

of Boolean operations *per se* is relatively straightforward [9], control of signal propagation, routing and multimplication of signals is of most importance when considering circuits not simply singe gates. To multiply a signal or to change wave-fragment trajectory we can temporarily apply illumination impurities to change local properties of the medium on a way the wave. Thus we can cause the wave-fragment to split (Fig. 6ab) or deflect (Fig. 6cd). A control impurity (Fig. 6bd), or deflector, consists of a few segments of sites which illumination level is slightly above or below overall illumination level of the medium. Combining these excitatory and inhibitory segments we can precisely control wave's trajectory, e.g. realize U-turn of a signal (Fig. 6cd). A simple logical gates implemented in collision of two wave-fragments is shown in Fig. 6e.

4   Multi-layered RD Processors: Co-programming

Ideally, it would be reasonable to have two excitable chemical systems physically co-existing in one reactor, so space-time dynamics of one chemical medium 'programs' (influences) space-time dynamics of another chemical medium. We did not have yet experimental implementations of such medium-medium programming, however our computational experiments on guiding a virtual robots indicate that the idea is feasible. Namely, to guide a robot we assume that the robot is attracted by wave-fronts of one system — which represents a target — and repelled by wave-fronts of the other system — which represents obstacles.

In [10] we navigated a virtual robot using two separate and isolated from each other chemical reactors containing the BZ medium. Obstacles are mapped onto one reactor and targets onto another. We assume the robot detects concentration of the chemical species using optical sensors from spatial snapshots of the BZ medium activity. We constructed a software model of 'pixbot' [10] — a pixel size robot which moves in discrete steps on images (attractive medium $\mathbf{A}$ and repelling medium $\mathbf{R}$) of the spatial excitation dynamics of the BZ medium.

The pixbot behaves as follows. Let a_{ij} and r_{ij} be blue color values of pixel (i,j) in images $\mathbf{A}$ and $\mathbf{R}$, and $(x,y)^t$ be the pixbot's coordinates at time step t. At each step of discrete time the pixbot can move to one of eight pixels closest to $(x,y)^t$. The pixbot coordinates are calculated as follows, $p^t = (x,y)^t$:

$$p^{t+1} = p^t + \vartheta(t, t-m)[f(p^t, g, \mathbf{A}, \mathbf{R})\chi(f(p^t, g, \mathbf{A}, \mathbf{R}))+$$

$$(1 - \chi(f(p^t, g, \mathbf{A}, \mathbf{R})))(\varrho(p^t, \mathbf{R}))]+$$

$$(1 - \vartheta(t, t-m)(\varrho(p^t, \mathbf{R}))$$

where $\chi(z) = 1$ if $z \neq 0$ and $\chi(z) = 0$ otherwise; $\vartheta(t, t-m) = 0$ if $|p^t - p^{t-m}| < k$ and $\vartheta(t, t-m) = 1$ otherwise;

$$f(p^t, g, \mathbf{A}, \mathbf{R}) = |\mathbf{V}|^{-1} \sum_{(u_i, u_j) \in \mathbf{V}} (u_i, u_j)$$

$$\mathbf{V} = \{(v_i, v_j) \in \{-1, 0, 1\} : |a_{p^t} - a_{p^t + (v_i, v_j)}| > g, \, r_{p^t + (v_i, v_j)} < c\}$$

and

$$\varrho(p^t, \mathbf{R}, m) = \mathtt{random}\{(v_i, v_j) \in \{-1, 0, 1\} : r_{p^t + (v_i, v_j)} < c\}$$

g and c are constant depending on initial concentration of reactants, in most experiments, $2 \leq c \leq 5$, $15 \leq g \leq 30$, $10 \leq m \leq 20$. The function ϑ plays a role of a 'kinetic energy accumulator': if the pixbot spends too much time wandering in the same local domain it is forced to jump randomly, this will allow pixbot to mount wave-fronts. The function $f()$ selects a site neighboring to p^t along the preferable descent of $\mathbf{A}$ and minimum values of $\mathbf{B}$. If such a site does not exist then a site with no obstacle wave is selected at random.

An example of the pixbot's collision-free movement towards a target is shown in Fig. 7, where attracting wave-fronts represent a target and repelling wave-fronts represent obstacles.

5   Discussion

Sluggishness, narrow range of computational tasks solved, and seeming unsusceptibility to a control are usually seen as main disadvantages of existing prototypes of RD computers. In the paper we briefly outlined several ways of external

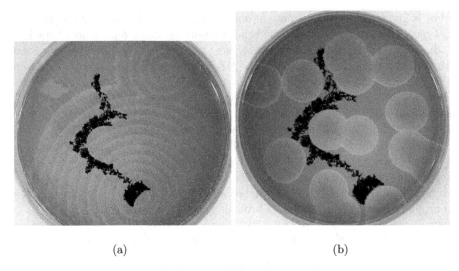

(a)   (b)

Fig. 7. Trajectories of pixbot moving towards the target through space with obstacles:
(a) trajectory of pixbot projected onto pattern of attracting wave-fronts, (b) trajectory
of pixbot projected onto pattern of repelling wave-fronts [10]

controlling, tuning, and ultimately programming, of spatially extended chemical devices. We have also indicated how to 'switch' a RD computer, with fixed
set of reactions but variable reaction rates, between several domains of problems, and thus make it more 'omnivorous'. Thus we made grounds for partial
dismissal of specialization and uncontrollability statements. As to the speed,
real-life RD processors are slow indeed, due to limitations on speed of diffusion
and phase waves traveling in a liquid layer or a gel. We can argue, however, that
future applications of the chemical processors lie in the field of micro-scale computing devices and soft robotic architectures, e.g. gel-made robots, where RD
medium forms an integral part of robot body [44]. A silicon fabrication is another way, however possibly a step back from material implementation point of
view, to improve speed of RD computers. This route seems to be well developed,
particularly in designing RD media in non-linear circuits and cellular neural
networks [20, 21, 10]. CMOS design and analog emulation of RD systems, BZ
medium in particular, have already demonstrated feasibility of mapping chemical dynamics onto silicon architectures [13, 14, 15, 16]. Semiconductor devices
based on minor carrier transport [16], like arrays of p-n-p-n diod based reaction
devices, give us a hope for forthcoming designs of nano-scale RD processors.

Acknowledgement

I thank Ben De Lacy Costello for numerous discussions on laboratory prototypes
of reaction-diffusion computers, Tetsuya Asai for enlightening me in electronic
reaction-diffusion devices, and participants of "Non-Linear Media Based Com-

puters" (Bristol, September, 2003) and "Unconventional Programming Paradigms" (Mont St Michel, 2004) workshops for help in shaping my ideas. I also thank Peter Dittrich for encouraging me to think about more computer-science related issues of reaction-diffusion computing.

References

1. Adamatzky, A.: Reaction-diffusion and excitable processors: a sense of the unconventional. Parallel and Distributed Computing **3** (2000) 113–132.
2. Adamatzky, A.: Computing in Nonlinear Media and Automata Collectives (Institute of Physics Publishing, 2001).
3. Adamatzky, A., De Lacy Costello, B. and Ratcliffe, N.M.: Experimental reaction-diffusion pre-processor for shape recognition. Physics Letters A **297** (2002) 344–352.
4. Adamatzky, A. and De Lacy Costello, B.P.J.: Experimental logical gates in a reaction-diffusion medium: The XOR gate and beyond. Phys. Rev. E **66** (2002) 046112.
5. Adamatzky, A. and De Lacy Costello, B.P.J.: On some limitations of reaction-diffusion computers in relation to Voronoi diagram and its inversion. Physics Letters A **309** (2003) 397–406.
6. Adamatzky, A. and De Lacy Costello, B.P.J.: Reaction-diffusion path planning in a hybrid chemical and cellular-automaton processor. Chaos, Solitons & Fractals **16** (2003) 727–736.
7. Adamatzky, A., De Lacy Costello, B., Melhuish, C. and Ratcliffe, N.: Experimental reaction-diffusion chemical processors for robot path planning. J. Intelligent & Robotic Systems **37** (2003) 233–249.
8. Adamatzky, A.: Computing with waves in chemical media: massively parallel reaction-diffusion processors. IEICE Trans. (2004), in press.
9. Adamatzky, A.: Collision-based computing in BelousovZhabotinsky medium. Chaos, Solitons & Fractals **21** (2004) 1259–1264.
10. Adamatzky, A., Arena, P., Basile, A., Carmona-Galan, R., De Lacy Costello, B., Fortuna, L., Frasca, M., Rodriguez-Vazquez, A.: Reaction-diffusion navigation robot control: from chemical to VLSI analogic processors. IEEE Trans. Circuits and Systems I, **51** (2004) 926–938.
11. Adamatzky, A. and Motoike, I.: Three-valued logic gates in excitable media, in preparation (2004).
12. Agladze, K., Magome, N., Aliev, R., Yamaguchi, T. and Yoshikawa, K.: Finding the optimal path with the aid of chemical wave. Physica D **106** (1997) 247–254.
13. Asai, T., Kato, H., and Amemiya, Y.: Analog CMOS implementation of diffusive Lotka-Volterra neural networks, INNS-IEEE Int. Joint Conf. on Neural Networks, P-90, Washington DC, USA, July 15–19, 2001.
14. Asai, T., Nishimiya, Y. and Amemiya, Y.: A CMOS reaction-diffusion circuit based on cellular-automaton processing emulating the Belousov-Zhabotinsky reaction. IEICE Trans. on Fundamentals of Electronics, Communications and Computer, **E85-A** (2002) 2093–2096.
15. Asai, T. and Amemiya, Y.: Biomorphic analog circuits based on reaction-diffusion systems. Proc. 33rd Int. Symp. on Multiple-Valued Logic (Tokyo, Japan, May 16–19, 2003) 197–204.

16. Asai, T., Adamatzky, A., Amemiya, Y.: Towards reaction-diffusion semiconductor computing devices based on minority-carrier transport. Chaos, Solitons & Fractals **20** (2004) 863–876.
17. Beato, V., Engel, H.: Pulse propagation in a model for the photosensitive Belousov-Zhabotinsky reaction with external noise. In: Noise in Complex Systems and Stochastic Dynamics, Edited by Schimansky-Geier, L., Abbott, D., Neiman, A., Van den Broeck, C. Proc. SPIE **5114** (2003) 353–62.
18. Bouzat, S. and Wio, H.S.: Pattern dynamics in inhomogeneous active media. Physica A **293** (2001) 405–420.
19. Brandtstädter, H., Braune, M., Schebesch, I. and Engel, H.: Experimental study of the dynamics of spiral pairs in light-sensitive BelousovZhabotinskii media using an open-gel reactor. Chem. Phys. Lett. **323** (2000) 145–154.
20. Chua, L.O.: CNN: A Paradigm for Complexity (World Scientific Publishing, 1998).
21. Chua, L.O. and Roska, T.: Cellular Neural Networks and Visual Computing: Foundations and Applications (Cambridge University Press, 2003).
22. De Kepper, P., Dulos, E., Boissonade, J., De Wit, A., Dewel, G. and Borckmans, P.: Reaction-diffusion patterns in confined chemical systems. J. Stat. Phys. **101** (2000) 495–508.
23. Feeney, R., Schmidt, S.L. and Ortoleva, P.: Experiments of electric field-BZ chemical wave interactions: annihilation and the crescent wave. Physica D **2** (1981) 536–544.
24. Gorecki, J., Yoshikawa, K., Igarashi, Y.: On chemical reactors that can count. J. Phys. Chem. A **107** (2003) 1664–1669.
25. Grill, S., Zykov, V. S., Müller, S. C.: Spiral wave dynamics under pulsatory modulation of excitability. J. Phys. Chem. **100** (1996) 19082–19088.
26. Kastánek P., Kosek, J., Snita,D., Schreiber, I. and Marek, M.: Reduction waves in the BZ reaction: Circles, spirals and effects of electric field, Physica D **84** (1995) 79–94.
27. Kuhnert, L.: Photochemische Manipulation von chemischen Wellen. Naturwissenschaften **76** (1986) 96–97.
28. Kuhnert, L., Agladze, K.L. and Krinsky, V.I.: Image processing using light-sensitive chemical waves. Nature **337** (1989) 244–247.
29. Masia, M., Marchettini, N., Zambranoa, V. and Rustici, M.: Effect of temperature in a closed unstirred Belousov-Zhabotinsky system. Chem. Phys. Lett. **341** (2001) 285–291.
30. Motoike, I.N. and Yoshikawa, K.: Information operations with multiple pulses on an excitable field. Chaos, Solitons & Fractals **17** (2003) 455–461.
31. Muenster, A.F, Watzl, M. and Schneider, F.W.: Two-dimensional Turing-like patterns in the PA-MBO-system and effects of an electric field. Physica Scripta **T67** (1996) 58–62.
32. Muñuzuri, A.P., Davydov, V.A., Pérez-Muñuzuri, V., Gómez-Gesteira, M. and Pérez-Villar, V.: General properties of the electric-field-induced vortex drift in excitable media. Chaos, Solitons, & Fractals **7** (1996) 585–595.
33. Ortoleva, P.: Chemical wave-electrical field interaction phenomena. Physica D **26** (1987) 67–84.
34. Rambidi, N.G. and Yakovenchuck, D.: Finding path in a labyrinth based on reaction–diffusion media. Adv. Materials for Optics and Electron. **7** (1999) 67–72.
35. Rambidi, N.: Chemical-based computing and problems of high computational complexity: The reaction-diffusion paradigm, In: Seinko, T., Adamatzky, A., Rambidi, N., Conrad, M., Editors, Molecular Computing (The MIT Press, 2003).

36. Sakurai, T., Miike, H., Yokoyama, E. and Muller, S.C.: Initiation front and an-nihilation center of convection waves developing in spiral structures of Belousov-Zhabotinsky reaction. J. Phys. Soc. Japan **66** (1997) 518–521.
37. Schebesch, I., Engel, H.: Wave propagation in heterogeneous excitable media. Phys. Rev. E **57** (1998) 3905-3910.
38. Seipel, M., Schneider, F.W. and Mnster, A.F.: Control and coupling of spiral waves in excitable media. Faraday Discussions **120** (2001) 395–405.
39. Sielewiesiuka, J. and Górecki, J.: On the response of simple reactors to regular trains of pulses. Phys. Chem. Chem. Phys. **4** (2002) 1326-1333.
40. Sevćikova, H. and Marek, M.: Chemical waves in electric field. Physica D **9** (1983) 140–156.
41. Sevćikova, H. and Marek, M.: Chemical front waves in an electric field. Physica D **13** (1984) 379–386.
42. Steinbock O., Schutze J., Muller, S.C.: Electric-field-induced drift and deformation of spiral waves in an excitable medium. Phys. Rev. Lett. **68** (1992) 248–251.
43. Steinbock, O., Tóth, A. and Showalter, K.: Navigating complex labyrinths: optimal paths from chemical waves. Science **267** (1995) 868–871.
44. Tabata, O., Hirasawa, H., Aoki, S., Yoshida, R. and Kokufuta, E.: Ciliary motion actuator using selfoscillating gel. Sensors and Actuators A **95** (2002) 234–238.
45. Tóth, A. and Showalter, K.: Logic gates in excitable media. J. Chem. Phys. **103** (1995) 2058–2066.
46. Wang, J.: Light-induced pattern formation in the excitable Belousov-Zhabotinsky medium. Chem. Phys. Lett. **339** (2001) 357–361.
47. Yoneyama, M.: Optical modification of wave dynamics in a surface layer of the Mn-catalyzed Belousov-Zhabotinsky reaction. Chem. Phys. Lett. **254** (1996) 191–196.

From Prescriptive Programming of Solid-State Devices to Orchestrated Self-organisation of Informed Matter

Klaus-Peter Zauner

School of Electronics and Computer Science,
University of Southampton, SO17 1BJ, United Kingdom
kpz@ecs.soton.ac.uk
www.ecs.soton.ac.uk/people/kpz/

Abstract. Achieving real-time response to complex, ambiguous, high-bandwidth data is impractical with conventional programming. Only the narrow class of compressible input-output maps can be specified with feasibly sized programs. Present computing concepts enforce formalisms that are arbitrary from the perspective of the physics underlying their implementation. Efficient physical realizations are embarrassed by the need to implement the rigidly specified instructions requisite for programmable systems. The conventional paradigm of erecting strong constraints and potential barriers that narrowly prescribe structure and precisely control system state needs to be complemented with a new approach that relinquishes detailed control and reckons with autonomous building blocks. Brittle prescriptive control will need to be replaced with resilient self-organisation to approach the robustness and efficiency afforded by natural systems. Structure-function self-consistency will be key to the spontaneous generation of functional architectures that can harness novel molecular and nano materials in an effective way for increased computational power.

1 Commanding the Quasi-universal Machine

The common conventional computer is an approximation of a hypothetical universal machine [1] limited by memory and speed constraints. Universal machines are generally believed to be in principle able to compute any computable function and are commonly used to define what can effectively be computed [2]. Correspondingly it is assumed that if processing speed and memory space of computers would indefinitely continue to increase, any computable information processing problem would eventually come within reach of practical devices. Accordingly time and space complexity of computation has been studied in detail [3] and technological advances have focused on memory capacity and switching speed [4]. But along with this there is another factor that limits realizable computing devices: the length of the program required to communicate a desired behaviour to the device [5]. The length of this program is limited by the state space of the

J.-P. Banâtre et al. (Eds.): UPP 2004, LNCS 3566, pp. 47–55, 2005.

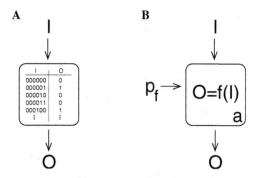

Fig. 1. Communicating a desired input-output map to a machine. The input-output map can in principle be thought of as a potentially very large lookup table that associates an output response with every input that can be discerned by the machine (**A**). For n bit input patterns (I) and a m bit output response (O) the, number of possible maps is 2^{m2^n}. To implement an arbitrary one of these maps on a quasi-universal machine, the mapping f has to be specified by the program p with respect of machine architecture a (**B**). Selecting an arbitrary map from the set of possible maps may require a specification of length: $\log_2 \left[2^{m2^n} \right] = m2^n$. Even for moderate pattern recognition problems (e.g., classifying low resolution images) the program length required for most mappings is impractical [6]

device and the capacity of the programmers. Even small problems can exhaust these practical limitations (cf. figure 1). As a consequence conventional computing architectures are restricted to the implementation of highly compressible input-output transforms [7]. The set of compressible maps is a small subset of the potential input-output functions—most behaviours cannot be programmed. Whether the inaccessible mappings would be useful for practical applications awaits further investigation. For complex ambiguous pattern recognition problems, a domain where organisms cope much better than existing technology, mappings of limited compressibility may be valuable.

The picture painted in figure 1 is optimistic with regard to the number of maps that can be implemented by a program of given size. It assumes that the machine architecture is not degenerate, i.e., any two programs that differ by at least one bit will give rise to distinct input-output maps. In practice, computing architectures often map many programs to the same input-output transformation. The transformation is usually implemented as a programmed sequence of elementary operations. The essence of each operation is to selectively discard information [8, 9]. As the number of elementary operations grows it becomes increasingly likely that all information regarding the input signals is dissipated and as a consequence the output of the computation is constant [10, 11]. Accordingly, the degeneracy of the mapping from program to input-output transform raises with increased program length in conventional architectures and the number input-output transforms accessible through programming is further reduced.

For a machine to be programmable, additional restrictions come into play. Programming is here equated with an engineering approach in which mental conception precedes physical creation (cf. [12]). It necessitates the possibility for the programmer to anticipate the actions of the available elementary operations. Only if the function of the elementary operations can be foreseen by the programmer can a desired input-output map be implemented by incrementally composing a program. Accordingly, the machine's architecture has to adhere to a fixed, finite user manual to facilitate programming. To achieve this, numerous potential interactions among the components of the machine need to be suppressed [13]. Programmability is achieved by using relatively large networks of components with fixed behaviour. This however does not allow for the efficiency afforded by networks of context sensitive components [14].

As outlined above, conventional programming is not always the most suitable way of implementing an input-output map. Some maps cannot be compressed into programs of practical length, and the need for programmability precludes hardware designs that elicit functionality from a minimum of material.

2   Learning, Adaptation, Self-organisation

Programmability is not a strict requirement for information processing systems. The enviable computing capabilities of cells and organisms are not implemented by programs. Non-programmed information processing is not limited to nature. Artificial neural networks provide a technological example of a system where programmability has been given up for the benefit of parallel operation [15]. Freeing the computing architecture from the need for predictable function of elementary components opens up new design degrees of freedom. Firstly, the fan-in for an elementary component could be increased by orders of magnitude. It may be interesting to note that neurons in the cortex of the mouse have on average 8000 input lines [16]. Secondly, there is no need for all components to operate according to identical specifications. This opens a path to broadening the material basis of computation by allowing for computational substrates the structure of which cannot be controlled in detail. And likewise, thirdly, the operation of the elementary components can depend on their context in the architecture, thus greatly increasing the number of interactions among the components that can be recruited for signal fusion.

Utilising these design degrees of freedom requires the development of new training algorithms for the resulting networks. Evolutionary methods that take the performance of a network as prediction for the performance of a randomly modified network are particularly suitable. They can cope with the complexity and inhomogeneity of architectures based on context sensitive components and benefit from the increased dimensionality in such networks [17, 18, 19]. Clearly, giving up programmability will not by itself increase the number of input-output transforms that can be implemented on a given system. The feasible length of training for the system draws the limit. However, the complexity of the input-output transformations is not restricted by the need for compact specification.

3   Orchestrating Informed Matter

Techniques for producing biomaterials and manufacturing nano-materials are rapidly developing. We already see materials with unprecedented characteristics arriving at an increasing rate. But so far computer science is not on a path to harnessing these new materials for increased computational power. Training the materials to act as logic gates is unlikely to be fruitful.

Present computing concepts enforce formalisms that are arbitrary from the perspective of the physics underlying their implementation. Nature's gadgets process information in starkly different ways than do conventionally programmed machines [20]. They exploit the physics of the materials directly and arrive at problem solutions driven by free energy minimisation while current computer systems are coerced by high potential barriers to follow a narrowly prescribed, contrived course of computation [21]. The latter is only possible in a macro-physical device and comes at the cost of using a large fraction of the material of the processing device for enforcing adherence to the formalism rather than actual information processing. As devices shrink to micro-physical scale it becomes increasingly difficult to isolate the operation of the device from the physics of their implementation. However, as outlined in the preceeding two sections, information processing can be implemented without a formalism that abstracts away from the underlying computing substrate.

Nature provides a large collection of implementations that employ computation driven directly by physics for sophisticated information processing tasks. This mode of computation is most clearly demonstrated by single-cell systems. A seed weighs time series of multiple ambiguous sensory signals to make the decision to grow, a vital decision from which it cannot retract [22]. Bacteria assess their chemical surroundings to adjust their motions in accordance with a complex trade-off among attractive and repulsive factors [23, 24]. Being too small to afford isolation from the micro-physics of their material components the information processing operations in these systems necessarily have to follow a course of computation inherent in molecular interactions.

In physics-driven information processing architectures the structure of an architecture and its processing function are inseparable. Accordingly physics-driven information processing is closely related to self-organisation. Self-organisation is taken here as a process that forms an organised functional structure and is essentially supported by the components of the structure themselves rather than a process conducted by an external infrastructure. The possibilities of self-organisation are exemplified by biological growth and development. Self-assembly of molecular structures is a relatively simple self-organisation process in the aforementioned sense. The formation of viruses [25] is the prototypic example of molecular self-assembly, but numerous functional structures in the cell, e.g., ribosomes [26] form in a similar fashion. Artificial self-assembly systems have been designed with inorganic [27], organic [28], and bio-molecules [29, 30] and provide a potential route to realizing artificial molecular information processors [31].

Fig. 2. Implementation paradigms for a computational device. Present conventional computer technology is indicated near the lower left corner. Random variation enters unintentionally in the production process. With increasing miniaturisation control will become increasingly more difficult (dashed arrow). Resilient architectures that can cope with wide component variation and the deliberate use of self-organisation processes provide the most likely path to complexification of computing architectures (bent arrow)

The practical implementation of an input-output map can adhere in varying degrees to different paradigms as illustrated in figure 2.

As engineering extends to base-components at nano meter scale, the fine-grained prescriptive control familiar from the macro-physical world becomes increasingly difficult to achieve. Accordingly the proportion of products conforming to specification is falling. To some extend it is possible to compensate for the loss of control during production in a subsequent selection procedure, as is common practice. Selecting functional structures from a pool of randomly created structures provides a first approach to nano-materials where detailed control is not feasible or not economical. If the process of structure formation is repeatable then the selection from random variation can be iterated for evolutionary progress.

A key driver for miniaturisation, however, is its potential for highly complex systems within a small volume. A production process relying on selection alone will not deliver such systems for two reasons. Firstly, the falling proportion of functional components will make the selection approach (indicated by the dashed arrow in figure 2) increasingly inefficient, particularly if systems with high component count are desired. Secondly, for selecting the products that exhibit correct functionality it is necessary to identify them. Doing so by testing incurs a high cost and exhaustive testing becomes prohibitive with rising system complexity.

To arrive at economic nano-scale systems of high complexity it is necessary to leave the implementation approach indicated by the baseline of the triangle in figure 2. One possible solution lies in the self-assembly properties of suitably formed base components. The challenge is to design base components in such a way that they will spontaneously form a desired architecture. This course of engineering (indicated by the bend arrow in figure 2) will require the considera-

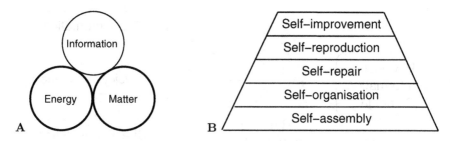

Fig. 3. To engineer self-organised systems, the traditional design considerations of energy and matter need to be augmented to include information (**A**). The potential gain of adding the information paradigm to our engineering toolkit can best be estimated by a view at nature. The biological world exhibits a hierarchy of self-processes that lead to increasingly more complex organisations of matter (**B**)

tion of information in addition to the traditional considerations of materials and energy (Figure 3A).

The concept of *informed matter* [32], i.e., molecules deliberately designed to carry information that enables them to interact individually, autonomously with other molecules, provides a basis for heterogeneous three-dimensional fabrication. Combining the abstract concepts of artifical chemistry [33] with the physics of supramolecular chemistry [28, 34] conceivably will enable the orchestration of self-organisation to arrive in practical time scales at physics-driven architectures.

This path to organising matter requires an information paradigm that does take physics into account. Molecules cannot be instructed in the way conventional computers are programmed, because their interactions and behaviour cannot be limited to simple abstractions. A methodology more akin to mechanical engineering than to software engineering, conceptually depicted in figure 4, is required.

4   Perspectives

Potential application domains for the principles outlined in the previous section are architectures in which the amount of matter necessary to implement a required function is important. Examples are pervasive computing and space exploration devices. A likely early application niche is the area of autonomous micro-robotic devices. With the quest for robots at a scale of a cubic millimetre and below molecular controllers become increasingly attractive [35, 36], and initial steps towards implementation are underway [37]. Coherent perception-action under real-time constraints with severely limited computational resources does not allow for the inefficiency of a virtual machine that abstracts physics away. For satisfactory performance the robot's control needs to adapt directly to the reality of its own body [38]. In fact the body structure can be an integral part of the computational infrastructure [39]. A second application domain is

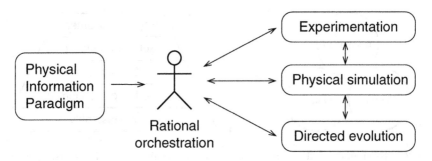

Fig. 4. Orchestration of informed matter. The interplay of experimental data, physical simulation of component behaviour in a systems context and adaptation methods such as directed evolution will play an important role in the process of engineering informed matter building-blocks that self-organise to spontaneously form architectures with desired functionality

bioimmersive computing. Components of a computational architecture could be encoded in the genome of a host cell and upon expression the computational machinery would autonomously form within the cell [40, 41, 42]. Any computational device small enough to fit within a cell will be severely limited in the amount of matter that can be used to implement it. It will need to employ the physics of its material directly for realizing its operations.

The 18 million organic compounds we known today comprise a negligible part of the space of possible organic molecules, estimated to 10^{63} substances [43]. Nature offers a glimpse at what is available in this space of possibilities with organised, adaptive, living, thinking, conscious matter. Following Lehn's trail-blazing call to "ultimately acquire the ability to create new forms of complex matter" [32] will require information processing concepts tailored to the microphysics of the underlying computational substrate.

Acknowledgements. Comments by Stefan Artmann, Srinandan Dasmahapatra, and Denis Nicole are gratefully acknowledged.

References

1. Turing, A.M.: On computable numbers with an application to the Entscheidungsproblem. In: Proceedings of the London Mathematical Society. Volume 42. (1937) 230–265 Corrections, Ibid vol. 43 (1937), pp. 544–546. Reprinted in *The Undecideable*, M. Davis, ed., Raven Press, New York, 1965.
2. Minsky, M.L.: Computation: Finite and Infinite Machines. Prentice-Hall, Englewood Cliffs, N.J. (1967)
3. Papadimitriou, C.H.: Computational Complexity. Addison-Wesley, Reading (1994)
4. Compañó, R.: Trends in nanoelectronics. Nanotechnology **12** (2001) 85–88
5. Chaitin, G.J.: On the length of programs for computing finite binary sequences. J. Assoc. Comput. Mach. **13** (1966) 547–569

6. Conrad, M., Zauner, K.P.: Conformation-based computing: a rational and a recipe. In Sienko, T., Adamatzky, A., Rambidi, N., Conrad, M., eds.: Molecular Computing. MIT Press, Cambridge, MA (2003) 1–31

7. Zauner, K.P., Conrad, M.: Molecular approach to informal computing. Soft Computing **5** (2001) 39–44

8. Landauer, R.: Irreversibility and heat generation in the computing process. IBM Journal **5** (1961) 183–191

9. Landauer, R.: Fundamental limitations in the computational process. Berichte der Bunsen-Gesellschaft **80** (1976) 1048–1059

10. Langdon, W.B.: How many good programs are there? How long are they? In Rowe, J., et al., eds.: Foundations of Genetic Algorithms FOGA-7, Torremolinos, 4-6 September, Morgan Kaufmann (2002)

11. Langdon, W.B.: The distribution of reversible functions is normal. In Riolo, R., ed.: Genetic Programming Theory and Practice, Ann Arbor, 15–17 May, Proceedings, Dordrecht, Kluwer Academic Publishers (2003)

12. Pfaffmann, J.O., Zauner, K.P.: Scouting context-sensitive components. In Keymeulen, D., Stoica, A., Lohn, J., Zebulum, R.S., eds.: The Third NASA/DoD Workshop on Evolvable Hardware—EH-2001, Long Beach, 12–14 July 2001, IEEE Computer Society, Los Alamitos (2001) 14–20

13. Conrad, M.: Scaling of efficiency in programmable and non-programmable systems. BioSystems **35** (1995) 161–166

14. Conrad, M.: The price of programmability. In Herken, R., ed.: The Universal Turing Machine: A Fifty Year Survey. Oxford University Press, New York (1988) 285–307

15. Partridge, D.: Non-programmed computation. Communications of the ACM **43** (2000) 293–302

16. Schüz, A.: Neuroanatomy in a computational perspective. In Arbib, M.A., ed.: The Handbook of Brain Theory and Neural Networks. MIT Press, Cambridge, MA (1995) 622–626

17. Cariani, P.: To evolve an ear: epistemological implications of Gordon Pask's electrochemical devices. Systems Research **10** (1993) 19–33

18. Thompson, A., Layzell, P., Zebulum, R.S.: Explorations in design space: Unconventional electronics design through artificial evolution. IEEE Trans. Evol. Comp. **3** (1999) 167–196

19. Miller, J.F., Downing, K.: Evolution in materio: Looking beyond the silicon box. In: 2002 NASA/DoD Conference on Evolvable Hardware (EH'02), July 15 - 18, 2002, Alexandria, Virginia, IEEE (2002) 167–176

20. Conrad, M.: Information processing in molecular systems. Currents in Modern Biology (now BioSystems) **5** (1972) 1–14

21. Zauner, K.P., Conrad, M.: Parallel computing with DNA: toward the anti-universal machine. In Voigt, H.M., Ebeling, W., Rechenberg, I., Schwefel, H.P., eds.: Parallel Problem Solving from Nature: PPSN IV. Volume 1141 of Lecture Notes in Computer Science., Berlin, Springer-Verlag, Berlin (1996) 696–705

22. Conrad, M.: The seed germination model of enzyme catalysis. BioSystems **27** (1992) 223–233

23. Adler, J., Tso, W.W.: "Decision"-making in bacteria: Chemotactic response of Escherichia coli to conflicting stimuli. Science **184** (1974) 1292–1294

24. Scharf, B.E., Fahrner, K.A., Turner, L., Berg, H.C.: Control of direction of flagellar rotation in bacterial chemotaxis. Proc. Natl. Acad. Sci. USA **95** (1998) 201–206

25. Wikoff, W.R., Johnson, J.E.: Virus assembly: Imaging a molecular machine. Current Biology **9** (1999) R296–R300

26. Ban, N., Nissen, P., Hansen, J., Moore, P.B., Steitz, T.A.: The complete atomic structure of the large ribosomal subunit at 2.4 å resolution. Science **289** (2000) 905–920
27. Müller, A., Beckmann, E., Bogge, H., Schmidtmann, M., Dress, A.: Inorganic chemistry goes protein size: a mo368 nano-hedgehog initiating nanochemistry by symmetry breaking. Angew. Chem. Int. Ed. Engl. **41** (2002) 1162–1167
28. Lehn, J.M.: Supramolecular chemistry—scope and perspectives: Molecules, super-molecules and molecular devices. Angewandte Chemie, Int. Ed. Engl. **27** (1988) 90–112
29. Seeman, N.C.: DNA in a material world. Nature (2003) 427–431
30. Zhang, S.: Fabrication of novel biomaterials through molecular self-assembly. Nature Biotechnology **21** (2003) 1171–1178
31. Conrad, M.: Quantum mechanics and cellular information processing: The self-assembly paradigm. Biomedica Biochimica Acta **49** (1990) 743–755
32. Lehn, J.M.: Supramolecular chemistry: from molecular information towards self-organization and complex matter. Reports on Progress in Physics **67** (2004) 249–265
33. Dittrich, P., Ziegler, J., Banzhaf, W.: Artificial chemistries—a review. Artificial Life **7** (2001) 225–275
34. Whiteside, G.M., Mathias, J.P., Seto, C.T.: Molecular self-assembly and nanochemistry: A chemical strategy for the synthesis of nanostructures. Science **254** (1991) 1312–1319
35. Ziegler, J., Dittrich, P., Banzhaf, W.: Towards a metabolic robot control system. In Holcombe, M., Paton, R., eds.: Information Processing in Cells and Tissues. Plenum Press, New York (1998) 305–317
36. Adamatzky, A., Melhuish, C.: Parallel controllers for decentralized robots: towards nano design. Kybernetes **29** (2000) 733–745
37. Adamatzky, A., de Lacy Costello, B., Melluish, C., Ratcliffe, N.: Experimental implementation of mobile robot taxis with onboard Belousov-Zhabotinsky chemical medium. Materials Science & Engineering C **24** (2004) 541–548
38. Elliott, T., Shadbolt, N.R.: Developmental robotics: manifesto and application. Phil. Trans. R. Soc. Lond. A **361** (2003) 2187–2206
39. Hasslacher, B., Tilden, M.W.: Living machines. Robotics and Autonomous Systems (1995) 143–169
40. Atkinson, M.R., Savageau, M.A., Myers, J.T., Ninfa, A.J.: Development of genetic circuitry exhibiting toggle switch or oscillatory behavior in Escherichia coli. Cell **113** (2003) 597–607
41. Benenson, Y., Gil, B., Ben-Dor, U., Adar, R., Shapiro, E.: An autonomous molecular computer for logical control of gene expression. Nature **429** (2004) 423–429
42. Blake, W.J., Isaacs, F.J.: Synthetic biology evolves. Trends in Biotechnology **22** (2004) 321–324
43. Scheidtmann, J., Weiß, P.A., Maier, W.F.: Hunting for better catalysts and materials—combinatorial chemistry and high throughput technology. Applied Catalysis A: General **222** (2001) 79–89

Relational Growth Grammars – A Graph Rewriting Approach to Dynamical Systems with a Dynamical Structure

Winfried Kurth[1], Ole Kniemeyer[1], and Gerhard Buck-Sorlin[1,2]

[1] Brandenburgische Technische Universität Cottbus, Department of Computer Science,
Chair for Practical Computer Science / Graphics Systems,
P.O.Box 101344, 03013 Cottbus, Germany
`{wk, okn}@informatik.tu-cottbus.de`
[2] Institute of Plant Genetics and Crop Plant Research (IPK), Dept. Cytogenetics,
Corrensstr. 3, 06466 Gatersleben, Germany
`Buck-Sorlin@ipk-gatersleben.de`

Abstract. Relational growth grammars (RGG) are a graph rewriting formalism which extends the notations and semantics of Lindenmayer systems and which allows the specification of dynamical processes on dynamical structures, particularly in biological and chemical applications. RGG were embedded in the language XL, combining rule-based and conventional object-oriented constructions. Key features of RGG and of the software GroIMP (Growth grammar related Interactive Modelling Platform) are listed. Five simple examples are shown which demonstrate the essential ideas and possibilities of RGG: signal propagation in a network, cellular automata, globally-sensitive growth of a plant, a "chemical" prime number generator, and a polymerisation model using a simple mass-spring kinetics.

1 Introduction

Rule-based programming is one of the traditionally acknowledged paradigms of programming [5], but its application has in most cases been restricted to logical inference or to spaces with restricted forms of topology: grids in the case of cellular automata [20], locally 1-dimensional branched structures in the case of classical L-systems [14]. Recently, there has been growing interest in rule-based simulation of dynamical systems with a dynamical structure, using diverse types of data structures and topologies, motivated by biological and chemical applications [7].

In this paper we propose a rewriting formalism, "relational growth grammars" (RGG), acting on relational structures, i.e. graphs with attributed edges, which generalizes L-systems and allows the specification of dynamical processes on changing structures in a wide field of applications. By associating the nodes of the graphs with classes in the sense of the object-oriented paradigm, we obtain a further degree of flexibility. Here we will explain the fundamental concepts and show simple examples with the aim to demonstrate the essential ideas and possibilities of this approach.

J.-P. Banâtre et al. (Eds.): UPP 2004, LNCS 3566, pp. 56 – 72, 2005.

Our work was motivated by the demand for a uniform modelling framework capable of representing genomes and macroscopic structures of higher organisms (plants), all in the same formalism [11]. Within the frame of a "Virtual Crops" project, we thus created the language XL, an extension of Java allowing a direct specification of RGG, and the software GroIMP (Growth-Grammar related Interactive Modelling Platform) enabling interpretation of XL code and easy user interaction during simulations [10].

2   Relational Growth Grammars

An RGG rule is a quintuple (L, C, E, R, P) with $L \cup C \neq \emptyset$. L, the *left-hand side proper* of the rule, is a set of graphs with node labels and edge labels. A *derivation step* of an RGG involves the removal of a copy ("match") of one rule's L from a (usually) larger graph and the insertion of the corresponding R, the *right-hand side proper* of the rule, which is also a set of graphs (with the underlying node sets not necessarily disjunct from those of L). C is again a set of labelled graphs (with the node set possibly but not necessarily overlapping with that of L) and is called the *context* of the rule. For a rule, in order to be applicable the set C must match with a set of subgraphs of the given graph in a way which is consistent with the match of L, but in the derivation step the context is not removed (except for the parts that are also in L). This notion of context generalizes the "left" and "right contexts" of context-sensitive L-systems [14] and enables a flexible control of subgraph replacement by specifying a local situation which must be given before a rule can be applied. E is a set of logical expressions in some syntax which we are not going to define in detail here. These expressions usually contain some parameters referring to node labels from $L \cup C$ and are interpreted as *conditions* which must be met before the rule can be applied. Conditions may also contain some function calls evoking a random number generator: if this is the case the rule is called *stochastic*. Finally, P is a (possibly empty) list of commands which are also not specified syntactically here, possibly involving parameters referring to node labels from $L \cup C \cup R$ and parameters from E. P specifies a procedural piece of code which is executed after rule application. We write RGG rules in the form

$$(* \ C \ *), \ L, \ (E) \ \texttt{==>} \ R \ \{ P \};$$

the order of the C, L and E parts being indeterminate.

Figure 1 illustrates a simple example of an RGG rule with $C = E = P = \emptyset$ (upper part) and its application to a graph (lower part). A possible text notation for this rule in our XL syntax would be `i -b-> j, j -a-> k, k -a-> i ==> j`.

In our applications, we found it useful to have a short notation for rules with $L = R = \emptyset$. In this case, only parameters from the context C (and possibly from E) appear in the procedural part, and we write

$$C , (E) \ \texttt{::>} \ P.$$

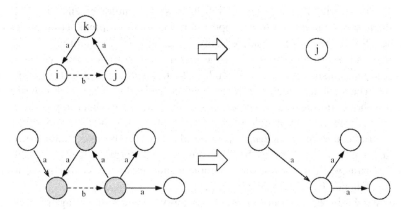

Fig. 1. An RGG rule in graphical notation (*upper part*) and its application to a given graph (*lower part*). The shaded nodes are matched by the left-hand side of the rule. From ([11])

An RGG is a set of RGG rules. In the language XL, RGG rules can be put together in blocks, thus enabling an additional hierarchy of rules and an explicit control of their order of application, like in table L-systems [16]. An RGG-based *derivation* is a sequence of discrete, successive derivation steps, starting from a given initial graph (axiom). In each step, one or all matching rules are applied, depending on the chosen mode of rule application (see below).

RGG were partly inspired by the PROGRES graph grammar system [18]. Further-more, features from parametric L-systems were incorporated into the RGG formalism. Particularly, commands from turtle geometry (cf. [14]) are allowed as nodes and can serve to interpret the derived graphs geometrically.

Pure rule-based programming does not in all situations allow an intuitive access. The notion of "programmed graph replacement systems" [17] was introduced to over-come this limitation: additional programming structures, following a different para-digm, are supported. In the RGG approach, the inclusion of *P* in our definition allows the execution of code from a conventional object-oriented language. Additionally, in XL such a language (Java) serves as a framework for the whole RGG and allows the user to define constants, variables, classes and methods. Furthermore, graph nodes in XL are Java objects and can carry arbitrary additional information and functionalities, e.g., concerning geometry, visual appearance or animated behaviour.

3 Key Features of RGG

Two issues require special consideration in graph grammars: the *mode of rule application* and the *embedding* of the right-hand side into the graph immediately after rule application. *Sequential* and *parallel* mode of application are well known from Chomsky grammars and L-systems, respectively. In most physical, chemical and biological applications, the parallel mode turns out to be more appropriate. However, the parallel application of rules requires the specification of a *conflict resolution strategy* for overlapping matches of left-hand sides. Future extensions of the RGG formalism will contain explicit support for the most common conflict resolution schemes. So far, we have considered only a special case: the multiple matching of *L* with one and the same copy of *L* in the graph. This always occurs where *L* allows some automorphism and where *C* and *E* do not enforce a selection between the matches. The standard mode of rule application realized in XL, which is basically the single-pushout approach (also known as the algebraic or Berliner approach) [3], tries to apply the rule to every match. In many applications it is more meaningful to apply a rule only once to an *underlying node set* of a match. The selection among the isomorphic matches has then to be done either nondeterministically or following a specified strategy. This option will be implemented in a later XL version; currently it must be emulated by additional conditions in part *E* of the rule.

Our standard mechanism of *embedding* simply transfers incoming (resp. outgoing) edges of the textually leftmost (resp. rightmost) nodes of *L* to the textually leftmost (resp. rightmost) nodes of *R*. Future versions of XL will allow other embedding strategies.

We have shown in another paper [11] that it is straightforward to represent typical *standard data structures* like sets, multisets, lists or multiple-scaled trees as labelled graphs. The RGG formalism provides standard types of edges (i.e., special edge labels) to represent common relations occurring in these data structures, like the successor relation in lists or the membership relation in sets. Because the successor relation is used so frequently, it is denoted by a blank in our notation, i.e., **a b** is equivalent to **a -successor-> b**. Additionally, the user can define new relations, using e.g. algebraic operators like the transitive hull, which can be employed in RGG rules in the same way as edges.

Several graph transformation software systems are already available, e.g., AGG [4] and PROGRES [18]. However, these systems—like most of the graph-grammar approaches from the Seventies and Eighties, see, e.g., [13, 8]—do not support the parallel mode of rule application which is essential for many biological applications. Neither do they allow a syntax which directly extends some well-established notations from L-system-based plant modelling [14]. Since our target group mainly consists of researchers from the plant sciences, there was sufficient motivation to create our own tool.

Nevertheless, advanced tools like PROGRES can serve as a model for further development of the RGG formalism. The PROGRES language, for example, provides built-in semantics for consistency verification of the graph structure; it supports user-definable derived attributes, post-conditions which are checked after application of graph productions, and a more versatile graph query language. At least some of these features will be included in future specifications of our RGG formalism.

4 GroIMP

The realisation of RGG-based models – by means of the language XL – is one of the aims of the software GroIMP (Growth-Grammar related Interactive Modelling

Platform). A sheer XL compiler would not be sufficient; at least an immediate visualisation of the outcome and basic user interaction has to be possible. These features are well-known in present modelling platforms, cf. [15] for a platform which is widely used in the field of L-system-based plant modelling. The software GroIMP includes these features; they are built on top of a general platform infrastucture which provides, among others,

- 3D visualisation and manipulation,
- property editors for objects of the scene,
- an integrated XL compiler,
- integrated text editors for XL source code,
- a file import/export to VRML, POV-Ray, cpfg [15],
- an HTML viewer for model documentation.

The platform is implemented in Java. Figure 2 shows a screenshot.

Compared to other integrated graph grammar systems, GroIMP focuses on a seamless integration of graph grammars into a 3D modelling platform. Hence, tools like graphical rule editors or topological graph viewers, which are present in PROGRES or AGG, are missing at the moment; on the other hand, GroIMP contains a rich set of node classes representing 3D geometry (geometric primitives, parametric surfaces, lights) which can be visualized and interactively modified within GroIMP.

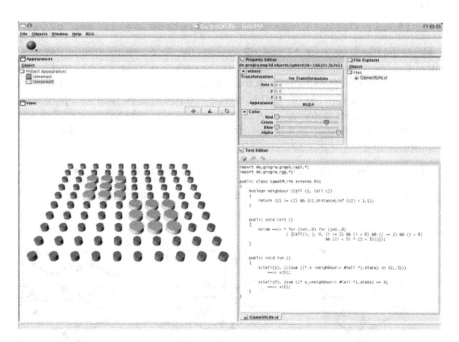

Fig. 2. Screenshot of GroIMP, showing the initial situation of the "Game of Life" example (see Example 2 below)

Though our RGG implementation XL is tightly integrated in GroIMP, both XL and GroIMP can be used separately; the coupling is established by XL's graph model interface. This interface can be implemented by other applications which contain graph-like structures and want XL's graph grammar capabilities to operate on these structures. This has been done for the commercial 3D modelling platform CINEMA 4D as part of a student's thesis [9].

GroIMP is an open-source project; it is distributed under the terms of the General Public License at **http://www.grogra.de**.

5 Examples

5.1 Example 1: Spreading of a Signal in a Network

We assume that a signal in each time step jumps from a given cell to all adjacent cells of a network and changes the state of each cell it reaches from "inactive" (0) to "active" (1). In our implementation in XL we make use of the possibility to use objects as nodes which can carry arbitrary additional data, in this case the state of the cell. "Cell" is a predefined class which contains a variable called "state", but such a class could also be defined by the user. The signal propagation requires only one RGG rule:

```
(* c1: Cell *) c2: Cell, (c1.state == 1) ==> c2(1).
```

Here, the blank between ***)** and **c2** denotes the successor relation in the network where the rule is to be applied. "**Cell**" is the node type (class), "**c1**" and "**c2**" are labels of nodes serving to distinguish them and to refer to them on the right-hand side, and "**state**" is a variable of "**Cell**" which can likewise be seen as a parameter of the nodes and which is forced to 1 at node **c2** on the right-hand side. The way in which the context is specified in this rule is a shorthand notation for the definition-conforming rule

```
(* c1: Cell c2: Cell *), c2, (c1.state == 1) ==> c2(1).
```

The result of two steps of rule application is illustrated in Figure 3.

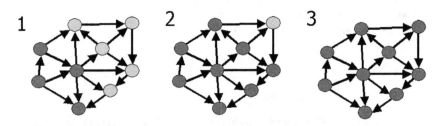

Fig. 3. Application of the signal propagation rule to a network. Dark nodes have state 1, light-grey nodes 0

This example simulates the dynamics of some state variable, but there is no dynamical structure; the topology of the network remains unchanged. Hence this is a simple case, however, using the same basic rule structure it is possible to simulate the dynamics of complex metabolic and gene regulation networks, using real-valued concentrations and Michaelis-Menten kinetics in the state-changing rules (see [2, 11] for examples).

5.2 Example 2: "Game of Life"

Cellular automata (CA) can easily be expressed as RGG. This is demonstrated at the example of the "Game of Life", a well-known 2-dimensional CA with nontrivial longterm behaviour [6]. We use again the class "Cell", with state values of 1, for "living", and 0, for "dead". The following snippet of XL code contains the complete specification of the CA in the form of one declaration of a function and three rules.

```
boolean neighbour(Cell c1, Cell c2)
  { return (c1 != c2) && (c1.distanceLinf(c2) < 1.1); }

public void init()
  [
  Axiom ==> XTranslation(-4) YTranslation(2) ZTranslation(-5)
            for(i=0..9) for(j=0..9)
            ([ Cell(i, j, (i>=2)&&(i<8)&&(j>=2)&&(j<8)
                          &&((i<5)^(j<5))) ]);
  ]

public void run()
  [
  x:Cell(1),
    (!(sum( (* x -neighbour-> #Cell *).state) in {2..3}))
      ==> x(0);
  x:Cell(0),
    ( sum( (* x -neighbour-> #Cell *).state) == 3)
      ==> x(1);
  ]
```

The declaration in the first two lines defines the Moore neighbourhood as a new edge type between "Cell" nodes, based upon a geometric relation (checkerboard distance, denoted **distanceLinf**, lower than 1.1). The block "**init**" contains only the start rule: The start symbol, **Axiom**, is transformed into a square (10×10) pattern of cells. The "**for**" construction generalizes the repetition operator used in L-systems [12]. It simply iterates the subsequent graph specification; the number of repetitions is given by the range of the variable in its argument. The state of the newly created cells (living/dead) is specified by a boolean expression, which is arbitrarily chosen here. The only purpose of the three translation commands is to provide a better initial view on the plane where the cells are arranged. This initialisation rule could also be replaced by a rule which enables interactive choice of living cell positions.

The block "**run**" contains the transition function of the CA in the form of two RGG rules. These rules cover only the cases where the state switches from 0 to 1 or vice versa; no rule is necessary to force a cell *not* to change its state. The conditions in both rules make use of an *arithmetical-structural operator*, **sum**, which was first introduced in the context of L-systems [12]. Its argument is iteratively evaluated for all nodes matching with the node marked by **#** in the context specification **(* ... *)** and added up. Figure 4 demonstrates the possibility of user interaction during RGG execution, which is provided by the GroIMP software. (a) and (b) show successive steps in the undisturbed development of a "Game of Life" configuration (living cells are black and enlarged). After every step, the user can stop the RGG derivation process and interfere manually; e.g., he may change the state of a cell. In (c), a cell was even removed from its position and placed at an irregular location on the grid. Rule application can nevertheless be resumed, leading to a "disturbed" dynamics (d).

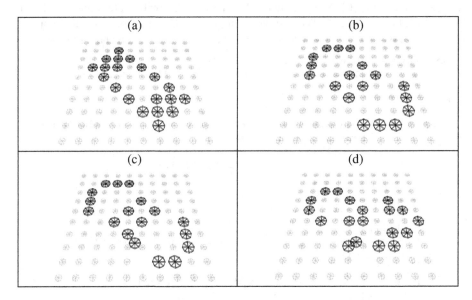

Fig. 4. A symmetric configuration in the Game of Life (a) and its successor configuration (b). In (c), one "living" cell from configuration (b) was moved upwards by the user. The disturbed configuration develops asymmetrically, as shown in (d) after several steps

In this example, structural change can only be obtained by user intervention. The next example shows the growth of a geometrical structure.

5.3 Example 3: A Distance-Sensitive Plant

The following rules simulate the growth of a plant which consists of a main axis, ending in an apical meristem **m**, and short lateral branches (emanating from invisible nodes of type "**s**") with the capacity of (terminal) flowering. The apical bud of such a branch is transformed into a visible flower only if there is no other bud or flower closer to the bud than a given threshold distance. This makes biological sense as it simulates the avoidance of overcrowding in branched structures, an important mechanism which prevents, e.g., mutual mechanical damage by friction, mutual shading, or the transfer of diseases. The corresponding RGG is similar to a classical L-system, but the global character of the sensitivity involved in the distance criterion excludes a realisation as a "context-sensitive" L-system ("context" being interpreted in this case with respect to strings).

```
module m(int x) extends Sphere(3);  /* apical meristem */
module s;                           /* lateral shoot   */
module inflor;                      /* inflorescence   */
module bud extends inflor;          /* flowering bud   */

public void init()
  [ Axiom ==> [m(10)] XTranslation(30) [m(10)]
                      XTranslation(30) [m(10)];
  ]

public void run()
  [
  m(x)   ==> F(12) if (x>0) ( RH(180) [s] m(x-1) );
  s      ==> RU(irandom(50, 70)) F(irandom(15, 18)) bud;
  b:bud ==> inflor
            if (forall(distance(b,(* #x:inflor,(b!=x)*)) > 13)
                ( RL(70) [ F(4) RH(50)
                          for (1..5) ( RH(72)
                                      [ RL(80) F(3) ]) ] );
  ]
```

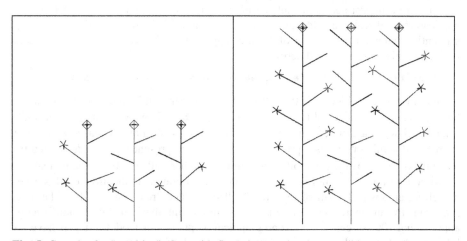

Fig. 5. Growth of a "sensitive" plant with flowering restricted to conditions where a distance threshold to the nearest competing object must be surpassed

The rule under "**init**" creates "seeds" (**m(10)**) for three plants, equidistantly spaced in x direction, using a translation command. In the "**run**" part, designed for modelling the growth process, the system uses the turtle commands **F** (creation of a cylinder) and **RH**, **RL**, **RU** (spatial rotations), cf. [14, 12]. The second rule of "**run**" is stochastic and introduces some randomness in the branching angles and branch lengths. The third rule makes again use of arithmetical-structural operators (**forall**, **distance**) and iterative evaluation of a set defined by a context definition. Note that the class hierarchy specified in the module declarations is used to count not only inflorescences, but also buds as potentially flower-inhibiting objects (**bud extends inflor**). Furthermore, conditional and loop structures (**if**, **for**) are used to organize the right-hand side. Figure 5 shows two stages of a derivation which started with three "m" nodes (meristems). Flowering turns out to be partially inhibited for the central plant, due to over-crowding.

5.4   Example 4: A Prime Number Generator

RGG can also be used for "chemical computing". The underlying paradigm is here that there is an unstructured "soup" of objects (molecules) which collide with each other at random and can undergo certain specified "reactions" when they collide. A very simple example, taken from [19], demonstrates this principle at a "soup of numbers". The objects are simply integers here. The first RGG rule generates therefore a large number (1000) of random integers, taken from a certain range (here, between 2 and 100):

```
Axiom ==> for (i=1..1000) ( irandom(2, 100), );
```

In contrast to the previous example, there is no graph structure and no geometrical information associated with these integer "molecules". In fact, our graph is degenerated to a set of "naked" nodes, carrying integers as attributes. To this set, which can be interpreted as a multiset of integers and which was generated by one application of the above rule, the following rule is now applied iteratively and in a sequential manner (in the case of parallel application, the same object could react twice, and this is not intended here):

```
(* a:int *), b:int, (a < b && b % a == 0) ==> `b / a`;
```

Only the integer object **b** is the left-hand side proper of this rule, and it is going to be replaced by an integer object carrying the value **b/a**. However, this happens only if another integer **a** can be found in the multiset (this is certainly the case in our large soup!), and if this integer is a proper divisor of **b**. The presence of **a** is demanded by the context **(* ... *)**, the divisibility condition (together with **a ≠ b**) by the logical expression forming the condition of the rule. The iterated application of this rule, modelling an abstract form of repeated "collisions" and "reactions", will in the long run lead to an increasing proportion of prime numbers in the soup, finally approaching 100 per cent. There is no graphical output of this model (integers have no "shape"), but we could include an output command printing the numbers on a text screen. We emphasize the purely declarative nature of this algorithm. For each rule application, the integers **b** and **a** are taken from the "soup" at random. Hence the convergence to a "prime number soup" can only be stated statistically.

5.5   Example 5: A Polymerisation Model with Mass-Spring Kinetics

Our last example will combine structural changes with dynamic, physically-based simulation of state variables. Furthermore, it shows again the applicability of RGG in the field of chemistry. We have once more a chemical "soup" here, but a simple geometrical—or mechanical—structure is now imposed on it: Each object has a position and a velocity.

Spherical "monomers" are enclosed in a rectangular "cubicle" and move in random initial directions with constant velocity. The cubicle's boundaries are reflecting. Each time two monomers have a close encounter, a chemical bond is formed between them which is modelled in analogy to a spring. Impulse is conserved in the resulting dimer. Reactions resulting in a bond can also take place between still unsaturated ends of a polymer. It is assumed that each monomer has only two binding sites. Thus the resulting polymers have either a chain or a ring topology (see Fig. 6).

The RGG specifying this behaviour essentially consists of not more than 2 module definitions ("Mon", i.e. monomer, and "Spring") and 4 rules: one for initialisation, one for constant movement with reflection at the walls, one for spring mechanics and one for chemical binding. (We have added line numbers in the listing for convenience.)

```
1 module Mon (float radius, float vx, float vy,
2                 float mass, int valence)
3                   extends Sphere (radius);
4 module Spring (float rate, float friction,
5               float dx, float dy)
6                 extends Cylinder (0.01);
7 const float D_T = 0.03;
8 static Mon newmon (float mass, float x, float y,
9                   float vx, float vy, int val)
10   { Mon a = new Mon (0.1*Math.pow(mass, 0.333),
11                     vx, vy, mass, val);
12     a.basis.set(x, y, 0);
13     return a;
14   }
15
16 public void init()
17   [ Axiom ==> for(i=1..15)
18               ( newmon(1, random(-1,1), random(-1,1),
19                 random(-0.1,0.1), random(-0.1,0.1), 0) ,)
20             Line(-1,-1,0,2,0,0) Line(1,-1,0,0,2,0)
21             Line(1,1,0,-2,0,0)  Line(-1,1,0,0,-2,0);
22   ]
23
24 public void run()
25   { apply("mechanics", 10); chemistry(); }
26
27 private void mechanics()
28   [ l:Mon s:Spring(rate, fr, dx, dy) r:Mon   ::>
29       { float fx = rate * (r.basis.x - l.basis.x - dx)
30               + fr * (r.vx - l.vx),
31             fy = rate * (r.basis.y - l.basis.y - dy)
32               + fr * (r.vy - l.vy);
33       l.vx :+= D_T*fx/l.mass; l.vy :+= D_T*fy/l.mass;
34       r.vx :-= D_T*fx/r.mass; r.vy :-= D_T*fy/r.mass;
35       s.basis.set(l.basis);
```

```
36              s.axis.set(r.basis.x - l.basis.x,
37                          r.basis.y - l.basis.y, 0);
38          }
39      a:Mon    ::>
40          { a.basis.x += D_T*a.vx; a.basis.y += D_T*a.vy;
41            if (((a.basis.x >  1) && (a.vx > 0)) ||
42                ((a.basis.x < -1) && (a.vx < 0)))
43               { a.vx = -a.vx; }    /* reflection */
44            if (((a.basis.y >  1) && (a.vy > 0)) ||
45                ((a.basis.y < -1) && (a.uy < 0)))
46               { a.vy = -a.vy; }    /* reflection */
47          }
48      ]
49
50 private void chemistry()
51    [ a:Mon, b:Mon, ((a.getId() < b.getId())
52                      && (a.valence <= 1) && (b.valence <= 1)
53                      && (a.basis.distance(b.basis)
54                          < 1.2 * (a.radius + b.radius))
55                      && !(b in (* a Spring #? *) ) ) )
56      ==>    a Spring(1, 0.2, b.basis.x - a.basis.x,
57                          b.basis.y - a.basis.y) b
58            { a.valence++; b.valence++; };
59    ]
```

The first three lines declare that a "**Mon**(omer)" object inherits all properties of a sphere, but has additionally the parameters **vx**, **vy** (velocity in x and y direction), **mass** and **valence**. Similarly, "**Spring**" (lines 4–6) is a subclass of **Cylinder**, carrying the additional parameters **rate**, **friction** (both used for calculating the effect of the spring on the movement of the monomers which it connects, lines 29–38) and **dx**, **dy** (extension of the spring in its stable state). Lines 7–14 declare the basic time interval for all dynamical calculations (**D_T**) and a constructor function for new monomers, initialising the parameters of the newly created monomer with the values given in the function call (this call appears only in line 18 when the scenery is initialised) and calculating the radius of the spherical monomer from its mass by the formula

$$r = 0.1 * \sqrt[3]{m} .$$

The initialisation rule (lines 17–21) creates 15 monomers, each with mass 1, placed at random positions inside a square extending from –1 to 1 in x and y direction, and with random velocities between –0.1 and 0.1 in each direction. The "valence", denoting the number of already saturated chemical binding sites, of these new monomers is 0, because they have not yet formed any bonds. Additionally, four lines delimiting the borders of the allowed space for the monomers are created in lines 20–21. The lines are given by the x, y, z coordinates of their start positions and direction vectors.

The block in lines 24–25 is some sort of "meta-rule" or table controlling the order of application of rules from different blocks. In our model, 10 steps of purely mechanical movements ("mechanics") alternate with 1 step of "chemistry" where the possibility to create new bonds is checked and such bonds are formed. The reason for this arrangement is that the "chemistry" rule (lines 50–59) with all its conditions takes more computation time, and so it would be inefficient to check it again after each minor movement.

The "mechanics" block consists of two "update" rules both consisting only of a context and a procedural part, therefore using a "::>" transformation arrow which ensures that only certain parameters specified on the left-hand side are modifed in the procedural part on the right-hand side, leaving the graph structure unchanged otherwise. The first rule (lines 28–38) calculates the impact of the spring force on the velocities of two monomers which are already connected by a spring. It also updates the spring parameters. The second rule (lines 39–47) calculates the new position of a monomer in the time interval **D_T**, based on its current velocity. It takes also care of the special situation that arises when the center of the monomer breaches one of the four borders: In this case, an "ideal" reflection law (without energy loss) is applied. (No deformation of the monomers or of the walls is considered in this simple model. Furthermore, a monomer can slightly overlap with the exterior because it is only its midpoint which is checked for collision.) As both rules consist largely of conventional imperative code, we do not comment on the details here. However, we draw attention to the use of the special colon-prefixed incrementation/decrementation operators **:+=** and **:-=** in lines 33–34: They enforce a quasi-parallel execution of the intended modification of values of variables, in contrast to the ordinary incrementation operators in line 40 where this parallel treatment is not necessary (the rule manipulates only one monomer anyway). The necessity for a quasi-parallel mode of incrementation in lines 33–34 arises from the possibility that a monomer is connected with several springs; in this case, the increments coming from all rule applications are internally summed up and applied to **vx** and **vy** only at the end.

The "chemistry" rule (lines 50–59) looks for two unsaturated monomers **a** and **b**. "Unsaturated" means that the valence has not yet reached its maximal value, i.e. two. The rule must be applicable to each pair only once; this is ensured by a "trick", namely to compare the unique identifiers of each of the two objects (line 51) and to impose the condition that they are in ascending order. (As already mentioned in section 3, later versions of XL will provide a more intuitive way of guaranteeing this application "to each subset only once".) A further condition for the formation of a new bond is that both monomers are close enough to each other (lines 53–54). Finally, it has to be checked whether they are already connected by a spring (line 55). This is done by testing if **b** belongs to a certain, locally defined context **(* a Spring #? *)**. On the right-hand side of the rule, a new spring is created and initialized between **a** and **b** (lines 56–57), and the valence of both monomers is increased by 1 (line 58). Because of the valence condition, the resulting "polymers" can only have linear or ring structure (Fig. 6). An animated display of the resulting movements would show that the velocity of the larger spring-connected chains is normally slower than that of the single monomers.

The XL code given above can easily be modified into a 3D model with monomers and polymers moving in the interior of a box; see Fig. 7 for a snapshot of the corresponding output.

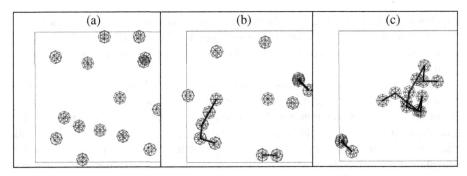

Fig. 6. Development simulated by the polymerisation model. (a) initial situation: 15 separate monomers, (b) after several collisions, two chains and one ring (of three monomers, one of them being hidden in the picture) have formed, (c) finally one large chain and the small ring remain

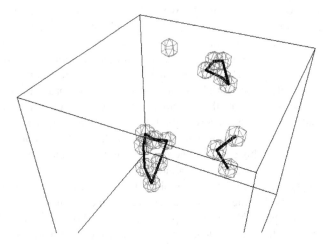

Fig. 7. Snapshot of the 3D version of the polymerisation model after several collisions

6 Conclusions

Relational growth grammars permit the writing of short and comprehensible model specifications for a wide field of scientific applications, ranging from physical and chemical simulations (Example 5) to the growth of plants (Example 3), genetic processes and metabolic networks [2, 11]. In particular at the example of a multi-scaled ecophysiological model of barley (*Hordeum vulgare* L.) [2], we have shown that both the new formalism (RGG) and the modelling language we have implemented it into (XL) are flexible and versatile enough to yield validable results that can compete with standard methods for the modelling of genetic model and crop plants (instead of simplified "toy models"); yet with the advantage that sometimes cumbersome interfaces between different modules can now be disposed of, as various biological phenomena such as metabolic and genetic regulatory networks, signal and nutrient transport processes and morphogenesis which take place at a single or several different scales of observation synchronously can now be represented in one and the same formalism.

RGG are essentially rule-based, but because they operate on unordered *sets* of graphs, they share also some characteristics with chemical computing. However, they do not (yet) have the full complexity of advanced forms of chemical computing where rules can also be dealt with as parts of the chemical solution ("active molecules"), cf. [1]. Instead, in the language XL the "unconventionality" of rule-based and chemical computing is moderated by an implementation of RGG that enables straightforward combination with procedural and object-oriented constructions, i.e., with "conventional" programming. This hybrid approach enhances the accessibility of RGG-based modelling for scientists who are accustomed to classical imperative languages. Hence we see an important potential for future applications.

The current state of the implementation of the language XL is far from complete. Not all features of the Java language have been integrated, and especially the graph query language has to be extended by more powerful node patterns and path expressions. In addition, more conditions on rule application, more specific embedding prescriptions and strategies for conflict resolution of overlapping matches have to be developed and implemented. Another topic for improvement is the implementation of efficient graph matching algorithms, since these play the key role in runtime efficiency of grammar-based systems. However, even in its current state, XL by far exceeds the modelling capabilities of traditional, widely-used L-system-based approaches.

Particularly, the potential of RGG for the representation of processes in the fields of genetics and genomics has only just begun to be explored by us [2, 11]: In the future, more complicated biological examples involving multiple interactions between DNA, RNA and proteins (e.g., posttranscriptional and posttranslational control) would be within reach, given further consequent implementation of RGG principles into the XL language and the corresponding software environment, GroIMP [10].

Acknowledgements

This research was funded by the DFG under grant Ku 847/5-1 in the framework of the research group "Virtual Crops". The third author thanks the IPK, in particular Dr. Patrick Schweizer, for providing office facilities while being a guest researcher. All support is gratefully acknowledged.

References

1. Banâtre, J.-P., Fradet, P., Radenac, Y.: Chemical specification of autonomic systems. In: Proceedings of the 13th International Conference on Intelligent and Adaptive Systems and Software Engineering (IASSE'04), July 2004,
   http://www.irisa.fr/paris/Biblio/Papers/Banatre/BanFraRad04IASSE.pdf.

2. Buck-Sorlin, G. H., Kniemeyer, O., Kurth, W.: Barley morphology, genetics and hormonal regulation of internode elongation modelled by a Relational Growth Grammar. New Phytologist 166 (2005), in press.

3. Ehrig, H., Korff, M., Löwe, M., Ribeiro, L., Wagner, A., Corradini, A.: Algebraic approaches to graph transformation—part II: Single pushout approach and comparison with double pushout approach. In: G. Rozenberg (ed.): Handbook of Graph Grammars and Computing by Graph Transformation, Vol. 1, Foundations. World Scientific, Singapore (1997) 247–312.

4. Ermel, C., Rudolf, M., Taentzer, G.: The AGG-approach: Language and tool environment. In: G. Rozenberg (ed.): Handbook of Graph Grammars and Computing by Graph Transformation, Vol. 2, Applications, Languages and Tools. World Scientific, Singapore (1999) 551–604.

5. Floyd, R.: The paradigms of programming. Communications of the ACM 22 (1979) 455–460.

6. Gardner, M.: Wheels, Life, and Other Mathematical Amusements. W.H. Freeman, New York (1983).

7. Giavitto, J.-L., Michel, O.: MGS: A rule-based programming language for complex objects and collections. Electronic Notes in Theoretical Computer Science 59 (4) (2001).

8. Göttler, H.: Graph grammars, a new paradigm for implementing visual languages. In: N. Dershowitz (ed.): Rewriting Techniques and Applications. Springer, Berlin (1989) 152–166.

9. Herzog, R.: Ausbau eines bereits implementierten Graphtransformationstools zu einem Plugin für Cinema 4D. Bachelor Thesis, BTU Cottbus, 2004.

10. Kniemeyer, O.: Rule-based modelling with the XL/GroIMP software. In: H. Schaub, F. Detje, U. Brüggemann (eds.): The Logic of Artificial Life. Proceedings of 6th GWAL, April 14–16, 2004, Bamberg, Germany. AKA, Berlin (2004) 56–65.

11. Kniemeyer, O., Buck-Sorlin, G., Kurth, W.: A graph grammar approach to Artificial Life. Artificial Life 10 (4) (2004) 413–431.

12. Kurth, W.: Some new formalisms for modelling the interactions between plant architecture, competition and carbon allocation. Bayreuther Forum Ökologie 52 (1998) 53–98.

13. Nagl, M.: A tutorial and bibliographical survey on graph-grammars. In: V. Claus, H. Ehrig, G. Rozenberg (eds.): Graph-Grammars and Their Application to Computer Science and Biology. Springer, Berlin (1979) 70–126.

14. Prusinkiewicz, P., Lindenmayer, A.: The Algorithmic Beauty of Plants. Springer, New York (1990).

15. Prusinkiewicz, P.: Art and science for life: Designing and growing virtual plants with L-systems. In: C. Davidson, T. Fernandez (eds.): Nursery Crops: Development, Evaluation, Production and Use: Proceedings of the XXVI International Horticultural Congress. Acta Horticulturae 630 (2004) 15–28.

16. Rozenberg, G.: T0L systems and languages. Information and Control 23 (1973) 357–381.

17. Schürr, A.: Programmed graph replacement systems. In: G. Rozenberg (ed.): Handbook of Graph Grammars and Computing by Graph Transformation, Vol. 1, Foundations. World Scientific, Singapore (1997) 479–546.

18. Schürr, A., Winter, A.J., Zündorf, A.: The PROGRES approach: Language and environment. In: G. Rozenberg (ed.): Handbook of Graph Grammars and Computing by Graph Transformation, Vol. 2, Applications, Languages and Tools. World Scientific, Singapore (1999) 487–550.

19. Skusa, A., Banzhaf, W., Busch, J., Dittrich, P., Ziegler, J.: Künstliche Chemie. Künstliche Intelligenz 1/00 (2000) 12–19.
20. Wolfram, S.: Cellular Automata and Complexity. Collected papers. Addison-Wesley, Reading (1994).

A New Programming Paradigm Inspired by Artificial Chemistries

W. Banzhaf[1] and C. Lasarczyk[2]

[1] Department of Computer Science, Memorial University of Newfoundland,
St. John's NL A1B 3X5, Canada
[2] Department of Computer Science, University of Dortmund,
D-44221 Dortmund, Germany

Abstract. In this contribution we shall introduce a new method of program execution, based on notions of Artificial Chemistries. Instead of executing instructions in a predefined sequential order, execution will be in random order in analogy to chemical reactions happening between substances. It turns out that such a model of program execution is able to achieve desirable goals if augmented by an automatic program searching method like Genetic Programming. We demonstrate the principle of this approach and discuss prospects and consequences for parallel execution of such programs.

1 Introduction

Is it possible to achieve reliable results by running a machine with unreliable elements? This was a question that already John von Neumann was pondering when thinking about the brain and its performance[14]. Computers had, for many years, a problem of the same type. Elements of computing machinery would break, sometimes without being noticed by the programmer or operator, and only the results of a computation would have indicated that something strange had happened.

Computer engineers have, through various draconic measures, succeeded in clamping down on indeterminism in computing machinery, for instance through binary coding of all information held in physical devices, or through introduction of error-correcting codes for transmission of information. These and other measures, however, come at a cost in efficiency. In order to make sure that a deterministic order of programs is followed, for example, a program counter requests execution of one instruction at a time. Time is clocked, and movement of data is heavily constricted. Sometimes two or more cycles are needed just to move information around, energy needs to be spent to readjust electrical voltages to binary levels, and more data need to be transmitted in order to secure error correction.

In recent years, however, the specter of unreliability has come back: Neural networks have demonstrated that non-binary (if nonlinear) elements are useful in computing for certain functions like, e.g. pattern recognition. Quantum computing devices have been invented that work with probability bits, called qu-bits, instead of deterministic bits as traditional. Parallel computers have achieved such processor density that unreliability in elements becomes a major concern again. IBM's BlueGene project, for instance, has so many processors that at least once a day, a cosmic radiation event will succeed in flipping a bit. Where and when this happens is unknown, that it happens is a statistical exercise to calculate.

Notably the community in parallel and distributed computing has gone to great length in securing that parallel and distributed computers provide some sort of synchronicity between processes.

Here we argue that a particular sort of radical indeterminism can be injected into a computing machine without prohibiting it from computing useful quantities. We speak of the enforced deterministic sequentiality of computer code that might be dissolved this way. When von Neumann et al. put forward their proposal for a stored program computer, the invention contained actually two important pieces, one being to store programs as data. This development opened the way for a much more efficient method of programming than was used before, and - at the same time - allowed for self-modifying code. The second aspect of the invention, however, frequently underestimated in its impact, was the program counter which would control execution of code residing in memory by providing the address of the next instruction in memory.

It is the behavior of the program counter that we shall change in this contribution, bringing it more in line in its behavior with execution of processes in the natural world. There, synchronicity is the effect of a highly intricate and complex construction, whereas at the lowest level of processes, things happen asynchronously. We shall ask the question whether it is possible to have a system without deterministic execution control. We shall put this question in the framework of artificial chemistries, an area recently sprung up to study algorithms that model and simulate chemical reaction systems for various purposes.

We shall introduce a program counter that is randomly selecting from a set of instructions, or multi-set of instructions, rather, where a repetition of instructions is allowed to appear in memory locations. Thus, computing understood as the transformation from input to output is different from a prescribed sequence of computational steps. Instead, instructions from a multi-set $I = \{I_1, I_2, I_3, I_2, I_3, I_1, ...\}$ are drawn in a random order to produce a transformation result. In this way we dissolve the sequential order usually associated with the notion of an algorithm. It will turn out, that such an arrangement is still able to produce useful results, though only under the reign of a programming method that banks on its stochastic character. This method will be Genetic Programming.

A program in this sense is thus not a sequence of instructions but rather an assemblage of instructions that can be executed in arbitrary order. By randomly choosing one instruction at a time, the program proceeds through its transformations until a predetermined number of instructions has been executed. In the present work we set the number of instructions to be executed at 3.5 times the size of the multi-set, this way giving ample chance to each instruction to be executed at least once and to exert its proper influence on the result.

Different multi-sets can be considered different programs, whereas different passes through a multi–set can be considered different behavioral variants of a single program. Programs of this type can be seen as artificial chemistries, where instructions interact with each other (by taking the transformation results from one instruction and feeding it into another). As it will turn out, many interactions of this type are, what in an Artificial Chemistry is called "elastic", in that nothing happens as a result, for instance because the earlier instruction did not feed into the arguments of the later.[1]

Because instructions are drawn randomly in the execution of the program, it is really the concentration of instructions that matters most. It is thus expected that "programming" of such a system requires the proper choice of concentrations of instructions, similar to what is required from the functioning of living cells, where at each given time many reactions happen simultaneously but without a need to synchronicity.

2   ACs and Law of Large Numbers

Algorithmic Chemistries were considered earlier in the work of Fontana [10]. Here we use the term for those kinds of artificial chemistries [8] that aim at algorithms. As opposed to terms like randomized or probabilistic algorithms, in which a certain degree of stochasticity is introduced explicitly, our algorithms have an implicit type of stochasticity. Executing the sequence of instructions every time in a different order has the potential of producing highly unpredictable results.

Its behaviour can be likened to that of a random program. Methods which can deal with random programs, and develop them into programs with proper behaviour, have been introduced in the past decade with considerable success [11, 5]. The trick is to evolve these programs by changing and combining them until the behaviour is of satisfying quality. This evolution is orchestrated by setting up a system which systematically explores the space of programs using random operations like mutation and recombination, and by subsequently selecting fitter programs over less fit ones.

Whereas in this way, random programs can be evolved into well behaved programs, these studies were all done under the premises of a deterministic program counter. Thus, each time the programs were executed under the same input, and starting from the same state, they would produce the same result. This gave evolution a guide as to which programs to prefer over which other.

In the present system, however, we do not only start from random programs as determined by the multiset of instructions, we stay random due to the program counter acting as a random number generator with each program being executed in a different order. How can we think of such a system as being able to profit under selection rules at all?

---

[1] Elastic interactions have some bearings on neutral code, but they are not identical.

There is a certain systematics even to programs with random execution order, which is revealed by looking at the data flow of such a program. Certain registers or memory locations will be used as input or output arguments of instructions. If it happens that an output register is also acting as an input register, the two instructions involved are connected, and a data flow is established between the input registers of the first and the output register of the second instruction. Irrespective of the order in which the instructions are executed (remember we allow repetition of execution), there will be a definite outcome through this contiguity.

It is this data-flow "logic" that is under the control of evolution, and which will be developed and optimized to the point that the entire multiset of instructions performs a certain function.

Suppose we want to compute the following function:

$$r_1 = \frac{r_2 - r_3}{r_4} \tag{1}$$

where r_1, r_2, r_3, r_4 are register addresses. This would entail the reuse of results from one instruction (subtracting together two numbers) and their subsequent division by another number. By setting up a number of training cases for the wished–for behavior, we could generate a fitness measure which would allow enforcement, under evolution, of such an algorithm.

It clearly becomes a matter of statistics, and thus of large numbers to evolve the proper algorithm. First we have to allow a sufficient chance for each instruction in the program (multiset) to be executed. If size of the multiset is n, a program should be executed m times. Next we have to execute a program sufficiently often (l times) to be able to capture its "typical" behavior on each fitness case. Then we have to rotate through the training data and compute all k or at least some $k' < k$ fitness cases. Finally we have to do this for a population of p individuals to be able to select. Our total effort is therefore $e = n * m * l * k * p$ instructions to be executed. For reasonable numbers $n = 100$, $m = 4$, $l = 20$, $k = 10$ and $p = 100$, we'd end up with 8 million instructions per generation. This could be executed in 4 ms on a 2 Ghz machine. We shall come back to this example in a later chapter.

Following previous work on Artificial Chemistries (see, for example [2, 6, 7, 15]) we introduced in [3] a very general analogy between chemical reaction and algorithmic computation, arguing that concentrations of results would be important. [4] was the first step in this new direction. In [12] tried to deepen our understanding of the resulting system by studying a well–known benchmark task from the GP area: even-parity. Here we continue our investigation by trying out variants on program counter behaviour.

3   The Method

Genetic Programming (GP) [11, 5] belongs to the family of Evolutionary Algorithms (EA). These heuristic algorithms try to improve originally random

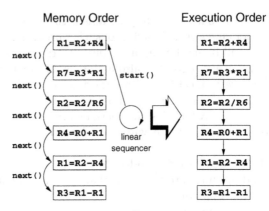

Fig. 1. Execution of an individual in linear GP. Memory order and execution order correspond to each other. Arrows indicate returned values of calls to the sequence generator

solutions to a problem via the mechanisms of recombination, mutation and selection. Many applications of GP can be described as evolution of models [9]. The elements of models are usually arithmetic expressions, logical expressions or executable programs.

Here, we shall use evolution of approximation and classification problems to demonstrate the feasibility of the approach. We represent a program as a set of instructions only stored as a linear sequence in memory due to technical limitations. These instructions are 2 and 3 address instructions which work on a set of registers.

3.1   Linear GP with Sequence Generators

Here we shall use 3-address machine instructions. The genotype of an individual is a list of those instructions. Each instruction consists of an operation, a destination register, and two source registers[2]. Initially, individuals are produced by randomly choosing instructions. As is usual, we employ a set of fitness cases in order to evaluate (and subsequently select) individuals.

Figure 1 shows the execution of an individual in linear GP. A sequence generator is used to determine the sequence of instructions. Each instruction is executed, with resulting data stored in its destination register. Usually, the sequence generator moves through the program sequence instruction by instruction. Thus, the location in memory space determines the particular sequence of instructions. Classically, this is realized by the program counter.[3]

1–*Point–Crossover* can be described using two sequence generators. The first generator is acting on the first parent and returns instructions at its beginning. These instructions form the first part of the offspring. The second sequence

---

[2] Operations which require only one source register simply ignore the second register.
[3] (Conditional) jumps are a deviation from this behavior.

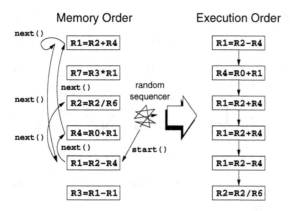

Fig. 2. Execution in the AC system. The sequence generator returns a random order for execution

generator operates on the other parent. We ignore the first instructions this generator returns[4]. The others form the tail of the offsprings instruction list.

Mutation changes single instructions by changing either operation, or destination register or the source registers according to a prescribed probability distribution.

3.2   A Register Machine as an Algorithmic Chemistry

There is a simple way to realize an chemistry by a register machine. By substituting the systematic incremental stepping of the sequence generator by a random sequence we arrive at our system. That is to say, the instructions are drawn randomly from the set of all instructions in the program[5]. Still, we have to provide the number of registers, starting conditions and determine a target register from which output is to be drawn.

As shown in Figure 2 the chemistry works by executing the instructions of an individual analogous to what would happen in a linear GP–System (cf. 1), except that the sequence order is different.

It should be noted that there are registers with different features: Some registers are read-only. They can only be used as source registers. These registers contain constant values and are initialized for each fitness case at the start of program execution. All other registers can be read from and written into. These are the connection registers among which information flows in the course of the computation. Initially they are set to zero.

How a program behaves during execution will differ from instance to instance. There is no guarantee that an instruction is executed, nor is it guaranteed that this happens in a definite order or frequency. If, however, an instruction is more

---

[4] Should crossover generate two offspring, the instructions not copied will be used for a second offspring.

[5] For technical reasons instructions are ordered in memory space, but access to an instruction (and subsequent execution) are done in random order.

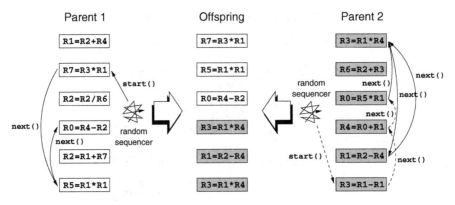

Fig. 3. Crossover in an Artificial Chemistry

frequent in the multi-set, then its execution will be more probable. Similarly, if it should be advantageous to keep independence between data paths, the corresponding registers should be different in such a way that the instructions are not connecting to each other. Both features would be expected to be subject to evolutionary forces.

3.3   Evolution of an Algorithmic Chemistry

Genetic programming of this algorithmic chemistry (ACGP) is similar to other GP variants. The use of a sequence generator should help understand this similarity. We have seen already in Section 3.2 how an individual in ACGP is evaluated.

Initialization and Mutation. Initialization and mutation of an individual are the same for both the ACGP and usual linear GP.

Mutation will change operator and register numbers according to a probability distribution. In the present implementation register values are changed using a Gaussian with mean at present value and standard deviation 1.

Crossover. Crossover makes use of the randomized sequences produced by the sequence generator. As shown in Figure 3 a random sequence of instructions is copied from the parents to the offspring. Though the instructions inherited from each of the parents are located in contiguous memory locations, the actual sequence of the execution is not dependent on that order. The probability that a particular instruction is copied into an offspring depends on the frequency of that instruction in the parent. Inheritance therefore is inheritance of frequencies of instructions, rather than of particular sequences of instructions.

Constant register values will be copied with equal probability from each parent, as is done for choice of the result register.

4   Results

Figure 4 shows data flow graphs of the best individual in generation 0, 25 and 50. Each line shows a single time step. Result register is read after $t = n$. Within

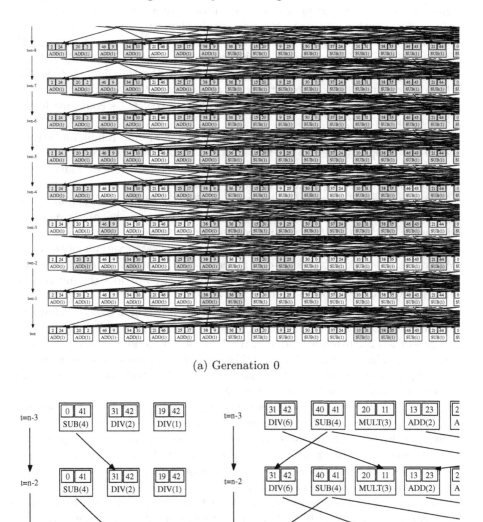

(a) Gerenation 0

(b) Gerenation 25   (c) Gerenation 50

Fig. 4. Best individuals data flow graphs at different time steps during evolution. These individuals try to describe data point generated by Eq. (1)

a line each node represents an unequal instructions participating in any data flow. Instructions, just reading registers, that no other instruction use as target register, and write to register not read by any other instruction and unequal to result register, do not participate in data flow considered here and are therefore ignored. Nodes show the instructions' operation name, addresses of source registers and frequency of this instruction within chemistry in brackets. Each line shows the same set of instructions, because each instruction could be executed in each time step. Additionally we mark those nodes gray, that possibly influence the value of the result register. In the last time steps (bottom line) these are just those instructions, that use result register as their target register. In the previous time step instructions writing to source of those instructions could modify the results, and so on.

Figure 4 shows a part of the possible data flow of an initial individual during last 9 time steps. As we can see there are two instructions writing to the result register and nearly all instructions executed 5 time steps before evaluation could influence the result. All instruction show single concentration.

Things changed after 25 generations (cf. Fig. 4). Just a small number of instructions participate in data flows as considered here(see above). Two instruction write to the individuals result register (gray nodes on bottom line). They look very similar, so we can assume that one is a mutated variant of the other. While the right instructions divides an empty(=0) connection register thru r_4 $((r_2, r_3, r_4) \rightarrow (R[40], R[41], R[42]))$, the left instruction divides the difference of an other empty(=0) register and r_3 thru r_4.

After 50 generations the desired solution is already found. Figure 4 shows the important part of the best individual, which is similar to the individual in ancestor generation 25. Just one kind of instruction uses the result register as its target register and also the remaining data flow toward result register is unambiguous. An other important point here is, that frequency of instructions correlates with their position/important in data flow. While we can not generalize this statement yet, the observed behavior matches our expectations. After a good solution is found, individuals could increase probability of execution in required order by adjusting the instructions concentration appropriately. While it is important to execute all instructions part of the data flow to get the correct results, instruction next to the result register need a higher probability of execution, because their timeframe for successful execution is much smaller. The timeframe for successful execution is limited by the point of time their source registers contain the required values and the time required to execute the remaining part of the data flow.

5   Results and Outlook

Using examples from regression and classification we show that goal-oriented behaviour is possible with a seemingly uncoordinated structure of program elements.

The similarity of this approach to dataflow architectures [1] is obvious. Traditional restrictions of that architecture, however, can be loosened with the present model of non-deterministic computation, "programmed" by evolution. Recent work in the dataflow community [13] might therefore find support in such an approach.

The strength of this approach will only appear if distributedness is taken into account. The reasoning would be the following: Systems of this kind should consist of a large number of processing elements which would share program storage and register content. Elements would asynchroneously access storage and register. The program's genome wouldn't specify an order for the execution of instructions. Instead, each element would randomly pick instructions and execute them. Communication with the external world would be performed via a simple control unit.

It goes without saying that such a system would be well suited for parallel processing. Each additional processing element would accelerate the evaluation of programs. There would be no need for massive communication and for synchronization between processing elements. The system would be scalable at run-time: New elements could be added or removed without administrative overhead. The system as a whole would be fault-tolerant, failure of processing elements would appear merely as a slowed-down execution. Loss of information would not be a problem, and new processes need not be started instead of lost ones. Reducing the number of processors (and thus slowing down computation) could be allowed even for power management.

Explicit scheduling of tasks would not be necessary. Two algorithmic chemistries executing different tasks could be unified into one even, provided they used different connection registers. Would it be necessary that one task should be prioritized a higher concentration of instructions would be sufficient to achieve that.

Acknowledgement

The authors gratefully acknowledge support from a grant of the Deutsche Forschungsgemeinschaft DFG to W.B. under Ba 1042/7–3 and from an NSERC discovery grant to W.B. under RGPIN 283304-04.

References

1. ARWIND, AND KATHAIL, V. A multiple processor data flow machine that supports generalized procedures. In *International Conference on Computer Architecture (Minneapolis 1981)* (Los Alamitos, CA, 1981), IEEE Computer Society.
2. BANZHAF, W. Self-replicating sequences of binary numbers. *Comput. Math. Appl.* *26* (1993), 1–8.
3. BANZHAF, W. Self-organizing Algorithms Derived from RNA Interactions. In *Evolution and Biocomputing*, W. Banzhaf and F. Eeckman, Eds., vol. 899 of *LNCS*. Springer, Berlin, 1995, pp. 69–103.
4. BANZHAF, W., AND LASARCZYK, C. W. G. Genetic programming of an algorithmic chemistry. In *Genetic Programming Theory and Practice II*, U.-M. O'Reilly, T. Yu, R. Riolo, and B. Worzel, Eds., vol. 8 of *Genetic Programming*. Kluwer/Springer, Boston MA, 2005, pp. 175–190.

5. BANZHAF, W., NORDIN, P., KELLER, R., AND FRANCONE, F. *Genetic Programming - An Introduction*. Morgan Kaufmann, San Francisco, CA, 1998.

6. DI FENIZIO, P. S., DITTRICH, P., BANZHAF, W., AND ZIEGLER, J. Towards a Theory of Organizations. In *Proceedings of the German 5th Workshop on Artificial Life* (Bayreuth, Germany, 2000), M. Hauhs and H. Lange, Eds., Bayreuth University Press.

7. DITTRICH, P., AND BANZHAF, W. Self-Evolution in a Constructive Binary String System. *Artificial Life 4*, 2 (1998), 203–220.

8. DITTRICH, P., ZIEGLER, J., AND BANZHAF, W. Artificial Chemistries - A Review. *Artificial Life 7* (2001), 225–275.

9. EIBEN, G., AND SMITH, J. *Introduction to Evolutionary Computing*. Springer, Berlin, Germany, 2003.

10. FONTANA, W. Algorithmic chemistry. In *Artificial Life II* (Redwood City, CA, 1992), C. G. Langton, C. Taylor, J. D. Farmer, and S. Rasmussen, Eds., Addison-Wesley, pp. 159–210.

11. KOZA, J. *Genetic Programming*. MIT Press, Cambridge, MA, 1992.

12. LASARCZYK, C. W. G., AND BANZHAF, W. An algorithmic chemistry for genetic programming. In *EuroGP 2005* (2005). (submitted).

13. SWANSON, S., MICHELSON, K., AND OSKIN, M. Wavescalar. Tech. Rep. UW-CSE-03-01-01, University of Washington, Dept. of Computer Science and Engineering, 2003.

14. VON NEUMANN, J. Probabilistic logics and the synthesis of reliable organisms from unreliable components. In *Automata Studies* (Princeton, NJ, 1956), C. Shannon and J. McCarthy, Eds., Princeton Univ.Press.

15. ZIEGLER, J., AND BANZHAF, W. Evolving Control Metabolisms for a Robot. *Artificial Life 7* (2001), 171–190.

Higher-Order Chemical Programming Style

J.-P. Banâtre[1], P. Fradet[2], and Y. Radenac[1]

[1] IRISA, Campus de Beaulieu, 35042 Rennes Cedex, France
{jbanatre, yradenac}@irisa.fr
[2] INRIA Rhône-Alpes, 655 avenue de l'Europe, 38330 Montbonnot, France
Pascal.Fradet@inria.fr

Abstract. The chemical reaction metaphor describes computation in terms of a chemical solution in which molecules interact freely according to reaction rules. Chemical solutions are represented by multisets of elements and reactions by rewrite rules which consume and produce new elements according to conditions. The chemical programming style allows to write many programs in a very elegant way. We go one step further by extending the model so that rewrite rules are themselves molecules. This higher-order extension leads to a programming style where the implementation of new features amounts to adding new active molecules in the solution representing the system. We illustrate this style by specifying an autonomic mail system with several self-managing properties.

1   Introduction

The chemical reaction metaphor has been discussed in various occasions in the literature. This metaphor describes computation in terms of a chemical solution in which molecules (representing data) interact freely according to reaction rules. Chemical solutions are represented by multisets. Computation proceeds by rewritings of the multiset which consume and produce new elements according to reaction conditions and transformation rules.

To the best of our knowledge, the Gamma formalism was the first "chemical model of computation" proposed as early as in 1986 [4] and later extended in [5]. A Gamma program is a collection of reaction rules acting on a multiset of basic elements. A reaction rule is made of a condition and an action. Execution proceeds by replacing elements satisfying the reaction condition by the elements specified by the action. The result of a Gamma program is obtained when a stable state is reached, that is to say, when no reaction can take place anymore (the solution is said to be inert).

Figure 1 gives three small examples illustrating the style of programming of Gamma. The reaction *max* computes the maximum element of a non empty set. The reaction replaces any couple of elements x and y such that the reaction condition $(x \geq y)$ holds by x. This process goes on till a stable state is reached, that is to say, when only the maximum element remains. The reaction *primes* computes the prime numbers lower or equal to a given number N when applied to the multiset of all numbers between 2 and N ($multiple(x, y)$ is true if and

J.-P. Banâtre et al. (Eds.): UPP 2004, LNCS 3566, pp. 84–95, 2005.

$$max = \textbf{replace } x, y \textbf{ by } x \textbf{ if } x \geq y$$
$$primes = \textbf{replace } x, y \textbf{ by } y \textbf{ if } multiple(x, y)$$
$$maj = \textbf{replace } x, y \textbf{ by } \{\} \textbf{ if } x \neq y$$

Fig. 1. Examples of Gamma programs

only if x is a multiple of y). The majority element of a multiset is an element which occurs more than $card(M)/2$ times in the multiset. Assuming that such an element exists, the reaction maj yields a multiset which only contains instances of the majority element just by removing pairs of distinct elements. Let us emphasize the conciseness and elegance of these programs. Nothing had to be said about the order of evaluation of the reactions. If several disjoint pairs of elements satisfy the condition, the reactions can be performed in parallel.

Gamma makes it possible to express programs without artificial sequentiality. By artificial, we mean sequentiality only imposed by the computation model and unrelated to the logic of the program. This allows the programmer to describe programs in a very abstract way. In some sense, one can say that Gamma programs express the very idea of an algorithm without any unnecessary linguistic idiosyncrasies. The interested reader may find in [5] a long series of examples (string processing problems, graph problems, geometry problems, *etc.*) illustrating the Gamma style of programming and in [1] a review of contributions related to the chemical reaction model. Gamma has inspired many other models like the Chemical Abstract Machine [7], membrane computing [11], *etc.*

This article presents a higher-order extension of the Gamma model where all the computing units are considered as molecules reacting in a solution. In particular, reaction rules are molecules which can react or be manipulated as any other molecules. In Section 2, we exhibit a minimal higher-order chemical calculus, called the γ-calculus, which expresses the very essence of chemical models. This calculus is then enriched with conditional reactions and the possibility of rewriting atomically several molecules. The resulting higher-order chemical language suggests a programming style where the implementation of new features amounts to adding new active molecules in the solution representing the system. Section 3 illustrates the characteristics of our language through the example of an autonomic mail system with several self-managing features. Section 4 concludes and suggests several research directions.

2 A Minimal Chemical Calculus

In this section, we introduce a higher-order calculus, the γ-*calculus* [3], that can be seen as a formal and minimal basis for the chemical paradigm in much the same way as the λ-calculus is the formal basis of the functional paradigm.

2.1 Syntax and Semantics

The fundamental data structure of the γ-calculus is the multiset. Computation can be seen either intuitively, as chemical reactions of elements agitated

$$
\begin{array}{lll}
M ::= & x & ; \text{ variable} \\
\mid & \gamma\langle x\rangle.M & ; \text{ } \gamma\text{-abstraction} \\
\mid & M_1, M_2 & ; \text{ multiset} \\
\mid & \langle M\rangle & ; \text{ solution}
\end{array}
$$

Fig. 2. Syntax of γ-molecules

$$
\begin{array}{llll}
(\gamma\langle x\rangle.M), \langle N\rangle & \longrightarrow_\gamma & M[x := N] & \text{if } \textit{Inert}(N) \vee \textit{Hidden}(x, M) \text{ ; } \gamma\text{-reduction} \\
\gamma\langle x\rangle.M & \equiv & \gamma\langle y\rangle.M[x := y] \text{ with } y \text{ fresh} & ; \text{ } \alpha\text{-conversion} \\
M_1, M_2 & \equiv & M_2, M_1 & ; \text{ commutativity} \\
M_1, (M_2, M_3) & \equiv & (M_1, M_2), M_3 & ; \text{ associativity}
\end{array}
$$

Fig. 3. Rules of the γ-calculus

by Brownian motion, or formally, as higher-order, associative and commutative (AC), multiset rewritings. The syntax of γ-terms (also called *molecules*) is given in Figure 2. A γ-abstraction is a reactive molecule which consumes a molecule (its argument) and produces a new one (its body). Molecules are composed using the AC multiset constructor ",". A solution encapsulates molecules and keeps them separate. It serves to control and isolate reactions.

The γ-calculus bears clear similarities with the λ-calculus. They both rely on the notions of (free and bound) variable, abstraction and application. A λ-abstraction and a γ-abstraction both specify a higher-order rewrite rule. However, λ-terms are tree-like whereas the AC nature of the application operator "," makes γ-terms multiset-like. Associativity and commutativity formalize Brownian motion and make the notion of solution necessary, if only to distinguish between a function and its argument.

The conversion rules and the reduction rule of the γ-calculus are gathered in Figure 3. Chemical reactions are represented by a single rewrite rule, the γ-reduction, which applies a γ-abstraction to a solution. A molecule $(\gamma\langle x\rangle.M), \langle N\rangle$ can be reduced only if:

Inert(N): the content N of the solution argument is a closed term made exclusively of γ-abstractions or exclusively of solutions (which may be active),

or *Hidden*(x, M): the variable x occurs in M only as $\langle x\rangle$. Therefore $\langle N\rangle$ can be active since no access is done to its contents.

So, a molecule can be extracted from its enclosing solution only when it has reached an inert state. This is an important restriction that permits the ordering of rewritings. Without this restriction, the contents of a solution could be extracted in any state and the solution construct would lose its purpose. Reactions can occur in parallel as long as they apply to disjoint sub-terms. A molecule is in normal form if all its molecules are inert.

In order to illustrate γ-reduction, consider the following molecules:

$$
\Delta \equiv \gamma\langle x\rangle.x, \langle x\rangle \qquad \Omega \equiv \Delta, \langle\Delta\rangle \qquad I \equiv \gamma\langle x\rangle.\langle x\rangle
$$

Clearly, Ω is an always active (non terminating) molecule and I an inert molecule (the identity function in normal form). The molecule $\langle\Omega\rangle, \langle I\rangle, \gamma\langle x\rangle.\gamma\langle y\rangle.x$ reduces as follows:

$$\langle\Omega\rangle, \langle I\rangle, \gamma\langle x\rangle.\gamma\langle y\rangle.x \longrightarrow \langle\Omega\rangle, \gamma\langle y\rangle.I \longrightarrow I$$

The first reduction is the only one possible: the γ-abstraction extracts x from its solution and $\langle I\rangle$ is the only inert molecule ($Inert(I) \wedge \neg Hidden(x, \gamma\langle y\rangle.x)$). The second reduction is possible only because the active solution $\langle\Omega\rangle$ is not extracted but removed ($\neg Inert(\Omega) \wedge Hidden(y, I)$).

Like in the λ-calculus, constants can be defined using basic constructs. For example, booleans and conditionals can be encoded as follows:

$$\textbf{true} \equiv \gamma\langle x\rangle.\gamma\langle y\rangle.x$$
$$\textbf{false} \equiv \gamma\langle x\rangle.\gamma\langle y\rangle.y$$
$$\textbf{if } C \textbf{ then } M_1 \textbf{ else } M_2 \equiv \langle\langle C\rangle, \gamma\langle x\rangle.x, \langle M_1\rangle\rangle, \gamma\langle y\rangle.y, \langle M_2\rangle$$

In the encoding of the conditional, when the molecule C reduces to **true** (resp. **false**) the whole expression reduces to M_1 (resp. M_2). Other standard constructions (pairs, tuples, integers, recursion, *etc.*) can be encoded as well. Actually, the λ-calculus can easily be encoded within the γ-calculus (see [3] for more details).

In fact, the γ-calculus is more expressive than the λ-calculus since it can also express non-deterministic programs. For example, let A and B two distinct normal forms, then:

$$(\gamma\langle x\rangle.\gamma\langle y\rangle.x), \langle A\rangle, \langle B\rangle \equiv (\gamma\langle x\rangle.\gamma\langle y\rangle.x), \langle B\rangle, \langle A\rangle$$
$$\downarrow_\gamma \qquad\qquad\qquad \downarrow_\gamma$$
$$(\gamma\langle y\rangle.A), \langle B\rangle \qquad\qquad (\gamma\langle y\rangle.B), \langle A\rangle$$
$$\downarrow_\gamma \qquad\qquad\qquad \downarrow_\gamma$$
$$A \qquad\qquad \not\equiv \qquad\qquad B$$

The γ-calculus is not confluent.

2.2   Extensions

The γ-calculus is a quite expressive higher-order calculus. However, compared to the original Gamma [5] and other chemical models [10, 11], it lacks two fundamental features:

- *Reaction condition.* In Gamma, reactions are guarded by a condition that must be fulfilled in order to apply them. Compared to γ where inertia and termination are described syntactically, conditional reactions give these notions a semantic nature.
- *Atomic capture.* In Gamma, any fixed number of elements can take part in a reaction. Compared to a γ-abstraction which reacts with one element at a time, a n-ary reaction takes atomically n elements which cannot take part in any other reaction at the same time.

These two extensions are orthogonal and enhance greatly the expressivity of chemical calculi. So from now, γ-abstractions (also called *active molecules*) can react according to a condition and can extract elements using pattern-matching. Furthermore, we consider the γ-calculus extended with booleans, integers, arithmetic and booleans operators, tuples (written $x_1{:}\ldots{:}x_n$) and the possibility of naming molecules (*ident* $= M$). The syntax of γ-abstractions is extended to:

$$\gamma P\lfloor C\rfloor.M$$

where M is the action, C is the reaction condition and P a pattern extracting the elements participating in the reaction. If the condition C is **true**, we omit it in the definition of the γ-abstraction.

Patterns have the following syntax:

$$P ::= x \mid \omega \mid ident = P \mid P, P \mid \langle P \rangle$$

where

- x stands for variables which match basic elements (integers, booleans, tuples, *etc.*),
- ω is a named wild card that matches any molecule (even the empty one),
- *ident* $= P$ matches any molecule m named *ident* matched by P,
- P_1, P_2 matches any molecule (m_1, m_2) such that P_1 matches m_1 and P_2 matches m_2,
- $\langle P \rangle$ matches any solution $\langle m \rangle$ such that P matches m.

For example, the pattern Sol $= \langle x, y, \omega \rangle$ matches any solution named "Sol" containing at least two basic elements. The rest of the solution (that may be empty) is matched by ω.

γ-abstractions are one-shot: they are consumed by the reaction. However, many programs are naturally expressed by applying the same reaction an arbitrary number of times. We introduce recursive (or n-shot) γ-abstractions which are not consumed by the reaction. We denote them by the following syntax:

replace P by M if C

Such a molecule reacts exactly as $\gamma P\lfloor C\rfloor.M$ except than it remains after the reaction and can be used as many times as necessary. If needed, a reactive molecule can be removed by another molecule, thanks to the higher-order nature of the language.

A higher-order Gamma program is an unstable solution of molecules. The execution of that program consists in performing the reactions (modulo A/C) until a stable state is reached (*i.e.*, no more reaction can occur). A standard Gamma program can be represented in our extended calculus by encoding its reaction rules by n-shot abstractions placed in the multiset.

For example, the Gamma program computing the maximum element of a multiset of integers is represented by a reaction rule (*max* in Figure 1) to be applied to the multiset. In our higher-order model, that rule is considered as a

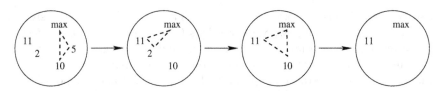

Fig. 4. A possible execution of the program computing the maximum

molecule in the solution of integer molecules. Figure 4 illustrates such a solution and its reduction. Like in the original Gamma, the program terminates when no more reactions can occur. In our example, the solution becomes inert when only one integer (the maximum) remains.

The following solution computes the greatest common divisor (gcd) of its two integers:

$$\langle \text{init}, \text{gcd}, \text{clean}, 15, 21 \rangle$$

where

$$\text{init} = \gamma(x,y)\lfloor x \geq y \rfloor.x{:}y$$
$$\text{gcd} = \textbf{replace } x{:}y \textbf{ by } y{:}(x \bmod y) \textbf{ if } y \neq 0$$
$$\text{clean} = \gamma(x{:}y, \text{gcd})\lfloor y = 0 \rfloor.x$$

First, only the abstraction "init" can react. It places the two integers in a pair and disappears (one-shot abstraction). Then, the molecule "gcd" transforms sequentially the pair until the second place is null ($x \bmod y$ yields the rest of the division of x by y). Finally, the one-shot abstraction "clean" reacts: it extracts the result (x) from the pair and removes the gcd molecule.

Names can be used to tag any molecule: abstractions, solutions, *etc.* For example, if we name "Gcd" the following solution computing the gcd of two integers:

$$\text{Gcd} = \langle \text{init}, \text{gcd}, \text{clean} \rangle$$

then the abstraction computing the gcd of two parameters can be written:

$$\gamma(\text{Gcd} = \langle \omega \rangle, x, y).\langle \omega, x, y \rangle$$

It builds a solution made of the molecules init, gcd, clean (*i.e.*, Gcd) and the two parameters x and y (assumed to be integers). When the solution becomes inert, only the gcd of x and y remains.

N-shot abstractions are well fitted to express self-management properties. For example, computing the prime numbers up to 5 can be expressed as:

$$\langle \text{primes}, 2, 3, 4, 5 \rangle \longrightarrow_\gamma \langle \text{primes}, 2, 3, 5 \rangle$$

where *primes* is the reaction of Figure 1. The molecule "primes" is part of the result (stable state). If new integers are added (perturbation), reactions may start again until a new inert solution is reached (new stable state). For example, if we need the prime numbers up to 10, we may just add integers to the previous inert solution:

$$\langle \text{primes}, 2, 3, 4, 5 \rangle, \ \gamma\langle x \rangle.\langle x, 6, 7, 8, 9, 10 \rangle$$

and the solution will re-stabilize to $\langle \text{primes}, 2, 3, 5, 7 \rangle$. The molecule "primes" can be seen as an invariant: it describes the valid inert states (here, set of prime numbers). In the next section, we make use of this property to add several self-management features to a mail system.

3   Towards an Autonomic Mail System

In this section, we describe an autonomic mail system within our higher-order chemical framework. This example illustrates the adequacy of the chemical paradigm to the description of autonomic systems.

3.1   General Description: Self-organization

The mail system consists in servers, each one dealing with a particular address domain, and clients sending their messages to their domain server. Servers forward messages addressed to other domains to the network. They also get messages addressed to their domain from the network and direct them to the appropriate clients. The mail system (see Figure 5) is described using several molecules:

- Messages exchanged between clients are represented by basic molecules whose structure is left unspecified. We just assume that relevant information (such as sender's address, recipient's address, *etc.*) can be extracted using appropriate functions (such as *sender, recipient, senderDomain, etc.*).
- Solutions named ToSend_{d_i} contain the messages to be sent by the client i of domain d.
- Solutions named Mbox_{d_i} contain the messages received by the client i of domain d.
- Solutions named Pool_d contain the messages that the server of domain d must take care of.
- The solution named Network represents the global network interconnecting domains.
- A client i in domain d is represented by two active molecules send_{d_i} and recv_{d_i}.
- A server of a domain d is represented by two active molecules put_d and get_d.

Clients send messages by adding them to the pool of messages of their domain. They receive messages from the pool of their domain and store them in their mailbox. The send_{d_i} molecule sends messages of the client i (*i.e.*, messages in the ToSend_{d_i} solution) to the client's domain pool (*i.e.*, the Pool_d solution). The recv_{d_i} molecule places the messages addressed to client i (*i.e.*, messages in the Pool_d solution whose recipient is i) in the client's mailbox (*i.e.*, the Mbox_{d_i} solution).

Servers forward messages from their pool to the network. They receive messages from the network and store them in their pool. The put_d molecule forwards

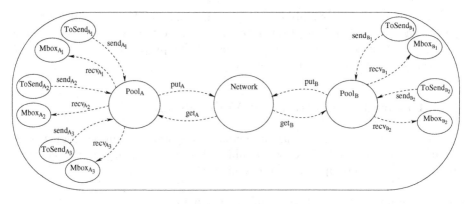

Fig. 5. Mail system

$$\text{send}_{d_i} = \textbf{replace } \text{ToSend}_{d_i} = \langle msg, \omega_t \rangle, \ \text{Pool}_d = \langle \omega_p \rangle$$
$$\textbf{by } \text{ToSend}_{d_i} = \langle \omega_t \rangle, \ \text{Pool}_d = \langle msg, \omega_p \rangle$$

$$\text{recv}_{d_i} = \textbf{replace } \text{Pool}_d = \langle msg, \omega_p \rangle, \text{Mbox}_{d_i} = \langle \omega_b \rangle$$
$$\textbf{by } \text{Pool}_d = \langle \omega_p \rangle, \text{Mbox}_{d_i} = \langle msg, \omega_b \rangle$$
$$\textbf{if } recipient(msg) = i$$

$$\text{put}_d = \textbf{replace } \text{Pool}_d = \langle msg, \omega_p \rangle, \text{Network} = \langle \omega_n \rangle$$
$$\textbf{by } \text{Pool}_d = \langle \omega_p \rangle, \text{Network} = \langle msg, \omega_n \rangle$$
$$\textbf{if } recipientDomain(msg) \neq d$$

$$\text{get}_d = \textbf{replace } \text{Network} = \langle msg, \omega_n \rangle, \text{Pool}_d = \langle \omega_p \rangle$$
$$\textbf{by } \text{Network} = \langle \omega_n \rangle, \text{Pool}_d = \langle msg, \omega_p \rangle$$
$$\textbf{if } recipientDomain(msg) = d$$

$$\text{MailSystem} = \langle\ \text{send}_{A_1},\ \text{recv}_{A_1},\ \text{ToSend}_{A_1} = \langle \ldots \rangle,\ \text{Mbox}_{A_1} = \langle \ldots \rangle,$$
$$\text{send}_{A_2},\ \text{recv}_{A_2},\ \text{ToSend}_{A_2} = \langle \ldots \rangle,\ \text{Mbox}_{A_2} = \langle \ldots \rangle,$$
$$\text{send}_{A_3},\ \text{recv}_{A_3},\ \text{ToSend}_{A_3} = \langle \ldots \rangle,\ \text{Mbox}_{A_3} = \langle \ldots \rangle,$$
$$\text{put}_A,\ \text{get}_A,\ \text{Pool}_A,\ \text{Network},\ \text{put}_B,\ \text{get}_B,\ \text{Pool}_B,$$
$$\text{send}_{B_1},\ \text{recv}_{B_1},\ \text{ToSend}_{B_1} = \langle \ldots \rangle,\ \text{Mbox}_{B_1} = \langle \ldots \rangle,$$
$$\text{send}_{B_2},\ \text{recv}_{B_2},\ \text{ToSend}_{B_2} = \langle \ldots \rangle,\ \text{Mbox}_{B_2} = \langle \ldots \rangle$$
$$\rangle$$

Fig. 6. Self-organization molecules

only messages addressed to other domains than d. The molecule get_d extracts messages addressed to d from the network and places them in the pool of domain d. The system is a solution, named MailSystem, containing molecules representing clients, messages, pools, servers, mailboxes and the network. Figure 5 represents graphically the solution with five clients grouped into two domains A and B and Figure 6 provides the definition of the molecules.

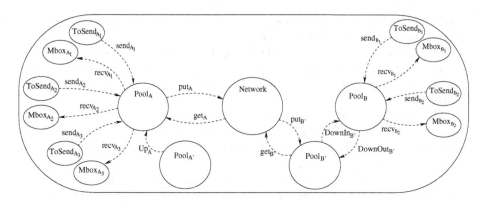

Fig. 7. Highly-available mail system

$$\text{crashServer}_d = \textbf{replace } \text{put}_d, \text{ get}_d, \text{ Up}_d$$
$$\textbf{by } \text{put}_{d'}, \text{ get}_{d'}, \text{DownIn}_d, \text{ DownOut}_d$$
$$\textbf{if } \textit{failure}(d)$$

$$\text{repairServer}_d = \textbf{replace } \text{put}_{d'}, \text{ get}_{d'}, \text{DownIn}_d, \text{ DownOut}_d$$
$$\textbf{by } \text{put}_d, \text{ get}_d, \text{ Up}_d$$
$$\textbf{if } \textit{recover}(d)$$

$$\text{DownOut}_d = \textbf{replace } \text{Pool}_d = \langle msg, \omega_p \rangle, \text{Pool}_{d'} = \langle \omega_n \rangle$$
$$\textbf{by } \text{Pool}_d = \langle \omega_p \rangle, \text{Pool}_{d'} = \langle msg, \omega_n \rangle$$
$$\textbf{if } domain(msg) \neq d$$

$$\text{DownIn}_d = \textbf{replace } \text{Pool}_d = \langle \omega_p \rangle, \text{Pool}_{d'} = \langle msg, \omega_n \rangle$$
$$\textbf{by } \text{Pool}_d = \langle msg, \omega_p \rangle, \text{Pool}_{d'} = \langle \omega_n \rangle$$
$$\textbf{if } domain(msg) = d$$

$$\text{Up}_d = \textbf{replace } \text{Pool}_{d'} = \langle msg, \omega_p \rangle, \text{Pool}_d = \langle \omega_n \rangle$$
$$\textbf{by } \text{Pool}_{d'} = \langle \omega_p \rangle, \text{Pool}_d = \langle msg, \omega_n \rangle$$

$$\text{MailSystem} = \langle \ldots, \text{ Up}_A, \text{ Up}_B, \text{ Pool}_{A'}, \text{ Pool}_{B'}, \text{ crashServer}_A, \text{ repairServer}_A,$$
$$\text{crashServer}_B, \text{ repairServer}_B \rangle$$

Fig. 8. Self-healing molecules

3.2   Self-healing

We now assume that a server may crash. To prevent the mail service from being discontinued, we add an emergency server for each domain (see Figure 7). The emergency servers work with their own pool as usual but are active only when the corresponding main server has crashed. The modeling of a server crash can be done using the reactive molecules described in Figure 8. When a failure occurs, the active molecules representing a main server are replaced by molecules representing the corresponding emergency server. The boolean *failure* denotes a (potentially complex) failure detection mechanism. The inverse reaction repairServer represents the recovery of the server.

The two molecules Up_d and $(DownIn_d, DownOut_d)$ represent the state of the main server d in the solution, but they are also active molecules in charge of transferring pending messages from $Pool_d$ to $Pool_{d'}$; then, they may be forwarded by the emergency server.

The molecule $DownOut_d$ transfers all messages bound to another domain than d from the main pool $Pool_d$ to the emergency pool $Pool_{d'}$. The molecule $DownIn_d$ transfers all messages bound to the domain d from the emergency pool $Pool_{d'}$ to the main pool $Pool_d$.

After a transition from the $Down$ state to the Up state, there may remain some messages in the emergency pools. So, the molecule Up_d brings back all the messages of the emergency pool $Pool_{d'}$ into the main pool $Pool_d$ to be then treated by the repaired main server. In our example, self-healing can be implemented by two emergency servers A' and B' and boils down to adding the molecules of Figure 8 into the main solution.

3.3   Self-protection

Self-protection can be decomposed in two phases: a detection phase and a reaction phase. Detection consists in filtering data and reactions in preventing offensive data to spread (and sometimes also in counter-attacking). It can easily be expressed with the condition-reaction scheme of the chemical paradigm. In our mail system, self-protection is simply implemented with active molecules of the following form:

$$\text{self-protect} = \textbf{replace } x, \omega \textbf{ by } \omega \textbf{ if } \textit{filter}(x)$$

If a molecule x is recognized as offensive data by a filter function then it is suppressed. Variants of self-protect would consist in generating molecules to counter-attack or to send warnings.

Offensive data can take various forms such as spam, virus, $etc.$ A protection against spam can be represented by the molecule:

$$\text{rmSpam} = \textbf{replace } msg, \omega \textbf{ by } \omega \textbf{ if } \textit{isSpam}(msg)$$

which is placed in a $Pool_d$ solution. The contents of the pool can only be accessed when it is inert, that is when all spam messages have been suppressed by the active molecule rmSpam.

Two other self-management features for the mail system have been developed in [2]: self-optimization (by enabling the emergency server and load-balancing messages between it and the main server) and self-configuration (managing mobile clients).

Our description should be regarded as a high-level parallel and modular specification. It allows to design and reason about autonomic systems at an appropriate level of abstraction. Let us emphasize the elegance of the resulting programs which rely essentially on the higher-order and chemical nature of Gamma. A direct implementation of our chemical specifications is likely to be quite inefficient and further refinements are needed; this is another exciting research direction, not tackled here.

4   Conclusion

We have presented a higher-order multiset transformation language which can be described using the chemical reaction metaphor. The higher-order property of our model makes it much more powerful and expressive than the original Gamma [5] or than the Linda language as described in [8]. In this article, we have shown the fundamental features of the chemical programming paradigm. The γ-calculus embodies the essential characteristics (AC multiset rewritings) in only four syntax rules. This minimal calculus has been shown to be expressive enough to express the λ-calculus and a large class of non-deterministic programs [3]. However, in order to come close to a real chemical language, two fundamental extensions must be considered: reaction conditions and atomic capture. Along with appropriate syntactic sugar (recursion, constants, operators, pattern-matching, *etc.*), the extended calculus can easily express most of the existing chemical languages.

In this higher-order model, reactive molecules (γ-abstractions) can be seen as catalysts that perform computations and implement new features. This programming style has been illustrated by the specification of an autonomic mail system in terms of solutions of molecules. Some molecules react as soon as a predefined condition holds without external intervention. In other words, the system configures and manages itself to face predefined situations. Our chemical mail system shows that our approach is well-suited to the high-level description of autonomic systems. Reaction rules exhibit the essence of "autonomy" without going into useless details too early in the development process. A distinctive and valuable property of our description is its modularity. Properties are described by independent collections of molecules and rules that are simply added to the system without requiring other changes.

An interesting research direction is to take advantage of these high-level descriptions to carry out proofs of properties of autonomic systems (in the same spirit as [6]). For example, "not losing any messages" would be an important property to prove for our mail system. Another research direction would be to pursue the extension of our language to prevent clumsy encodings (*e.g.*, using advanced data structures and others high-level facilities).

Other models use a kind of "higher-order" chemical metaphor like [9]: it considers multisets of reacting λ-terms, and it studies the self-organization property.

References

1. Jean-Pierre Banâtre, Pascal Fradet, and Daniel Le Métayer. Gamma and the chemical reaction model: Fifteen years after. In *Multiset Processing*, volume 2235 of *LNCS*, pages 17–44. Springer-Verlag, 2001.

2. Jean-Pierre Banâtre, Pascal Fradet, and Yann Radenac. Chemical specification of autonomic systems. In Walter Dosch and Narayan Debnath, editors, *Proc. of the 13th Int. Conf. on Intelligent and Adaptive Systems and Software Engineering (IASSE'04)*. ISCA, 2004.

3. Jean-Pierre Banâtre, Pascal Fradet, and Yann Radenac. Principles of chemical programming. In S. Abdennadher and C. Ringeissen, editors, *Proceedings of the 5th International Workshop on Rule-Based Programming (RULE 2004)*, volume 124 of *ENTCS*, pages 133–147. Elsevier, June 2004.

4. Jean-Pierre Banâtre and Daniel Le Métayer. A new computational model and its discipline of programming. Technical Report RR0566, INRIA, September 1986.

5. Jean-Pierre Banâtre and Daniel Le Métayer. Programming by multiset transformation. *Communications of the ACM (CACM)*, 36(1):98–111, January 1993.

6. Hector Barradas. *Systematic derivation of an operating system kernel in Gamma*. Phd thesis (in french), University of Rennes, France, July 1993.

7. Gérard Berry and Gérard Boudol. The chemical abstract machine. *Theoretical Computer Science*, 96:217–248, 1992.

8. Nicholas Carriero and David Gelernter. Linda in Context. *Communications of the ACM*, 32(4):444–458, 1989.

9. Walter Fontana and Leo Buss. Algorithmic chemistry. In J. Farmer C. Langton, C. Taylor and S. Rasmussen, editors, *Artificial Life II*, volume X, pages 159–209. Addison-Wesley, 1992.

10. Daniel Le Métayer. Higher-order multiset programming. In American Mathematical Society, editor, *Proc. of the DIMACS workshop on specifications of parallel algorithms*, volume 18 of *Dimacs Series in Discrete Mathematics*, 1994.

11. Gheorghe Păun. Computing with membranes. *Journal of Computer and System Sciences*, 61(1):108–143, 2000.

Amorphous Computing

Introduction to Amorphous Computing

Daniel Coore

The University of the West Indies, Mona. Jamaica, WI

Abstract. The study of amorphous computing aims to identify useful programming methodologies that will enable us to engineer the emergent behaviour of a myriad, locally interacting computing elements (agents). We anticipate that in order to keep such massively distributed systems cheap, the elements must be bulk manufactured. Therefore, we use a conservative model in which the agents run asynchronously, are interconnected in unknown and possibly time-varying ways, communicate only locally, and are identically programmed. We present a description of this model, and some of the results that have been obtained with it, particularly in the areas of pattern formation and the development of programming languages that are specifically suited to our model. Finally, we briefly describe some of the ongoing efforts in amorphous computing, and we present some of the interesting and important problems that still remain open in amorphous computing.

1 Introduction

The collection of cells in an embryo self-organize, under the control of a common genetic program, to form a single organism. When we consider this phenomenon in computing terms, it is indeed remarkable that organisms reproduce so reliably and consistently. If we suppose that each cell is a computing element whose program is encoded in DNA, then an embryo would be a massively distributed system that runs a single program on all its elements and produces a globally coherent result. The study of amorphous computing seeks to identify and apply the engineering principles behind the coordination of such a multitudinous distributed system.

An amorphous computing system is a large collection of irregularly placed, locally interacting, identically-programmed, asynchronous computing elements [1]. We assume that these elements (agents) communicate within a fixed radius, which is large relative to the size of an element, but small relative to the diameter of the system. We also assume that most agents do not initially have any information to distinguish themselves from other agents; this includes information such as position, identity and connectivity. The challenge of amorphous computing is to develop computing paradigms that enable us to write programs that when executed on each agent produce some pre-specified emergent behaviour.

We are motivated by recent advances in microfabrication and in cellular engineering [10, 4, 18, 19] – technologies that will enable us to build systems with several orders of magnitude more computing elements than we currently can. If

J.-P. Banâtre et al. (Eds.): UPP 2004, LNCS 3566, pp. 99–109, 2005.

such systems could be controlled with the reliability and precision with which we control present day computers, then these systems could be used in a variety of applications including: molecular-scale circuit factories, smart drugs, and smart building materials. The challenge, in anticipation of realising these systems in the near future, is to find programming techniques for controlling these systems.

1.1   The Amorphous Computing Model

The amorphous computing model is not explicit about the assumed capabilities of a single agent – only that it has limited memory to work with because of its size. It has become commonplace to assume that each agent, operating in isolation, can:

- maintain and update state (read and write to memory)
- access a timer (a piece of state that changes uniformly with time, but not necessarily at the same rate as happens on other agents)
- access a source of random bits
- perform simple arithmetic and logic operations.

In addition, the ensemble of agents are assumed to:

- **run asynchronously:** each agent has a clock whose period is uniformly distributed between 1 and some fixed upper bound b, which limits the maximal permitted ratio between any two agents.
- **be irregularly located:** each agent is fixed at a location that is unknown to itself and to its neighbours. Neither is any *a priori* knowledge about the number or placement of the agent's neighbours available.
- **communicate via short-range broadcast only:** each agent communicates by broadcasting a short range signal that is felt by only those agents within some fixed distance from the agent, which we call the *communication radius*. The communication radius is generally large relative to the size of a single agent, but small compared to the diameter of the system. This way, each neighbourhood contains several agents, yet there are several neighbourhoods within the system.
- **have limited computational resources at hand:** each agent is presumed to have limited storage capacity. This sometimes places limitations on the types of information that an agent can be expected to compute.
- **run a common program:** there is a single program that is uploaded to every agent. Any differences in behaviours of individual agents must arise from differentiation of state variables, which is generally coordinated through local communication, and ultimately must arise from the initial conditions set on the system.
- **be initialised uniformly with only a few special cases:** the number of agents that need special attention for setting the initial conditions should be kept small, since each one must be initiated from the user.

1.2   Execution

Executing a program on an amorphous computer involves loading the common program onto each agent (the program could be an intrinsic part of the agent's definition – e.g. stored in ROM), and setting up the initial conditions of the system. The initial conditions of the system are comprised of all initial states of the agents in the system. The initial state of an agent determines its entry point into the common program. By this mechanism, the user has the opportunity to supply "initial conditions" after the system has booted and its program has been loaded.

More precisely, when an amorphous system boots, all of the agents are in the same initial state, and therefore the collection of states of all agents is the same immediately after each boot. This initial state is essentially a quiescent state in which agents are listening for messages to respond to, but never sending any. The user sets an initial state on an agent by producing a stimulus at one of its sensors, which is treated as a message that causes it to begin executing a different part of the program. Observe that this is potentially different from the typical notion of "initial conditions" in a mathematical system, where the initial conditions are regarded as the state of the system as it was captured at some designated reference time. In particular, delays between user-supplied stimuli and differing clock speeds on each agent will cause the collection of all initial state transitions to not be perfectly simultaneous. Any undesirable side-effects of this must be addressed by the user, e.g. through judicious selection of loci for initial conditions, or by using synchronizers where necessary.

2   Progress to Date

Most of the problems that were tackled at first (1997–2000) were related to pattern formation: suppose that each agent may take on one of several predefined states each of which has been associated with a single colour. If we are given a pattern comprised of these colours, is it possible to write a program that directs the adoption of state at an agent, and to find suitable initial conditions for that program, that together cause the given pattern to emerge? For example, the pattern shown in Figure 1 is the result of a program that was designed to form the letters "M I T" above a line. It used initial conditions that required special states to be defined for only four agents.

Out of these initial efforts at pattern formation have emerged a number of useful routines, as well as a few programming languages that allow the user to think more about the global objectives rather than the local interactions. More recent work, such as Beal's work on *persistent nodes* [2], has focused on producing robust logical structures that can cooperatively perform a simple task.

2.1   The Coordinate System Problem

In the early days of the project, we believed that a coordinate system would be important for describing and generating patterns. Since then, we have found

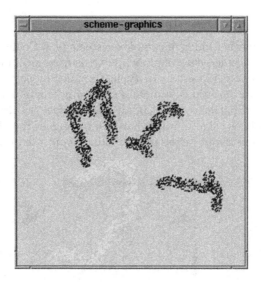

Fig. 1. Self-organizing text. The initial conditions include two neighbouring points to generate the reference line (in yellow), and two others that establish the left-to-right direction and initiates the first letter. The program producing this pattern encodes instructions for generating each letter, and for sequencing them along the reference line. It was implemented as a GPL program

that while it can be useful, the computation involved in setting up a coordinate system implies that it is probably not the most ideal method for generating patterns. Nevertheless, having a coordinate system still seems like a useful tool that will probably find many applications in problems that are highly dependent on the geometric properties of the amorphous ensemble.

One idea for generating a coordinate system was to use triangulation: distances, represented by hop counts, were obtained from three distinguished agents to each agent. Using trigonometric relations, the three distances were translated into a coordinate. This approach was fairly straightforward to implement, but suffered from large errors in regions near the reference points. These results are summarised by Nagpal in [12].

Another approach uses a single distinguished agent to establish the origin of the coordinate system. That agent then establishes an approximately circular boundary around itself, along which each agent computes its coordinates from an approximation to the angle around the boundary. These coordinates are then used as boundary values for an iterative solution of Laplace's equations within the circular boundary. When convergence is achieved, each agent within the boundary has been assigned a coordinate that is consistent with the boundary. This approach requires more effort to implement, and takes longer to generate coordinates, but produces smaller errors than the triangulation method. A brief account of the method is given in [8].

2.2   Languages for Describing Patterns

As it is in so many other kinds of complex systems (e.g. Cellular Automata), we are interested in the emergence of global patterns from local interactions [17, 3], but from a different perspective. In typical studies of pattern formation, researchers investigate variations of models of local interaction and try to classify the emergent global patterns (e.g. [20, 14]). In contrast, we are more interested in exercising this knowledge in ways that give a designer the ability to generate emergent patterns, without necessarily thinking about the local interactions in-

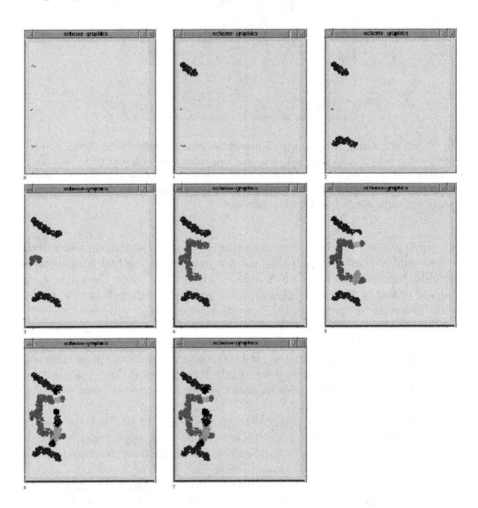

Fig. 2. Snapshots from the self-organization of the CMOS layout of an inverter. The first image, labeled 0 shows the locations of the five points that make up the initial conditions. Each dot represents an agent, the thickness of one of the lines represents the diameter of a typical neighbourhood. Each colour reflects a computational state taken on by the agent at that point. The colours used were deliberately chosen to correspond to those of a real CMOS design

volved. In general, our approaches to this problem have been to design languages that specify global patterns in terms of points in space that are computationally active. These global descriptions are then systematically compiled to the appropriate local interactions.

The Growing Point Language (GPL) [7] is a language for describing patterns of topological relations (i.e. patterns of the form "point A is connected to point B, which is connected to points C and D ..."). Perhaps the most useful example of this kind of pattern is an electrical circuit. Figure 2 shows the execution of a GPL coded CMOS inverter as an example. GPL is also capable of describing a number of other types of patterns, for example the self-organising text shown in Figure 1 was generated by a GPL program. The invention of GPL led us to recognise that it was viable to abstract the lower level local processes in ways that related to the global arrangements that we were trying to achieve.

Another language for specifying patterns is the Origami Shape Language (OSL) [13], which allows the user to specify patterns as sequences of Origami-like folds. In this situation, we imagine that the agents are equipped with actuators that can allow them to effect folds in the surface on which they have been distributed. A sequence of folds encoded in OSL is automatically compiled into agent level instructions, which when executed by the ensemble, yields an appropriately folded surface. Figure 3 shows the sequence of Origami folds that make a paper cup. Figure 4 shows the behaviour of the agents when executing the OSL encoding of those folds.

Other work has focused on producing patterns in a variation of the amorphous computing model [11]. In this work, Kondacs described a method for producing system-level patterns on a system in which agents reproduce and multiply to occupy space. The pattern produced at the end of execution was the shape of the space that was occupied by the agents. Kondacs used small overlapping coordinate patches to generate patterns. To code a pattern, first it was analysed in terms of overlapping circular regions, each of which could be grown by pro-

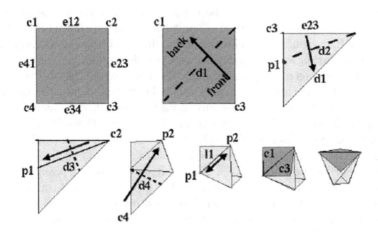

Fig. 3. An Origami cup, defined as a sequence of folds on a square piece of paper

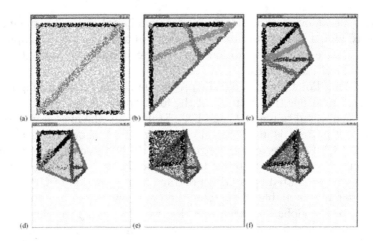

Fig. 4. The result of executing the OSL instructions for folding the Origami cup

liferation of the agents. Geometric relations for these circular regions were then used to guide their construction.

Currently, the most recent efforts at tackling the pattern formation problem has been to develop a language that attempts to unify the ideas presented in GPL and OSL [6]. This work is still on-going and we hope that it will yield powerful languages that can be used to express highly complex global behaviours, yet remain compilable to simple agent-level interactions.

2.3   Other Progress

Not all of the work on amorphous computing systems has been solely about describing patterns. Agents are expected to fail frequently. So we are keen to find ways to engineer robust systems, but without putting undue burden on the designer (that is, we would like the designer to worry about the unreliability of the agents as little as possible). Clement and Nagpal showed in [5] how the pattern of a line segment could be robustly maintained between its end points. In this implementation, state assignments were transient and had to be continuously reasserted. If an agent, anywhere along the line (except for the end points), failed completely then nearby agents would be recruited into the line to take the place of the failed one(s) and circumvent the break. The mechanism used was implemented directly in terms of low-level interactions. It remains to be extended and generalised so that robust lines can become an available feature in high level amorphous programming languages.

Beal describes how to create a persistent logical blob of agents who share some information. The logical blob is called a *persistent node*, and it has the remarkable property that even when large swathes of agents are oblated from it, it can migrate to another part of the amorphous substrate, to regenerate itself. Throughout all that, it retains enough coherence to maintain some shared information that was provided to it upon its creation.

In all of our work so far, we have relied upon simulations for testing our ideas for amorphous computing. This has led to the development of an agent-level programming language, called ECOLI, that encourages the programmer to focus on the messages exchanged between agents, rather than on the sequential processing occurring on each agent.

In ECOLI agents are expected to communicate, so programs are organised into groups of related message handlers, called *dictionaries*, which in turn are grouped together to form *behaviours*. At any one time, within a behaviour, only one dictionary is active, and it determines which handlers may be activated by incoming messages on the agent. In this way, we can implement modal responses from agents, which can be used to achieve behavioural differentiation and specialisation by agents. If biological systems are any indication, this is an evidently important ability to have in order to build complex hierarchical (logical) structures. The simplifying ideas of ECOLI were key to the first implementation of a self-organizing inverter, which was then generalised into what is today called GPL.

Although the initial ideas for ECOLI were developed so long ago, we believe that there are still more benefits to be reaped from it, and so there are still ongoing efforts to enhance and improve it. There are also some efforts currently underway at adapting communications protocols for the amorphous computing environment. In yet another project, we are investigating the use of redundant paths through an amorphous system between distant agents to improve the reliability of message delivery.

The amorphous computing environment has also been used as a simulation platform, often to investigate what rules of interaction are the amorphous equivalents of those in other complex systems in which there is more regularity either in space or time. For example reaction-diffusion systems are usually simulated on regular grids using finite difference rules for simulating the differential operator in diffusion. In [9] we showed that there are approximating rules for the amorphous environment that are at least capable of producing qualitatively similar patterns as those generated on regular grids [14]. Rauch [15] has also shown that some differential operators can be simulated amorphously quite effectively; in particular, wave motion can be simulated amorphously. This is particularly interesting because one would intuitively expect that the underlying irregular network would introduce errors that would ultimately disrupt the oscillating patterns.

3   Summary and Future Directions

Pattern formation [17, 14, 16] inspired the earliest results from amorphous computing. The work that was generated in trying to generate global patterns from local interactions has led to a number of programming languages (e.g. GPL and OSL) being developed. These languages are system-level languages that demonstrate that one effective approach to the amorphous computing challenge is to capture system-level concepts in programming constructs that are readily compilable to an agent-level language, such as ECOLI.

There is still much work to be done, however. Both GPL and OSL have relatively narrow scopes of application, and there is room for generalisation, which we are actively pursuing. Even when we achieve a more general pattern description language, it remains to be seen whether that language is Turing-complete, or whether some other ingredients are needed in it to capture all amorphously computable functions.

Several avenues for research remain wide open in this area. For example, little work has been done on mobile agents. It is quite natural to expect that in many amorphous systems agents will not be stationary as they are in most of our current simulations. None of the current languages are fully capable of dealing with this phenomenon. It remains to be seen whether the motion of agents can actually be exploited to compute some functions more efficiently than when the agents are stationary. Such an outcome would be counter-intuitive, but not implausible as we recognise that agents that are constantly bumping into each other can exchange information about a wider region than agents that are stationarily positioned.

Another area for pursuing in amorphous computing is the development of languages for self-organizing functionality, as opposed to pattern formation which is self-organizing form. In other words, when we form logical patterns now, they are just assignments of local state; but can we create programs that ascribe functionality and behaviour to agents based on their positions relative to others. Following on from this idea, we would also like to create powerful mechanisms for specifying automatic cooperative distributed computing. For example, given a large set of records, all of which are too numerous to be stored at a single agent, is there a way to have the amorphous system partition itself into specialised functional groups that cooperate to sort the set?

There are also open questions about forming dynamic patterns, which would involve getting patterns that are constructed using the methods we have already discovered to become animated to explore configurations other than the one in which they were created. One application of this could be to the circuit diagrams that we already produce. In reality, the CMOS masks that would be generated from the circuits that we can produce today would often be in violation of some of the design rules. If we could get patterns to re-organize as coherent structures, then we could potentially produce circuits that used space optimally, with little more effort than it took to draw them in the first instance. However, we still do not have a good idea how to engineer coherence for arbitrarily shaped structures that can migrate across agents in the system.

In conclusion, amorphous computing is still an active area of research. Currently, much of the research effort is being spent on developing special purpose programming languages for solving particular classes of amorphous computing problems. There still remain many challenging open problems that are likely to be most adequately addressed by a broad, cross-disciplinary approach to them.

References

1. ABELSON, H., D. Allen, D. Coore, C. Hanson, G. Homsy, T. Knight, R. Nagpal, E. Rauch, G. Sussman, and R. Weiss. Amorphous Computing. *Communications of the ACM*, **43**(5), May 2000.
2. BEAL, Jacob, "Persistent Nodes for Reliable Memory in Geographically Local Networks", *AI Memo 2003-011*, Massachusetts Institute of Technology, Artificial Intelligence Laboratory, Apr. 2003.
3. BERLEKAMP, E., J. Conway, R. K. Guy, *Winning Ways for your Mathematical Plays, Vol 2: Games in Particular.*, Academic Press. London. 1982.
4. BENENSON, Yaakov., Rivka Adar,Tamar Paz-Elizur, Zvi Livneh, and Ehud Shapiro, "DNA molecule provides a computing machine with both data and fuel." in *Proceedings National Academy of Science, USA* **100**, 2191-2196. 2003.
5. CLEMENT, Lauren, and Radhika Nagpal, " Self-Assembly and Self-Repairing Topologies", in *Workshop on Adaptability in Multi-Agent Systems*, RoboCup Australian Open, Jan. 2003.
6. COORE, Daniel, "Towards a Universal Language for Amorphous Computing", in *International Conference on Complex Systems (ICCS2004)*, May 2004.
7. COORE, Daniel, *Botanical Computing: A Developmental Approach to Generating Interconnect Topologies on an Amorphous Computer*. PhD thesis, MIT, Dept. of Electrical Engineering and Computer Science, Feb. 1999.
8. COORE, Daniel. "Establishing a Coordinate System on an Amorphous Computer". In *Proceedings of 1998 MIT Student Workshop on High-Performance Computing in Science and Engineering*. Technical Report 737, MIT Laboratory for Computer Science. 1998.
9. COORE, Daniel, Radhika Nagpal, "Implementing Reaction-Diffusion on an Amorphous Computer". In *Proceedings of 1998 MIT Student Workshop on High-Performance Computing in Science and Engineering*. Technical Report 737, MIT Laboratory for Computer Science. 1998.
10. KNIGHT, Tom, Gerald J. Sussman, "Cellular Gate Technologies", in *First International Conference on Unconventional Models of Computation (UMC98)*, 1998.
11. KONDACS, Attila, "Biologically-Inspired Self-Assembly of Two-Dimensional Shapes Using Global-to-Local Compilation", in *International Joint Conference on Artificial Intelligence (IJCAI)*, Aug. 2003.
12. NAGPAL, Shrobe, Bachrach, "Organizing a Global Coordinate System from Local Information on an Ad Hoc Sensor Network", *2nd International Workshop on Information Processing in Sensor Networks (IPSN '03)*, Palo Alto, April 2003.
13. NAGPAL, Radhika, *Programmable Self-Assembly: Constructing Global Shape using Biologically-inspired Local Interactions and Origami Mathematics*. PhD thesis, MIT, Dept. of Electrical Engineering and Computer Science, June 2001.
14. PEARSON, J. E., "Complex Patterns in a Simple System", *Science* **261**, 189–192, July 1993.
15. RAUCH, E., *Discrete, Amorphous Physical Models*. MS thesis, MIT, Dept. Electrical Engineering and Computer Science, 1999.
16. SLACK, J. M. W., *From Egg to Embryo: Regional Specification in Early Development (2nd ed)*. Cambridge University Press. Cambridge, UK. 1991.
17. TURING, A., "The Chemical Basis of Morphogenesis", *Phil. Trans. Royal Society*, **B 237**, 37–72. 1952.
18. WEISS, Ron, *Cellular Computation and Communications using Engineered Genetic Regulatory Networks*. PhD thesis, MIT, Dept. of Electrical Engineering and Computer Science, Sep. 2001.

19. WEISS, R., T. F. Knight, "Engineered Communications for Microbial Robotics", Sixth International Meeting on DNA-based computers (DNA6), June 2000.
20. WOLFRAM, S., "Computation Theory of Cellular Automata", *Communications in Mathematical Physics* **96**, 15–57, 1984.

Abstractions for
Directing Self-organising Patterns

Daniel Coore

The University of the West Indies,
Mona, Jamaica, WI

Abstract. We present an abstraction for pattern formation, called *pattern networks*, which are suitable for constructing complex patterns from simpler ones in the amorphous computing environment. This work builds upon previous efforts that focused on creating suitable system-level abstractions for engineering the emergence of agent-level interactions. Our pattern networks are built up from combinations of these system-level abstractions, and may be combined to form bigger pattern networks. We demonstrate the power of this abstraction by illustrating how a few complex patterns could be generated by a combination of appropriately defined pattern networks. We conclude with a discussion of the challenges involved in parameterising these abstractions, and in defining higher-order versions of them.

1   Introduction

An amorphous computing system is a collection of irregularly placed, locally interacting, identically-programmed, asynchronous computing elements [1]. We assume that these elements (agents) communicate within a fixed radius, which is large relative to the size of an element, but small relative to the diameter of the system. We also assume that most agents do not initially have any information to distinguish themselves from other agents; this includes information such as position, identity and connectivity. The challenge of amorphous computing is to systematically produce a program that when executed by each agent (in parallel) produces some pre-specified system-wide behaviour.

So far, one of the most important results of Amorphous Computing is that despite the constraints of the computing model, in which so little positional information is available, it is still possible to engineer the emergence of certain types of globally defined patterns [6, 9, 4, 8, 2]. In each of these works, the principal mechanism used to control emergence was to define a system-level language that could describe an interesting class of patterns, but that could also be systematically transformed to agent-level computations.

1.1   A Unifying Pattern Description Language

Recently, we proposed a unifying language [5] that is capable of describing the same patterns as those produced by the programming languages defined

J.-P. Banâtre et al. (Eds.): UPP 2004, LNCS 3566, pp. 110–120, 2005.

in [6, 9, 4, 8]. The language aims to capture system-level programming motifs by providing primitive operations that implement them by transparently initiating and managing the necessary agent-level processes. The motifs supported are those that were found to be common among the programming languages cited. In [5], we argued that, these primitves could be combined in simple ways to describe more interesting higher (system) level behaviour, such as self-organizing lines and regions. These primitively supported motifs include:

- diffusing values to form gradients,
- querying neighbourhoods for the value of a variable,
- selecting a neighbouring agent on which to invoke a computation,
- using majority among neighbourhoods to smooth their boundaries,
- competing for leadership among a connected set of agents (they need not belong to a single neighbourhood),
- monitoring conditions local to a neighbourhood

In this language, the system is regarded as a collection of points. Each point has a *neighbourhood* which is the set of points that lie within some fixed distance of the original point. Points can be named and some operations may yield points as results, which may be used in any context in which a point is expected. We can execute blocks of commands at any point. Computations that are specified to occur at multiple points are performed in parallel, but generally computations specified at a single point are carried out sequentially (although threaded computations are permitted at a point).

All computations are either entirely internal to an agent or may be derived from local communication between neighbouring agents. All primitive operations, whether they can be computed by an agent in isolation or only through neighbourhoods, have a mechanism for indicating to the originating point when the computation is considered completed. This means that any operations performed at a point may be sequenced together, even if the operation involves computations at many points.

An Example. By way of example, we shall briefly review some of the features of this language to give the reader a feel for it. This should help to establish a basis for the network abstraction presented in the remainder of the paper.

One way to draw a line segment is to diffuse a signal from one end, far enough that it encounters the other end of the line. The other end then labels itself a part of the line, performs a neighbourhood query, and examines each neighbour's concentration of the diffused signal. The neighbour with the strongest signal towards the source is selected to repeat the process. The combined computations yield a gradient-descent (or hill-climbing) process that will label a sequence of points from one end point to the other as being a part of the line. Notice that in this discussion, the two end points are provided as inputs to the line drawing process. In the context of the amorphous environment, this means that they would be provided as initial conditions to the agent-level program. Below is the code listing that implements this idea, it was excerpted from [5].

```
1              Diffusable B-stuff
2              PointSet ABLine
3              at B: diffuse (B-stuff, linear-unbounded)
4              at A:do SearchForB {
5                  addTo(ABLine)
6                  nbrConcs := filter(queryNbhd(B-stuff),
7                                     lt(B-stuff))
8                  at select(nbrConcs, min):
9                      do SearchForB
10             }
```

The two end points have been named A and B respectively. The at command initiates computation at a point. The primitive function diffuse initiates a diffusion process that is centred at the point at which it is invoked. Its first argument is the name of the substance being diffused, the second is a function that determines the shape of the gradient of the diffusion. In this example, the builtin function linear-unbounded specifies a gradient that increases from the centre and propagates as far as possible in all directions. So, line 3 causes a gradient to be established that is centred at the point named B. Its extent is the entire connected component within which B lies. The gradient's values increase with the distance from the centre, so a "stronger" signal in this context means a smaller value of diffused substance.

In parallel with the process initiated at B, a named block of code (called SearchForB) is evaluated at point A. The addTo command adds the point (at which it is evaluated) to the set given as the argument to addTo. The form queryNbhd is a special form that takes the name of a substance whose concentration is to be queried on each neighbour. The predicate lt(B-stuff) is a curried version of the usual less than comparator. The interpreter first evaluates the name B-stuff to yield the concentration of B-stuff at that point (in this case A); it then generates a predicate of one argument that returns true whenever that argument is less than the supplied currying value of B-stuff at the time the predicate was constructed. The filter operation is an ordinary list filter. So lines 6 and 7 together produce a list of neighbourhood concentrations that are smaller than that at the centre of the neighbourhood, which based on the gradient laid down by B must all be closer to the point labeled B than the centre of the neighbourhood (currently labeled A) is. Lines 8 and 9 selects the neighbour with the smallest concentration and invokes the entire SearchForB block on it, thereby propagating the computation to a neighbour of the point A. When the computation reaches the point B, the filter procedure will produce an empty set of neighbours (since the concentration at the source of a diffusion that is shaped by the linear-unbounded function is smaller than all other concentrations in its neighbourhood). This then terminates the process, since the `at` command in line 8 will have no points on which to execute.

One of the most interesting aspects to this type of programming is that when we think of this program as if it were running on a single machine (the abstraction we would like to present), the `SearchForB` block appears as a recursive process. However, when it is actually evaluated, it is in fact a computation that executes at a separate point in space. In this way, the `at` command gives us the ability to distribute recursive computation over space – a notion that hints at elegant expressions of interesting geometric patterns[1].

2   Pattern Networks

The recently proposed pattern description language [5] is not rich in abstractions. It provides primitives that abstract over the agent-level interactions, but it does not provide any abstractions over the patterns that may be described. For example, it is possible to describe four lines that form a square, but it is not possible to name that pattern of four lines and invoke it whenever we need a square. Instead we must describe the four constituent lines, each time a square is desired.

We propose a plausible abstraction for patterns, called a *pattern network*, that is compatible with this language. This abstraction is similar to the network abstractions for GPL described in [6]. The implementation of this abstraction in our pattern description language is in progress, so any sample outputs illustrating the idea have been taken from the GPL version of the abstraction.

Pattern networks describe patterns in terms of a set of given points in the domain (the *input* points). Special points that arise from the generation of these patterns (the *output* points) may be named and used as inputs to other pattern networks. The `network` construct defines a pattern network. Its syntax is:

```
network ⟨name⟩ [⟨inputs⟩] [⟨outputs⟩] {
        ⟨pattern-defn⟩
}
```

2.1   An Example

As an illustration of how this abstraction can be used, let us reuse the code, presented in [5], that draws a line segment between two given points. We present below, the original code surrounded by a box to highlight the minimal syntax of the pattern network abstraction.

---

[1] The constraints are actually topological, but in the amorphous environment, because neighbourhoods are determined by points being within a specified proximity, topological constraints are concomitant with geometric constraints.

```
network segment[A, B] [] {
```

```
Diffusable B-stuff
PointSet ABLine
at B: diffuse (B-stuff, linear-unbounded)
at A:do SearchForB {
    addTo(ABLine)
    nbrConcs := filter(queryNbhd(B-stuff),
                       lt(B-stuff))
    at select(nbrConcs, min):
        do SearchForB
}
```

```
}
```

In this example, the network is called segment and has two input points (A, B) and zero output points. Whenever the segment network is invoked, a logical substance named B-stuff is diffused from the point supplied as B. Simultaneously from A, a process is started that locally seeks the source of the B-stuff diffusion, and propagates from point to point until it is found. This process labels each visited point with the ABLine label to identify the line segment that would have formed from A to B after the process is completed. In this example, both the logical substance B-stuff and the set label ABLine are local to the network, so they are actually renamed on each invocation of the network so that the actual labels exchanged at the agent level are unique to the invocation of the network. This avoids unwanted interference between separate invocations of the same network. As an example, to define a triangle between three points, we might implement the following network:

```
network triangle [A, B, C] [] {
    segment[A,B]
    segment[B,C]
    segment[C,A]
}
```

2.2   Combining Patterns

Pattern networks can be defined in terms of combinations of smaller pattern networks. We have already seen an example of this in the triangle network defined above, however that was simply the simultaneous invocation of three instances of the segment network. We can go further by using the output of one network to feed into another. A special operation has to be introduced for associating output points of one network with inputs of another. We introduced the cascade operation to conveniently implement the simple chaining of networks together. Its syntax is:

$$\text{cascade}(\langle points \rangle, \langle net_1 \rangle, \ldots, \langle net_n \rangle, [points])$$

To illustrate the operation of cascade, let us assume that we already have three pattern networks, each with one input and one output, named up, right

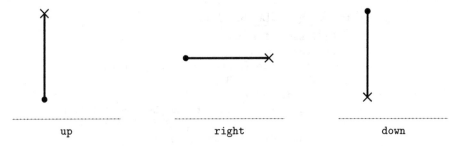

up   right   down

Fig. 1. Three networks, each having one input and one output have been defined, and named *up*, *right* and *down*. Each one draws a short line in the indicated direction relative to a reference line (produced by some other pattern). In each case, a dot indicates the location of the input point and an 'x' indicates the output point

and `down`. Each one draws a short line relative to some reference line (constructed by some other pattern) in the indicated direction. The termination point of each line is the output point of its network. These networks are illustrated in Figure 1. We could now define a new network, called `rising` with one input and one output that is the result of cascading `up` with `right`. A similar network, called `falling`, could be composed from cascading `down` with `right`. To get one period of a square wave, we could `cascade` `rising` and `falling` together. The effect of the `cascade` operation in these definitions is illustrated in Figure 2.

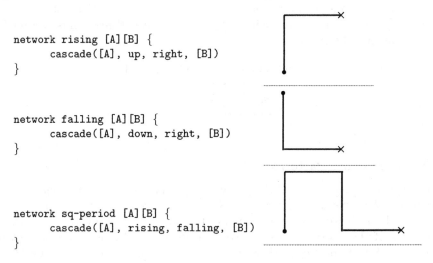

```
network rising [A][B] {
      cascade([A], up, right, [B])
}


network falling [A][B] {
      cascade([A], down, right, [B])
}


network sq-period [A][B] {
      cascade([A], rising, falling, [B])
}
```

Fig. 2. The composition of networks with the `cascade` operation. Pattern networks can be composed and abstracted to build compound patterns that would otherwise be tedious to construct

We could now further build upon this network by constructing a square wave of several periods, by cascading many instances of `sq-period` together. It should be clear that the cascade operation has provided considerable expressive power by enabling the composition of a large pattern from sub-patterns.

When there are multiple inputs and outputs, the cascade operation associates outputs with inputs according to the order in which they appear. In some instances, the user may want the association between outputs of one network and inputs of another to be some permutation other than the identity permutation. This re-ordering of points can be achieved with the use of a binding construct that permits intermediate points to be named and used in any context in which a point expression may legally appear. The let-points construct facilitates this; its syntax is defined as:

$$
\text{let-points } [\langle id_1 \rangle, \ \ldots, \ \langle id_n \rangle]
$$
$$
\{\langle point\text{-}defns \rangle\}
$$
$$
\text{in } \{\langle pattern\text{-}defn \rangle\}
$$

The point-defns expression may be any expression that is capable of yielding points as outputs. These points are bound to the names id_1, id_2 for use in evaluating the pattern-defn expression, which itself is also any expression that may have legally appeared in the body of a pattern network. The let-points construct allows outputs to be permuted when cascaded with other networks.

For example, suppose that net1 and net2 are two pattern networks each with two inputs and two outputs. Now, suppose we want to cascade the outputs of net1 to the inputs of net2 but with the orderings exchanged (i.e. first output to second input and vice-versa). In addition, we shall make the connected structure a new pattern network. The following network definition uses the let-points construct to accomplish this.

```
network crossed [A, B][C, D] {
    let-points[out1, out2]
             {cascade([A, B], net1, [out1, out2])}
    in {cascade([out2, out1], net2, [C, D])}
}
```

The let-points command not only provides a generic means for supporting arbitrary permutations of output points, but it also provides a means for connecting the outputs of two pattern networks to the inputs of a single network. The following example shows how the outputs from the right and up networks (previously mentioned) can be connected to the inputs of net1. It creates a pattern network that has two inputs and two outputs. Each input point acts as the input to the single-input networks, their outputs are connected to the inputs of net1 and its outputs are the outputs of the overall network.

```
network two-to-one [A, B][C, D] {
    let-points[out1, out2]
                {
                  cascade([A], right, [out1])
                  cascade([B], up, [out2])
                }
    in {cascade([out1, out2], net1, [C, D])}
    }
```

3   Examples

Pattern networks provide a convenient high-level abstraction for describing patterns in a system-level language. In this section, we illustrate their versatility by showing how they were used in GPL to describe self-organising text and CMOS circuit layouts.

3.1   Text

As an example, let us use pattern networks to define patterns of self-organising text. The idea is that each letter of the alphabet is defined as a pattern network. Each letter is defined relative to a line, which will be generated along with the characters themselves. Each network has two input points and two output points. One input point defines the starting point for the letter, and the other the starting point for the segment of the reference line, upon which the letter sits. The letters are drawn from left to right, so the outputs represent the locations that a letter placed to the right of the current one would use as its inputs.

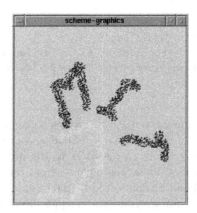

Fig. 3. The result of cascading the pattern networks for the letters 'M', 'I' and 'T' together. Observe that the reference line is subject to the variability in the distribution of the agents. A badly drawn reference line can often cause the desired letters to fail to form in a recognizable way

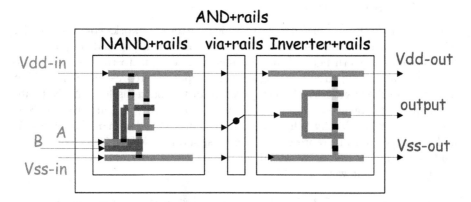

Fig. 4. The *NAND+rails* network has 4 inputs and 3 outputs, and both of *via+rails* and *Inverter+rails* have 3 inputs and 3 outputs. The arrows depict the connections between the outputs and inputs of the three networks. Each bordering rectangle depicts a network. Observe that the result of the cascade of the three networks is itself another network with 4 inputs (the number of inputs of the first network in the cascade) and 3 outputs (the number of outputs of the last network in the cascade)

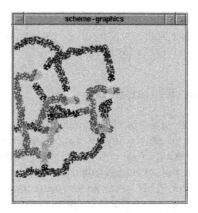

Fig. 5. The result of executing the **and+rails** network. Its **nand+rails** and **inverter+rails** components are readily identified. The pattern was drawn from left to right, in the order specified by the **cascade** command, so the starting points for the **inverter+rails** network were determined by the termination points of the **nand+rails** network. While the result is geometrically quite crude, it is nevertheless topologically correct

In this way, a word can be defined as a cascade of pattern networks each of which produces a single letter. Furthermore, each word is also now a network with exactly two inputs and two outputs that can be cascaded with other words and letters to form bigger networks. Figure 3 illustrates the result of using this technique in GPL with three letters, each separately defined as a network and then cascaded together.

3.2   CMOS Circuits

Another fruitful family of patterns to which pattern networks could be applied with great effect is that of circuit diagrams. Indeed, input and output points for a circuit's pattern network often directly correspond to the input and output terminals of the circuit. For example, the pattern representing the CMOS layout of an AND gate can be composed from the patterns for a NAND gate, a via (a connector across layers in the CMOS process), and an inverter. Suppose that we have already defined pattern networks called nand+rails, via+rails and inverter+rails to represent their corresponding CMOS circuit layouts (including the power rails). We would be able to define and+rails in a completely natural way as follows:

```
network and+rails [vdd-in, vss-in, a, b][vdd-out, vss-out, output] {
   cascade([vdd-in, vss-in, a, b],
           nand+rails,
           via+rails,
           inverter+rails,
           [vdd-out, vss-out, output])
}
```

Figure 4 illustrates how the various constituent networks of the AND circuit are combined, and Figure 5 shows a result of an actual execution of the GPL implementation of the and+rails network.

4   Challenges for Extensions

Since the input points involved in the definition of a pattern network, are not necessarily local to each other, the invocation of a network's computation is actually the parallel invocation of all computations specified at the input points. In particular, the output points that result from this parallel execution may also be non-local to each other. This poses some problems for attempting to create parameterised or higher-order abstractions of networks. For example, if pattern networks could accept parameters, their values would have to be available to all points participating in the invocation of these networks. This could probably be accomplished by passing around an environment specific to the pattern network, but in the context of cascaded networks, one challenge would be to propagate information from one output of a network to all inputs of its following network. Another problem is that any information available within the scope of the network must become available to all points that may participate in evaluating the network. Doing either of these represents a significant departure from the current macro-style implementation of pattern networks, in which all global knowledge is statically known, and therefore can be transmitted through the common agent level program.

One long-term challenge is that in the most general cases, amorphous systems will consist of mobile agents. This means that neighbourhoods will be dynamic and many of the techniques applied in the pattern description language will need to be adapted to that new situation. Currently none of our pattern formation processes actively maintain their forms, so even with slowly moving agents, our patterns would eventually dissolve away. To prevent this we will need to come up with new primitives that are capable of maintaining patterns, and that are accessible to higher level abstractions, such as the network abstraction described here.

5   Conclusions

Pattern networks provide a powerful means of expressing patterns that can be self-organised. They can capture simple patterns that are directly expressed in terms of local interactions, and they can be combined to form more complex pattern networks. In addition, the expression of these combinations are quite natural, yet they remain transformable to collections of local interactions that, under the appropriate conditions, cause the desired patterns to emerge. Pattern networks are currently not generalisable to higher order patterns nor can they even accept parameters to allow more general specifications. However, these limitations are currently self-imposed as a simplification exercise, and we expect some of them, at least, will be overcome in the near future.

References

1. ABELSON, H., D. Allen, D. Coore, C. Hanson, G. Homsy, T. Knight, R. Nagpal, E. Rauch, G. Sussman, and R. Weiss. Amorphous Computing. *Communications of the ACM*, **43**(5), May 2000.
2. BEAL, Jacob, "Persistent Nodes for Reliable Memory in Geographically Local Networks", *AI Memo 2003-011*, Massachusetts Institute of Technology, Artificial Intelligence Laboratory. Apr. 2003.
3. BENENSON, Yaakov., Rivka Adar,Tamar Paz-Elizur, Zvi Livneh, and Ehud Shapiro, "DNA molecule provides a computing machine with both data and fuel." in *Proceedings National Academy of Science, USA* **100**, 2191-2196. (2003).
4. CLEMENT, Lauren, and Radhika Nagpal, " Self-Assembly and Self-Repairing Topologies", in *Workshop on Adaptability in Multi-Agent Systems, RoboCup Australian Open*, Jan. 2003.
5. COORE, Daniel, "Towards a Universal Language for Amorphous Computing", in *International Conference on Complex Systems (ICCS2004)*, May 2004.
6. COORE, Daniel, *Botanical Computing: A Developmental Approach to Generating Interconnect Topologies on an Amorphous Computer*. PhD thesis, MIT, Dept. of Electrical Engineering and Computer Science, Feb. 1999.
7. KNIGHT, Tom, Gerald J. Sussman, "Cellular Gate Technologies", in *First International Conference on Unconventional Models of Computation (UMC98)*, 1998.
8. KONDACS, Attila, "Biologically-Inspired Self-Assembly of Two-Dimensional Shapes Using Global-to-Local Compilation", in *International Joint Conference on Artificial Intelligence (IJCAI)*, Aug. 2003.
9. NAGPAL, Radhika, *Programmable Self-Assembly: Constructing Global Shape using Biologically-inspired Local Interactions and Origami Mathematics*. PhD thesis, MIT, Dept. of Electrical Engineering and Computer Science, (June 2001).

Programming an Amorphous Computational Medium

Jacob Beal

Massachusetts Institute of Technology, Cambridge MA 02139, USA

Abstract. Amorphous computing considers the problem of controlling millions of spatially distributed unreliable devices which communicate only with nearby neighbors. To program such a system, we need a high-level description language for desired global behaviors, and a system to compile such descriptions into locally executing code which robustly creates and maintains the desired global behavior. I survey existing amorphous computing primitives and give desiderata for a language describing computation on an amorphous computer. I then bring these together in Amorphous Medium Language, which computes on an amorphous computer as though it were a space-filling computational medium.

1 Introduction

Increasingly, we are faced with the prospect of programming spatially embedded mesh networks composed of huge numbers of unreliable parts. Projects in such diverse fields as sensor networks (e.g. NEST [12]), peer-to-peer wireless (e.g. RoofNet [2]), smart materials (e.g. smart dusts [17, 26]), and biological computation [18, 29, 30] all envision deployed networks of large size (ranging from thousands to trillions of nodes) where only nodes nearby in space can communicate directly, and the network as a whole approximates the physical space through which it is deployed.

Any such large spatially embedded mesh network may be considered an amorphous computer. Amorphous computing studies the problem of controlling these networks from a perspective of group behavior, taking inspiration from biological processes such as morphogenesis and regeneration, in which unreliable simple processing units (cells) communicating locally (e.g. with chemical gradients) execute a shared program (DNA) and cooperate to reliably produce an organism's anatomy.

Controlling an amorphous computer presents serious challenges. Spatially local communication means networks may have a high diameter, and large numbers of nodes place tight constraints on sustainable communication complexity. Moreover, large numbers also mean that node failures and replacements are a continuous process rather than isolated events, threatening the stability of the network. If we are to program in this environment, we need high-level programming abstractions to separate the behaviors being programmed from the networking and robustness issues involved in executing that program on a spatially embedded mesh network.

J.-P. Banâtre et al. (Eds.): UPP 2004, LNCS 3566, pp. 121–136, 2005.

Let us define an **amorphous medium** to be a hypothetical continuous computational medium filling the space approximated by an amorphous computer. I propose that this is an appropriate basis for abstraction: high-level behavior can then be described in terms of geometric regions of the amorphous medium, then executed approximately by the amorphous computer.

In support of this hypothesis, I first detail the amorphous computing scenario, then survey existing amorphous computing primitives and describe how they can be viewed as approximating the behavior of an amorphous medium. I then present the Amorphous Medium Language, which describes program behavior in terms of nested processes occupying migrating regions of the space in which the network is embedded, describe AML's key design elements — spatial processes, active process maintenance, and homeostasis — and illustrate the language by means of examples.

2   The Amorphous Computing Scenario

The amorphous computing engineering domain presents a set of challenging requirements and prohibitions to the system designer, forcing confrontation of issues of robustness, distribution, and scalability. These constraints derive much of their inspiration from biological systems engaged in morphogenesis and regeneration, which must be accomplished by coordinating extremely large numbers of unreliable devices (cells).

The first and foremost requirement is **scalability**: the number of devices may be large, anywhere from thousands to millions or even billions. Biological systems, in fact, may comprise trillions of cells. Practically, this means that an algorithm is reasonable only if its per-device asymptotic complexity (e.g. space or bandwidth per device) are polynomial in $\log n$ (where n is the number of devices) — and any bound significantly greater than $O(\lg n)$ should be treated with considerable suspicion. Further, unlike ad-hoc networking and sensor networks scenarios, amorphous computing generally assumes **cheap energy, local processing, and storage** — in other words, as long as they do not have a high per-device asymptotic complexity, minimizing them is not of particular interest.

The network graph is determined by the **spatial distribution** of the devices in some Euclidean space, which collaborate via **local communication**. Devices are generally **immobile** unless the space in which they are embedded is moved (e.g. cutting and pasting "smart paper")[1]. A unit disc model is often used to create the network, in which a bidirectional link exists between two devices if and only if they are less than distance r apart. Local communication implies that the network is expected to have a high diameter, and, assuming a packet-based communication model, this means that the time for information to propagate through the network depends primarily on the number of hops it needs to travel. Local communication also means that communication complexity is best mea-

---

[1] Note that mobile devices might be programmed as immobile virtual devices [13, 14].

sured by **maximum communication density** — the maximum bandwidth required by a device — rather than by number of messages.

Due to the number of devices potentially involved, the system must not depend on much care and feeding of the individual devices. In general, it is assumed that every device is **identically programmed**, but that there can be a small amount of **differentiation via initial conditions**. Once the system is running, however, there is **no per-device administration** allowed.

There are strict limitations on the assumed network infrastructure. The system executes with **partial synchrony** — each device may be assumed to have a clock which ticks regularly, but the clocks may show different times, run at (boundedly) different rates, and have different phases. In addition, the system may not assume complex services not presently extended to the amorphous domain — this is applied particularly to mean **no global naming, routing, or coordinate service** may be assumed.

Finally, in a large, spatially distributed network of devices, failures are not isolated events. Due to the sheer number of devices, point failures are best measured by an expected **rate of device failure**. This suggests also that methods of analysis like half-life analysis [21] will be more useful than standard f-failure analysis. In addition, because the network is spatially embedded, outside events may cause **failure of arbitrary spatial regions** — larger region failures are assumed to occur less frequently. Generally stopping failures have been used, in which the failing device or link simply ceases operating. Finally, maintenance requires recovery or replacement of failed devices: in either case, the effect is that **new devices join** the network either individually or as a region.

3   Amorphous Computing Mechanisms

Several existing amorphous computing algorithms will serve as useful primitives for constructing a language. Each mechanism summarized here has been implemented as a code module and demonstrated in simulation. Together they are a powerful toolkit from which primitives for high-level languages can be constructed.

3.1   Shared Neighborhood Data

This simple mechanism allows neighboring devices to communicate by means of a shared-memory region, similar to the systems described in [7, 32]. Each device maintains a table of key-value pairs which it wishes to share (for example, the keys might be variable names and the values their bindings). Periodically each device transmits its table to its neighbors, informing them that it is still a neighbor and refreshing their view of its shared memory. Conversely, a neighbor is removed from the table if more than a certain time has elapsed since its last refresh. The module can then be queried for the set of neighbors, and the values its neighbors most recently held for any key in its table.

Shared neighborhood data can also be viewed as a sample of the amorphous medium within a unit neighborhood. Aggregate functions of the neighborhood data (e.g. average or maximum) are then approximations of the same functions on a neighborhood of the amorphous medium.

Maintaining shared neighborhood data requires storage and communication density proportional to the number of values being stored, size of the values, and number of neighbors.

3.2   Regions

The region module maintains labels for contiguous sets of devices, approximating connected regions of the amorphous medium, using a mechanism similar to that in [31]. A Region is defined by a name and a boolean membership function. When seeded in one or more devices, a Region spreads via shared neighborhood data to all adjoining devices that satisfy the membership test. When a Region is deallocated, a garbage collection mechanism spreads the deallocation throughout the participating devices, attempting to ensure that the defunct Region is removed totally.

Note that failures or evolving system state may separate a Region into disconnected components. While these are still logically the same Region, and may rejoin into a single connected component in the future, information will not generally pass between disconnected components. As a result, the state of disconnected components of a Region may evolve separately, and in particular garbage collection is only guaranteed to be effective in a connected component of a Region.

Regions are organized into a tree, with every device belonging to the root Region. In order for a device to be a member of a Region, it must also be a member of that Region's parent in the tree. This implicit compounding of membership tests allows Regions to exhibit stack-like behavior which will be useful for establishing execution scope in a high-level language.

Maintaining Regions requires storage and communication density proportional to the number of Regions being maintained, due to the maintenance of shared neighborhood data. Garbage collecting a Region requires time proportional to the diameter of the Region.

3.3   Gossip

The gossip communication module [6] propagates information throughout a Region via shared neighborhood data, after the fashion of flooding algorithms [22]. Gossip is all-to-all communication: each item of gossip has a merge function that combines local state with neighbor information to produce a merged whole. When an item of gossip is garbage-collected, the deallocation propagates slowly to prevent regrowth into areas which have already been garbage-collected.

Gossip requires storage and communication density proportional to the number and size of gossip items being maintained in each Region of which a device is a member, due to the maintenance of shared neighborhood data. Garbage collecting an item of gossip takes time proportional to the diameter of the region.

3.4   Consensus and Reduction

Non-failing devices participating in a strong consensus process must all choose the same value if any of them choose a value, and the chosen value must be held by at least one of the participants. Reduction is a generalization of consensus in which the chosen value is an aggregate function of values held by the participants (e.g. sum or average) — as before, all non-failing devices complete the operation holding the same value.

The Paxos consensus algorithm [20] has been demonstrated in an amorphous computing context [6], but scales badly. A gossip-based algorithm currently under development promises much better results: it appears that running a robust reduction process on a Region may require only storage and communication density logarithmic in the diameter of the Region and time linear in the diameter of the Region.

3.5   Read/Write Atomic Objects

Atomic consistency means that all transactions with an object can be viewed as happening in some order, even if they overlap in time. If we designate a Region of an amorphous medium as a read/write atomic object, then reading or writing values at any point in the Region produces a consistent view of the value held by the Region over time.

Using consensus and reduction, quorum-based atomic transactions can be supported by a reconfigurable set of devices [23,15]. This has been demonstrated in simulation for amorphous computing [6], and scales as the underlying consensus and reduction algorithms do.

3.6   Active Gradient

An active gradient [9, 11, 8] maintains a hop-count upwards from its source or sources — a set of devices which declare themselves to have count value zero — giving an approximation of radial distance in the amorphous medium, useful for establishing Regions. Points in the gradient converge to the minimum hop-count and repairs their values when they become invalid. The gradient runs within a Region, and may be further bounded (e.g. with a maximum number of hops). When the supporting sources disappear, the gradient is garbage-collected; as in the case of gossip items, the garbage collection propagates slowly to prevent unwanted regrowth into previously garbage collected areas. A gradient may also carry version information, allowing its source to change more smoothly. Figure 1 shows an active gradient being used to maintain a line.

Maintaining a gradient requires a constant amount of storage and communication density for every device in range of the gradient, and garbage collecting a gradient takes time linear in the diameter of its extent.

3.7   Persistent Node

A Persistent Node [4] is a robust mobile virtual object that occupies a ball in the amorphous medium (See Figure 2). A Persistent Node is a read/write

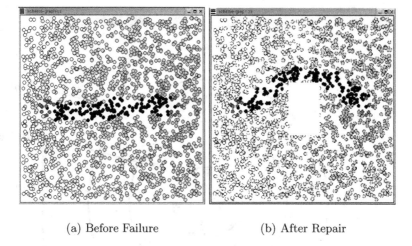

(a) Before Failure   (b) After Repair

Fig. 1. A line being maintained by active gradients, from [8]. A line (black) is constructed between two anchor regions (dark grey) based on the active gradient emitted by the right anchor region (light grays). The line is able to rapidly repair itself following failures because the gradient actively maintains itself

object supporting conditionally atomic transactions. A variant guaranteeing atomic transactions has been developed [6], which trades off liveness in favor of consistency and costs more due to underlying consensus and reduction algorithms.

A Persistent Node is implemented around an active gradient flowing outward from its center. All devices within r hops (the Persistent Node's *core*) are identified as members of the Persistent Node, while a heuristic calculation flows inward from all devices within $2r$ hops (the *reflector*) to determine which direction the center should be moving. The gradient is bounded to kr hops (the *umbra*), so every device in this region is aware of the existence and location of the Persistent Node. If any device in the core survives a failure, the Persistent Node will rebuild itself, although if the failure separates the core into disconnected components, the Persistent Node may be cloned. If the umbras of two clones come in contact, however, they will resolve back into a single Persistent Node via the destruction of one clone.

Persistent Nodes are useful as primitives for establishing regions, much like active gradients. A Persistent Node, however, can change its position within a larger region in response to changing conditions.

Maintaining a Persistent Node requires storage and communication density linear in the size of the data stored by it. A Persistent Node moves and repairs itself in time linear in its diameter.

3.8   Hierarchical Partitioning

A Region can be partitioned through the use of Persistent Nodes: [5] nodes of a characteristic radius are generated and allowed to drift, repelling one another,

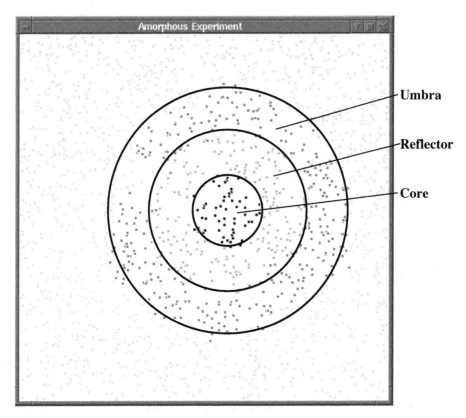

Fig. 2. Anatomy of a Persistent Node. The innermost circle is the core (black), which arts as a virtual node. Every device within middle circle is in the reflector (light grey), which calculates which direction the Persistent Node will move. The outermost circle (dark grey) is the umbra (k=3 in this example), which knows the identity of the Persistent Node, but nothing else

until every device in the Region is near some Persistent Node, and devices choose a node with which to associate, with some hysteresis. A set of partitions with exponentially increasing diameter can generate clustering relations which form a hierarchical partition of the Region. Although the partitions are not nested, the clusters which they generate are, and the resulting structure is highly resilient against failures — unlike other clustering algorithms, partitioning on the basis of persistent nodes bounds the extent of address changes caused by a failure linearly in the size of a circumscription of the failure. Figures 3 and 4 show an example of partitioning.

Maintaining a hierarchical partition takes storage and communication logarithmic in the diameter of the Region being partitioned, and creating the partition takes time log-linear in the diameter.

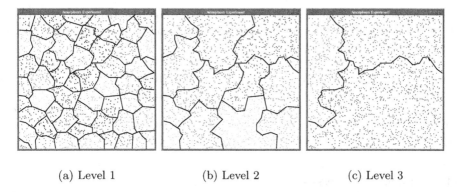

(a) Level 1   (b) Level 2   (c) Level 3

Fig. 3. Hierarchical partitioning via Persistent Nodes for a simulation with 2000 devices. There are five levels in the resulting hierarchy. The top and bottom levels of the hierarchy are uninteresting, as the top has every particle in the same group and the bottom has every particle in a different group; these images show the middle three levels of the hierarchy, with each ith level node a different color, and thick black lines showing the approximate boundaries. The logical tree is shown in Figure 4

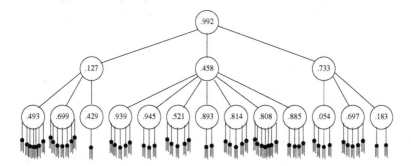

Fig. 4. A hierarchy tree produced by the hierarchical partitioning shown in Figure 3. The numbers are the names of Persistent Nodes in the top three levels; the level 1 nodes are shown as black dots and the 2000 leaf nodes are not explicitly enumerated

4   Amorphous Medium Language

I want to be able to program an amorphous computer as though it is a space filled with a continuous medium of computational material: the actual executing program should produce an approximation of this behavior on a set of discrete points. This means that there should be no explicit statements about individual devices or communication between them. Instead, the language should describe behavior in terms of spatial regions of the amorphous medium, which I will take to be the manifold induced by neighborhoods in the amorphous computer's mesh network.

The program should be able to be specified without knowledge of the particular amorphous medium on which it will be run. Moreover, the geometry and topology of the medium should be able to change as the program is executing, through failure and addition of devices, and the running program adjust to its new environment gracefully.

Finally, since failures and additions may disconnect and reconnect the medium, a program which is separated into two different executions must be able to reintegrate when the components of the medium rejoin.

Amorphous Medium Language combines mechanisms from the previous section to fulfill these goals via three key design components: spatial processes, aggregate state, active process maintenance, and homeostasis.

4.1   Spatial Processes

In AML each active process is associated with a region of space. The programs that direct a process are written to be executed at a generic place in their region. Every device in the region is running the process, continually sharing process variables with those neighbors (in the region) that are running the same process.

A process may designate (perhaps overlapping) subregions of its region to execute subprocesses. These subregions may be delineated by an active gradient, a Persistent Node, or some characteristic function. Thus, the collection of processes forms a tree, whose root operates on a region that covers the entire network.

The set of devices constituting a region that is participating in a processes may migrate, expand, or contract in response to changing conditions in the network or in its state, subject to the constraint that it remains in the region owned by its parent process (This constraint yields subroutine compositional semantics). Since regions assigned to processes may overlap, the devices in the overlap will be running all of the processes associated with that part of space, and all of the parent processes that cover that region.

Many copies of the same process may run at the same device, as long as they have different parameters or different parent processes. So if process FOO calls (FIBONACCI 5) and (FIBONACCI 10), it creates two different processes, and if FOO and BAR both call (FIBONACCI 5) it creates two different processes, but if FOO calls (FIBONACCI 5) twice it creates only a single process.

4.2   Aggregate State

Processes have state, described as the values of program variables. The values of these variables are determined by aggregation across the set of participating devices. Depending on the requirements of the computation, a variable may be implemented by gossip, by reduction, or as a distributed atomic object. Gossip is the cheapest mechanism, but it provides no consistency guarantees and can be used only for certain aggregation functions (e.g. maximum or union). Reduction is similar, but somewhat more costly and allows non-idempotent aggregation functions (e.g. average or sum). An atomic object gives guaranteed consistency, but it is expensive and may not be able to progress in the face of partition or high failure rates.

If a process is partitioned by a failure into two parts that cannot communicate then each part is an independent process, which evolves separately. Differences between the parts must be resolved if the parts later merge.

4.3   Active Process Maintenance

To remain active a process must be actively supported by its parent process. If a process is not supported it will die. The root process is eternally supported. Support is implemented by an active gradient mechanism. When a process loses support and dies the resources held by that process in each device are recycled by a garbage collector.[2]

4.4   Homeostasis and Repair

In AML processes are specified by procedures that describe conditions to be maintained and actions to be taken if those conditions are not satisfied. If a failure is small enough the actions are designed by the programmer to repair the damage and restore the desired conditions.

As a result, incomplete computation and disruption caused by failures can be handled uniformly. Failures produce deviations in the path towards homeostasis, and if the system state converges toward homeostasis faster than failures push it away, then eventually the process will complete its computation.

4.5   Examples

I will illustrate how AML programs operate by means of examples. These examples use the CommonLISP formatting processed by my AML compiler. These examples are meant to illustrate how ideas are expressed in AML.

Maximum Density. Calculating maximum density is the AML equivalent of a "hello world" program. To run this, we will need only one simple process (See Figure 5).

The AML process ROOT is the entry point for a program, similar to a MAIN function in C or Java. When an AML program runs, the ROOT process runs across the entire space, and is automatically supported everywhere so it will never be garbage collected.

Processes are defined with the command (DEFPROCESS *name* (*arguments*) *statement* ...). In this case, the name is ROOT and there are no arguments, since there are no initial conditions. The statements of a process are variable definitions and homeostasis conditions; while the process is active, it runs cyclically, clocked by the shared neighbor data refreshes. Each cycle the process first updates variable aggregate values, then maintains its homeostasis conditions in the order they are defined.

The first statement creates a variable, X, which we will use to aggregate the density. Variables are defined with the command (DEFVARIABLE *name*

---

[2] This is much the same problem as addressed in [3].

```
(defprocess root ()
  (defvariable x #'max :base 0)
  (maintain
   (eq (local x) (density))
   (set! x (density)))
  (always
   (actuate 'color (regional x))))
```

Fig. 5. Code to calculate maximum density (number of neighbors). The density at each point is written to variable X, which aggregates them using the function MAX. Each point then colors itself using the aggregate value for X

aggregation-function arguments). In this case, since we want to calculate maximum density, the aggregation function will be MAX.

Aggregation in AML is executed by taking a base aggregate value and updating it by merging it with other values or aggregates — this also means that if there are no values to aggregate, the variable equals the base value. Since the default base value, NIL, is not a reasonable value for density, we use the optional BASE argument to set it to zero instead.

Now we have a variable which will calculate its maximum value over the process region, but haven't specified how it gets any values to start with. First, though, a word about the different ways in which we can talk about the value of variable X. Every variable has three values: a local value, a neighborhood aggregate value, and a regional aggregate value. Setting a variable sets only its local value, though the aggregates may change as a result. Reading any value from a variable is instantaneous, based on the current best estimate, but the neighborhood aggregate may be one cycle stale, and the regional aggregate may be indefinitely out of date.

The second statement is a homeostasis condition that deals only with the local value of X. The function (DENSITY) is a built-in function that returns the estimated density of the device's neighborhood,[3] so the MAINTAIN condition may be read as: if the local value for X isn't equal to the density, set it equal to the density.

These local values for density are then aggregated by the variable, and the current best estimate can be read using (REGIONAL X), as is done in the third statement. The third statement is an ALWAYS homeostasis condition, which is syntactic sugar for (MAINTAIN NIL ...), so that it is never satisfied and runs its action every cycle. The action, in this case, reads the regional value of X and sends it to the device's color in a display — (ACTUATE *actuator value*) is a built-in function to allow AML programs to write to an external interface (its converse (READ-SENSOR *sensor*) reads from the external interface).

When this program is run, all the devices in the network start with the color for zero, then turn all different colors as each writes its density to X locally. The

---

[3] Density is most simply calculated as number of neighbors, but might be smoothed for more consistent estimates.

highest value colors then spread outward through their neighbors until each connected component on the network is colored uniformly according to the highest density it contains.

Blob Detection. With only slightly more complexity, we can write a program to detect blobs in a binary image (See Figure 6). In this scenario, an image is mapped onto a space and devices distributed to cover the image. The image is input to the network via a sensor named IMAGE, which reads BLACK for devices located at black points of the image and WHITE for devices located at white points of the image. The goal of the program is to find all of the contiguous regions of black, and measure their areas.

Unlike the maximum density program, the ROOT process for blob detection takes an argument — FUZZINESS — which specifies how far apart two black regions can be and still be considered contiguous.

The first statement in the ROOT process declares its one variable, BLOBS, which uses UNION to aggregate the the blobs detected throughout the network into a global list.

```
(defprocess root (fuzziness)
  (defvariable blobs #'union)
  (always
    (when (eq (read-sensor 'image) 'black)
      (subprocess (measure-blob) :gradient fuzziness)
      (setf blobs
        (list (get-from-sub (measure-blob) blob)))))
  (avoid
    (read-sensor 'query)
    (let ((q (first (read-sensor 'query))))
      (cond
        ((eq q 'blobs)
         (actuate 'response (regional blobs)))
        ((eq q 'area)
         (actuate 'response
           (fold #'+ (mapcar #'second
                             (regional blobs)))))))))

(defprocess measure-blob ()
  (defvariable uid #'max :atomic :base 0 :init (random 1))
  (defvariable area #'sum :reduction :base 0 :init 1)
  (defvariable blob :local)
  (always
    (setf blob (list uid area))))
```

Fig. 6. Code to find a set of fuzzy blobs and their areas in a binary image. Each contiguous black area of the image runs a connected MEASURE-BLOB process that names it and calculates its area. The set of blobs is collected by the ROOT process and made accessible to the user on the RESPONSE actuator in response to requests on the QUERY sensor

The second statement is an ALWAYS condition which runs a blob measuring process anywhere that there is black. The MEASURE-BLOB process takes no arguments, and its extent is defined by an active gradient going out FUZZINESS hops from each device where the image sensor reads BLACK.

This elegantly segments the image into blobs: from each black device a gradient spreads the process out for FUZZINESS hops in all directions, so any two black devices separated by at most twice-FUZZINESS hops of white devices will be in a connected component of the MEASURE-BLOB process. Where there are more than twice-FUZZINESS hops of white devices separating two black points, however, the MEASURE-BLOB process is not connected and each component calculates independently — effectively as a separate blob!

The MEASURE-BLOB process has two responsibilities: give itself a unique name, and calculate its area. The UID variable, whose aggregate will be the name of the blob, uses two arguments which we haven't seen before. The ATOMIC argument means that the regional aggregate value of UID will be consistent across the process and as a side effect will be more stable in its value. We use the INIT argument, on the other hand, to start UID with a random value at each point. As a result, UID will eventually have a random number as its regional aggregate value which is unlikely to be the same as that of another blob.

The AREA variable also uses an INIT argument, which sets everything to be 1. This serves as the point mass of a device, which we integrate across the process to find its area using SUM as an aggregator. We must ensure that no point is counted more than once, however, so we use the REDUCTION argument to specify that the aggregation must be done that way rather than defaulting to gossip.

Finally, we declare the BLOB variable and add an ALWAYS statement to make it a list of UID and AREA, packaging a result for the MEASURE-BLOB process to be read by the ROOT process. The ROOT process can read variables in with child processes with the command (GET-FROM-SUB (*name parameters*) *variable*), and uses this to set the local value of BLOBS.

The final statement of the ROOT process sets up a user interface in terms of an AVOID homeostasis condition. When there is a request queued up on the QUERY sensor, it upsets homeostasis, which the repair action attempts to rectify by placing an answer, calculated from the regional aggregate value of BLOBS, on the RESPONSE actuator. The user would then remove the serviced request from the queue, restoring homeostasis.

Thus, given a binary image, each contiguous region of black will run a MEASURE-BLOB process which names it and calculates its area. The ROOT process then records this information, which propagates throughout the network until there is a consistent list of blobs everywhere.

4.6   Related Languages

In sensor networks research, a number of other high-level programming abstractions have been proposed to enable programming of large mesh networks. For example, GHT [28] provides a hash table abstraction for storing data in the network, and TinyDB [24] focuses on gathering information via query processing.

Both of these approaches, however, are data-centric rather than computation-centric, and do not provide guidance on how to do distributed manipulation of data, once gathered.

More similar is the Regiment [27] language, which uses a stream-processing abstraction to distribute computation across the network. Regiment is, in fact, complementary to AML: its top-down design allows it to use the well-established formal semantics of stream-processing, while AML's programming model is still evolving. Regiment's robustness against failure, however, has not yet clearly been established, and there are significant challenges remaining in adapting its programming model to the sensor-network environment.

Previous work on languages in amorphous computing, on the other hand, has worked with much the same failure model, but has been directed more towards problems of morphogenesis and pattern formation than general computation. For example, Coore's work on topological patterns [10], and the work by Nagpal [25] and Kondacs [19] on geometric shape formation. A notable exception is Butera's work on paintable computing [7], which allows general computation, but operates at a lower level of abstraction than AML.

5   Conclusion

Considering the space occupied by an amorphous computer as an amorphous medium provides a useful programming abstraction. The amorphous medium abstraction can be programmed in terms of the behavior of spaces defined using geometric primitives, and the amorphous computer can approximate execution on the actual network.

Amorphous Medium Language is an example of how one can program using the amorphous medium abstraction. Processes are distributed through space, and run while there is demand from their parent processes. Within a connected process region, data is shared via variables aggregated over the region, and computation executes in response to violated homeostasis conditions.

An AML compiler in progress is being used as a workbench for further language development, concurrent with investigation of more lightweight implementations of robust primitives and of analysis techniques capable to dealing with the challenges of an amorphous environment. All of the mechanisms described above have been implemented, but only gossip, regions, and shared data are fully integrated with the compiler, which is run on a few test programs whose behavior is demonstrated in simulation on 500 nodes.

AML does not solve all of the problems in its domain, but it has exposed a clear set of problems, some of which appear to be challenges inherent to programming space. These outstanding challenges are the basis of current investigation.

- It is not clear at this time how large a range of behaviors can be specified as homeostatic conditions. It does seem adequate to allow the construction and maintenance of arbitrary graphs and some geometric constructions. The code that is executed when a condition is violated is intended to remedy the situation, but there is no guarantee that the repair behavior is actually making progress.

- AML programs can be composed with subroutine semantics, but it is less clear how to implement functional composition, particularly when the two programs may occupy different regions of space.
- Moving information between processes logically separated in the process tree is awkward, since information must be routed through a common parent.
- Integration of other programming ideas, such as streaming, may help to address some of these problems. We may also need to develop robust primitives better suited for our environment.
- At a more fundamental level, the tradeoff between consistency and liveness needs continued exploration, as does the problem of how to merge state when separated regions of a process rejoin.
- Failures which involve unpredictable behavior of a device are not currently dealt with, and may cause widespread disruption in the network.

Indeed, even analyzing the behavior of an aggregate in which devices are continually failing and being replaced is not a well understood problem.

References

1. H. Abelson, D. Allen, D. Coore, C. Hanson, G. Homsy, T. Knight, R. Nagpal, E. Rauch, G. Sussman and R. Weiss. Amorphous computing. AI Memo 1665, MIT, 1999.
2. Daniel Aguayo, John Bicket, Sanjit Biswas, Douglas S. J. De Couto, and Robert Morris, "MIT roofnet implementation," 2003.
3. H. Baker and C. Hewitt, "The incremental garbage collection of processes.," in *ACM Conference on AI and Programming Languages*, 1977, pp. 55–59.
4. J. Beal. "Persistent nodes for reliable memory in geographically local networks." Tech Report AIM-2003-11, MIT, 2003.
5. J. Beal. A robust amorphous hierarchy from persistent nodes. In *CSN*, 2003.
6. Jacob Beal and Seth Gilbert, "RamboNodes for the metropolitan ad hoc network," in *Workshop on Dependability in Wireless Ad Hoc Networks and Sensor Networks, part of the International Conference on Dependable Systems and Networks*, June 2003.
7. William Butera, *Programming a Paintable Computer*, Ph.D. thesis, MIT, 2002.
8. L. Clement and R. Nagpal, "Self-assembly and self-repairing topologies," in *Workshop on Adaptability in Multi-Agent Systems, RoboCup Australian Open*, Jan. 2003.
9. Daniel Coore. "Establishing a Coordinate System on an Amorphous Computer." MIT Student Workshop on High Performance Computing, 1998.
10. Daniel Coore, "Botanical Computing: A Developmental Approach to Generating Interconnect Topologies on an Amorphous Computer." Ph.D. thesis, MIT, 1999.
11. Daniel Coore, Radhika Nagpal and Ron Weiss. "Paradigms for structure in an amorphous computer." MIT AI Memo 1614.
12. DARPA IXO, "Networked embedded systems technology program overview," .
13. S. Dolev, S. Gilbert, N. Lynch, A. Shvartsman, and J. Welch., "Geoquorums: Implementing atomic memory in mobile ad hoc networks," in *Proceedings of the 17th International Symposium on Distributed Computing (DISC 2003)*, 2003.

14. Shlomi Dolev, Seth Gilbert, Nancy A. Lynch, Elad Schiller, Alex A. Shvartsman, and Jennifer L. Welch, "Virtual mobile nodes for mobile ad hoc networks," in *DISC04*, Oct. 2004.
15. Seth Gilbert, Nancy Lynch, and Alex Shvartsman, "RAMBO II:: Rapidly reconfigurable atomic memory for dynamic networks," in *DSN*, June 2003, pp. 259–269.
16. Frederic Gruau, Philippe Malbos. "The Blob: A Basic Topological Concept for "Hardware-Free" Distributed Computation." in *Unconventional Models of Computation* (UMC 2002). Springer, 2002.
17. V. Hsu, J. M. Kahn, and K. S. J. Pister, "Wireless communications for smart dust," Tech. Rep. Electronics Research Laboratory Technical Memorandum Number M98/2, Feb. 1998.
18. Thomas F. Knight Jr. and Gerald Jay Sussman. "Cellular gate technology." In *Unconventional Models of Computation*, pages 257-272, 1997.
19. Attila Kondacs, "Biologically-inspired self-assembly of 2d shapes, using global-to-local compilation," in *International Joint Conference on Artificial Intelligence (IJCAI)*, 2003.
20. Leslie Lamport, "The part-time parliament," *ACM Transactions on Computer Systems*, vol. 16, no. 2, pp. 133–169, 1998.
21. D. Liben-Nowell, H. Balakrishnan, D. Karger. Analysis of the evolution of peer-to-peer systems. In *PODC*, 2002.
22. Nancy Lynch, *Distributed Algorithms*, Morgan Kaufman, 1996.
23. Nancy Lynch and Alex Shvartsman., "RAMBO: A reconfigurable atomic memory service for dynamic networks," in *DISC*, 2002, pp. 173–190.
24. Samuel R. Madden, Robert Szewczyk, Michael J. Franklin, and David Culler, "Supporting aggregate queries over ad-hoc wireless sensor networks," in *Workshop on Mobile Computing and Systems Applications*, 2002.
25. Radhika Nagpal, *Programmable Self-Assembly: Constructing Global Shape using Biologically-inspired Local Interactions and Origami Mathematics*, Ph.D. Thesis, MIT, 2001.
26. "NMRC scientific report 2003," Tech. Rep., National Microelectronics Research Centre, 2003.
27. Ryan Newton and Matt Welsh, "Region streams: Functional macroprogramming for sensor networks," in *First International Workshop on Data Management for Sensor Networks (DMSN)*, Aug. 2004.
28. Sylvia Ratnasamy, Brad Karp, Li Yin, Fang Yu, Deborah Estrin, Ramesh Govindan, and Scott Shenker, "GHT: a geographic hash table for data-centric storage," in *Proceedings of the 1st ACM international workshop on Wireless sensor networks and applications*. 2002, pp. 78–87, ACM Press.
29. Ron Weiss and Tom Knight "Engineered Communications for Microbial Robotics" in *Proceedings of the Sixth International Meeting on DNA Based Computers (DNA6)*, June 2000
30. Ron Weiss and Subhyu Basu. "The device physics of cellular logic gates." In *NSC-1: The First Workshop on NonSilicon Computing*, pages 54–61, 2002.
31. Matt Welsh and Geoff Mainland, "Programming sensor networks using abstract regions," in *Proceedings of the First USENIX/ACM Symposium on Networked Systems Design and Implementation (NSDI '04)*, Mar. 2004.
32. Kamin Whitehouse, Cory Sharp, Eric Brewer, and David Culler, "Hood: a neighborhood abstraction for sensor networks," in *Proceedings of the 2nd international conference on Mobile systems, applications, and services*. 2004, ACM Press.

Computations in Space and Space in Computations

Jean-Louis Giavitto, Olivier Michel, Julien Cohen,
and Antoine Spicher

LaMI, umr 8042 du CNRS, Université d'Évry – Genopole
Tour Évry-2, 523 Place des Terrasses de l'Agora
91000 Évry, France
{giavitto, michel}@lami.univ-evry.fr

> *The Analytical Engine weaves algebraic*
> *patterns just as the Jacquard loom weaves*
> *flowers and leaves.*
>
> Ada Lovelace

1 Goals and Motivations

The emergence of terms like *natural computing, mimetic computing, parallel problem solving from nature, bio-inspired computing, neurocomputing, evolutionary computing*, etc., shows the never ending interest of the computer scientists for the use of "natural phenomena" as "problem solving devices" or more generally, as a fruitful source of inspiration to develop new programming paradigms. It is the latter topic which interests us here. The idea of *numerical experiment* can be reversed and, instead of using computers to simulate a fragment of the real world, the idea is to use (a digital simulation of) the real world to compute. In this perspective, the processes that take place in the real world are the objects of a new calculus:

$$\text{description of the world's laws} = \text{program}$$
$$\text{state of the world} = \text{data of the program}$$
$$\text{parameters of the description} = \text{inputs of the program}$$
$$\text{simulation} = \text{the computation}$$

This approach can be summarized by the following slogan: "programming *in* the language of nature" and was present since the very beginning of computer science with names like W. Pitts and W. S. McCulloch (formal neurons, 1943), S. C. Kleene (inspired by the previous for the notion of finite state automata, 1951), J. H. Holland (connectionist model, 1956), J. Von Neumann (cellular automata, 1958), F. Rosenblatt (the perceptron, 1958), etc.

This approach offers many advantages from the *teaching, heuristic* and *technical* points of view: it is easier to explain concepts referring to real world processes that are actual examples; the analogy with the nature acts as a powerful source

J.-P. Banâtre et al. (Eds.): UPP 2004, LNCS 3566, pp. 137–152, 2005.

of inspirations; and the studies of natural phenomena by the various scientific disciplines (physics, biology, chemistry...) have elaborated a large body of concepts and tools that can be used to study computations (some concrete examples of this cross fertilization relying on the concept of dynamical system are given in references [6, 5, 34, 12]).

There is a *possible fallacy* in this perspective: the description of the nature is not unique and diverse concurent approaches have been developed to account for the same objects. Therefore, there is not a unique "language of nature" prescribing a unique and definitive programming paradigm. *However*, there is a common concern shared by the various descriptions of nature provided by the scientific disciplines: *natural phenomena take place in time and space.*

In this paper, we propose the use of spatial notions as structuring relationships *in* a programming language. Considering space in a computation is hardly new: the use of spatial (and temporal) notions is at the basis of computational complexity *of* a program; spatial and temporal relationships are also used in the implementation of parallel languages (if two computations occur at the same time, then the two computations must be located at two different places, which is the basic constraint that drives the scheduling and the data distribution problems in parallel programming); the methods for building domains in denotational semantics have also clearly topological roots, but they involve the *topology of the set of values*, not the *topology of a value*. In summary, spatial notions have been so far mainly used to describe the running of a program and not as *means to design new programs*.

We want to stress this last point of view: we are not concerned by the organization of the resources used by a program run. What we want is to develop a spatial point of view on the entities built by the programmer when he designs his programs. From this perspective, a program must be seen as a space where computation occurs and a computation can be structured by spatial relationships. We hope to provide some evidences in the rest of this paper that the concept of space can be as fertile as mathematical logic for the development of programming languages. More specifically, we advocate that the concepts and tools developed for the algebraic construction and characterization of shapes[1] provide interesting teaching, heuristic and technical alternatives to develop new data structures and new control structures for programming.

The rest of this paper is organized as follows. Section 2 and section 3 provide an informal discussion to convince the reader of the interest of introducing a topological point of view in programming. This approach is illustrated through the experimental programming language MGS used as a vehicle to investigate and validate the topological approach.

---

[1] G. Gaston-Granger in [23] considers three avenues in the formalization of the concept of space: *shape* (the algebraic construction and the transformation of space and spatial configurations), *texture* (the continuum) and *measure* (the process of counting and coordinatization [39]). In this work, we rely on elementary concepts developed in the field of combinatorial algebraic topology for the construction of spaces [24].

Section 2 introduces the idea of seeing a data structure as a space where the computation and the values move. Section 3 follows the spatial metaphor and presents control structures as path specifications. The previous ideas underlie MGS. Section 4 sketches this language. The presentation is restricted to the notions needed to follow the examples in the next section. Section 5 gives some examples and introduces the (DS)^2 class of dynamical systems which exhibit a dynamical structure. Such kind of systems are hard to model and simulate because the state space must be computed jointly with the running state of the system. To conclude in section 6 we indicate some of the related work and we mention briefly some perspectives on the use of spatial notions.

2   Data Structures as Spaces[2]

The relative accessibility from one element to another is a key point considered in a data structure definition:

- In a simply linked list, the elements are accessed linearly (the second after the first, the third after the second, etc.).
- In a circular buffer, or in a double-linked list, the computation goes from one element to the following *or* to the previous one.
- From a node in a tree, we can access the sons.
- The neighbors of a vertex V in a graph are visited after V when traveling through the graph.
- In a record, the various fields are locally related and this localization can be named by an identifier.
- Neighborhood relationships between array elements are left implicit in the array data-structure. Implementing neighborhood on arrays relies on an index algebra: index computations are used to code the access to a neighbor. The standard example of index algebra is integer tuples with linear mappings $\lambda x.x \pm 1$ along each dimension (called "Von Neumann" or "Moore" neighborhoods).

This accessibility relation defines a logical neighborhood. The concept of logical neighborhood in a data structure is not only an abstraction perceived by the programmer and vanishing at the execution, but it does have an actual meaning for the computation. Very often the computation indeed complies with the logical neighborhood of the data elements and it is folk's knowledge that most of the algorithms are structured either following the structure of the input data or the structure of the output data. Let us give some examples.

The recursive definition of the `fold` function on lists propagates an action to be performed along the traversal of a list. More generally, recursive computations on data structures respect so often the logical neighborhood, that standard high-order functions (e.g. *primitive recursion*) can be automatically defined from the

---

[2] The ideas exposed in this section are developed in [19, 14].

data structure organization (think about catamorphisms and other polytypic functions on inductive types [29, 26]).

The list of examples can be continued to convince ourselves that a notion of logical neighborhood is fundamental in the definition of a data structure. So to define a data organization, we adopt a *topological* point of view: *a data structure can be seen as a space*, the set of positions between which *the computation moves. Each position possibly holds a value*[3]. The set of positions is called the *container* and the values labeling the positions constitute the *content*.

This topological approach is constructive: one can define a data type by the set of moves allowed in the data structure. An example is given by the notion of "Group Based Fields" or GBF in short [21, 16]. In a uniform data structure, i.e. in a data structure where any elementary move can be used against any position, the set of moves possesses the structure of a mathematical group $\mathcal{G}$. The neighborhood relationship of the container corresponds to the Cayley graph of $\mathcal{G}$. In this paper, we will use only two very simple groups $\mathcal{G}$ corresponding to the moves |north> and |east> allowed in the usual two-dimensional grid and to the moves allowed in the hexagonal lattice figured at the right of Fig. 3.

3   Control Structures as Paths

In the previous section, we suggested looking at data structure as spaces in which computation moves. Then, when the computation proceeds, a path in the data structure is traversed. This path is driven by the control structures of the program. So, a control structure can be seen as a path specification in the space of a data structure. We elaborate on this idea into two directions: concurrent processes and multi-agent systems.

3.1   Homotopy of a Program Run

Consider two sequential processes A and B that share a semaphore s. The current state of the parallel execution P = A ‖ B can be figured as a point in the plane $A \times B$ where A (resp. B) is the sequence of instructions of A (resp. B). Thus, the running of P corresponds to a path in the plane $A \times B$. However, there are two constraints on paths that represent the execution of P. Such a path must be "increasing" because we suppose that at least one of the two subprocesses A or B must progress. The second constraint is that the two subprocesses cannot be simultaneously in the region protected by the semaphore s. This constraint has a clear geometrical interpretation: the increasing paths must avoid an "obstruction region", see Fig. 1. Such representation is known at least from the 1970's as "progress graph" [7] and is used to study the possible deadlocks of a set of concurrent processes.

Homotopy (the continuous deformation of a path) can be adapted to take into account the constraint of increasing paths and provides effective tools to

---

[3] *A point in space is a placeholder awaiting for an argument*, L. Wittgenstein, (Tractatus Logico Philosophicus, 2.0131).

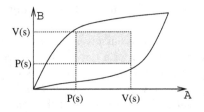 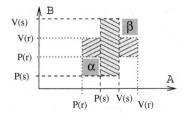

Fig. 1. *Left:* The possible path taken by the process A ∥ B is constrained by the obstruction resulting of a semaphore shared between the processes A and B. *Right:* The sharing of two semaphores between two processes may lead to deadlock (corresponding to the domain α) or to the existence of a "garden of Eden" (the domain β cannot be accessed from outside β and can only be leaved.)

detect deadlocks or to classify the behavior of a parallel program (for instance in the previous example, there are two classes of paths corresponding to executions where the process A or B enters the semaphore first). Refer to [22] for an introduction to this domain.

3.2   The Topological Structure of Interactions[4]

In a multi-agent system (or an object based or an actor system), the control structures are less explicit and the emphasis is put on the local interaction between two (sometimes more) agents. In this section, we want to show that the interactions between the elements of a system exhibit a natural topology.

The starting point is the decomposition of a system into subsystems defined by the requirement that the elements into the subsystems interact together and are truly independent from all other subsystems parallel evolution.

In this view, the decomposition of a system S into subsystems $S_1, S_2, \ldots, S_n$ is *functional*: state $s_i(t + 1)$ of the subsystem S_i depends solely of the previous state $s_i(t)$. However, the decomposition of S into the S_i can depend on the time steps. So we write $S^t = \{S_1^t, S_2^t, \ldots, S_{n_t}^t\}$ for the decomposition of the system S at time t and we have: $s_i(t + 1) = h_i^t(s_i(t))$ where the h_i^t are the "local" evolution functions of the S_i^t. The "global" state $s(t)$ of the system S can be recovered from the "local" states of the subsystems: there is a function φ^t such that $s(t) = \varphi^t(s_1(t), \ldots, s_{n_t}(t))$ which induces a relation between the "global" evolution function h and the local evolution functions: $s(t + 1) = h(s(t)) = \varphi^t(h_1^t(s_1(t)), \ldots, h_{n_t}^t(s_{n_t}(t)))$.

The successive decomposition $S_1^t, S_2^t, \ldots, S_{n_t}^t$ can be used to capture the *elementary parts* and the *interaction structure* between these elementary parts of S. Cf. Figure 2. Two subsystems S' and S'' of S interact if there are some t such that $S', S'' \in S^t$. Two subsystems S' and S'' are *separable* if there some t such that $S' \in S^t$ and $S'' \notin S^t$ or vice-versa. This leads to consider the set $\mathcal{S}$, called the *interaction structure* of S, defined by the smaller set closed by intersection that contains the S_j^t.

---

[4] This section is adapted from [36].

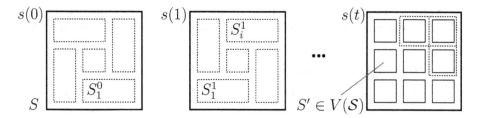

Fig. 2. The interaction structure of a system S resulting from the subsystems of elements in interaction at a given time step

Set $\mathcal{S}$ has a *topological structure*: $\mathcal{S}$ corresponds to an *abstract simplicial complex*. An abstract simplicial complex [24] is a collection $\mathcal{S}$ of finite nonempty set such that if A is an element of $\mathcal{S}$, so is every nonempty subset of A. The element A of $\mathcal{S}$ is called a *simplex* of $\mathcal{S}$; its *dimension* is one less that the number of its elements. The dimension of $\mathcal{S}$ is the largest dimension of one of its simplices. Each nonempty subset of A is called a *face* and the *vertex set* $V(\mathcal{S})$, defined by the union of the one point elements of $\mathcal{S}$, corresponds to the *elementary functional parts* of the system S. The abstract simplicial complex notion generalizes the idea of *graph*: a simplex of dimension 1 is an edge that links two vertices, a simplex f of dimension 2 can be thought of as a surface whose boundaries are the simplices of dimension 1 included in f, etc.

4   MGS Principles

The two previous sections give several examples to convince the reader that a topological approach of the data and control structures of a program present some interesting perspectives for language design: a data structure can be defined as a space (and there are many ways to build spaces) and a control structure is a path specification (and there are many ways to specify a path).

Such a topological approach is at the core of the MGS project. Starting from the analysis of the interaction structure in the previous section, our idea is to define directly the set $\mathcal{S}$ with its topological structure and to specify the evolution function h by specifying the set S_i^t and the functions h_i^t:

- the interaction structure $\mathcal{S}$ is defined as a new kind of data structures called *topological collections*;
- a set of functions h_i^t together with the specification of the S_i^t for a given t are called a *transformation*.

We will show that this abstract approach enables an homogeneous and uniform handling of several computational models including cellular automata (CA), lattice gas automata, abstract chemistry, Lindenmayer systems, Paun systems and several other abstract reduction systems.

These ideas are validated by the development of a language also called MGS. This language embeds a complete, strict, impure, dynamically or statically typed functional language.

4.1 Topological Collections

The distinctive feature of the MGS language is its handling of entities structured by *abstract topologies* using *transformations* [20]. A set of entities organized by an abstract topology is called a *topological collection*. Here, topological means that each collection type defines a neighborhood relation inducing a notion of *subcollection*. A subcollection S' of a collection S is a subset of connected elements of S and inheriting its organization from S. Beware that by "neighborhood relation" we simply mean a relationship that specify if two elements are neighbors. From this relation, a cellular complex can be built and the classical "neighborhood structure" in terms of open and closed sets can be recovered [35].

A topological collection can be thought as a function with a finite support from a set of positions (the elements of $V(\mathcal{S})$) to a set of values (the support of a function is the set of elements on which the function takes a well defined value). Such a data structure is called a *data field* [13]. This point of view is only an abstraction: the data structure is not really implemented as a function. This approach makes a distinction between the content and the container. The notions of *shape* [25] and *shape type* [11] also separate the set of positions of a data structure from the values it contains. Often there is no need to distinguish between the positions and their associated values. In this case, we use the term "element of the collection".

Collection Types. Different predefined and user-defined collection types are available in MGS, including sets, bags (or multisets), sequences, Cayley graphs of Abelian groups (which include several unbounded, circular and twisted grids), Delaunay triangulations, arbitrary graphs, quasi-manifolds [36] and some other arbitrary topologies specified by the programmer.

Building Topological Collections. For any collection type T, the corresponding empty collection is written ():T. The join of two collections C_1 and C_2 (written by a comma: C_1, C_2) is the main operation on collections. The comma operator is overloaded in MGS and can be used to build any collection (the type of the arguments disambiguates the collection built). So, the expression 1, 1+2, 2+1, ():set builds the set with the two elements 1 and 3, while the expression 1, 1+2, 2+1, ():bag computes a bag (a set that allows multiple occurrences of the same value) with the three elements 1, 3 and 3. A set or a bag is provided with the following topology: in a set or a bag, any two elements are neighbors. To spare the notations, the empty sequence can be omitted in the definition of a sequence: 1, 2, 3 is equivalent to 1, 2, 3, ():seq.

4.2 Transformations

The MGS experimental programming language implements the idea of transformations of topological collections into the framework of a functional language:

collections are just new kinds of values and transformations are functions acting on collections and defined by a specific syntax using rules. Transformations (like functions) are first-class values and can be passed as arguments or returned as the result of an application.

The *global transformation* of a topological collection s consists in the *parallel application* of a set of *local transformations*. A local transformation is specified by a rule r that specifies the replacement of a subcollection by another one. The application of a rewriting rule $\sigma \Rightarrow f(\sigma, ...)$ to a collection s:

1. selects a subcollection s_i of s whose elements match the *pattern* σ,
2. computes a new collection s_i' as a function f of s_i and its neighbors,
3. and specifies the insertion of s_i' in place of s_i into s.

One should pay attention to the fact that, due to the parallel application strategy of rules, *all distinct instances s_i of the subcollections matched by the σ pattern are "simultaneously replaced"* by the $f(s_i)$.

Path Pattern. A pattern σ in the left hand side of a rule specifies a subcollection where an interaction occurs. A subcollection of interacting elements can have an arbitrary shape, making it very difficult to specify. Thus, it is more convenient (and not so restrictive) to enumerate sequentially the elements of the subcollection. Such enumeration will be called a *path*.

A path pattern *Pat* is a sequence or a repetition *Rep* of *basic filters*. A basic filter *BF* matches one element. The following fragment of the grammar of path patterns reflects this decomposition:

$$Pat ::= Rep \mid Rep\,,\,Pat \qquad Rep ::= BF \mid BF/exp \qquad BF ::= \mathtt{cte} \mid \mathrm{id} \mid \mathtt{<undef>}$$

where $\mathtt{cte}$ is a literal value, id ranges over the pattern variables and exp is a boolean expression. The following explanations give an interpretation for these patterns:

literal: a literal value $\mathtt{cte}$ matches an element with the same value.

empty element the symbol $\mathtt{<undef>}$ matches an element whose position does not have an associated value.

variable: a pattern variable a matches exactly one element with a well defined value. The variable a can then occur elsewhere in the rest of pattern or in the r.h.s. of the rule and denotes the value of the matched element.

neighbor: b,p is a pattern that matches a path which begins by an element matched by b and continues by a path matched by p, the first element of p being a neighbor of b.

guard: p/exp matches a path matched by p when the boolean expression exp evaluates to $\mathtt{true}$.

Elements matched by basic filters in a rule are distinct. So a matched path is without self-intersection. The identifier of a pattern variable can be used only once as a basic filter. That is, the path pattern x,x is forbidden. However, this pattern can be rewritten for instance as: $x,y\ /\ y=x$.

Right Hand Side of a Rule. The right hand side of a rule specifies a collection that replaces the subcollection matched by the pattern in the left hand side. There is an alternative point of view: because the pattern defines a sequence of elements, the right hand side may be an expression that evaluates to a sequence of elements. Then, the substitution is done element-wise: element i in the matched path is replaced by the element i in the r.h.s. This point of view enables a very concise writing of the rules.

A Very Simple Transformation. The *map* function which applies a function to each element of a collection is an example of a simple transformation:

```
trans map[f=\z.z] = {    x => f(x)    }
```

This transformation is made of only one rule. The syntax must be obvious (the default value of the optional parameter f is the identity written using a lambda-notation). This transformation implements a *map* since each element e of the collection is matched by the pattern x and will be replaced by $f(e)$ in a parallel application strategy of the rule.

5   Examples

5.1   The Modeling of Dynamical Systems

In this section, we show through one example the ability of MGS to concisely and easily express the state of a dynamical system and its evolution function. More examples can be found on the MGS web page and include: cellular automata-like examples (game of life, snowflake formation, lattice gas automata...), various resolutions of partial differential equations (like the diffusion-reaction *à la* Turing), Lindenmayer systems (e.g. the modeling of the heterocysts differentiation during Anabaena growth), the modeling of a spatially distributed signaling pathway, the flocking of birds, the modeling of a tumor growth, the growth of a meristem, the simulation of colonies of ants foraging for food, etc.

The example given below is an example of a discrete "classical dynamical system". We term it "classical" because it exhibits a *static structure*: the state of the system is statically described and does not change with the time. This situation is simple and arises often in elementary physics. For example, a falling stone is statically described by a position and a velocity and this set of variables does not change (even if the value of the position and the value of the velocity change in the course of time). However, in some systems, it is not only the values of state variables, but also the *set* of state variables *and/or* the evolution function, that changes over time. We call these systems *dynamical systems with a dynamic structure* following [17], or (DS)² in short. As pointed out by [15], many biological systems are of this kind. The rationale and the use of MGS in the simulation of (DS)² is presented in [14, 15].

Diffusion Limited Aggregation (DLA). DLA, is a fractal growth model studied by T.A. Witten and L.M. Sander, in the eighties. The principle of the model is

Fig. 3. From left to right: the final state of a DLA process on a torus, a chess pawn, a Klein's bottle and an hexagonal meshes. The chess pawn is homeomorphic to a sphere and the Klein's bottle does not admit a concretization in Euclidean space. These two topological collections are values of the *quasi-manifold* type. Such collection are build using *G-map*, a data-structure widely used in geometric modeling [27]. The torus and the hexagonal mesh are GBFs

simple: a set of particles diffuses randomly on a given spatial domain. Initially one particle, the seed, is fixed. When a mobile particle collides a fixed one, they stick together and stay fixed. For the sake of simplicity, we suppose that they stick together forever and that there is no aggregate formation between two mobile particles. This process leads to a simple CA with an asynchronous update function or a lattice gas automata with a slightly more elaborate rule set. This section shows that the MGS approach enables the specification of a simple generic transformation that can act on arbitrary complex topologies.

The transformation describing the DLA behavior is really simple. We use two symbolic values `'free` and `'fixed` to represent respectively a mobile and a fixed particle. There are two rules in the transformation:

1. the first rule specifies that if a diffusing particle is the neighbor of a fixed seed, then it becomes fixed (at the current position);
2. the second one specifies the random diffusion process: if a mobile particle is neighbor of an empty place (position), then it may leave its current position to occupy the empty neighbor (and its current position is made empty).

Note that the order of the rules is important because the first has priority over the second one. Thus, we have :

```
trans dla = {
    'free, 'fixed   =>  'fixed, 'fixed
    'free, <undef>  =>  <undef>, 'free
}
```

This transformation is polytypic and can be applied to any kind of collection, see Fig. 3 for a few results.

5.2   Programming in the Small: Algorithmic Examples

The previous section advocates the adequacy of the MGS programming style to model and simulate various dynamical systems. However, it appears that the MGS programming style is also well fitted for the implementation of algorithmic tasks. In this section, we show some examples that support this assertion. More examples can be found on the MGS web page and include: the analysis of the Needham-Schroeder public-key protocol [30], the Eratosthene's sieve, the normalization of boolean formulas, the computation of various algorithms on graphs like the computation of the shortest distance between two nodes or the maximal flow, etc.

Gamma and the Chemical Computing Metaphor. In MGS, the topology of a multiset is the topology of a complete connected graph: each element is the neighbor of any other element. With this topology, transformations can be used to easily emulate a Gamma transformations [2, 3]. The Gamma transformation:

```
M = do
    rp x₁,...,xₙ
    if  P(x₁,...,xₙ)
    by  f₁(x₁,...,xₙ),...,fₘ(x₁,...,xₙ)
```

is simply translated into the following MGS transformation:

```
trans M = {
    x₁,...,xₙ
    /  P(x₁,...,xₙ)
    => f₁(x₁,...,xₙ),...,fₘ(x₁,...,xₙ) }
```

and the application M(b) of a Gamma transformation M to a multiset b is replaced in MGS by the computation of the fixpoint iteration M[iter='fixpoint](b). The optional parameter iter is a system parameter that allows the programmer to choose amongst several predefined application strategies:

$$f[\text{iter}='\text{fixpoint}](x_0)$$

computes $x_1 = f(x_0), x_2 = f(x_1), ..., x_n = f(x_{n-1})$ and returns x_n such that $x_n = x_{n-1}$.

As a consequence, the concise and elegant programming style of Gamma is enabled in MGS: refer to the Gamma literature for numerous examples of algorithms, from knapsack to the maximal convex hull of a set of points, through the computation of prime numbers. See also the numerous applications of multiset rewriting developped in the projects Elan [38] and Maude [37].

One can see MGS as "Gamma with more structure". However, one can note that the topology of a multiset is "universal" in the following sense: it embeds any other neighborhood relationship. So, it is always possible to code (at the price of explicit coding the topological relation into some value inspected at run-time) any specific topology on top of the multiset topology. We interpret the development of "structured Gamma" [10] from this perspective. In addition, transformations are functions and functions are first citizen values in MGS. So the higher-order features of the higher-order chemical programming style (see the article by Banâtre et al. in this volume) can be easely achieved in MGS.

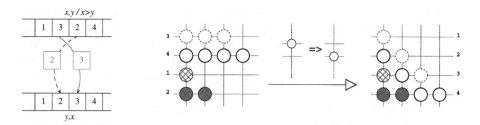

Fig. 4. *Left:* Bubble sort. *Right:* Bead sort [1]

Two Sorting Algorithms. A kind of bubble-sort is straightforward in MGS; it is sufficient to specify the exchange of two non-ordered adjacent elements in a sequence, see Fig. 4. The corresponding transformation is defined as:

```
trans BubbleSort = {   x,y / x>y ⇒ y,x   }
```

The transformation *BubbleSort* must be iterated until a fixpoint is reached. This is not a real a bubble sort algorithm because swapping of elements happen at arbitrary places; hence an out-of-order element does not necessarily bubble to the top in the characteristic way.

Bead sort is a new sorting algorithm [1]. The idea is to represent positive integers by a set of beads, like those used in an abacus. Beads are attached to vertical rods and appear to be suspended in the air just before sliding down (a number is read horizontally, as a row). After their falls, the rows of numbers have been rearranged such as the smaller numbers appears on top of greater numbers, see Fig. 4. The corresponding one-line MGS program is given by the transformation:

```
trans BeadSort = { 'empty |north> 'bead ⇒ 'bead, 'empty }
```

This transformation is applied on the usual grid. The constant 'empty is used to give a value to an empty place and the constant 'bead is used to represent an occupied cell. The l.h.s. of the only rule of the transformation *BeadSort* selects the paths of length two, composed by an occupied cell at north of an empty cell. Such a path is replaced by a path computed in the r.h.s. of the rule. The r.h.s. in this example computes a path of length two with the occupied and the empty cell swapped.

Hamiltonian Path. A graph is a MGS topological collection. It is very easy to list all the Hamiltonian paths in a graph using the transformation:

```
trans H = {
    x* / size(x) = size(self) / Print(x) / false => !(false)
}
```

This transformation uses an iterated pattern x* that matches a path (a sequence of elements neighbor two by two). The keyword self refers to the collection on which the transformation is applied, that is, the entire graph. The size of a graph returns the number of its vertices. So, if the length of the path x is the same as the number of vertices in the graph, then the path x is an Hamiltonian path because matched paths are simple (no repetition of an element). The second guard prints the Hamiltonian path as a side effect and returns its argument which is not a false value. Then the third guard is checked and returns false, thus, the r.h.s. of the rule is never triggered (the ! operator introduces an assertion and !(false) raises an exception that stops the evaluation process if it is evaluated). The matching strategy ensures a maximal rule application. In other words, if a rule is not triggered, then there is no instance of a possible path that fulfills the pattern. This property implies that the previous rule must be checked on all possible Hamiltonian paths and $H(g)$ prints all the Hamiltonian path in g before returning g unchanged.

6   Current Status and Related Work

The topological approach we have sketched here is part of a long term research effort [21] developed for instance in [13] where the focus is on the substructure, or in [16] where a general tool for uniform neighborhood definition is developed. Within this long term research project, MGS is an experimental language used to investigate the idea of associating computations to paths through rules. The application of such rules can be seen as a kind of rewriting process on a collection of objects organized by a topological relationship (the neighborhood). A privileged application domain for MGS is the modeling and simulation of dynamical systems that exhibit a dynamic structure.

Multiset transformation is reminiscent of multiset-rewriting (or rewriting of terms modulo AC). This is the main computational device of Gamma [2], a language based on a chemical metaphor; the data are considered as a multiset M of molecules and the computation is a succession of chemical reactions according to a particular rule. The CHemical Abstract Machine (CHAM) extends these ideas with a focus on the expression of semantic of non deterministic processes [4]. The CHAM introduces a mechanism to isolate some parts of the chemical solution. This idea has been seriously taken into account in the notion of P systems. P systems [31] are a recent distributed parallel computing model based on the notion of a membrane structure. A membrane structure is a nesting of cells represented, e.g, by a Venn diagram without intersection and with a unique superset: the skin. Objects are placed in the regions defined by the membranes and evolve following various transformations: an object can evolve into another object, can pass trough a membrane or dissolve its enclosing membrane. As for Gamma, the computation is finished when no object can further evolve. By using nested multisets, MGS is able to emulate more or less the notion of P systems. In addition, patterns like the iteration + go beyond what is possible to specify in the l.h.s. of a Gamma rule.

Lindenmayer systems [28] have long been used in the modeling of (DS)² (especially in the modeling of plant growing). They loosely correspond to transformations on sequences or string rewriting (they also correspond to tree rewriting, because some standard features make particularly simple to code arbitrary trees,

Cf. the work of P. Prusinkiewicz [32]). Obviously, L systems are dedicated to the handling of linear and tree-like structures.

There are strong links between GBF and cellular automata (CA), especially considering the work of Z. Róka which has studied CA on Cayley graphs [33]. However, our own work focuses on the construction of Cayley graphs as the shape of a data structure and we develop an operator algebra and rewriting notions on this new data type. This is not in the line of Z. Róka which focuses on synchronization problems and establishes complexity results in the framework of CA.

A unifying theoretical framework can be developed [18, 20], based on the notion of *chain complex* developed in algebraic combinatorial topology. However, we do not claim that we have achieved a useful theoretical framework encompassing the previous paradigms. We advocate that few topological notions and a single syntax can be consistently used to allow the merging of these formalisms *for programming* purposes.

The current MGS interpreter is freely available at the MGS home page: mgs.lami.univ-evry.fr. A compiler is under development where a static type discipline can be enforced [8, 9]). There are two versions of the type inference systems for MGS: the first one is a classical extension of the Hindley-Milner type inference system that handles homogeneous collections. The second one is a soft type system able to handle heterogeneous collection (e.g. a sequence containing both integers and booleans is heterogeneous).

Acknowledgments

The authors would like to thanks Franck Delaplace at LaMI, Frédéric Gruau at University of Paris-Sud, Florent Jacquemard at INRIA/LSV-Cachan, C. Godin and P. Barbier de Reuille at CIRAD-Montpellier, Pierre-Etienne Moreau at Loria-Nancy, Éric Goubault at CEA-Saclay, P. Prusinkiewicz at the University of Calgary (who coined the term "computation in space") and the members of the Epigenomic group at GENOPOLE-Évry, for stimulating discussions, thoughtful remarks and warm support. We gratefully acknowledge the financial support of the CNRS, the GDR ALP, IMPBIO, the University of Évry and GENOPOLE.

References

1. J. Arulanandham, C. Calude, and M. Dinneen. Bead-sort: A natural sorting algorithm. *Bulletin of the European Association for Theoretical Computer Science*, 76:153–162, Feb. 2002. Technical Contributions.

2. J.-P. Banatre, A. Coutant, and D. L. Metayer. A parallel machine for multiset transformation and its programming style. *Future Generation Computer Systems*, 4:133–144, 1988.

3. J.-P. Banâtre, P. Fradet, and D. L. Métayer. Gamma and the chemical reaction model: Fifteen years after. *Lecture Notes in Computer Science*, 2235:17–44, 2001.

4. G. Berry and G. Boudol. The chemical abstract machine. In *Conf. Record 17th ACM Symp. on Principles of Programmming Languages, POPL'90, San Francisco, CA, USA, 17–19 Jan. 1990*, pages 81–94. ACM Press, New York, 1990.

5. R. W. Brockett. Dynamical systems that sort lists, diagonalize matrices, and solve linear programming problems. *Linear Algebra and its Applications*, 146:79–91, 1991.

6. K. M. Chandy. Reasoning about continuous systems. *Science of Computer Programming*, 14(2–3):117–132, Oct. 1990.

7. E. G. Coffman, M. J. Elphick, and A. Shoshani. System deadlocks. *Computing Surveys*, 3(2):67–78, 1971.

8. J. Cohen. Typing rule-based transformations over topological collections. In J.-L. Giavitto and P.-E. Moreau, editors, *4th International Workshop on Rule-Based Programming (RULE'03)*, pages 50–66, 2003.

9. J. Cohen. Typage fort et typage souple des collections topologiques et des transformations. In V. Ménissier-Morain, editor, *Journées Francophones des Langages Applicatifs (JFLA 2004)*, pages 37–54. INRIA, 2004.

10. P. Fradet and D. L. Métayer. Structured Gamma. *Science of Computer Programming*, 31(2–3):263–289, July 1998.

11. P. Fradet and D. L. Mtayer. Shape types. In *Proc. of Principles of Programming Languages*, Paris, France, Jan. 1997. ACM Press.

12. F. Geurts. Hierarchy of discrete-time dynamical systems, a survey. *Bulletin of the European Association for Theoretical Computer Science*, 57:230–251, Oct. 1995. Surveys and Tutorials.

13. J.-L. Giavitto. A framework for the recursive definition of data structures. In *ACM-Sigplan 2nd International Conference on Principles and Practice of Declarative Programming (PPDP'00)*, pages 45–55, Montral, Sept. 2000. ACM-press.

14. J.-L. Giavitto. Invited talk: Topological collections, transformations and their application to the modeling and the simulation of dynamical systems. In *Rewriting Technics and Applications (RTA'03)*, volume LNCS 2706 of *LNCS*, pages 208 – 233, Valencia, June 2003. Springer.

15. J.-L. Giavitto, C. Godin, O. Michel, and P. Prusinkiewicz. *Modelling and Simulation of biological processes in the context of genomics*, chapter "Computational Models for Integrative and Developmental Biology". Hermes, July 2002. Also republished as an high-level course in the proceedings of the Dieppe spring school on "Modelling and simulation of biological processes in the context of genomics", 12-17 may 2003, Dieppes, France.

16. J.-L. Giavitto and O. Michel. Declarative definition of group indexed data structures and approximation of their domains. In *Proceedings of the 3nd International ACM SIGPLAN Conference on Principles and Practice of Declarative Programming (PPDP-01)*. ACM Press, Sept. 2001.

17. J.-L. Giavitto and O. Michel. Mgs: a rule-based programming language for complex objects and collections. In M. van den Brand and R. Verma, editors, *Electronic Notes in Theoretical Computer Science*, volume 59. Elsevier Science, 2001.

18. J.-L. Giavitto and O. Michel. MGS: a programming language for the transformations of topological collections. Technical Report 61-2001, LaMI – Université d'Évry Val d'Essonne, May 2001.

19. J.-L. Giavitto and O. Michel. Data structure as topological spaces. In *Proceedings of the 3nd International Conference on Unconventional Models of Computation UMC02*, volume 2509, pages 137–150, Himeji, Japan, Oct. 2002. Lecture Notes in Computer Science.

20. J.-L. Giavitto and O. Michel. The topological structures of membrane computing. *Fundamenta Informaticae*, 49:107–129, 2002.
21. J.-L. Giavitto, O. Michel, and J.-P. Sansonnet. Group based fields. In I. Takayasu, R. H. J. Halstead, and C. Queinnec, editors, *Parallel Symbolic Languages and Systems (International Workshop PSLS'95)*, volume 1068 of *LNCS*, pages 209–215, Beaune (France), 2–4 Oct. 1995. Springer-Verlag.
22. E. Goubault. Geometry and concurrency: A user's guide. *Mathematical Structures in Computer Science*, 10:411–425, 2000.
23. G.-G. Granger. *La pense de l'espace*. Odile Jacob, 1999.
24. M. Henle. *A combinatorial introduction to topology*. Dover publications, 1994.
25. C. B. Jay. A semantics for shape. *Science of Computer Programming*, 25(2–3):251–283, 1995.
26. J. Jeuring and P. Jansson. Polytypic programming. *Lecture Notes in Computer Science*, 1129:68–114, 1996.
27. P. Lienhardt. Topological models for boundary representation : a comparison with n-dimensional generalized maps. *Computer-Aided Design*, 23(1):59–82, 1991.
28. A. Lindenmayer. Mathematical models for cellular interaction in development, Parts I and II. *Journal of Theoretical Biology*, 18:280–315, 1968.
29. E. Meijer, M. Fokkinga, and R. Paterson. Functional Programming with Bananas, Lenses, Envelopes and Barbed Wire. In *5th ACM Conference on Functional Programming Languages and Computer Architecture*, volume 523 of *Lecture Notes in Computer Science*, pages 124–144, Cambridge, MA, August 26–30, 1991. Springer.
30. O. Michel and F. Jacquemard. *An Analysis of a Public-Key Protocol with Membranes*, pages 281–300. Natural Computing Series. Springer Verlag, 2005.
31. G. Paun. From cells to computers: Computing with membranes (P systems). *Biosystems*, 59(3):139–158, March 2001.
32. P. Prusinkiewicz and J. Hanan. L systems: from formalism to programming languages. In G. Ronzenberg and A. Salomaa, editors, *Lindenmayer Systems, Impacts on Theoretical Computer Science, Computer Graphics and Developmental Biology*, pages 193–211. Springer Verlag, Feb. 1992.
33. Z. Róka. One-way cellular automata on Cayley graphs. *Theoretical Computer Science*, 132(1–2):259–290, 26 Sept. 1994.
34. M. Sintzoff. Invariance and contraction by infinite iterations of relations. In *Research directions in high-level programming languages, LNCS*, volume 574, pages 349–373, Mont Saint-Michel, France, june 1991. Springer-Verlag.
35. R. D. Sorkin. A finitary substitute for continuous topology. *Int. J. Theor. Phys.*, 30:923–948, 1991.
36. A. Spicher, O. Michel, and J.-L. Giavitto. A topological framework for the specification and the simulation of discrete dynamical systems. In *Sixth International conference on Cellular Automata for Research and Industry (ACRI'04)*, volume 3305 of *LNCS*, Amsterdam, October 2004. Springer.
37. The MAUDE project. Maude home page, 2002. `http://maude.csl.sri.com/`.
38. The PROTHEO project. Elan home page, 2002. `http://www.loria.fr/equipes/protheo/SOFTWARES/ELAN/`.
39. H. Weyl. *The Classical Groups (their invariants and representations)*. Princeton University Press, 1939. Reprint edition (October 13, 1997). ISBN 0691057567.

Bio-inspired Computing

Bio-inspired Computing Paradigms
(Natural Computing)

Gheorghe Păun

Institute of Mathematics of the Romanian Academy,
PO Box 1-764, 014700 Bucureşti, Romania and
Research Group on Natural Computing,
Department of Computer Science and Artificial Intelligence,
University of Sevilla,
Avda. Reina Mercedes s/n, 41012 Sevilla, Spain
`george.paun@imar.ro`, `gpaun@us.es`

Abstract. This is just a glimpse to the fruitful and continuous preoccupation of computer science to try to get inspired by biology, at various levels. Besides briefly discussing the main areas of natural computing (genetic algorithms–evolutionary computing, neural computing, DNA computing, and membrane computing), we mention some of the hopes and the difficulties/limits of this enterprise.

1 From Turing to Present Days

In some sense, the whole history of computer science is the history of a series of continuous attempts to discover, study, and, if possible, implement computing ideas, models, paradigms from the way nature – the humans included – computes. We do not enter here into the debate whether or not the processes taking place in nature are by themselves "computations", or we, *homo sapiens*, interpret them as computations, but we just recall the fact that when defining the computing model which is currently known as *Turing machine* and which provides the standard definition of what is computable, A. Turing (in 1935–1936) explicitly wanted to abstract and model what a clerk in a bank is doing when computing with numbers. One decade later, McCullock, Pitts, Kleene founded the finite automata theory starting from modelling the neuron and the neural nets; still later, this led to the area called now *neural computing* – whose roots can be found in unpublished papers of the same A. Turing (see also Section 3 below). *Genetic algorithms* and evolutionary computing/programming are already well established (and much applied practically) areas of computer science. One decade ago, the history making Adleman's experiment of computing with DNA molecules was reported, proving that one can not only get inspired from biology for designing computers and algorithms for electronic computers, but one can also use a biological support (a bio–ware) for computing. In the last years, the

J.-P. Banâtre et al. (Eds.): UPP 2004, LNCS 3566, pp. 155–160, 2005.

search of computing ideas/models/paradigms in biology, in general in nature, became explicit and systematic under the general name of *natural computing*[1].

This trend of computer science is not singular, many other areas of science and technology are scrutinizing biology in the hope (confirmed in many cases) that life has polished for billions of years numerous wonderful processes, tools, and machineries which can be imitated in domains apparently far from biology, such as materials and sensor technology, robotics, bionics, nanotechnology.

2   A Typical Case: Evolutionary Computing

In order to see the (sometimes unexpected) benefits we can have in this framework, it is instructive to examine the case of genetic algorithms. Roughly speaking, they try to imitate the bio–evolution in solving optimization problems: the candidate solutions to a problem are encoded as "chromosomes" (strings of abstract symbols), which are evolved by means of crossover and point mutation operations, and selected from a generation to the next one by means of a fitness mapping; the trials to improve the fitness mapping continue until either no essential improvement is done for a number of steps, or until a given number of iterations are performed. The biological metaphors are numerous and obvious. What is not obvious (from a mathematical point of view) is why such a brute force approach – searching randomly the space of candidate solutions, with the search guided by random crossover and point mutations – is as successful as it happens to be (with a high probability, in many cases, the genetic algorithms provide a good enough solution in a large number of applications). The most convincing "explanation" is probably "because nature has used the same strategy in improving species". This kind of bio–mystical "explanation" provides a rather optimistic motivation for related researche.

3   Neural Computing

A special mentioning deserves another "classic" area included nowadays in natural computing, namely neural computing. In short, the challenge is now to learn something useful from the brain organization, from the way the neurons are linked; the standard model consists of neuron–like computing agents (finite state machines, of very reduced capabilities), placed in the vertices of a net, with numerical weights on edges, aiming to compute a function; in a first phase, the net is "trained" for the task to carry out, and the weights are adjusted, then the net is used for solving a real problem. Pattern recognition problems are typical to

---

[1] As a proof of the popularity of this syntagm, it is of interest to point out that there are conferences with this topic explicitly included in their scope, a new journal with this name is published by Kluwer, a new series of the Elsevier *Theoretical Computer Science* journal is devoted to natural computing, a new series of books published by Springer–Verlag and a column in the *Bulletin of the European Association for Theoretical Computer Science* also have this name.

be addressed via neural nets. The successes (and the promises) are comparable with those of genetic algorithms, without having a similarly wide range of applications. However, the brain remains such a misterious and efficient machinery that nobody can underestimate the progresses in any area trying to imitate the brain. (It also deserves to mention the rather interesting detail that Alan Turing himself, some years after introducing Turing machines, had a paper where he proposed a computing device in the form of a net of very simple computing units, able to learn, and then to solve an optimization problem – nothing else than neural computing *avant la lettre*. Unfortunately, his paper remained unpublished and was only recently reevaluated; see `http://www.AlanTuring.net` and [12] for details.)

4   DNA Computing

Coming back to the history making Adleman's experiment mentioned above [1], it has the merit of opening (actually, confirming, because speculations about using DNA as a support for computations were made since several decades, while theoretical computing models inspired from the DNA structure and operations were already proposed in eighties, see, e.g., [7]) a completely new research vista, not looking for better algorithms for existing computers, but for a new type of hardware, based on bio–molecules. Specifically, Adleman has solved in a lab, just handling DNA by techniques already standard in bio–chemistry, a computationally hard problem, the well–known Hamiltonian Path problem. The problem is **NP**–complete, among those considered intractable for the usual computers, but Aldeman has solved it in linear time (the number of lab operations carried out was linear in terms of the number of nodes). The graph used in the experiment had only 7 nodes, a toy–problem by all means, while the actual working time was of seven days, but the *demo* (in terms of [6]) was convincing: we can compute using DNA!

It is worth emphasizing the fundamental novelty of this event: the dream is to find an essentially new type of computers – sometimes called "wet computer". The great promise is to solve hard problems in a feasible time, by making use of the massive parallelism made possible by the very compact way of storing information on DNA molecules (bits at the molecular level, with some orders of efficiency over silicon supports). In this way, billions of "computing chips" can be accommodated in a tiny test tube, much more than on electronic supports. The possible (not yet very probable for the near future...) "DNA computer" also has other attractive features: energetical efficiency, reversibility, evolvability.

5   The Marvelous DNA Molecule

For the practical computer science, DNA computing fuels several hopes, mainly related to the massive parallelism mentioned above; on this basis, we can simulate non-determinism (which is anyway present in biochemistry), so that one can address in this framework computationally hard problems, with the possibility to push with some steps forward the feasibility barriers – at least for certain problems.

There are mentioned also other good features of DNA as a support for computations (energy efficiency, stability, reversibility of certain processes), but we switch here to a purely theoretical observation, which is simply spectacular from a general computability point of view: in certain sense, *all Turing computable languages are "hidden" in the DNA molecules, and any particular language can be "read off" from this blue print of computability by the simplest transducer, the finite state one!*.

This newspaper–style statement has a precise mathematical counterpart, first mentioned in [11]. Everything starts with an old characterization of recursively enumerable (RE) languages, as the projection of the intersection of a twin–shuffle language with a regular language. However, both the projection and the intersection with a regular language, and the decoding of the symbols of an arbitrary alphabet from codes over a binary alphabet can be computed by a sequential transducer. Therefore, every RE language is the image through a sequential transducer of the twin–shuffle language over the alphabet with two symbols. Now, a clever observation from [11] relates the twin–shuffle language over two symbols with "readings" of DNA molecules (one goes along the two strands of a molecule, step by step but with non-deterministically varying speed, and producing a single string, by interleaving the visited nucleotides; this reading can be done either starting from the same end of a double stranded molecule, or from opposite ends, for instance, according to the directionality of the two strands). Thus: every RE language can be obtained through a finite state transducer from the pool of readings of DNA molecules! The double stranded data structure, with the corresponding nucleotides related by the Watson–Crick complementarity relation, is intrinsically universal from a computational point of view!

This observation (a presentation and variants of the mathematical details can also be found in [10]) should bring to theoretical DNA computing a similar degree of optimism as genetic algorithms bring to practical natural computing.

6   Recent Attempts

Another component of this general intellectual enterprise is membrane computing, which starts from the observation that the cell is the smallest living thing, and at the same time it is a marvellous tiny machinery, with a complex structure, an intricate inner activity, and an exquisite relationship with its environment – the neighboring cells included. Then, the challenge is to find in the structure and the functioning of the cell those elements useful for computing. Distribution, parallelism, non-determinism, decentralization, (non)synchronization, coordination, communication, robustness, scalability, are only a few keywords related to this challenge. For instance, a problem which cannot be easily solved in terms of silicon engineering, but which was misteriously and very efficiently solved by nature at the level of the cell is related to the coordination of processes, the control pathways which keep the cell alive, without a high cost of coordination (in parallel computing the communication complexity is sometimes higher than the time and space complexity). Then, interesting questions appear in connection with the organization of cells into tissues, and this is also related to the way the neurons cooperate in the brain.

Similar issues are addressed by several other recent research directions belonging to natural computing, for instance, trying to learn computing ideas/models/paradigms from the way certain colonies of insects are organized and work together, the way bacteria populations develop in a given environment, the way flocks of birds maintain their "organization", the (amazing) way ciliates unscramble their chromosomes after reproduction [5], and so on. Most of these areas still wait for producing a *demo*, many of them are still in the stage of "craftsmanship", with *ad-hoc* ideas involved in *ad-hoc* models/tools handling *ad-hoc* problems, but the whole approach is both intellectually appealing and practically promising (sometimes through "by–products", useful for biology, medicine, robotics, etc).

7   Hopes and Limits

As mentioned above, there are many convincing achievements of natural computing, many bio–inspired areas of computer science have important practical applications, or/and they are appealing from a theoretical point of view. Sometimes, the usefulness of the bio–inspired models and tools has a somewhat misterious source/explanation, in other cases the matter is simpler and more transparent. Anyway, we try here to compose a list of attractive features of this attempt, of learning from the living nature to the benefit of computer science (most of these features can be called "hopes", as not being confirmed by current natural computing): in many cases, we look for ideas for improving the use of the existing computers, for new types of algorithms; in other cases, a new hardware is sought for; as new ideas to be found in nature, we can learn new data structures (such as the double strand with complementary pairs of symbols), or new operations (crossover and point mutations, splicing, annealing, and so on and so forth); bio–computing can make available a massive parallelism, reversible computations, non-determinism, energy efficiency, maybe also evolvable hardware/software, self–healing, robust; new ideas learnt from biology can lead to a complete reconstruction of computability theory, on non-standard bases (e.g., using the splicing operation, quite different from the rewriting operation, which is standard in computability); nature can suggest new computer architectures, ways to cope with such difficulties of parallel computing as communication, (de)centralization, synchronization, controlling distributed processes, etc.

The list might be probably continued, but we want to make here a point which we find important: when discussing about new computing paradigms inspired from biology, most authors are enthusiastic or even over–enthusiastic. For promoting a young research area, this is understandable – but natural computing is no longer an young area. A more lucid position is similarly helpful as a blindly optimistic one, so that we balance here the previous list with another one, of difficulties of implementing bio–ideas in computer science: nature has (in a certain sense, unlimited) time and resources, nature is cruel, kills what is not fit (all these are difficult to incorporate in computers, let them be based on electronic hardware or on a hypothetic bio–ware); nature has other goals than computing; many bio–chemical processes have a degree of non-determinism which we cannot afford in our computations; the life processes are complex, with a high degree of redundancy; biology seems to deal with non-crisp mathematics, with probabilities, with fuzzy estimations, which are not fully manageable in computations. And, last but not least, maybe we dream too much even from a theoretical point of view. First, the space–time trade–off specific to molecular computing, cannot redefine complexity classes, and it is sometimes too costly in space (in the size of used bio–ware). Then, M. Conrad [4] warned us that programmability (universality), efficiency, and evolvability are three contradictory features of any computing model... Both these observations indicate that there is no free lunch in computer science, even in the bio–inspired one.

References

1. L.M. Adleman, Molecular Computation of Solutions to Combinatorial Problems. *Science*, 226 (November 1994), 1021–1024.
2. B. Alberts, A. Johnson, J. Lewis, M. Raff, K. Roberts, P. Walter, *Molecular Biology of the Cell*, 4th ed. Garland Science, New York, 2002.
3. J.A. Anderson, *An Introduction to Neural Networks*. The MIT Press, Cambridge, MA, 1996.
4. M. Conrad, The Price of Programmability. In *The Universal Turing Machine: A Half–Century Survey* (R. Herken, ed.), Kammerer and Unverzagt, Hamburg, 1988, 285–307.
5. A. Ehrenfeucht, T. Harju, I. Petre, D.M. Prescott, G. Rozenberg, *Computations in Living Cells*. Springer–Verlag, Berlin, 2004.
6. J. Hartmanis, About the Nature of Computer Science. *Bulletin of the EATCS*, 53 (June 1994), 170–190.
7. T. Head, Formal Language Theory and DNA: An Analysis of the Generative Capacity of Specific Recombinant Behaviors. *Bulletin of Mathematical Biology*, 49 (1987), 737–759.
8. J.H. Koza, J.P. Rice, *Genetic Algorithms: The Movie*. MIT Press, Cambridge, Mass., 1992.
9. Gh. Păun, *Computing with Membranes: An Introduction*. Springer–Verlag, Berlin, 2002.
10. Gh. Păun, G. Rozenberg, A. Salomaa, *DNA Computing. New Computing Paradigms*. Springer–Verlag, Berlin, 1998.
11. G. Rozenberg, A. Salomaa, Watson–Crick Complementarity, Universal Computations, and Genetic Engineering. *Techn. Report* 96–28, Department of Computer Science, Leiden Univ., Oct. 1996.
12. C. Teuscher, *Alan Turing. Life and Legacy of a Great Thinker*. Springer–Verlag, Berlin, 2003.

Inverse Design of Cellular Automata by Genetic Algorithms: An Unconventional Programming Paradigm

Thomas Bäck[1,2], Ron Breukelaar[1,*], and Lars Willmes[2]

[1] Universiteit Leiden, LIACS, P.O. Box 9512, 2300 RA Leiden, The Netherlands
{baeck, rbreukel}@liacs.nl
[2] NuTech Solutions GmbH, Martin Schmeißer Weg 15,
44227 Dortmund, Germany
{baeck, willmes}@nutechsolutions.de

Abstract. Evolving solutions rather than computing them certainly represents an unconventional programming approach. The general methodology of evolutionary computation has already been known in computer science since more than 40 years, but their utilization to program other algorithms is a more recent invention. In this paper, we outline the approach by giving an example where evolutionary algorithms serve to program cellular automata by designing rules for their iteration. Three different goals of the cellular automata designed by the evolutionary algorithm are outlined, and the evolutionary algorithm indeed discovers rules for the CA which solve these problems efficiently.

1 Evolutionary Algorithms

Evolutionary Computation is the term for a subfield of Natural Computing that has emerged already in the 1960s from the idea to use principles of natural evolution as a paradigm for solving search and optimization problem in high-dimensional combinatorial or continuous search spaces. The algorithms within this field are commonly called evolutionary algorithms, the most widely known instances being genetic algorithms [6, 4, 5], genetic programming [8, 9], evolution strategies [12, 13, 14, 15], and evolutionary programming [3, 2]. A detailed introduction to all these algorithms can be found e.g. in the Handbook of Evolutionary Computation [1].

Evolutionary Computation today is a very active field involving fundamental research as well as a variety of applications in areas ranging from data analysis and machine learning to business processes, logistics and scheduling, technical engineering, and others. Across all these fields, evolutionary algorithms have

---

* Part of the research was funded by the Foundation for Fundamental Research on Matter (FOM), Utrecht, The Netherlands, *project: "An evolutionary approach to many-parameter physics"*.

convinced practitioners by the results obtained on hard problems that they are very powerful algorithms for such applications. The general working principle of all instances of evolutionary algorithms today is based on a program loop that involves simplified implementations of the operators mutation, recombination, selection, and fitness evaluation on a set of candidate solutions (often called a population of individuals) for a given problem. In this general setting, mutation corresponds to a modification of a single candidate solution, typically with a preference for small variations over large variations. Recombination corresponds to an exchange of components between two or more candidate solutions. Selection drives the evolutionary process towards populations of increasing average fitness by preferring better candidate solutions to proliferate with higher probability to the next generation than worse candidate solutions. By fitness evaluation, the calculation of a measure of goodness associated with candidate solutions is meant, i.e., the fitness function corresponds to the objective function of the optimization problem at hand.

This short paper does not intend to give a complete introduction to evolutionary algorithms, as there are many good introductory books on the topic available and evolutionary algorithms are, meanwhile, quite well known in the scientific community. Rather, we would like to briefly outline the general idea to use evolutionary algorithms to solve highly complex problems of parameterizing other algorithms, where the evolutionary algorithm is being used to find optimal parameters for another algorithm to perform its given task at hand as good as possible. One could also view this as an inverse design problem, i.e., a problem where the target design (behavior of the algorithm to be parameterized) is known, but the way to achieve this is unknown. The example we are choosing in this paper is the design of a rule for a 2 dimensional cellular automaton (CA) such that the cellular automaton solves a task at hand in an optimal way. We are dealing with 2 dimensional CA where the cells have just binary states, i.e., can have a value of one or zero. The behavior of such a CA is fully characterized by a rule which, for each possible pattern of bit values in the local neighborhood of a cell (von Neumann neighborhood: the cell plus its four vertical and horizontal direct nearest neighbors; Moore neighborhood: the cell plus its 8 nearest neighbors, also including the diagonal cells), defines the state of this cell in the next iteration of the CA evolution process. In the next section, we will explain the concept of a CA in some more detail. Section 5 reports experimental results of our approach with a 5 by 5 CA where the goal is to find rules which evolve from a standardized initial state of the CA to a target bit pattern, such that the rule rediscovers (i.e., inversely designs) this bit pattern. Finally, we give some conclusions from this work.

2   Cellular Automata

According to [16] Cellular Automata (CA) are mathematical idealizations of physical systems in which space and time are discrete, and physical quantities take on a finite set of discrete values. The simplest CA is one dimensional and looks a bit like an array of ones and zeros of width N, where the first position of the array is linked to the last position. In other words, defining a row of positions $C = \{a_1, a_2, ..., a_N\}$ where C is a CA of width N and a_N is adjacent to a_1.

The neighborhood s_n of a_n is defined as the local set of positions with a distance to a_n along the connected chain which is no more than a certain radius (r). This for instance means that $s_2 = \{a_{148}, a_{149}, a_1, a_2, a_3, a_4, a_5\}$ for $r = 3$ and $N = 149$. Please note that for one dimensional CA the size of the neighborhood is always equal to $2r + 1$.

The values in a CA can be altered all at the same time (synchronous) or at different times (asynchronous). Only synchronous CA are considered in this paper. In the synchronous approach at every timestep (t) every cell state in the CA is recalculated according to the states of the neighborhood using a certain transition rule $\Theta : \{0,1\}^{2r+1} \rightarrow \{0,1\}$, $s_i \rightarrow \Theta(s_i)$. This rule basically is a one-to-one mapping that defines an output value for every possible set of input values, the input values being the 'state' of a neighborhood. The state of a_n at time t is written as a_n^t, the state of s_n at time t as s_n^t and the state of the entire CA C at time t as C^t so that C^0 is the initial state and $\forall n = 1, \ldots, N$ $a_n^{t+1} = \Theta(s_n^t)$. Given $C^t = \{a_1^t, ..., a_N^t\}$, C^{t+1} can be defined as $\{\Theta(s_1^t), ..., \Theta(s_N^t)\}$.

Because $a_n \in \{0,1\}$ the number of possible states of s_n equals 2^{2r+1}. Because all possible binary representations of m where $0 \leq m < 2^{2r+1}$ can be mapped to a unique state of the neighborhood, Θ can be written as a row of ones and zeros $R = \{b_1, b_2, ..., b_{2^{2r+1}}\}$ where b_m is the output value of the rule for the input state that maps to the binary representation of $m - 1$. A rule therefore has a length that equals 2^{2r+1} and so there are $2^{2^{2r+1}}$ possible rules for a binary one dimensional CA. This is a huge number of possible rules (if $r = 3$ this sums up to about $3,4 \times 10^{28}$) each with a different behavior.

One of the interesting things about these and other CA is that certain rules tend to exhibit organizational behavior, independently of the initial state of the CA. This behavior also demonstrates there is some form of communication going on in the CA over longer distances than the neighborhood allows directly. In [10] the authors examine if these simple CA are able to perform tasks that need positions in a CA to work together and use some form of communication. One problem where such a communication seems required in order to give a good answer is the Majority Problem (as described in section 4.1). A genetic algorithm is used to evolve rules for one dimensional CA that do a rather good job of solving the Majority Problem [10] and it is shown how these rules seem to send "particles" and communicate by using these particles [11]. These results imply that even very simple cells in one dimensional cellular automata can communicate and work together to form more complex and powerful behavior.

It is not unthinkable that the capabilities of these one dimensional CA are restricted by the number of directions in which information can "travel" through a CA and that using multiple dimensions might remove these restriction and therefore improve performance. Evolving these rules for the Majority Problem for two dimensional CA using a Moore neighborhood (explained in section 4) is reported in [7] showing that the GA did not clearly outperform random search.

The goal of the research is to find a generalization and report phenomena observed on a higher level, with the future goal to use this research for identification and calibration of higher-dimensional CA applications to real world systems like parallel computing and modeling social and biological processes. The approach is described and results are reported on simple problems such as the Majority Problem, AND, XOR, extending into how it can be applied to pattern generation processes.

3   The Genetic Algorithm

As mentioned before, this research was inspired by earlier work [10, 11] in which transition rules for one dimensional CA were evolved to solve the Majority Problem (as defined in section 4.1). The GA is a fairly simple algorithm using binary representation of the rules, mutation by bit inversion, truncation selection, and single-point crossover. The algorithm determined the fitness by testing the evolved rules on 100 random initial states. Every iteration the best 20% of the rules (the 'elite' rules) were copied to the next generation and the other 80% of the rules were generated using single-point crossover with two randomly chosen 'elite' rules and then mutated by flipping exactly 2 bits in the rule.

To be able to compare two dimensional CA with one dimensional CA the GA used in section 4.1 is a copy of the the GA used in [10, 11]. The GA's in section 4.2 and 5 on the other hand are modified to fit the different problem demands, as will be explained in these sections.

4   Experimental Results for Two Dimensional CA

The two dimensional CA in this document are similar to the one dimensional CA discussed so far. Instead of a row of positions, C now consists of a grid of positions. The values are still only binary (0 or 1) and there still is only one transition rule for all the cells. The number of cells is still finite and therefore CA discussed here have a width, a height and borders.

The big difference between one dimensional and two dimensional CA is the rule definition. The neighborhood of these rules is two dimensional, because there are not only neighbors left and right of a cell, but also up and down. That means that if $r = 1$, s_n would consist of 5 positions, being the four directly adjacent plus a_n. This neighborhood is often called "the von Neumann neighborhood" after its inventor. The other well known neighborhood expands the Neumann neighborhood with the four positions diagonally adjacent to a_n and is called "the Moore neighborhood" also after its inventor.

Rules are defined with the same rows of bits (R) as defined in the one dimensional case. For a von Neumann neighborhood a rule can be defined with $2^5 = 32$ bits and a rule for a Moore neighborhood needs $2^9 = 512$ bits. This makes the Moore rule more powerful, for it has a bigger search space. Yet, a bigger search space also implies a longer search time and finding anything usefull might be a lot more difficult. In [7] the authors discourage the use of the Moore neighborhood, yet in section 4.2 and section 5 results clearly show successes using the Moore neighborhood, regardless of the larger search space.

In a one dimensional CA the leftmost cell is connected to the rightmost cell. In the two dimensional CA this is also common such that it forms a torus structure.

4.1   Majority Problem

The Majority Problem can be defined as follows: *Given a set $A = \{a_1, ..., a_n\}$ with n odd and $a_m \in \{0, 1\}$ for all $1 \leq m \leq n$, answer the question: 'Are there more ones than zeros in A?'.*

The Majority Problem first does not seem to be a very difficult problem to solve. It seems only a matter of counting the ones in the set and then comparing them to the number of zeros. Yet, when this problem is assigned to a CA it becomes a lot more difficult. This is because the rule in a CA does not let a position look past its neighborhood and that is why the cells all have to work together and use some form of communication.

Given that the relative number of ones in C^0 is written as λ, in a simple binary CA the Majority Problem can be defined as: *Find a rule that, given an initial state of a CA with N odd and a finite number I of iterations to run, will result in an 'all zero' state if $\lambda < 0.5$ and an 'all one' state otherwise.*

The fitness (f) of a rule is therefore defined as the relative number of correct answers to 100 randomly chosen initial states, where a 'correct answer' corresponds to an 'all zero' state if $\lambda < 0.5$ and an 'all one' state otherwise. In [10] the authors found that using a uniform distribution over λ for the initial states enhanced performance greatly; this is used here as well. The best runs will be tested using randomly chosen initial states with a normal distribution over the number of ones. The relative number of correct classifications on these states is written as $F_{n,m}$ where n is the width of the CA and m is the number of tests conducted.

Preliminary experiments showed that it took much more time to evolve rules for the Moore neighborhood than for the von Neumann neighborhood. The tests that were done with the Moore neighborhood also did not result in any encouraging results, this being in line with [7]. That is why the von Neumann neighborhood was chosen for this experiment. Because this neighborhood consists of five positions, the search space for CA rules is a lot smaller than in the one dimensional experiment. Instead of the $2^7 = 128$ bits in the rule, R now consists of $2^5 = 32$ bits, thus drastically decreasing the search space. This means that the search space decreased from 2^{128} to 2^{32} and is now $2^{(128-32)} = 2^{96}$ times smaller!

For this experiment we used a CA with width $= 13$ and height $= 13$. This means that these CA have $13 \times 13 = 169$ cells (N) and are $169 - 149 = 20$ cells larger than the one dimensional CA used in the original experiment.

This algorithm was run 300 times and each winning rule was tested by calculating $F_{N,M}$ using $F_{169,10^3}$. These results are plotted against results of our own

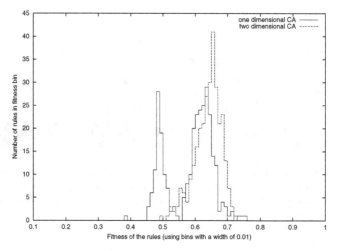

Fig. 1. This figure displays the number of rules that have a certain fitness value in the two dimensional experiment and compares this to the one dimensional experiment. The fitness bins are 0.01 in width and for both algorithm $F_{169,10^3}$ is calculated for 300 rules

Fig. 2. This figure shows a correct classification of the Majority Problem by a two dimensional CA with both width and height equal to 13 and $\lambda = 84/169$. The transition rule was one of the best tested in the experiment and scored $F_{169,10^3} = 0.715$

one dimensional experiment (not reported here, analogue to [10, 11]) in Figure 1. The striking difference between this distribution of fitness and the distribution of fitness in the one dimensional experiment is the absence of the peak around $F_{N,M} \approx 0.5$ in the two dimensional results. In those results almost all the evolved rules have a fitness above 0.58. A fitness around 0.66 seems to be average and the best rules have a fitness above 0.7. That is all very surprising taking into account that the von Neumann neighborhood only consists of 5 cells.

The Majority Problem is a good example of a problem that forces cells in a CA to 'communicate' with each other. The communication 'particles' can be seen in the one dimensional experiment, but are not easily spotted in the two dimensional experiment. That does not mean there are no 'particles' traveling in the two dimensional CA, because it might be very hard to identify these particles. In a two dimensional CA 'particles' are no longer restricted to traveling in only one direction, but can travel to multiple directions at the same time. Traveling particles in two dimensional CA can therefore look like expanding

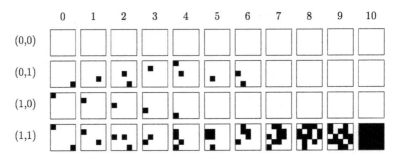

Fig. 3. This figure displays the iterations of a CA solving the AND problem. Every row shows the iteration of the rule using a different initial state. Note that in the first column ($t = 0$) the initial states are clearly visible and in the last column the coloring matches the output of an AND port

areas with a distinct border. But there might be multiple particles traveling at the same time, meeting each other and thereby creating new particles. This is why communication between cells in a two dimensional CA is not very visible in the Majority Problem, although results show that this communication is present.

4.2   AND and XOR Problem

To show the communication between cells in a two dimensional CA a different experiment was conducted. A genetic algorithm was used to evolve rules for two dimensional CA that could solve the simple binary operators AND and XOR. These operators both have two input values and one output value which can only be determined if both input values are known. This is unlike the OR operator for example where the output value is always one if one or more of the input values is one, so if only one input value is known to be one then the value of the other input value is not needed. This may look very trivial, but it is very important in order to force the CA to combine the two values and thereby communicate.

The AND Problem. To show the communications in a CA the information that needs to be combined must be initialized as far apart as possible. The following problem definition takes this into account: *Given a square CA with two 'input cells', one top left and one bottom right: find a rule that iterates the CA so that after I iterations the CA is in an 'all one' state if both the 'input cells' were one in the initial state and in an 'all zero' state otherwise.*

Small two dimensional CA were used with a width and a height of 5 cells and I was set to 10. The borders of the CA were unconnected to allow a larger virtual distance between the two corner cells. This means that the leftmost cell in a row was not connected to the rightmost cell in the same row and the topmost cell was not connected to the bottommost cell as was done with the Majority Problem experiment. Instead every cell on the border of the CA was connected to so called 'zero-cells'. These 'zero-cells' stay zero whatever happens.

When using two input cells, there are four different initial states. These states are written as $S_{(v_1,v_2)}$ where v_1 and v_2 are the two input values. All cells other than the two input cells are initialized with zero.

The fitness of a rule is defined as the total number of cells that have the correct values after I iterations. The number of ones in iteration t is written as $O^t_{(v_1,v_2)}$. The total fitness of the AND problem is defined as $f = (N - O^I_{(0,0)}) + (N - O^I_{(0,1)}) + (N - O^I_{(1,0)}) + O^I_{(1,1)}$. This makes the maximum fitness equal to $4 \times 5 \times 5 = 100$.

In this experiment another variation of the simple genetic algorithm was used. A generation step starts by sorting the rules according to their fitness. Then it selects the top ten% of the rules as 'elite' rules and copies them without changes to the next generation. Every 'elite' rule is then copied nine times or is used in single-point crossover to make the other 90% of the population. Both methods were tested and compared. The generated rules are mutated and also moved to the next generation. Mutation is done by flipping every bit in the rule with a probability p_m. The algorithm stops if it finds a rule with $f = 100$ or it reaches 1000 generations. In preliminary experiments a number of different values of p_m were tested. Setting p_m to a rather high value of 0.05 turned out to be the most effective choice, confirming our insight that with increasing selection strength higher mutation rates than the usual $\frac{1}{l}$ (l being the the length of the binary string) are performing better [1].

The algorithm was run 100 runs with and without single-point crossover and using both the von Neumann and the Moore neighborhoods. The results are shown in Table 1.

Although rules evolved with the von Neumann neighborhood are not able to solve the problem perfectly, it is already surprising that it finds rules which work for 93%, for such a rule only misplaces 7 cells in the final state. All the other 93 cells have the right value. This suggests that the information was combined, but the rule could not fill or empty the whole square using the same logic.

The Moore neighborhood is clearly more powerful and was able to solve the problem perfectly. The rules that are able to do this clearly show communicational behavior in the form of "traveling" information and processing this information at points where information "particles" meet.

Table 1. Fitness values found in the AND problem

| | Number of runs | | | |
| | Neumann | | Moore | |
Fitness	with crossover	without crossover	with crossover	without crossover
100	0	0	31	21
98-99	0	0	41	54
95-97	0	0	14	25
90-94	77	93	14	0
80-89	23	7	0	0
70-79	0	0	0	0
< 70	0	0	0	0

It is also surprising that using crossover in combination with a Neumann neighborhood does not outperform the same algorithm without the crossover. This may be due to the order of the bits in the transition rule and their meaning. This is worth exploring in future work. Maybe using other forms of crossover might give better results in combination with multi dimensional CA.

The XOR Problem. The XOR Problem is not much different from the AND problem. We used the same genetic algorithm and the same CA setup. The only difference is the fitness function. We defined the XOR problem as follows: *Given a square CA with two 'input cells', one top left and one bottom right: find a rule that iterates the CA so that after I iterations the CA is in an 'all one' state if only one of the 'input cells' was one in the initial state and in an 'all zero' state otherwise.* This means that the total fitness of the XOR problem is defined as $f = (N - O^I_{(0,0)}) + O^I_{(0,1)} + O^I_{(1,0)} + (N - O^I_{(1,1)})$.

The algorithm was run with $p_m = 0.05$ for a maximum of 1000 generations for 100 runs with both Neumann and Moore neighborhoods with and without single point crossover. The results are shown in Table 2.

Table 2. Fitness values found in the XOR problem

| | Number of runs | | | |
| | Neumann | | Moore | |
Fitness	with crossover	without crossover	with crossover	without crossover
100	0	0	0	1
98-99	0	0	4	4
95-97	0	0	7	6
90-94	2	1	19	21
80-89	76	96	69	66
70-79	18	3	1	2
< 70	4	0	0	0

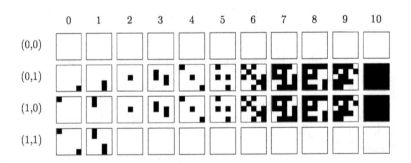

Fig. 4. This figure displays the iterations of a CA solving the XOR problem. Every row shows the iteration of the rule using a different initial state. Note that in the first column ($t = 0$) the initial states are clearly visible and in the last column the coloring matches the output of an XOR port

These results support earlier finding in suggesting that single-point crossover doesn't really improve the performance when used in a two dimensional CA. The results show that the algorithm using only mutation has found ways to solve this rather difficult communicational problem. The Neumann neighborhood seemed unable to perform for 100%, yet it came rather close with one rule classifying the problem for 92%. The algorithm found one transition rule using the Moore neighborhood that is able to solve the problem for the full 100%. This rule depicted in Figure 4 shows clear signs of "traveling particles" and is another example of how a local rule can trigger global behavior.

5   Evolving Bitmaps

Now that it is shown that two dimensional CA can communicate, it is time to increase the challenge for the CA a bit. The aim of this experiment is to evolve rules for two dimensional CA that generate patterns (or bitmaps).

The Bitmap Problem is defined as follows: *Given an initial state and a specific desired end state: find a rule that iterates from the initial state to the desired state in less than I iterations.* Note that this does not require the number of iterations between the initial and the desired state to be fixed.

The CA used in this experiment is not very different from the one used in the AND/XOR experiment (section 4.2). In preliminary experiments we tried different sizes of CA, but decided to concentrate on small square bitmaps with a width and a height of 5 cells (as done in section 4.2). To make the problem harder and to stay in line with earlier experiments the CA have unconnected borders like in section 4.2. The von Neumann neighborhood was chosen instead of the Moore neighborhood and therefore s_n consist of 5 cells ($r = 1$) and a rule can be described with $2^5 = 32$ bits. The search space therefore is $2^{32} = 4294967296$.

After testing different initial states, the 'single seed' state was chosen and defined as the state in which all the positions in the CA are zero except the position ($\lfloor width/2 \rfloor, \lfloor height/2 \rfloor$) which is one. For the GA we used the same algorithm as we used in the AND and XOR experiments. Because this experiment uses a Neumann neighborhood and the AND and XOR experiments suggested that the combination between the von Neumann neighborhood and single point crossover was not a good idea, this experiment used only mutation. Like in section 4.2 mutation is performed by flipping every bit in the rule with a probability p_m. In this experiment $p_m = 1/32 = 0.03125$.

In trying to be as diverse as possible five totally different bitmaps were chosen, they are shown in Figure 5. The algorithm was run 100 times for every bitmap for a maximum of 5000 generations. The algorithm was able to find a rule for all the bitmaps, but some bitmaps seemed a bit more difficult than others. Table 3

Fig. 5. The bitmaps used in the pattern generation experiment

Table 3. Number of successful rules found per bitmap

Bitmap	Successful rules (out of a 100)
"square"	80
"hourglass"	77
"heart"	35
"smiley"	7
"letter"	9

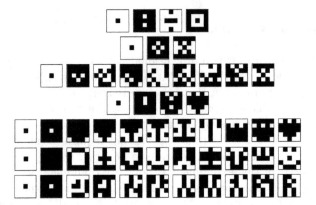

Fig. 6. This figure shows some iteration paths of successful transition rules

shows the number of successful rules for every bitmap. Note that symmetrical bitmaps seem to be easier to generate then asymmetric ones.

Although this experiment is fairly simple, it does show that a GA can be used to evolve transition rules in two dimensional CA that are able to generate patterns even with a simple von Neumann neighborhood. Ongoing experiments with bigger CA suggest that they don't differ much from these small ones, although the restrictions on what can be generated from a single-seed state using only a von Neumann neighborhood seem to be bigger when size of the CA increases.

6 Conclusions

The aim of the experiment reported in this paper was to demonstrate the capability of evolutionary algorithms, here a fairly standard genetic algorithm, to parameterize other methods such as, specifically, cellular automata. From the experimental results reported, one can conclude that this kind of inverse design of CA is possible by means of evolutionary computation in a clear, straightforward, and very powerful way. The results clearly indicate that real world applications of CA could also be tackled by this approach, and the unconventional programming of CA by means of EA's is not only a possibility, but a useful and efficient method to parameterize this kind of algorithm.

References

1. Th. Bäck, D. B. Fogel, and editors Michalewicz, Z., editors. *Handbook of Evolutionary Computation.* Oxford University Press and Institute of Physics Publishing, Bristol/New York, 1997.
2. D. B. Fogel. *Evolutionary Computation: Toward a New Philosophy of Machine Intelligence.* IEEE Press, Piscataway, New York, 1995.
3. L. Fogel, A. Owens, and M. Walsh. *Artificial Intelligence through Simulated Evolution.* John Wiley and Sons, 1966.
4. D. E. Goldberg. *Genetic Algorithms in Search, Optimization and Machine Learning.* Addison-Wesley, 1989.
5. D. E. Goldberg. *The Design of Invocation:Lessons from and for Competent Genetic Algorithms.* Kluwer Academic Publishers, 2002.
6. J. H. Holland. *Adaptation in Natural and Artificial Systems.* The University of Michigan Press, Ann Arbor, 1975.
7. S. Inverso, D. Kunkle, and C. Merrigan. Evolutionary methods for 2-d cellular automata computation. www.cs.rit.edu/~drk4633/mypapers/gacaProj.pdf, 2002.
8. J. R. Koza. *Genetic Programming: On the Programming of Computers by Natural Selection.* MIT Press, Cambridge, MA, 1992.
9. J. R. Koza, M. A. Keane, M. J. Streeter, W. Mydlowec, J. Yu, and G. Lanza. *Genetic Programming IV: Routine Human-Competitive Machine Intelligence.* Kluwer Academic Publishers, 2003.
10. M. Mitchell and J.P. Crutchfield. The evolution of emergent computation. Technical report, Proceedings of the National Academy of Sciences, SFI Technical Report 94-03-012, 1994.
11. M. Mitchell, J.P. Crutchfield, and P.T. Hraber. Evolving cellular automata to perform computations: Mechanisms and impediments. *Physica D*, 75:361–391, 1994.
12. I. Rechenberg. *Evolutionsstrategie: Optimierung technischer Systeme nach Prinzipien der biologischen Evolution.* Fromman-Holzboog Verlag, Stuttgart, 1973.
13. I. Rechenberg. *Evolutionsstrategie '94.* Fromman-Holzboog Verlag, Stuttgart, 1994.
14. H. P. Schwefel. Numerische optimierung von computer-modellen mittels der evolutionsstrategie. *Interdisciplinary Systems Research*, 26, 1977.
15. H. P. Schwefel. *Evolution and Optimum Seeking.* Wiley, New York, 1995.
16. S. Wolfram. Statistical mechanics of cellular automata. *Reviews of Modern Physics*, 55, 1983.

Design, Simulation, and Experimental Demonstration of Self-assembled DNA Nanostructures and Motors

John H. Reif, Thomas H. LaBean, Sudheer Sahu,
Hao Yan, and Peng Yin

Department of Computer Science, Duke University,
Box 90129, Durham, NC 27708-0129, USA
{reif, thl, sudheer, hy1, py}@cs.duke.edu

Abstract. Self-assembly is the spontaneous self-ordering of substructures into superstructures, driven by the selective affinity of the substructures. Complementarity of DNA bases renders DNA an ideal material for programmable self-assembly of nanostructures. DNA self-assembly is the most advanced and versatile system that has been experimentally demonstrated for programmable construction of patterned systems on the molecular scale. The methodology of DNA self-assembly begins with the synthesis of single strand DNA molecules that self-assemble into macromolecular building blocks called DNA tiles. These tiles have single strand "sticky ends" that complement the sticky ends of other DNA tiles, facilitating further assembly into larger structures known as DNA tiling lattices. In principle, DNA tiling assemblies can form any computable two or three-dimensional pattern, however complex, with the appropriate choice of the tiles' component DNA. Two-dimensional DNA tiling lattices composed of hundreds of thousands of tiles have been demonstrated experimentally. These assemblies can be used as programmable scaffolding to position molecular electronics and robotics components with precision and specificity, facilitating fabrication of complex nanoscale devices. We overview the evolution of DNA self-assembly techniques from pure theory, through simulation and design, and then to experimental practice. In particular, we begin with an overview of theoretical models and algorithms for DNA lattice self-assembly. Then we describe our software for the simulation and design of DNA tiling assemblies and DNA nano-mechanical devices. As an example, we discuss models, algorithms, and computer simulations for the key problem of error control in DNA lattice self-assembly. We then briefly discuss our laboratory demonstrations of DNA lattices and motors, including those using the designs aided by our software. These experimental demonstrations of DNA self-assemblies include the assembly of patterned objects at the molecular scale, the execution of molecular computations, and the autonomous DNA walking and computing devices.

1   Introduction

Self-assembly is the spontaneous self-ordering of substructures into superstructures driven by the selective affinity of the substructures. This paper focuses on a method for self-assembly known as *DNA self-assembly*, where DNA provides a molecular scale material for effecting this programmable self-assembly, using the selective affinity of

J.-P. Banâtre et al. (Eds.): UPP 2004, LNCS 3566, pp. 173–187, 2005.

pairs of DNA strands to form DNA nanostructures. Self-assembling nanostructures composed of DNA molecules offer great potential for bottom-up nanofabrication of materials and objects with smaller features than ever previously possible [13, 30, 37]. The methodology of DNA self-assembly begins with the synthesis of single-strand DNA molecules that self-assemble into macromolecular building blocks called DNA tiles. These tiles have sticky ends that match the sticky ends of other DNA tiles, facilitating further assembly into larger structures known as DNA tiling lattices. In principle, DNA tiling assemblies can be made to form any computable two- or three-dimensional pattern, however complex, with the appropriate choice of the tiles' component DNA.

DNA self-assembly is an emerging subfield of nanoscience with the development of its theoretical basis and a number of moderate to large-scale experimental demonstrations. Recent experimental results indicate that this technique is scalable. Periodic 2D DNA lattices have been successfully constructed with a variety of DNA tiles [15, 23, 52, 56]. These lattices are composed of up to hundreds of thousands of tiles. Molecular imaging devices such as atomic force microscopes and transmission electron microscopes allow visualization of these self-assembled two-dimensional DNA tiling lattices. These assemblies can be used as scaffolding on which to position molecular electronics and other components such as molecular sensors with precision and specificity. The programmability lets this scaffolding have the patterning required for fabricating complex devices made of these components. Potential applications of DNA self-assembly and scaffolding include nanoelectronics, biosensors, and programmable/autonomous molecular machines.

In addition to manufacturing DNA lattices, DNA has also been demonstrated to be a useful material for molecular computing systems [1, 3, 6, 21, 22] and mechanical devices [19, 24, 57, 63]. In particular, the self-assembly of DNA tiles can also be used as a powerful computational mechanism [16, 27, 47, 49], which in theory holds universal computing power [53]. See [32] for a more detailed survey of current experimental work in self-assembled DNA nanostructures. Also, see [26] and [30] for comprehensive surveys of the larger field of DNA computation (also known as biomolecular computation).

In this paper, we overview the evolution of DNA self-assembly techniques from pure theory, through simulation and design, and then to experimental practice. The rest of the paper is organized as follows. In Section 2, we overview the theoretical work in self-assembly. In Section 3, we describe software for the simulation and design of DNA nanostructures and motors. As a concrete example, in Section 4 we discuss error control, which we feel is a major theoretical and practical challenge remaining in the area of DNA self-assembly. Finally, in Section 5 we give a discussion of experimental practice in DNA nanostructures.

2   The Theory of Self-assembly

This section overviews the emerging theory of self-assembly.

Domino Tiling Problems. The theoretical basis for self-assembly has its roots in *Domino Tiling Problems* (also known as Wang tilings) as defined by Wang [45]. For comprehensive text, see [10]. The input is a finite set of unit size square tiles. The sides of each square are labeled with symbols over a finite alphabet. Additional restrictions may include the initial placement of a subset of the these tiles, and the dimensions of the region where tiles must be placed. Assuming an arbitrarily large supply of each tile, the problem is to place the tiles, without rotation (a criterion that cannot apply to physical tiles), to completely fill the given region so that each pair of abutting tiles have identical symbols on their contacting sides.

Turing-universal and NP-Complete Self-assemblies. Domino tiling problems over an infinite domain with only a constant number of tiles were first proved by Berger to be undecidable [7]. This and subsequent proofs [7, 33] rely on constructions where tiling patterns simulate single-tape Turing machines or cellular arrays [53]. Winfree later showed that computation by self-assembly is Turing-universal [53] and so tiling self-assemblies can theoretically provide arbitrarily complex assemblies even with a constant number of distinct tile types. Winfree also demonstrated various families of assemblies which can be viewed as computing languages from families of the Chomsky hierarchy [47]. It has been proved that Domino tiling problems over polynomial-size regions are NP-complete [17]. Subsequently, [47], [11, 12], and [16] proposed the use of self-assembly processes (in the context of DNA tiling and nanostructures) to solve NP-complete combinatorial search problems such as SAT and graph coloring.

Program-size Complexity of Tiling Self-assemblies. The programming of tiling assemblies is determined simply by the set of tiles, their pads, and sometimes the choice of the initial seed tile (a special tile from which the growth of the assembly starts). A basic issue is the number of distinct tile types required to produce a specified tile assembly. The *program size complexity* of a specified tiling is the number of distinct tiles (with replacement) to produce it. Rothemund and Winfree showed that the assembly of an $n \times n$ size square can be done using $\Theta(\log n / \log \log n)$ distinct tiles and that the largest square uniquely produced by a tiling of a given number of distinct tiles grows faster than any computable function [34]. Adleman recently gave program size complexity bounds for tree shaped assemblies [3].

Massively Parallel Computation by Tiling. Parallelism reveals itself in many ways in computation by self-assembly. Each superstructure may contain information representing a different calculation (*global parallelism*). Due to the extremely small size of DNA strands, as many as 10^{18} DNA tiling assemblies may be made simultaneously in a small test tube. Growth on each individual superstructure may also occur at many locations simultaneously via *local parallelism*. The *depth* of a tiling superstructure is the maximum number of self-assembly reactions experienced by any substructure (the depth of the graph of reaction events), and the *size* of a superstructure is the number of tiles it contains. Likewise we can define the number of layers for a superstructure. For example, a superstructure consisting of an array of $n \times m$ tiles, where $n > m$ has m layers. Tiling systems with low depth, small size, and few layers are considered desirable, motivating the search for efficient computations performed by such systems. Reif was the first to consider the parallel depth complexity of tiling assemblies and gave DNA self-assemblies of linear size and logarithmic depth for a number of fundamental problems (e.g., prefix computation, finite state automata simulation, and string fingerprinting, etc.) that form the basis for the design of many parallel algorithms [27]. Furthermore, [27] showed that these elementary operations can be combined to perform more complex computations, such as bitonic sorting and general circuit evaluation with polylog depth assemblies.

Linear Self-assemblies. Tiling systems that produce only superstructures with k layers, for some constant k, are said to use *linear self-assembly*. [27] gave some simple linear tiling self-assemblies for integer addition as well as related operations (e.g., prefix XOR summing of n Boolean bits). Seeman's group demonstrated the first example of DNA computation using DNA tiling self-assembly [22], as described in Section 5. These linear tilings were refined in [51] to a class of String tilings that have been the basis for further DNA tiling experiments in [54] described in Section 5.

Kinetic Models of Tiling Self-assembly Processes. Domino tiling problems do not presume or require a specific process for tiling. Winfree first observed that self-assembly processes can be used for computation via the construction of DNA tiling lattices [46]. The sides of the tiles are assumed to have some methodology for selective affinity, which we call *pads*. Pads function as programmable binding domains, which hold together the tiles. Each pair of pads have specified binding strengths. The self-assembly process is initiated by a singleton tile (the *seed tile*) and proceeds by tiles binding together at their pads to form aggregates known as *tiling assemblies*. The preferential matching of tile pads facilitates the further assembly into tiling assemblies. Using the kinetic modeling techniques of physical chemistry, Winfree developed a kinetic model for the self-assembly of DNA tiles [48]. Following the classical literature of models for crystal assembly processes, Winfree considers assembly processes where the tiling assembly is only augmented by single tiles (known in crystallography as *monomers*) which bind to the assembly at their tile pads [46]. The likelihood of a particular tile binding at (or dissociating from) a particular site of the assembly is assumed to be a fixed probability dependent on that tile's concentration, the respective pad's binding affinity, and a temperature parameter. In addition, Adleman developed stochastic differential equation models for self-assembly of tiles and determined equilibrium probability distributions and convergence rates for some 1-dimensional self-assemblies [2, 4]. His model allowed for binding between subassemblies and assumed a fixed probability for tile binding events independent of the size of tile assemblies. Since the movement of tile assemblies may depend on their size (and thus mass), this model might in the future be refined to make the probability for tile binding events dependent on the size of tile assemblies.

Optimization of Tiling Assembly Processes. There are various techniques that may promote assembly processes in practice. One important technique is the tuning of the parameters (tile concentration, temperature, etc.) governing the kinetics of the process. Adleman considers the problem of determining tile concentrations for given assemblies and conjectures this problem is $\sharp$P-complete [3]. Various other techniques may improve convergence rates to the intended assembly. A blockage of tiling assembly process can occur if an incorrect tile binds in an unintended location of the assembly. While such a tile may be dislodged by the kinetics of subsequent time steps, it still may slow down the convergence rate of the tiling assembly process to the intended final assembly. To reduce the possibility of blockages of tiling assembly processes, Reif proposed the use of distinct tile pads for distinct time steps during the assembly [27]. [27] also described the use of self-assembled tiling *nano-frames* to constrain the region of the tiling assemblies.

3   Simulation and Design Software

Software for Kinetic Simulation of Tiling Assembly Processes. Winfree developed software for discrete time simulation of the tiling assembly processes, using approximate probabilities for the insertion or removal of individual tiles from the assembly [48]. These simulations gave an approximation to the kinetics of self-assembly chemistry and provided some validation of the feasibility of tiling self-assembly processes. Using this software as a basis, our group developed an improved simulation software package (sped up by use of an improved method for computing on/off likelihood suggested by Winfree) with a Java interface for a number of example tilings, such as string tilings for integer addition and XOR computations. In spite of an extensive literature on the kinetics of the assembly of regular crystalline lattices, the fundamental thermodynamic and kinetic aspects of self-assembly of tiling assemblies are still not yet well understood. For example, the effect of distinct tile concentrations and different relative numbers of tiles is not yet known; probably it will require an application of Le Chatelier's principle.

Software for Kinetic Simulation of Nanomechanical Devices. We have developed a software to simulate autonomous nanomechanical DNA devices driven by ligase and restriction enzymes in a solution system. This software does discrete time simulation of the ligation and restriction events on the DNA duplex fragments of the nanomechanical device. The approximate probabilities of ligation is calculated based on the concentrations of individual DNA fragments present in the solution system. These simulations can provide insight to the kinetics of such nanomechanical systems. We have used this software to simulate a DNA walker and a universal DNA Turing machine.

Software for Design of DNA Lattices and Nanomechanical Devices. A major computational challenge in constructing DNA objects is to optimize the selection of DNA sequences so that the DNA strands can correctly assemble into desired DNA secondary structures. A commonly used software package, *Sequin*, was developed by Seeman, which uses the symmetry minimization algorithm [35]. Sequin, though very useful, only provides a text-line interface and generally requires the user to step through the entire sequence selection process. Our lab recently developed a software package, *TileSoft*, which exploits an evolution algorithm and fully automates the sequence selection process [58]. TileSoft also provides the user with a graphical user interface, on which DNA secondary structure and accompanying design constraints can be directly specified and the optimized sequence information can be pictorially displayed. TileSoft is initially designed to solve optimization problem for a set of multiple tiles, but can also be used to design individual DNA objects, such as DNA nanomechanical devices.

4   Error Control in DNA Tiling Assemblies

A chief challenge in DNA tiling self-assemblies is the control of assembly errors. This is particularly relevant to computational self-assemblies, which, with complex patterning at the molecular scale, are prone to a quite high rate of error, ranging from approximately between 0.5% to 5%, and the key barrier to large-scale experimental implementation of 2D computational DNA tilings exhibiting patterning is this significant error rate in the self-assembly process. The limitation and/or elimination of these errors in self-assembly is perhaps the single most important major challenge to nanostructure self-assembly.

There are a number of possible methods to decrease errors in DNA tilings:

(a) Annealing Temperature Optimization. This is a well known technique used in hybridization and also crystallization experiments. It can be used to decrease the defect rates at the expense of increased overall annealing time duration. In the context of DNA tiling lattices, the parameters for the temperature variation that minimize defects have not yet been determined.

(b) Error Control by Step-wise Assembly. Reif suggested the use of serial self-assembly to decrease errors in self-assembly [26].

(c) Error Control by Redundancy. There are a number of ways to introduce redundancy into a computational tiling assembly. In [31] we describe a simple method that can be developed for linear tiling assemblies: we replace each tile with a stack of three tiles executing the same function, and then add additional tiles that essentially 'vote' on the pad associations associated with these redundant tiles. This results in a tiling of increased complexity but still linear size. This error resistant design can easily be applied to the integer addition linear tiling described above, and similar redundancy methods may be applied to higher dimension tilings.

Work in 2003 by Winfree provided a method to decrease tiling self-assembly errors without decreasing the intrinsic error rate of assembling a single tile, however, his technique resulted in a final assembled structure that is four times the size of the original one [50].

Recently we have developed improved methods for compact error-resilient self-assembly of DNA tiling assemblies and analyzed them by probabilistic analysis, kinetic analysis, and computer simulation [29]; and plan to demonstrate these error-resilient self-assembly methods by a series of laboratory experiments. Our compact error-resilient tiling methods do not increase the size of the tiling assembly. They use 2-way overlay redundancy such that a single pad mismatch between a tile and its immediate neighbor forces at least one further pad mismatch between a pair of adjacent tiles in the neighborhood of this tile. Theoretical probabilistic analysis and empirical studies of the computer simulation of Sierpinsky Triangle tilings have been used to validate these error-resilient 2-way overlay redundancy tiling results; the analysis shows that the error rate is considerably reduced.

5 Experimental Progress

DNA Hybridization. Single strand DNA is a polymer that consists of a sequence of four types of bases grouped into two disjoint pairs known as Watson-Crick complementary pairs that can bind together through hydrogen bonding in an operation known as hybridization. DNA enjoys a unique advantage for a nanostructure construction material because two single strands of DNA can be designed and constructed by the experimental scientist to be selectively sticky and bind together to form doubly stranded DNA. Hybridization is much more likely to occur if the DNA base sequences are complementarythat is, if the component bases are Watson-Crick pairs and the temperature and ionic composition of the solution are set appropriately. The resulting doubly stranded DNA is relatively rigid and forms the well-known double-helix geometry. If the sticky single-strand segments that hybridize abut doubly stranded segments of DNA, one can use an enzymic reaction known as ligation to concatenate these segments.

DNA Nanostructures. Seeman first pioneered DNA structure nanofabrication in the 1980s by assembling a multitude of DNA nanostructures (such as rings, cubes, and octahedrons) using DNA branched junctions and remains a leader in this area [38, 36, 39]. However, these early DNA nanostructures were not very rigid. To increase the rigidity of DNA nanostructures, Seeman made use of a DNA nanostructure known as a DNA crossover (also known as a *branched Holiday junction*), which consists of two doubly stranded DNA, each having a single strand that crosses over to the other. Pairs of crossovers, known as double crossovers, provide a significant increase in rigidity of a DNA nanostructure. Also, certain crossovers (known as antiparallel crossovers) cause a reversal in the direction of strand propagation following the exchange of the strand to a new helix.

DNA Tiles. These are quite rigid and stable DNA nanostructures that are formed from multiple DNA antiparallel crossovers. DNA tiles typically have a roughly rectangular geometry. These tiles come in multiple varieties that differ from one another in the geometry of strand exchange and the topology of the strand paths through the tile. The first DNA tiles developed were known as double-crossover(DX) tiles and composed of two DNA double helices with two crossovers [52]. LaBean, Reif, and Seeman have developed some novel DNA tiles known as triple-crossover (TX) tiles that are composed of three DNA double helices with four crossovers [15]. These TX tiles have properties that can facilitate one and two dimensional tiling assemblies and computations. Each DNA tile is designed to match the ends of certain other DNA tiles, a process that facilitates the assembly into tiling lattices. In particular, DNA tiles are designed to contain several short sections of unpaired, single-strand DNA (ssDNA) extending from the ends of selected helices (often called "sticky ends") that function as programmable binding domains, which are the *tile pads*. Both double- and triple-crossover tiles are useful for doing tiling assemblies. The DX tiles provide up to four pads for encoding associations with neighboring tiles, whereas the TX tiles provide up to six pads that are designed to function as binding domains with other DNA tiles. Use of pads with complementary base sequences provides control for the neighbor relations of tiles in the final assembly. In particular, the tile pads hybridize to the pads of other chosen DNA tiles. Individual tiles interact by binding with other specific tiles through hybridization of their pads to self-assemble into desired superstructures.

DNA Tiling Lattices. These are superstructures built up from smaller component structures (DNA tiles). Individual DNA tiles interact by annealing with other specific tiles via their ssDNA pads to self-assemble into desired superstructures. These lattices can be either: (a) *non-computational*, containing a fairly small number of distinct tile types in a repetitive, periodic pattern; or (b) *computational*, containing a larger number of tile types with more complicated association rules which perform a computation during lattice assembly. The direct assembly of DNA lattices from component single strand

DNA has been demonstrated for non-computational DNA lattices described below. Winfree and Seeman demonstrated the self-assembly of two-dimensional periodic lattices consisting of at hundreds of thousands of double-crossover tiles, which is strong evidence of this approach's scalability [52]. In addition, LaBean, Reif, and Seeman have constructed DNA TX molecules which produced tiling lattices of even larger numbers of tiles [15]. Both classes of self-assembled DNA lattices were observed through atomic force microscopy (AFM), a mechanical scanning process that provides images of molecular structures on a two-dimensional plate, as well as by use of transmission electron microscopy (TEM). Distinguishing surface features can be designed into individual tiles by slightly modifying the DNA strands comprising the tiles. These modified DNA strands form short loops that protrude above the tile. To enhance definition, we have also affixed metallic balls to these DNA loops using known methods for affixing gold balls to DNA. Surface features, such as two-dimensional banding patterns, have been programmed into these DNA lattices using DNA tiles that assemble into regular repetitive patterns. These topographical features were observed on the DNA tiling lattices with atomic force and transmission electron microscopy imaging devices [23, 20, 52]. These tiling assemblies had no fixed limit on their size. Recall that Reif introduced the concept of a *nano-frame*, which is a self-assembled nanostructure that constrains the subsequent timing assembly (*e.g.*, to a fixed size rectangle) [26]. A tiling assembly might be designed to be *self-delineating* (growing to only a fixed size) by the choice of tile pads that essentially "count" to their intended boundaries in the dimensions to be delineated. In addition, our lab recently developed a "waffle"-like DNA lattice composed of a novel type of DNA tiles (4 x 4 tile) [56]. We further used the 4 x 4 tiling lattices as templates for organizing nanoscale ligands, *e.g.* proteins and gold nano-particles [18, 25]. In addition, we have recently developed a new method for the assembly of aperiodic patterns [55].

Directed Nucleation Assembly Techniques. We have recently developed another method for assembly of complex patterns, where an input DNA strand is synthesized that encodes the required pattern, and then specified tiles assemble around blocks of this input DNA strand, forming the required 1D or 2D pattern of tiles [55]. This method uses artificially synthesized DNA strands that specify the pattern and around which 2D DNA tiles assemble into the specified pattern; in this method, the permanent features of the 2D pattern are generated uniquely for each case.

Computation by DNA Self-assembly. We now focus on another approach: computation by self-assembly. Adleman made use of a simple form of computation by self-assembly in his original experiment [1]: instead of blindly generating all possible sequences of vertices; instead, the oligonucleotide sequences and the logic of Watson-Crick complementarity guide the self-assembly processes so that only valid paths are generated.

Programming Self-assembly of DNA Tilings. Programming DNA self-assembly of tilings amounts to the design of the pads of the DNA tiles (recall these are sticky ends of single strand DNA that function as programmable binding domains, and that individual tiles interact by annealing with other specific tiles via their single strand DNA pads to self-assemble into desired superstructures). The use of pads with complementary base sequences allows the neighbor relations of tiles in the final assembly to be intimately controlled; thus the only large-scale superstructures formed during assembly are those that encode valid mappings of input to output. The self-assembly approach for computation only uses four laboratory steps:(i) mixing the input oligonucleotides to form the DNA tiles, (ii) allowing the tiles to self-assemble into superstructures, (iii) ligating strands that have been co-localized, and (iv) then performing a single separation to identify the correct output.

The Speed of Computing via DNA Tiling Assemblies (Compared with Silicon-based Computing). The speed of DNA tiling assemblies is limited by the annealing time, which can be many minutes, and can be 10^{10} slower than a conventional computer. A DNA computation via self-assembly must take into account the fact that the time to execute an assembly can range from a few minutes up to hours. Therefore, a reasonable assessment of the power of DNA computation must take into account both the speed of operation as well as the degree of massive parallelism. Nevertheless, the massive parallelism (both within assemblies and also via the parallel construction of distinct assemblies) possibly ranging up to 10^{18} provides a potential that may be advantageous for classes of computational problems that can be parallelized.

String-Tiles: A Mechanism for Small-Depth Tiling. An approach for small-depth computations is to compress several tile layers into single tiles, so that the simplest form of linear self-assembly suffices. Linear self-assembly schemes for integer addition were first described by [26]; in this scheme each tile performed essentially the operation of a single carry-bit logic step. This linear self-assembly approach works particularly well when the topology and routing of the strands in the DNA tiles is carefully considered, leading to the notion of string tiles. The concept of string tile assemblies derives from the observation that allowing neighboring tiles in an assembly to associate by two sticky ends on each side, one could increase the computational complexity of languages generated by linear self-assembly [51] showed that by allowing contiguous strings of DNA to trace through individual tiles and the entire assembly multiple times, surprisingly sophisticated calculations can be performed with one-layer linear assemblies of string tiles. The TAE tiles recently developed by LaBean [15] are particularly useful as string tiles. An experimental demonstration of the string tiles was achieved in our lab [54].

Input/Output to Tiling Assemblies Using Scaffold and Reporter Strands. Recall that the TX tiles are constructed of three double-helices linked by strand exchange. The TX tiles have an interesting property, namely that certain distinguished single stranded DNA (to be called scaffold and reporter strands, respectively) wind through all the tiles of a tiling assembly. This property provides a more sophisticated method for input and output of DNA computations in string tiling assemblies. In particular, there are two types. The TAE tile contains an Even (and the TAO tiles contains an Odd) number of helical half-turns between crossover points. Even spacing of crossovers of the TAE tile allows reporter strands to stretch straight through each helix from one side of the tile to the other. These reporter segments are used for building up a long strand which records inputs and outputs for the entire assembly computations.

(a) **Input via Scaffold Strands:** We take as input the scaffold strands and which encode the data input to the assembly computation. They are long DNA strands capable of serving as nucleation points for assembly. Preformed, multimetric scaffold strands are added to the hybridization/annealing mixture in place of the monomeric oligo corresponding to the tile's reporter segment. The remaining portion of the component ssDNA comprising the tiles are also added. In the resulting annealing process, tiles assemble around the scaffold strand, automatically forming a chain of connected tiles which can subsequently be used as the input layer in a computational assembly.

(b) **Output via Reporter Strands:** After ligation of the tiling assembly (this joins together each tile's segments of the reporter strands), the reporter strand provides an encoding of the output of the tiling assembly computation (and typically also the inputs). Note this input/output can occur in parallel for multiple distinct tiling assemblies. Finally, the tiling assembly is disassembled by denaturing (*e.g.*, via heating) and the resulting ssDNA Reporter Strands provide the result (these may be used as scaffold strands for later cycles of assembly computation, or the readout may be by PCR, restriction cutting, sequencing, or DNA expression chips).

One Dimensional DNA Tiling Computations for Parallel Arithmetic. We now outline procedures for using the string tiles described above that self-assemble into linear tiling assemblies to perform massively parallel arithmetic. LaBean *et. al.* describes tile systems that compute binary number addition (where the binary numbers are encoded by strands of DNA) by using two distinct sets of sticky-ends between adjacent tiles in the assembly to effectively communicate the values of the carry-bits [14]. (They can also be used for computation of bit-wise XOR of Boolean vectors encoded by strands of DNA.) The assemblies result in the appending of these strands to the addition sums. For computations on specific inputs, these procedures make use of the scaffold strands mentioned above. The inputs are self-assembled strands of DNA composed of sequences DNA words encoding the pairs of binary numbers to be summed. Otherwise, the input tiles can be (using known techniques uses for the assembly of combinatorial libraries of DNA strands) randomly assembled and thereby generate a molecular look-up table in which each reporter strand encodes the random inputs and resultant outputs of a single calculation. After denaturing the assemblies back to individual strands, one may sample the resulting reporter strands to verify the outputs are correctly computed. A sufficient number of DNA tile molecules provide full coverage of all possible n-bit input strings. Such look-up tables may be useful as input for further computations as they represent a unique library of sequences with a complex structural theme. An experimental demonstration of an XOR tiling computation based on TAO tiles is reported in [22].

Two Dimensional DNA Tiling Computations. In the immediate future, it may be possible to extend the one dimensional DNA tiling assembly methods to two dimensional tilings, and to demonstrate these methods experimentally. One interesting goal is integer multiplication. The most direct and relatively straightforward way is to multiply via repeated additions and bit shifts, applying known VLSI systolic array architecture designs for integer multiplication. This would require a two dimensional $n \times n$ tiling assembly, with some increased complexity over the linear assembly for integer addition. On the other hand, it will provide the first demonstration of computation of a two dimensional DNA self-assembly. Two dimensional computational tilings may also be used to do logical processing. Lagoudakis and LaBean proposed a 2D DNA self-assembly for Boolean variable satisfiability, which uses parallel construction of multiple self-assembling 2D DNA lattices to solve the problem [16]. Such methods for solving combinatorial search problems do not scale well with the input size (the number of parallel tiling assemblies grows exponentially with the number of Boolean variables of the formula). However, similar constructions may be used for evaluating Boolean queries and circuits in massively parallel fashion, for multiple input settings of the input Boolean variable, and in this context it may be appropriate to consider the Boolean formula to be of fixed size.

Three Dimensional DNA Tiling Computations. There is a number of possible methods for executing computations experimentally on 3D DNA lattices, providing computations with (implicit) data movement in three dimensions. Matrix inner product might be executed by a three dimensional computational tiling by applying known VLSI systolic array architecture designs for matrix inner product. Another possible three dimensional computational tiling is that of the time-evolution (time is the third dimension of the tiling) of a 2D cellular automata, *e.g.*, 2D cellular automata simulation of fluid flow.

DNA Robotics. Existing DNA nanomechanical devices can exhibit motions such as open/close [42, 43, 63], extension/contraction [5, 9, 19], and rotation [24, 57]. These motions are mediated by external environmental changes such as the addition and removal of DNA fuel strands [5, 9, 19, 42, 43, 57, 63] or the change of ionic strength of the solution [24]. Our lab has recently constructed a robust sequence-dependent DNA nanomechanical actuator and have incorporated it into a 2D parallelogram DNA lattice [23]. The actuator can be switched reversibly between two states, mediated by the addition and removal of fuel DNA strands.

An improvement of the above devices is the construction of DNA nanomechanical devices that achieve autonomous and non-localized motions, *e.g.* walking motion. Turberfield and colleagues have designed a free running DNA machine [44] using DNA as fuels. Mao's group recently constructed autonomous DNA tweezers powered by a DNA enzyme [8]. Seeman's group and Pierce's group respectively constructed a non-autonomous DNA walking device powered by the addition and removal of DNA fuel strands [40, 41]. In our group, Reif designed an autonomous DNA walking device and an autonomous DNA rolling device that move in a random bidirectional fashion along DNA tracks [28]. Building on Reif's original designs, we designed a suite of unidirectional autonomous DNA walking devices [60] and experimentally implemented one walking device in which a DNA fragment makes a 3-stop unidirectional motion along a self-assembled linear DNA track autonomously [62]. Based on this device, we further designed an autonomous universal DNA Turing machine [61] and autonomous universal DNA cellular automata [59]; their operations were verified with computer simulation.

6   Conclusion

The self-assembly of DNA is a promising emerging method for molecular scale constructions and computations. We have overviewed the area of DNA tiling self-assemblies and noted a number of open problems. We have discussed the potential approaches for error-control in self-assembly techniques for DNA computation; particularly the use of error-resilient modified tiling methods. We have identified some technological impacts of DNA assemblies, such as using them as platform for constructing molecular electronic and robotic devices. Important future work includes further investigating potential broader technological impacts of DNA lattices. Many applications of DNA lattices rely on the development of appropriate attachment methods between DNA lattice and other nanoparticles, which itself is a key challenge in DNA based nanoscience.

Acknowledgement

This work was supported by DARPA/AFSOR Contract F30602-01-2-0561, NSF ITR Grant EIA-0086015, DARPA/NSF Grant CCR-9725021, NSF QuBIC Grant EIA-0218376, and NSF QuBIC Grant EIA-0218359.

References

1. L. Adleman. Molecular computation of solutions to combinatorial problems. *Science*, 266:1021–1024, 1994.
2. L. Adleman. Towards a mathematical theory of self-assembly. Technical Report 00-722, University of Southern California, 2000.
3. L. Adleman, Q. Cheng, A. Goel, M.D. Huang, D. Kempe, P.M. de Espans, and P.W.K. Rothemund. Combinatorial optimization problems in self-assembly. In *Proceedings of the thirty-fourth annual ACM symposium on Theory of computing*, pages 23–32. ACM Press, 2002.
4. L. Adleman, Q. Cheng, A. Goel, M.D. Huang, and H. Wasserman. Linear self-assemblies: Equilibria, entropy, and convergence rate. In *Sixth International Conference on Difference Equations and Applications*, 2001.
5. P. Alberti and J.L. Mergny. DNA duplex-quadruplex exchange as the basis for a nanomolecular machine. *Proc. Natl. Acad. Sci. USA*, 100:1569–1573, 2003.
6. Y. Benenson, T. Paz-Elizur, R. Adar, E. Keinan, Z. Livneh, and E. Shapiro. Programmable and autonomous computing machine made of biomolecules. *Nature*, 414:430–434, 2001.
7. R. Berger. The undecidability of the domino problem. *Memoirs of the American Mathematical Society*, 66, 1966.
8. Y. Chen, M. Wang, and C. Mao. An autonomous DNA nanomotor powered by a DNA enzyme. *Angew. Chem. Int. Ed.*, 43:3554–3557, 2004.
9. L. Feng, S.H. Park, J.H. Reif, and H. Yan. A two-state DNA lattice switched by DNA nanoactuator. *Angew. Chem. Int. Ed.*, 42:4342–4346, 2003.
10. B. Grunbaum and G.C. Shepard. *Tilings and Patterns*, chapter 11. H Freeman and Company, 1986.
11. N. Jonoska and S. Karl. Ligation experiments in computing with dna. In *Proceedings of 1997 IEEE International Conference on Evolutionary Computation (ICEC'97)*, pages 261–265, 1997.
12. N. Jonoska, S.A. Karl, and M. Saito. Graph structures in dna computing. *Computing with Bio-Molecules, theory and experiments*, pages 93–110, 1998.

13. T.H. LaBean. Introduction to self-assembling DNA nanostructures for computation and nanofabrication. In *Computational Biology and Genome Informatics eds. J.T.L. Wang and C.H. Wu and and P. P. Wang ISBN 981-238-257-7 World Scientific Publishing Singapore*, 2003.
14. T.H. LaBean, E. Winfree, and J.H. Reif. Experimental progress in computation with DNA molecules. In *Proc. DNA Based Computers V*, 1999.
15. T.H. LaBean, H. Yan, J. Kopatsch, F. Liu, E. Winfree, J.H. Reif, and N.C. Seeman. The construction, analysis, ligation and self-assembly of DNA triple crossover complexes. *J. Am. Chem. Soc.*, 122:1848–1860, 2000.
16. M.G. Lagoudakis and T.H. LaBean. 2-D DNA self-assembly for satisfiability. In *DNA Based Computers V*, volume 54 of *DIMACS*, pages 141–154. American Mathematical Society, 2000.
17. H.R. Lewis and C.H. Papadimitriou. *Elements of the Theory of Computation*. Prentice-Hall, 1981.
18. H. Li, S.H. Park, J.H. Reif, T.H. LaBean, and H. Yan. DNA templated self-assembly of protein and nanoparticle linear arrays. *Journal of American Chemistry Society*, 126(2):418–419, 2004.
19. J. Li and W. Tan. A single DNA molecule nanomotor. *Nano Lett.*, 2:315–318, 2002.
20. D. Liu, S.H. Park, J.H. Reif, and T.H. LaBean. DNA nanotubes self-assembled from triple-crossover tiles as templates for conductive nanowires. *Proceedings of the National Academy of Science*, 101:717–722, 2004.
21. Q. Liu, L. Wang, A.G. Frutos, A.E. Condon, R.M. Corn, and L.M. Smith. DNA computing on surfaces. *Nature*, 403:175–179, 2000.
22. C. Mao, T.H. LaBean, J.H. Reif, and N.C. Seeman. Logical computation using algorithmic self-assembly of DNA triple-crossover molecules. *Nature*, 407:493–496, 2000.
23. C. Mao, W. Sun, and N.C. Seeman. Designed two-dimensional DNA holliday junction arrays visualized by atomic force microscopy. *J. Am. Chem. Soc.*, 121:5437–5443, 1999.
24. C. Mao, W. Sun, Z. Shen, and N.C. Seeman. A DNA nanomechanical device based on the B-Z transition. *Nature*, 397:144–146, 1999.
25. S.H. Park, P. Yin, Y. Liu, J.H. Reif, T.H. LaBean, and H. Yan. Programmable DNA self-assemblies for nanoscale organization of ligands and proteins. 2004. Submitted for publication.
26. J.H. Reif. Paradigms for biomolecular computation. In C. S. Calude, J. Casti, and M. J. Dinneen, editors, *First International Conference on Unconventional Models of Computation, Auckland, New Zealand*, pages 72–93. Springer Verlag, 1998.
27. J.H. Reif. Local parallel biomolecular computation. In H. Rubin and D. H. Wood, editors, *DNA-Based Computers 3*, volume 48 of *DIMACS*, pages 217–254. American Mathematical Society, 1999.
28. J.H. Reif. The design of autonomous DNA nanomechanical devices: Walking and rolling DNA. *Lecture Notes in Computer Science*, 2568:22–37, 2003. Published in Natural Computing, DNA8 special issue, Vol. 2, p 439-461, (2003).
29. J.H. Reif, S. Sahu, and P. Yin. Compact error-resilient computational DNA tiling assemblies. *Tenth International Meeting on DNA Based Computers (DNA10)*, 2004.
30. J.H. Reif. The emergence of the discipline of biomolecular computation. *Biomolecular Computing, New Generation Computing*, 20(3):217–236, 2002.
31. J.H. Reif. Molecular assembly and computation: From theory to experimental demonstrations. In *29-th International Colloquium on Automata, Languages, and Programming(ICALP), Mlaga, Spain*, pages 1–21, 2002.
32. J.H. Reif, T.H. LaBean, and N.C. Seeman. Challenges and applications for self-assembled dna nanostructures. In *Lecture Notes in Computer Science*, volume 2054, pages 173–198. Springer-Verlag, Berlin Heidelberg, 2001.

33. R.M. Robinson. Undecidability and non periodicity of tilings of the plane. *Inventiones Math*, 12:177–209, 1971.
34. P.W.K. Rothemund and E. Winfree. The program-size complexity of self-assembled squares (extended abstract). In *Proceedings of the thirty-second annual ACM symposium on Theory of computing*, pages 459–468. ACM Press, 2000.
35. N.C. Seeman. *De novo* design of sequences for nucleic acid structural engineering. *J. Biomol. Struct. Dyn.*, 8:573–581, 1990.
36. N.C. Seeman. Nucleic acid nanostructures and topology. *Angew. Chem. Int. Ed.*, 37:3220–3238, 1998.
37. N.C. Seeman. DNA in a material world. *Nature*, 421:427–431, 2003.
38. N.C. Seeman, Y. Zhang, and J. Chen. DNA nanoconstructions. *J. Vac. Sci. Technol.*, 12:4:1895–1903, 1994.
39. R. Sha, F. Liu, M.F. Bruist, and N.C. Seeman. Parallel helical domains in DNA branched junctions containing 5', 5' and 3', 3' linkages. *Biochemistry*, 38:2832–2841, 1999.
40. W.B. Sherman and N.C. Seeman. A precisely controlled DNA biped walking device. *Nano Lett.*, 4:1203–1207, 2004.
41. J.S. Shin and N.A. Pierce. A synthetic DNA walker for molecular transport. *J. Am. Chem. Soc.*, 126:10834–10835.
42. F.C. Simmel and B. Yurke. Using DNA to construct and power a nanoactuator. *Phys. Rev. E*, 63:041913, 2001.
43. F.C. Simmel and B. Yurke. A DNA-based molecular device switchable between three distinct mechanical states. *Appl. Phys. Lett.*, 80:883–885, 2002.
44. A.J. Turberfield, J.C. Mitchell, B. Yurke, Jr. A.P. Mills, M.I. Blakey, and F.C. Simmel. DNA fuel for free-running nanomachines. *Phys. Rev. Lett.*, 90:118102, 2003.
45. H. Wang. Proving theorems by pattern recognition ii. *Bell Systems Technical Journal*, 40:1–41, 1961.
46. E. Winfree. Complexity of restricted and unrestricted models of molecular computation. In R. J. Lipton and E. B. Baum, editors, *DNA Based Computers*, volume 27 of *DIMACS*, pages 187–198. American Mathematical Society, 1995.
47. E. Winfree. On the computational power of DNA annealing and ligation. In R. J. Lipton and E. B. Baum, editors, *DNA Based Computers 1*, volume 27 of *DIMACS*, pages 199–221. American Mathematical Society, 1996.
48. E. Winfree. *Algorithmic Self-Assembly of DNA*. PhD thesis, California Institute of Technology, 1998.
49. E. Winfree. Simulation of computing by self-assembly. Technical Report 1998.22, Caltech, 1998.
50. E. Winfree and R. Bekbolatov. Proofreading tile sets: logical error correction for algorithmic self-assembly. In *DNA Based Computers 9*, volume 2943 of *LNCS*, pages 126–144, 2004.
51. E. Winfree, T. Eng, and G. Rozenberg. String tile models for DNA computing by self-assembly. In *DNA Based Computers 6*, pages 63–88, 2000.
52. E. Winfree, F. Liu, L.A. Wenzler, and N.C. Seeman. Design and self-assembly of two-dimensional DNA crystals. *Nature*, 394(6693):539–544, 1998.
53. E. Winfree, X. Yang, and N.C. Seeman. Universal computation via self-assembly of DNA: Some theory and experiments. In L. F. Landweber and E. B. Baum, editors, *DNA Based Computers II*, volume 44 of *DIMACS*, pages 191–213. American Mathematical Society, 1996.
54. H. Yan, L. Feng, T.H. LaBean, and J.H. Reif. Parallel molecular computation of pair-wise xor using DNA string tile. *J. Am. Chem. Soc.*, 125(47), 2003.
55. H. Yan, T.H. LaBean, L. Feng, and J.H. Reif. Directed nucleation assembly of DNA tile complexes for barcode patterned DNA lattices. *Proc. Natl. Acad. Sci. USA*, 100(14):8103–8108, 2003.

56. H. Yan, S.H. Park, G. Finkelstein, J.H. Reif, and T.H. LaBean. DNA-templated self-assembly of protein arrays and highly conductive nanowires. *Science*, 301(5641):1882–1884, 2003.

57. H. Yan, X. Zhang, Z. Shen, and N.C. Seeman. A robust DNA mechanical device controlled by hybridization topology. *Nature*, 415:62–65, 2002.

58. P. Yin, B. Guo, C. Belmore, W. Palmeri, E. Winfree, T.H. LaBean, and J.H. Reif. TileSoft: Sequence optimization software for designing DNA secondary structures. Technical Report CS-2004-09, Duke University, Computer Science Department, 2004.

59. P. Yin, S. Sahu, A.J. Turberfield, and J.H. Reif. Design of autonomous DNA cellular automata. 2004. In preparation.

60. P. Yin, A.J. Turberfield, and J.H. Reif. Designs of autonomous unidirectional walking DNA devices. In *DNA Based Computers 10*, 2004.

61. P. Yin, A.J. Turberfield, S. Sahu, and J.H. Reif. Design of an autonomous DNA nanomechanical device capable of universal computation and universal translational motion. In *DNA Based Computers 10*, 2004.

62. P. Yin, H. Yan, X.G. Daniell, A.J. Turberfield, and J.H. Reif. A unidirectional DNA walker moving autonomously along a linear track. *Angew. Chem. Int. Ed.*, 43:4906–4911, 2004.

63. B. Yurke, A.J. Turberfield, Jr. A.P. Mills, F.C. Simmel, and J.L. Neumann. A DNA-fuelled molecular machine made of DNA. *Nature*, 406:605–608, 2000.

Membrane Systems: A Quick Introduction

Gheorghe Păun

Institute of Mathematics of the Romanian Academy,
PO Box 1-764, 014700 Bucureşti, Romania and
Research Group on Natural Computing,
Department of Computer Science and Artificial Intelligence,
University of Sevilla, Avda. Reina Mercedes s/n, 41012 Sevilla, Spain
george.paun@imar.ro, gpaun@us.es

Abstract. Membrane Computing (MC) is part of the powerful trend in computer science known under the name of Natural Computing. Its goal is to abstract computing models from the structure and the functioning of the living cell. The present paper is a short and informal introduction to MC, presenting the basic ideas, the central (types of) results, and the main directions of research.

1 Membrane Computing – Starting from Cells

In the last decade, the continuous and mutually beneficial collaboration of informatics with biology became simply spectacular. Two landmark examples are the completion of the genome project, a great success of bio–informatics, of using computer science in biology, and the successful Adleman's experiment (1994) of using DNA molecules as a support for computing. The latter example is illustrative for the direction of research opposite to the traditional one, of using computers in biology: in Adleman's experiment, biological materials and techniques were used in order to solve a computational problem. This was the "official birth certificate" of what is now called DNA Computing, and this gave a decisive impulse to *Natural Computing.*

Membrane Computing is the youngest branch of Natural Computing. It starts from the observation that one of the most marvellous machineries evolved by nature are the cells. The cell is the smallest living unit, a microscopic "enterprise", with a complex structure, an intricate inner activity, and an exquisite relationship with its environment. Both substances, from ions to large macromolecules, and information are processed in a cell, according to involved reactions, organized in a robust and at the same time sensitive manner, having as the goal the processes themselves, the life itself of the cell and of the structures where the cells are included – organs, organisms, populations.

Thus, a double challenge emerged: to check whether or not the often made statements about the "computations" taking place in a cell (see, e.g., [2] and [3]) are mere metaphoras or they correspond to computations in the standard (mathematical) understanding of this term, and, more ambitiously, having in mind the encouraging experience of other branches of Natural Computing, to get

J.-P. Banâtre et al. (Eds.): UPP 2004, LNCS 3566, pp. 188–195, 2005.

inspired from the structure and the functioning of the living cell and define new computing models, possibly of interest for computer science, for computability in general.

Membrane computing emerged as an answer to this double challenge, proposing a series of models (actually, a general framework for devising models) inspired from the cell structure and functioning, as well as from the cell organization in tissues. These models, called P systems, were investigated as mathematical objects, with the main goals being of a (theoretical) computer science type: computation power (in comparison with Turing machines and their restrictions), and usefulness in solving computationally hard problems. The field (founded in 1998; the paper [4] was first circulated on web) simply flourished at this level. Comprehensive information can be found in the web page at `http://psystems.disco.unimib.it`; see also [5].

In this paper we discuss only the cell–like P systems, whose study is much more developed than that of tissue–like P systems or of neural–like P systems, which were only recently investigated in more details.

In short, such a system consists of a hierarchical arrangement of *membranes* (understood as three–dimensional vesicles), which delimits *compartments* (also called *regions*), where abstract *objects* are placed. These objects correspond to the chemicals from the compartments of a cell, and they can be either unstructured, a case when they can be represented by symbols from a given alphabet, or structured. In the latter case, a possible representation of objects is by strings over a given alphabet. Here we discuss only the case of symbol–objects. Corresponding to the situation from reality, where the number of molecules from a given compartment matters, also in the case of objects from the regions of a P system we have to take into consideration their multiplicity, that is why we consider *multisets* of objects assigned to the regions of P systems. These objects evolve according to *rules*, which are also associated with the regions. The intuition is that these rules correspond to the chemical reactions from cell compartments and the reaction conditions are specific to each compartment, hence the evolution rules are localized. The rules say both how the objects are changed and how they can be moved (we say *communicated*) across membranes. By using these rules, we can change the *configuration* of a system (the multisets from its compartments); we say that we get a *transition* among system configurations. The way the rules are applied imitates again the biochemistry (but goes one further step towards computability): the reactions are done in *parallel*, and the objects to evolve and the rules by which they evolve are chosen in a *nondeterministic* manner, in such a way that the application of rules is maximal. A sequence of transitions forms a *computation*, and with computations which *halt* (reach a configuration where no rule is applicable) we associate a *result*, for instance, in the form of the multiset of objects present in the halting configuration in a specified membrane.

All these basic ingredients of a membrane computing system (a P system) will be discussed further below. This brief description is meant, on the one hand, to show the passage from the "real cell" to the "mathematical cell", as considered in MC, and, on the other hand, to give a preliminary idea about the computing model we are investigating.

It is important to note at this stage the generality of the approach. We start from the cell, but the abstract model deals with very general notions: membranes interpreted as separators of regions, objects and rules assigned to regions; the basic data structure is the multiset; the rules are used in the non-deterministic maximally parallel manner, and in this way we get sequences of transitions, hence computations. In such terms, MC can be interpreted as a *bio–inspired framework for distributed parallel processing of multisets*.

We close this introductory discussion by stressing the basic similarities and differences between MC and the other areas of Natural Computing. All these areas start from biological facts and abstract computing models. Neural and Evolutionary Computing are already implemented (rather successfuly, especially in the case of Evolutionary Computing) on the usual computer. DNA Computing has a bigger ambition, that of providing a new hardware, leading to bio–chips, to "wet computers". For MC it seems that the most realistic attempt for implementation is *in silico* (this started already to be a trend and some successes are already reported) rather than *in vitro* (no attempt was made yet).

2   The Basic Classes of P Systems

We introduce now the fundamental ideas of MC in a more precise way. What we look for is a computing device, and to this aim we need *data structures, operations* with these data structures, an *architecture* of our "computer", a systematic manner to define *computations* and *results* of computations.

Inspired from the cell structure and functioning, the basic elements of a *membrane system* (*P system*) are (1) the *membrane structure* and the sets of (2) *evolution rules* which process (3) *multisets* of (4) *objects* placed in the compartments of the membrane structure.

A membrane structure is a hierarchically arranged set of membranes. A suggestive representation is as in the figure from the next page. We distinguish the external membrane (corresponding to the plasma membrane and usually called the *skin* membrane) and several internal membranes (corresponding to the membranes present in a cell, around the nucleus, in Golgi apparatus, vesicles, etc); a membrane without any other membrane inside is said to be *elementary*. Each membrane uniquely determines a compartment, also called *region*, the space delimited from above by it and from below by the membranes placed directly inside, if any exists.

In the basic class of P systems, each region contains a multiset of symbol–objects, which correspond to the chemicals swimming in a water solution in a cell compartment; these chemicals are considered here as unstructured, that is why we describe them by symbols from a given alphabet.

The objects evolve by means of evolution rules, which are also localized, associated with the regions of the membrane structure. The rules correspond to the chemical reactions possible in the compartments of a cell. The typical form of such a rule is $aab \rightarrow (c, here)(d, out)(d, in)(d, in)$, with the following meaning: two copies of object a and one copy of object b react and the reaction produces one copy of c and three copies of d; the new copy of c remains in the same region (indication $here$), one of the copies of d exits the compartment, going to the surrounding region (indication out) and the others two enter one or two of the directly inner membranes (indication in). We say that the objects c, d, d, d are *communicated* as indicated by the commands associated with them in the right hand member of the rule. When an object exits a membrane, it will go to the surrounding compartment; in the case of the skin membrane this is the environment, hence the object is "lost", it never comes back into the system. If no inner membrane exists (that is, the rule is associated with an elementary membrane), then the indication in cannot be followed, and the rule cannot be applied.

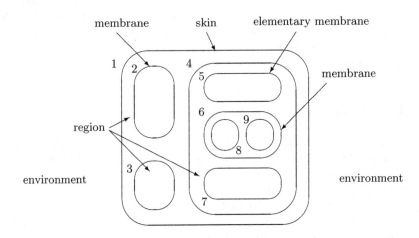

The communication of objects through membranes reminds the fact that the biological membranes contain various (protein) channels through which the molecules can pass (in a passive way, due to concentration difference, or in an active way, with a consumption of energy), in a rather selective manner. The fact that the communication of objects from a compartment to a neighboring compartment is controlled by the "reaction rules" is attractive mathematically, but not quite realistic from a biological point of view, that is why there also were considered variants where the two processes are separated: the evolution is controlled by rules as above, without target indications, and the communication is controlled by specific rules (by symport/antiport rules – see below).

A rule as above, with several objects in its left hand member, is said to be *cooperative*; a particular case is that of *catalytic* rules, of the form $ca \rightarrow cx$, where a is an object and c is a catalyst, appearing only in such rules, never changing. A rule of the form $a \rightarrow x$, where a is an object, is called *non-cooperative*.

The rules associated with a compartment are applied to the objects from that compartment, in a *maximally parallel way*: all objects which can evolve by means of local rules should do it (we assign objects to rules, until no further assignment is possible). The used objects are "consumed", the newly produced objects are placed in the compartments of the membrane structure according to the communication commands assigned to them. The rules to be used and the objects to evolve are chosen in a non-deterministic manner. In turn, all compartments of the system evolve at the same time, synchronously (a common clock is assumed for all membranes). Thus, we have two layers of parallelism, one at the level of compartments and one at the level of the whole "cell".

A membrane structure and the multisets of objects from its compartments identify a *configuration* of a P system. By a non-deterministic maximally parallel use of rules as suggested above we pass to another configuration; such a step is called a *transition*. A sequence of transitions constitutes a *computation*. A computation is successful if it halts, it reaches a configuration where no rule can be applied to the existing objects. With a halting computation we can associate a *result* in various ways. The simplest possibility is to count the objects present in the halting configuration in a specified elementary membrane; this is called *internal output*. We can also count the objects which leave the system during the computation, and this is called *external output*. In both cases the result is a number. If we distinguish among different objects, then we can have as the result a vector of natural numbers. The objects which leave the system can also be arranged in a sequence according to the moments when they exit the skin membrane, and in this case the result is a string. This last possibility is worth emphasizing, because of the qualitative difference between the data structure used inside the system (multisets of objects, hence numbers) and the data structure of the result, which is a string, it contains a positional information, a syntax.

Because of the non-determinism of the application of rules, starting from an initial configuration, we can get several successful computations, hence several results. Thus, a P system *computes* (one also uses to say *generates*) a set of numbers, or a set of vectors of numbers, or a language.

Of course, the previous way of using the rules from the regions of a P system reminds the non-determinism and the (partial) parallelism from cell compartments, with the mentioning that the maximality of parallelism is mathematically oriented (rather useful in proofs); when using P systems as biological models, this feature should be replaced with more realistic features (e.g., reaction rates, probabilities, partial parallelism).

An important way to use a P system is the automata–like one: an *input* is introduced in a given region and this input is *accepted* if and only if the computation halts. This is the way for using P systems, for instance, in solving decidability problems.

We do not give here a formal definition of a P system. The reader interested in mathematical and bibliographical details can consult the mentioned monograph [5], as well as the relevant papers from the web bibliography mentioned above. Of course, when presenting a P system we have to specify: the alphabet of objects, the membrane structure (usually represented by a string of labelled matching parentheses), the multisets of objects present in each region of the system (represented by strings of symbol–objects, with the number of occurrences of a symbol in a string being the multiplicity of the object identified by that symbol in the multiset represented by the considered string), the sets of evolution rules associated with each region, as well as the indication about the way the output is defined.

Many modifications/extensions of the very basic model sketched above are discussed in the literature, but we do not mention them here. Instead, we only briefly discuss the interesting case of *computing by communication*.

In the systems described above, the symbol–objects were processed by multiset rewriting–like rules (some objects are transformed into other objects, which have associated communication targets). Coming closer to the trans–membrane transfer of molecules, we can consider purely communicative systems, based on the three classes of such transfer known in the biology of membranes: *uniport, symport*, and *antiport* (see [1] for details). Symport refers to the transport where two (or more) molecules pass together through a membrane in the same direction, antiport refers to the transport where two (or more) molecules pass through a membrane simultaneously, but in opposite directions, while the case when a molecule does not need a "partner" for a passage is referred to as uniport.

In terms of P systems, we can consider object processing rules of the following forms: a symport rule (associated with a membrane i) is of the form (ab, in) or (ab, out), stating that the objects a and b enter/exit together membrane i, while an antiport rule is of the form $(a, out; b, in)$, stating that, simultaneously, a exits and b enters membrane i. A natural generalization is to move more than two objects simultaneously, for instance, considering antiport rules of the form $(x, out; y, in)$, where x, y are arbitrary multisets of objects.

A P system with symport/antiport rules has the same architecture as a system with multiset rewriting rules: alphabet of objects, membrane structure, initial multisets in the regions of the membrane structure, sets of rules associated with the membranes, possibly an output membrane – with one additional component, the set of objects present in the environment. This is an important detail: because by communication we do not create new objects, we need a supply of objects, in the environment, otherwise we are only able to handle a finite population of objects, those provided in the initial multiset. Also the functioning of a P system with symport/antiport rules is the same as for systems with multiset rewriting rules: the transition from a configuration to another configuration is done by applying the rules in a non-deterministic maximally parallel manner, to the objects available in the regions of the system and in the environment, as requested by the used rules. When a halting configuration is reached, we get a result, in a specified output membrane.

3   Computational Completeness; Universality

As we have already mentioned, many classes of P systems, combining various ingredients as those described above, are able to simulate Turing machines, hence they are *computationally complete*. Always, the proofs of results of this type are constructive, and this have an important consequence from the computability point of view: there are *universal* (hence *programmable*) P systems. In short, starting from a universal Turing machine (or an equivalent universal device), we get an equivalent universal P system. Among others, this implies that in the case of Turing complete classes of P systems, the hierarchy on the number of membranes always collapses (at most at the level of the universal P systems). Actually, the number of membranes sufficient in order to characterize the power of Turing machines by means of P systems is always rather small.

We only mention here two of the most interesting universality results:

1. P systems with symbol–objects with catalytic rules, using only two catalysts and two membranes, are universal.
2. P systems with symport/antiport rules of a rather restricted size (example: three membranes, symport rules with two objects each and no antiport rules, or only minimal symport and antiport rules) are universal.

We can conclude that the compartmental computation in a cell–like membrane structure (using various ways of communicating among compartments) is rather powerful. The "computing cell" is a powerful "computer".

4   Computational Efficiency

The computational power is only one of the important questions to be dealt with when defining a new computing model. The other fundamental question concerns the computing *efficiency*. Because P systems are parallel computing devices, it is expected that they can solve hard problems in an efficient manner – and this expectation is confirmed for systems provided with ways for producing an exponential workspace in a linear way. Three main such possibilities have been considered so far in the literature, and *all of them were proven to lead to polynomial solutions to* **NP**-*complete problems*: *membrane division, membrane creation,* and *string replication*. Using them, polynomial solutions to SAT, the Hamiltonian Path problem, the Node Covering problem, the problem of inverting one–way functions, the Subset–sum, and the Knapsack problems were reported (note that the last two are numerical problems, where the answer is not of the yes/no type, as in decidability problems). Details can be found in [5], [6], as well as in the web page of the domain.

Roughly speaking, the framework for dealing with complexity matters is that of *accepting P systems with input*: a family of P systems of a given type is constructed starting from a given problem, and an instance of the problem is introduced as an input in such systems; working in a deterministic mode (or a *confluent* mode: some non-determinism is allowed, provided that the branching converges after a while to a unique configuration), in a given time one of the answers yes/no is obtained, in the form of specific objects sent to the environment. The family of systems should be constructed in a uniform mode (starting from the size of instances) by a Turing machine, working a polynomial time.

This direction of research is very active at the present moment. More and more problems are considered, the membrane computing complexity classes are refined, characterizations of the $\mathbf{P}{\neq}\mathbf{NP}$ conjecture were obtained in this framework, improvements are looked for. An important recent result concerns the fact that $\mathbf{PSPACE}$ was shown to be included in $\mathbf{PMC}_D$, the family of problems which can be solved in polynomial time by P systems with the possibility of dividing both elementary and non-elementary membranes [7].

5   Concluding Remarks

This paper was intended as a quick and general introduction to Membrane Computing, an invitation to this recent branch of Natural Computing.

The starting motivation of the area was to learn from the cell biology new ideas, models, paradigms useful for informatics – and we have informally presented a series of details of this type. The mathematical development was quite rapid, mainly with two types of results as the purpose: computational universality and computational efficiency. Recently, the domain started to be used as a framework for modelling processes from biology (but also from linguistics, management, computer graphics, etc.), and this is rather important in view of the fact that P systems are (reductionistic, but flexible, easily scallable, algorithmic, intuitive) models of the whole cell; modelling the whole cell was often mentioned as an important challenge for the bio–computing in the near future – see, e.g., [8].

We have recalled only a few classes of P systems and only a few (types of) results. A detailed presentation of the domain is not only beyond the scope of this text, but also beyond the dimensions of a monograph; furthermore, the domain is fastly emerging, so that, the reader interested in any research direction, a more theoretical or a more practical one, is advised to follow the developments, for instance, through the web page mentioned in Section 2.

References

1. B. Alberts, A. Johnson, J. Lewis, M. Raff, K. Roberts, P. Walter, *Molecular Biology of the Cell*, 4th ed., Garland Science, New York, 2002.
2. D. Bray, Protein Molecules as Computational Elements in Living Cells. *Nature*, 376 (July 1995), 307–312.
3. S. Ji, The Cell as the Smallest DNA–Based Molecular Computer, *BioSystems*, 52 (1999), 123–133.
4. Gh. Păun, Computing with Membranes, *Journal of Computer and System Sciences*, 61, 1 (2000), 108–143 (and Turku Center for Computer Science–TUCS Report 208, November 1998, www.tucs.fi).
5. Gh. Păun, *Computing with Membranes: An Introduction*, Springer, Berlin, 2002.
6. M. Pérez–Jiménez, A. Romero–Jiménez, F. Sancho–Caparrini, *Teoría de la Complejidad en Modelos de Computatión Celular con Membranas*, Kronos, Sevilla, 2002.
7. P. Sosik, The Computational Power of Cell Division in P Systems: Beating Down Parallel Computers? *Natural Computing*, 2, 3 (2003), 287–298.
8. M. Tomita, Whole–Cell Simulation: A Grand Challenge of the 21st Century, *Trends in Biotechnology*, 19 (2001), 205–210.

Cellular Meta-programming over Membranes

Gabriel Ciobanu[1] and Dorel Lucanu[2]

[1] Romanian Academy, Institute of Computer Science, Iaşi
`gabriel@iit.tuiasi.ro`
[2] "A.I.Cuza" University of Iaşi, Faculty of Computer Science
`dlucanu@info.uaic.ro`

Abstract. Adaptable executions inspired by the cell behaviour can be described by a cellular meta-programming paradigm. The cell adaptability and meta-programming are related to the notions of behavioural reflection, which allows a program to modify, even at run-time, its own code as well as the semantics of its own programming language. We present the cellular meta-programming considering the membrane systems and a specification language based on rewriting and allowing meta-level strategies and use of reflection.

1 Introduction

In this paper we present cellular meta-programming, a computing paradigm inspired by the dynamic nature of the cell behaviour, described with the help of membrane systems representing abstract models inspired by the compartments of a cell. The root of this approach is given by the high adaptability and flexibility of the cell behaviour. Identifying the principles that govern the design and function of this adaptability is a central goal of our research. The adaptation of cells to the changing environment requires sophisticated processing mediated by interacting genes and proteins. In computing terms, we say that a cell is able to adapt its execution according to various developmental and environmental stimuli, causing corresponding changes in its behaviour. We refer mainly to adaptability at the software level.

Adaptable executions are generated in computer science by meta-programming, as well as by just-in-time compilation, aspect-oriented programming, generative programming, dynamic linking, partial evaluation. Meta-programming is the act of writing meta-programs, and a meta-program is a program that manipulates itself and possibly other programs as its data, allowing execution modification. Meta-programming is related to the notions of reflection [12]. In the programming languages, reflection is defined as the ability of a program to manipulate the encoding of the state of the program during its own execution. The mechanism for encoding execution states (as data) is called reification. The reflective mechanisms are both structural and behavioural. Structural reflection is the ability to work with the structures and processes of a programming system within the programming system itself. This form of reflection is easier to implement, and languages as Lisp, Smalltalk, and Java have

J.-P. Banâtre et al. (Eds.): UPP 2004, LNCS 3566, pp. 196–206, 2005.

structural reflection mechanisms. However, the cell adaptability is close to the behavioural reflection which allows a program to modify, even at run-time, its own code as well as the semantics and the implementation of its own programming language. Our main interest is in behaviour reflection.

The cell is able to modify its activity according to its foregoing processes, to observe and change its behaviour at run-time. This aspect is more than the reification process by which a program is used as a representation (data structures, procedures) expressed in the language itself, and made available at run-time as ordinary data. The cells programming languages allow to step into the meta-level, where implementation of the language is explicitly available. This capability enables various customizations including new structures, changing the behaviour, going up and down in a tower of meta-levels by using a reflection mechanism.

We use a rather mathematical language (called Maude) which is able to provide executable specification, and an abstract model of membranes inspired by the compartments of a cell (called P systems). In order to present the cellular meta-programming paradigm, we provide the executable specifications of P systems in Maude, a software system supporting reflection. Despite the theoretical limits, Meseguer and Clavel have defined a general theory of reflection for Maude in [9]. They propose meta-logical axioms for reflection, as well as general axioms for computational strategies in rewriting logic.

2   Membrane Systems

Membrane systems represent a new abstract model of parallel and distributed computing inspired by cell compartments and molecular membranes [10, 11]. A cell is divided in various compartments, each compartment with a different task, and all of them working simultaneously to accomplish a more general task of the whole system. The membranes of a P system determine regions where objects and evolution rules can be placed. The objects evolve according to the rules associated with each region, and the regions cooperate in order to maintain the proper behaviour of the whole system. P systems provide a nice abstraction for parallel systems, and a suitable framework for distributed and parallel algorithms [2]. It is desirable to find more connections with various fields of computer science, including implementations and executable specifications. From the programming point of view, a sequential software simulator of membrane systems is presented in [4], and a parallel simulator implemented on a cluster of computers is presented in [3]. It does not exist yet a programming language based on, or inspired of, the membrane systems.

A detailed description of the P systems can be found in [11]. A *P system* consists of several membranes that do not intersect, and a *skin membrane*, surrounding them all. The membranes delimit *regions*, and contain multisets of *objects*, as well as *evolution rules*. Only rules in a region delimited by a membrane act on the objects in that region. Moreover, the rules can contain target indications, specifying the membrane where objects are sent after applying the rule. The objects can pass through membranes, in two directions: they can be sent *out* of the membrane which delimits a region from outside, or can be sent *in* one of the membranes which delimit a region from inside, precisely identified by its label. The membranes can be *dissolved*; this action is important when discussing about adaptive executions. When such an action takes place, all the objects of the dissolved membrane remain free in the membrane placed immediately outside, but the evolution rules of the dissolved membranes are lost. The skin membrane is never dissolved. The application of evolution rules is done in parallel, and it is eventually regulated by *priority* relationships between rules.

A P system has a certain structure represented by a tree (with the skin as its root), or by a string of correctly matching parentheses, placed in a unique pair of matching parentheses; each pair of matching parentheses corresponds to a membrane. Graphically, a membrane structure is represented by a Venn diagram in which two sets can be either disjoint, or one the subset of the other. The membranes are labelled in a one-to-one manner. A membrane without any other membrane inside is said to be *elementary*. The space outside the skin membrane is called the *outer region*.

Formally, a P system $\Pi = (O, \mu, w_1, \ldots, w_m, R_1, \ldots, R_m, i_o)$ is a structure where:

(i) O is an alphabet of objects;
(ii) μ is a membrane structure consisting of labelled membranes;
(iii) w_i are multisets over O associated with the regions defined by μ;
(iv) R_i are finite sets of evolution rules over O associated with the membranes, of typical forms $u \to v$, with v containing paired symbols of the form $(c, here)$, (c, in_j), (c, out), with $(c, here)$ usually written simply c;
(v) i_o is either a number between 1 and m specifying the *output* membrane of Π, or it is equal to 0 indicating the environment as the output region.

The membrane structure and the multisets in Π determine the initial configuration of the system. We can pass from a configuration to another one by using the evolution rules. This is done in parallel: all objects, from all membranes, which can be the subject of local evolution rules, as prescribed by the priority relation, should evolve simultaneously. However, an object introduced by a rule cannot evolve at the same step by means of another rule. The use of a rule $u \to v$ in a region with a multiset w means to subtract the multiset identified by u from w, and then adding the objects of v according to the form of the rule. If an object appears in v in the form $(c, here)$, then it remains in the same region; if we have (c, in_j), then a copy of c is introduced in the membrane with the label j, providing that it is adjacent to the region of the rule $u \to v$, otherwise the rule cannot be applied; if we have (c, out), then a copy of the object c is introduced in the membrane placed immediately outside the region of the rule $u \to v$; if the special symbol δ appears in v, then the membrane which delimits the region is dissolved; in this way, all the objects in this region become elements of the region placed immediately outside, while the rules of the dissolved membrane are removed.

Example: We consider a P system generating symbols b and c with the properties that the number of c's is double of the number of b's, and the total number of b's and c's is a multiple of 6.

$$\Pi_1 = (O, \mu, w_1, w_2, R_1, R_2, i_o),$$
$$O = \{a, b, c\},$$
$$\mu = [_1 [_2 \;]_2]_1,$$
$$w_1 = a^2,$$
$$w_2 = \lambda,$$
$$R_1 = \{a \rightarrow a(b, in_2)(c, in_2)^2, \; a^2 \rightarrow (a, out)^2\},$$
$$R_2 = \emptyset,$$
$$i_o = 2.$$

The initial configuration is:

3   Evaluation Strategies and Reflection

We discuss in this section about meta-programming and reflection aspects, presenting in the same time some distinctive features of the membrane computing.

We express the evolution rules of a membrane system as rewriting rules. We consider the following maximal parallel application of rules: in a transition step, the rules of each membrane are used against its resources such that no more rules can be applied. Considering an elementary membrane $M = (R_M, w_M)$, where R_M is the finite set of evolution rules and w_M is the initial multiset, a computation step transition is defined as a rewriting rule by

$$\frac{x_1 \rightarrow y_1, \ldots, x_n \rightarrow y_n \in R_M, z \text{ is } R_M\text{-irreducible}}{x_1 \ldots x_n z \Rightarrow y_1 \ldots y_n z} \tag{1}$$

z is R_M-irreducible whenever there does not exist rules in R_M applicable to z. A *composite membrane*, that is a membrane with other membranes $M_1, \ldots, M_k$ inside it, is denoted by $(R_M, init, M_1, \ldots, M_k)$, where each M_i $(1 \leq i \leq k)$ is an elementary or a composite membrane. R_M represents the finite set of evolution rules of M, and $init$ is its initial configuration of form $(w, (w_1, \ldots, w_k))$, where

w_i is the multiset associated with the membrane M_i. A computational step of a composite membrane is defined as a rewriting rule by

$$\frac{w \Rightarrow w', w_1 \Rightarrow w'_1, \ldots, w_n \Rightarrow w'_n}{(w, (w_1, \ldots, w_k)) \Rightarrow (w', (w'_1, \ldots, w'_k))} \tag{2}$$

In this way, the objects of the membranes are the subject of local evolution rules that evolve simultaneously. A sequence of computation steps represents a computation. A computation is successful if this sequence is finite, namely there is no rule applicable to the objects present in the last configuration. In a final configuration, the result of a successful computation is the total number of objects present in the membrane considered as the output membrane. In this paper we simplify this procedure; no internal membrane is specified as an output membrane, and so the result is given by the number of objects in the skin membrane.

Maude and Rewriting Logic

Maude is essentially a mathematical language. The OBJ theory and languages [7] have influenced the Maude design and philosophy. A Maude program is a logical theory, and a Maude computation is a logical deduction using the axioms specified in the program. The foundations of Maude is given by membership equational logic and rewriting logic. A rewriting specification $\mathcal{R}$ is a 4-tuple $\mathcal{R}=(\Sigma, E, L, R)$ where (Σ, E) is a rewriting logic signature, L is a set whose elements are called labels, and R is a set of labelled rewriting rules (sentences) written as $r : [t(\overline{x})]_E \rightarrow [t'(\overline{x})]_E$. The inference rules of rewriting logic allow to deduce general (concurrent) transitions which are possible in a system satisfying $\mathcal{R}$. We say that $\mathcal{R}$ *entails the sentence* $[t] \rightarrow [t']$ and write $\mathcal{R} \vdash [t] \rightarrow [t']$ iff $[t] \rightarrow [t']$ can be obtained by finite application of its inference rules. The general theory of the rewriting logic allows conditional sentences and conditional rewriting rules. The interested reader is invited to read [5].

The basic programming statements of Maude are equations, membership assertions, and rules. A Maude program containing only equations and membership assertions is called a functional module. The equations are used as rules (equational rewriting), and the replacement of equals for equals is performed only from left to right. A Maude program containing both equations and rules is called a system module. Rules are not equations, they are local transition rules in a possibly concurrent system. Unlike for equations, there is no assumption that all rewriting sequences will lead to the same final result, and for some systems there may not be any final states.

The rewriting performed for membranes is a multiset rewriting. In Maude this is specified by declaring that the multiset union operator satisfies the associativity and commutativity equations, and has also an identity. This is done simply by using attributes, and this information is used to generate a multiset matching algorithm. Further expressiveness is gained by various features as equational pattern matching, user-definable syntax and data, generic types and modules, and reflection.

We emphasize the *evaluation strategies* and *reflection property*. Evaluation strategies control the positions in which equations can be applied, giving the user the possibility of indicating which arguments to evaluate before simplifying a given operator with the equations. Reflection allows a complete control of the rewriting (execution) using the rewriting rules in the theory. Reflective computations allow the link between meta-level and the object level, whenever possible.

Rewriting logic is *reflective* [9], i.e., there is a finitely presented *universal rewriting specification* $\mathcal{U}$ such that for any finitely presented rewriting specification $\mathcal{R}$ (including $\mathcal{U}$ itself), we have the following equivalence:

$$\mathcal{R} \vdash [t] \rightarrow [t'] \;\; \text{iff} \;\; \mathcal{U} \vdash \langle \overline{\mathcal{R}}, \overline{t} \rangle \rightarrow \langle \overline{\mathcal{R}}, \overline{t'} \rangle,$$

where $\overline{\mathcal{R}}$ and $\overline{t}$ are terms representing $\mathcal{R}$ and t as data elements of $\mathcal{U}$. Since $\mathcal{U}$ is representable in itself, it is possible to achieve a "reflective tower" with an arbitrary number of reflection levels:

$$\mathcal{R} \vdash [t] \rightarrow [t'] \; \text{iff} \; \mathcal{U} \vdash \langle \overline{\mathcal{R}}, \overline{t} \rangle \rightarrow \langle \overline{\mathcal{R}}, \overline{t'} \rangle \; \text{iff} \; \mathcal{U} \vdash \langle \overline{\mathcal{U}}, \overline{\langle \overline{\mathcal{R}}, \overline{t} \rangle} \rangle \rightarrow \langle \overline{\mathcal{U}}, \overline{\langle \overline{\mathcal{R}}, \overline{t'} \rangle} \rangle \dots$$

This interesting and powerful concept is supported by Maude through a built-in module called `META-LEVEL`. This module has sorts `Term` and `Module` such that the representation $\overline{t}$ of a term t is of sort `Term` and the representation $\overline{SP}$ of a specification SP is of sort `Module`. There are also functions like `metaReduce`$(\overline{SP}, \overline{t})$ which returns the representation of the reduced form of a term t using the equations in the module SP.

`META-LEVEL` module can be extended by the user to specify strategies of controlling the rewriting process. We use `META-LEVEL` in order to define the "maximal parallel rewriting" strategy. In fact the meta-level is needed for two main reasons: to locate the set of rules corresponding to a certain membrane in the structured Maude specification of a composite P system, and to describe the maximal parallel application of the located rules as a rewriting strategy.

The `META-LEVEL` module is used to provide a clear algorithmic description given by `maxParRew` of the "nondeterministic and maximal parallel" applications of evolution rules in the P systems. Using `maxParRew` as a transition step between meta-level configurations, we then provide an operational semantics of the P systems. Using the power given by the tower of reflection levels in Maude, we define operations over modules and strategies to guide the deduction process. Finally we can use a meta-metalevel to analyze and verify the properties of the P systems [1].

This conceptual description of the P systems based on meta-programming capabilities given by reflection is called cellular meta-programming, and it could become a useful paradigm for further investigations in programming systems, and in a new holistic view of molecular biology called systems biology [8]. Adding new abstractions, discrete models and methods able to help our understanding of the biological phenomena, systems biology may provide predictive power, useful classifications, new paradigms in computing and new perspectives on the dynamics of various biological systems.

4   Membrane Systems Specification in Maude

This section presents executable specifications for membrane systems. Each P system Π is naturally represented as a collection of Maude system modules such that each membrane is represented by a corresponding Maude system module. The sort Obj is for object names, and its subsort Output is for results. We add a sort Soup for the multisets of objects, and a sort Config for the states of a P system. An expression of the form $\langle M \mid S \rangle$ represents a configuration corresponding to an elementary membrane M with its multiset S, and an expression of the form $\langle M \mid S; C_1, \ldots, C_n \rangle$ represents a configuration corresponding to a composite membrane M in state S and with the component i having the configuration C_i. The Maude semantics of the module M is not the same with the P system semantics. Therefore we must associate with M the right semantics based on the maximal parallel rewrite relation. We use the facilities provided by reflection in Maude, defining this semantics at the meta-level.

For the elementary membranes, a computation step between configurations is defined as:

$$\frac{S \Rightarrow S'}{\langle M \mid S \rangle \Rightarrow \langle M \mid S' \rangle} \tag{3}$$

where $S \Rightarrow S'$ is defined in (1). $S \Rightarrow S'$ is not the ordinary rewriting defined by M; however they are strongly related:

$$S \Rightarrow S' \text{ iff } S \xrightarrow{+}_{R_M} S' \text{ s.t. } maxParCons(R_M, S, S') \tag{4}$$

Here $\xrightarrow{+}_{R_M}$ is the ordinary rewriting defined by R_M, and $maxParCons$ (R_M, S, S') represents the constraints defining the maximal parallel rewriting strategy over R_M. More precisely, we have:

1. if $S = S'$, then $maxParCons(R_M, S, S)$ holds iff S is R_M-irreducible;
2. if $S \neq S'$, then $maxParCons(R_M, S, S')$ holds iff there exists $S_1, S_1', \ell \to r \in R_M$ such that $S = \ell\, S_1$, $S' = r\, S_1'$, and $maxParCons(R_M, S_1, S_1')$.

Since $maxParCons$ has the set of rules of the module M as parameter, it follows that it can be decided only at meta-level.

We must say that we have an interleaving implementation of the maximal parallel rewriting over multisets. However, using the rewriting logic axioms, we can prove that two interleaving implementations of $S \Rightarrow S'$ are considered to be in fact the same. In this way, the class of interleaving implementations can express the parallel rewriting over multisets.

The transition between configurations for a composite membrane is defined as:

$$\frac{S \Rightarrow S', C_1 \Rightarrow C_1', \ldots, C_k \Rightarrow C_k'}{\langle M \mid S; C_1, \ldots, C_k \rangle \Rightarrow \langle M \mid S'; C_1', \ldots, C_k' \rangle} \tag{5}$$

Again we have an interleaving implementation of (5). The interleaving implementation is more complex now. For instance, at a time t we may have an elementary evolution step of the component C_i, and at time $t + 1$ we may have an elementary evolution step of the component C_j, where $j \neq i$. Rewriting logic does not distinguish between two interleaving implementations of the same evolution step of a composite membrane. This implies that our *simulation* of the parallel evolution of the P systems is faithful.

A computation is a sequence of transitions steps $C_0 \Rightarrow C_1 \Rightarrow C_2 \Rightarrow \ldots \Rightarrow C_n \Rightarrow \ldots$, where C_0 is the initial configuration. The result of a successful computation is extracted from the final configuration, and the result is given by the total number of objects present in the skin membrane.

Example: We consider the simple example of a membrane system presented in Section 2, describing and then executing its Maude specification. We present here only some important steps of the specification; more details can be found in [1]. Each membrane is specified in Maude by an independent system module. Actually, we ignore the membrane labelled by 2, change the rules accordingly, and specify Π_1 as follows:

```
(mod SKIN is
  inc CONFIG(OBJ-TO-ABC) .
  op init : -> Soup .
  eq init = a a .
  rl ['SKIN] : a => a b c c .
  rl ['SKIN] : a a => empty .
endm)
```

The Maude specification of a P system is a system module importing the modules corresponding to its component membranes. The structure of the system is specified in the initial configuration. The module describing Π_1 is:

```
(mod PSYS is
  inc SKIN .
  op initConf : -> Config .
  eq initConf = < 'SKIN | init > .
endm)
```

The rewriting rules defining the computation of P systems are included in a Maude system module called COMPS. For instance, the rewriting rules implementing (4) are described in Maude at the meta-level as:

```
crl maxParRewS(RS, T) =>
      (if (MP :: MatchPair)
        then maxParRewS(RS, (rl  X =>  Y [label(Q)] .), MP, T)
        else maxParRewS(RS1 RS2, T)
      fi)
    if RS1 (rl X => Y [label(Q)] .) RS2 := RS /\
      MP := metaXmatch(m, X, T, nil, 0, unbounded, 0) .

crl maxParRewS(RS, R, MP, T) =>
      '__[Y,  maxParRewS(RS, toTerm(getContext(MP)))]
      if (rl  X =>  Y [label(Q)] .) := R .

rl maxParRewS(none, T) => T .
```

The function maxParRewS(RS, T) is used to separate the processed part from the unprocessed part of a multiset. For instance, an intermediate form of (4) is written as u maxParRewS(RS, T), where u represents the processed part, and T is a meta-level representation of the unprocessed part which follows to be rewritten using the rules from RS. The first rewriting rule nondeterministically choses an evolution rule from the set RS, and the second rewriting rule simulates the execution of this evolution rule. Next evolution rule is chosen only after the execution of the previous one is completed. The rules implementing (5) are similar to the above ones.

We can use various Maude commands in order to make experiments with the P system specification. For instance, we use the command rew to see the result of maximal parallel rewritings:

```
Maude> select COMPS .
Maude> (down PSYS : rew  maxParReduce(up(PSYS),
                                       up(PSYS, initConf)))) .)
rewrites: 4784 in 130ms cpu (140ms real) (36800 rewrites/second)
result Config :
  < 'SKIN | a a b b b b b b c c c c c c c c c c c c >
Maude>
```

The function maxParReduce applies the maximal parallel rewriting strategy over the Maude description of a particular P system. The command down and the function up are used to move between two successive levels of the reflection tower. For instance, down COMPS interprets the result returned by rew in the module COMPS. The function call up(PSYS, initConf) returns the meta-level representation of the term initConf defined in PSYS.

The rew command with a limited number of steps is not useful to restrict the computation, because the number of rewriting steps in Maude is not the same with the number of computation steps of a P system. Therefore, the rewriting process is restricted by the configuration size:

```
crl rwf(X) => rwf(maxParRew(X)) if (X :: Term) /\ (#(X) < 20) .
crl rwf(X) => X if #(X) >= 20 .
```

The function maxParRew is similar to maxParRewS, but it separates the processed part from the unprocessed part of a configuration. The functions rwf controls the application of the maximal parallel rewriting strategy over configurations: the simulation of a next parallel evolution step start only after the simulation of the previous one is completed.

We consider a module METACOMPS defining a function out which removes the non-output objects, and a function #() which counts the occurrences of an object into a configuration. In our example, the function out simulates the membrane labelled by 2. Since these functions are applied to configurations obtained with metaRewrite command, module METACOMPS is defined at the meta-metalevel. Here we exemplify how the metaRewrite command is used:

```
Maude> (select METACOMPS .)
```

```
Maude> (down PSYS : down COMPS : red getTerm(metaRewrite(up(COMPS),
                    up(COMPS, maxParReduce(up(PSYS),
                    up(PSYS, initConf))), 100)) .)
rewrites: 26614 in 150ms cpu (140ms real) (177426 rewrites/second)
result Config :
   < 'SKIN | a a b b b b b b c c c c c c c c c c c c >
```

If we wish to investigate the properties of the result of a successful computation, we first compute the representation of this result at the meta-metalevel:

```
(mod PROOF is
   inc METACOMPS .
   op ql : -> QidList .
   eq ql = *** the representation at the meta-metalevel of
           *** metaRewrite(...,
           ***        maxParReduce(up(PSYS), up(PSYS, initConf)), 100)
endm)
```

We can check now that the number of objects c is double of the number of objects b, and the total number of b's and c's is a multiple of 6:

```
Maude> (red #(ql, ''c) == 2 * #(ql, ''b) .)
rewrites: 322 in 230ms cpu (230ms real) (1400 rewrites/second)
reduce in PROOF :
   #(ql,''c)== 2 * #(ql,''b)
result Bool :
   true
Maude> (red (#(ql, ''c) + #(ql, ''b)) rem 6 .)
rewrites: 326 in 10ms cpu (10ms real) (32600 rewrites/second)
reduce in PROOF :
   (#(ql,''c)+ #(ql,''b))rem 6
result Zero :
   0
```

Therefore we can check certain properties of a specific configuration or result. If we wish to check certain properties of a computation, or some properties for all the configurations, we may use the temporal formulas and a model checker implemented in Maude. Maude has a collection of formal tools supporting different forms of logical reasoning to verify program properties, including a model checker to verify temporal properties of finite-state system modules [6]. This model checker provides a useful tool to detect subtle errors, and to verify some desired temporal properties of a computation.

5   Conclusion

Starting from the cells ability to react and change their behaviour at run-time, we translate this adaptability in a meta-programming feature of a P systems implementation based on executable specifications. We view the cell as a complex system coordinating various membrane working in parallel. Adaptable executions inspired by the cell behaviour can be described by a cellular meta-programming paradigm. The cell adaptability and meta-programming are related to the notions of behavioural reflection. We present the cellular meta-programming with the help of membrane systems and a reflective specification language based on rewriting. The approach exploits the reflection property of the rewriting logic, property which provides a meta-programming abstraction. In this way, the abstract mechanism of reflection could describe the biological entities ability to react and change their behaviour according to various developmental and environmental stimuli. This paper focuses on the use of the meta-programming abilities and reflection power of Maude to implement a generic and adaptable P system interpreter; in this way we suggest a natural computing formalism with cellular meta-programming features.

Further research will investigate how to integrate these aspects with the the parallel executions of an implementation of the membrane systems on a cluster of computers [3]. Other research lines will use the cellular meta-programming, trying to harmonize theory and practice, fostering fertilization between biological principles and programming paradigms.

References

1. O. Andrei, G. Ciobanu, D. Lucanu. Executable Specifications of the P Systems. In *Membrane Computing. International Workshop WMC5*, Milano, June 2004, Lecture Notes in Computer Science vol.3365, Springer, 127-146, 2005.
2. G. Ciobanu. Distributed Algorithms over Communicating Membrane Systems. *BioSystems* vol.70(2), 123-133, 2003.
3. G. Ciobanu, W. Guo. P Systems Running on a Cluster of Computers. In *Membrane Computing. International Workshop WMC4*, Tarragona, June 2003, Lecture Notes in Computer Science vol.2933, Springer, 123-139, 2004.
4. G. Ciobanu, D. Paraschiv. P System Software Simulator. *Fundamenta Informaticae* vol.49, 61-66, 2002.
5. M. Clavel, F. Durán, S. Eker, P. Lincoln, N. Martí-Oliet, J. Meseguer, J.F. Quesada. Maude: Specification and Programming in Rewriting Logic. *Theoretical Computer Science* vol.285(2), 187-243, 2002.
6. S. Eker, J. Meseguer, A. Sridharanarayanan. The Maude LTL Model Checker and Its Implementation. In *Model Checking Software: 10th SPIN Workshop*, Lecture Notes in Computer Science vol.2648, Springer, 230-234, 2003.
7. J. Goguen, T. Winkler, J. Meseguer, K. Futatsugi, J.P. Jouannaud. Introducing OBJ. In *Software Engineering with OBJ*, Kluwer, 3-167, 2000.
8. H. Kitano. Computational Systems Biology. *Nature* vol.420, 206-210, 2002.
9. J. Meseguer, M. Clavel. Axiomatizing Reflective Logics and Languages. In G.Kiczales (Ed.): *Reflection'96*, Xerox PARC, 263-288, 1996.
10. Gh. Păun. Computing with membranes. *Journal of Computer and System Sciences* vol.61, 108-143, 2000.
11. Gh. Păun. *Computing with Membranes: An Introduction*, Springer, 2002.
12. J.M. Sobel, D.P. Friedman. An Introduction to Reflection-Oriented Programming. In G.Kiczales (Ed.): *Reflection'96*, Xerox PARC, 263-288, 1996.

Modelling Dynamically Organised Colonies of Bio-entities

Marian Gheorghe[1], Ioanna Stamatopoulou[2],
Mike Holcombe[1], and Petros Kefalas[3]

[1] Department of Computer Science, University of Sheffield, UK
{M.Gheorghe, M.Holcombe}@dcs.shef.ac.uk
[2] South-East European Research Center, Thessaloniki, Greece
istamatopoulou@seerc.info
[3] Department of Computer Science, CITY College, Thessaloniki, Greece
kefalas@city.academic.gr

Abstract. The dynamic nature of biological systems' structure, and
the continuous evolution of their components require new modelling approaches. In this paper it will be investigated how these systems composed of many dynamic components can be formally modelled as well as
how their configurations can be altered, thus affecting the communication between parts. We use two different formal methods, communicating
X-machines and population P systems, both with dynamic structures. It
will be shown that new modelling approaches are required in order to
capture the complex and dynamic nature of these systems.

1   Introduction

Biological systems are modelled in different ways depending on the aim of the
model. There are models trying to exhibit the general behaviour of the system
based mainly on continuous approaches. In this way a generic description of the
system's behaviour is defined in terms of mathematical functions evolving in
time. Another perspective is based on individual components interacting toward
achieving certain goals. In this latter case an emergent property of the system,
not obvious from the components' behaviour, is mostly envisaged. For example
the behaviours of the social insects are directed towards the benefit of the colony
as a whole, and this is done through self-organisation and specialisation. Local
interactions with other insects, and with the environment produce solutions to
problems that colonies face. No one insect in the colony can give a picture of the
whole environment, but information can be learnt through interaction. Bees, for
example, can determine how busy a colony is when they bring nectar to hive.
Instead of passing all this onto one bee (who will distribute it), small portions
of nectar will be passed onto many bees. The bee can determine how busy
the hive is by calculating how long it has to wait to pass nectar onto another
bee [11].

This perspective on modelling biological systems is investigated in this paper and mainly relies on describing components as agents. An agent is a fairly

J.-P. Banâtre et al. (Eds.): UPP 2004, LNCS 3566, pp. 207–224, 2005.

complex computer system that is situated in some environment and is capable of flexible, autonomous actions in order to meet its design objectives [16]. The extreme complexity of agent systems is due to substantial differences between the attributes of their components, high computational power required by the processes running within these components, huge volume of data manipulated by these processes and finally possibly extensive amount of communication in order to achieve coordination and collaboration. The use of a computational framework that is capable of modelling both the dynamic aspects (i.e. the continuous change of agents states together with their communication) and the static aspects (i.e. the amount of knowledge and information available), will facilitate modelling and simulation of such complex systems.

Many biological processes seem to behave like multi-agent systems, as for example a colony of ants or bees, a flock of birds, cell tissues etc. [6]. The vast majority of computational biological models based on an assumed, fixed system structure is not realistic. The concept of growth, division and differentiation of individual components (agents) and the communication between them should be addressed in order to create a complete biological system which is based on rules that are linked to the underlying biological mechanisms allowing a dynamic evolution.

For example, consider the case of an ant colony. Each ant has its own evolution rules that allow it to grow, reproduce and die over time or under other specific circumstances; other rules define the movement behaviour of the ants. The ants are arranged in some two- or three-dimensional space, and this layout implies the way ants interact with others in the local neighbourhood. The structure of the colony, changes over time, thus imposing a change in their interactions.

In the last years attempts have been made to devise biology inspired computational models in the form of generative devices [25], [26], unconventional programming paradigms [2], bio-engines solving NP hard problems [1], adequate mechanisms to specify complex systems [13]. In this paper we have selected two formal methods, X-machines and population P systems, in order to model biological systems with dynamic organisation as multi-agent systems. Each of these methods possesses different characteristics which will be examined through the modelling process. These modelling paradigms take their inspiration from biology and are used to specify problems occurring in nature.

The structure of this paper is as follows: Section 2 describes the biological system modelled in this paper. Sections 3 and 4 present the theory regarding communicating X-machines and population P systems, respectively. Section 5 presents the actual models developed for an ant colony behaviour. Section 6 discusses some issues concerning the experiments conducted. Finally, Section 7 concludes the paper.

2   Pharaoh's Ants

Monomorium pharaonis, the Pharaoh's ants, are species of small ants that originated from North Africa. They measure up to two millimetres in length. The small size of the ants make them ideal for studying in a laboratory as their living environment requires little room. Colonies have a rapid reproductive cycle, around five and half weeks from egg to an adult, which is another useful trait for a study colony.

Typically a Pharaoh's ant colony will contain anywhere between 100 and 5000 ants. The smallest natural colonies of around 100 ants usually contain: one queen, 35 workers, 12 pupae and some brood. The largest colonies tend to have over 100 queens. 200 ants are usually used for experimental purposes to keep the colony manageable.

The ants spend much of their time doing nothing; this redundancy in the colony allows them to respond rapidly to large food finds. This allows them to efficiently transport the food to the nest before their competitors. Ants doing nothing can be referred as inactive. An ant can become active in many different ways: spontaneously by hunger, being recruited to forage by another ant, another ant soliciting food or another ant offering food. These interactions tend to happen within the nest.

The problem that will be modelled further on in this study presents the behaviour of a simple colony of ants in a nest. The Pharaoh's ants behaviour takes into account a very simplified situation where the colony is sitting in an rectangular environment and consists only of workers. The ants are either inactive or move around looking for food and when this is not found then they go outside the hive to forage for food. When two ants come across they might exchange food if one is hungry and the other one is not - it was in an inactive state. The ants go out to forage when they are hungry, no source food is identified (i.e. no other ant that might provide some food) and a trail pheromone leading to an exit point from the hive is discovered.

This simple problem is of interest for a number of reasons:

- it is a simple and realistic enough case study
- it shows a combination of both independent behaviour of ants inside of the environment as well as synchronised behaviour, e.g. when two ants come across to exchange food
- it has an important degree of repetitiveness using the same type of ant in a number of instances but also slightly small variations between them through the food distribution across the ant colony and their different position in the environment
- it uses different activities that requires distinct execution time periods.

There are a number of thresholds associated to the level of food that is exchanged between two ants, the level of food defining the hungry state, the time to forage for food.

This case study will be modelled by using two approaches, the communicating X machine paradigm and the population P system approach. The two methods have complementary appealing characteristics. X-machines being a state-based formalism appear to be more suitable for representing their internal data and knowledge of each of the participating entities (ants), and how the stimuli received from the environment can change their internal state. They have also been extended so as to facilitate communication among components and this allows the modelling of a collection of units in an incremental manner that distinguishes between the individual components definitions and the communicating issues. Though work is being done towards this direction, the way X-machines are defined does not accommodate a straightforward way of dealing with systems dynamically reconfigured. In an attempt to find alternative ways towards this end, in the form of other computing devices that may exhibit this characteristic, effort is being dedicated to exploring the modelling prospects of Population P Systems, which naturally (by definition) employ the quality of reconstructing themselves. Finally, work has also been done on finding a formal relationship among the two formalisms [20] whereby simple rules are established for the transformation of P systems into X-machines.

3   Communicating X-Machines

The X-machines formal method [7], [12] forms the basis for a specification language with a great potential to software engineers. It is rather intuitive while at the same time formal descriptions of data types and functions can be written in any known mathematical notation.

For modelling systems containing more than one agent, the X-machine components need to be extended with new features, such as hierarchical decomposition and communication. A communicating X-machine model consists of several X-machines that are able to exchange messages. This involves the modelling of the participating agents and the definition of the rules of their communication.

The complete model is a *communicating X-machine system* Z defined as a tuple:

$$Z = ((C_i)_{i=1,\ldots,n}, CR)$$

where:

- C_i is the i-th communicating X-machine component, and
- CR is a relation defining the communication among the components, $CR \subseteq C \times C$ and $C = \{C_1, \ldots, C_n\}$. A tuple $(C_i, C_k) \in CR$ denotes that the X-machine component C_i can output a message to a corresponding input stream of the X-machine component C_k for any $i, k \in \{1, \ldots, n\}$, $i \neq k$.

A *communicating X-machine component* C_i is defined as a tuple [22]:

$$C_i = (\Sigma_i, \Gamma_i, Q_i, M_i, \Phi C_i, F_i, q_{0_i}, m_{0_i})$$

where:

- Σ_i and Γ_i are the input and output alphabets respectively.
- Q_i is the finite set of states.
- M_i is the (possibly) infinite set called memory.
- ΦC_i is a set of partial functions φ_i that map an input and a memory value to an output and a possibly different memory value, $\varphi_i : \Sigma_i \times M_i \to \Gamma_i \times M_i$.

There are four different types of functions in ΦC_i (in all of the following it is $\sigma \in \Sigma_i$, $\gamma \in \Gamma_i$, m, $m' \in M_i$; $(\sigma)_j$ means that input is provided by machine C_j whereas $(\gamma)_k$ denotes an outgoing message to machine C_k):

- the functions that read input from the standard input stream and write their output to the standard output stream:
$$\varphi_i (\sigma, m) = (\gamma, m')$$
- the functions that read input from a communication input stream and write their output to the standard output stream:
$$\varphi_i ((\sigma)_j, m) = (\gamma, m')$$
- the functions that read input from the standard input stream and write their output to a communication output stream:
$$\varphi_i (\sigma, m) = ((\gamma)_k, m')$$
- the functions that read input from a communication input stream and write their output to a communication output stream:
$$\varphi_i ((\sigma)_j, m) = ((\gamma)_k, m')$$

- F_i is the next state partial function, $F_i : Q_i \times \Phi C_i \rightarrow Q_i$, which given a state and a function from the type ΦC_i determines the next state. F_i is often described as a state transition diagram.
- q_{0_i} and m_{0_i} the initial state and initial memory respectively.

Graphically on the state transition diagram we denote the acceptance of input by a stream other than the standard by a solid circle along with the name C_j of the communicating X-machine component that sends it. Similarly, a solid diamond with the name C_k denotes that output is sent to the C_k communicating X-machine component. An abstract example of a Communicating X-machine component is depicted in Fig. 1.

The above allows the definition of systems of a static configuration. However, most multi-agent systems are highly dynamic and this requires that their structure and the communication among the agents is constantly changing. For this to happen in a communicating X-machine model, control has to be taken over by another system acting on a higher level. This controlling device can be modelled as a set of meta-rules that refer to the configuration of the system or as a meta-X-machine that will be able to apply a number of operators which will be affecting the structure of the communicating system [21]. These operators are defined below.

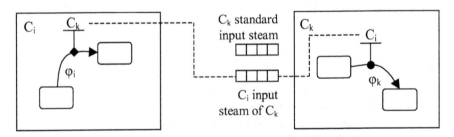

Fig. 1. An example of communication between two X-machine functions

Attachment Operator. This operator is responsible for establishing communication between an existing communicating X-machine component and a set of other existing components. Its definition is:

$$\textbf{ATT} : \mathcal{C} \times \mathcal{Z} \to \mathcal{Z}$$

where $\mathcal{C}$ is the set of communicating X-machine components, and $\mathcal{Z}$ is the set of communicating X-machine systems. For an existing component $C \in \mathcal{C}$ and a communicating X-machine system Z (to which C belongs to) a new communicating X-machine system Z' will be built that has different communication channels. The components remain the same except that for each function φ of the component machine C the streams of the other components, if any, it receives inputs from or sends outputs to are specified. Similarly, the communicating functions of the other components, with which C establishes communication, become related to the streams of the component C so that input can be received or output can be sent to it. It is this kind of relationships between the component C and the other components that define how the whole system is to communicate as a collection of units cooperating through streams of data.

Detachment Operator. This operator is used in order to remove communication channels between an existing communicating X-machine component and a set of other existing components with which it currently communicates. Its definition is:

$$\textbf{DET} : \mathcal{C} \times \mathcal{Z} \to \mathcal{Z}$$

where $\mathcal{C}$, $\mathcal{Z}$ are defined as previously. In this case all the relationships between the component C and its streams and the other components and their streams are broken down.

Generation Operator. A new communicating X-machine component is created and introduced into the system. If communication is required, according to the underlying communication rules, between the new and existing component(s), then communication channels are established. The definition of the operator is:

$$\textbf{GEN} : \mathcal{C} \times \mathcal{Z} \to \mathcal{Z}$$

where $\mathcal{C}$, $\mathcal{Z}$ are defined as previously.

Destruction Operator. This operator removes the component from the system along with all the communication channels that relate it to other components. This means that the corresponding streams that were used so that other components could send/receive messages to/from the removed component are also removed. The operator is defined as follows:

$$\textbf{DES} : \mathcal{C} \times \mathcal{Z} \to \mathcal{Z}$$

where $\mathcal{C}$, $\mathcal{Z}$ are defined as previously.

Conceptually, the meta-system could be considered to play the role of the environment to the actual communicating system. Because the meta-machine should be able to control the reconfiguration of the communicating system through the application of the above operators, it should possess the following information at all times:

- The communicating system $Z = ((C_1, \ldots, C_i, \ldots, C_n), CR)$,
- The current system state SZ of Z. SZ is defined as a set of tuples $SZ = \{sz \mid \exists C_i, 1 \leq i \leq n, \ sz = (q_c, M_c, \varphi_c)_i$, where q_c is the current state in which C_i is in, M_c is the current memory of C_i and φ_c is the last function that was applied in $C_i\}$,
- Definitions of all components that exist or may be added to the system. These definitions act as genetic codes (GC) for the system. GC is a set of tuples, $GC = \{\ldots (\Sigma, \Gamma, Q, M, \Phi, F, \Phi_R, \Phi_W)_j, \ldots\}$ where the first six elements are as in the definition of the X-machine given in the previous section and the last two the set of functions that may be involved in communication with other components (i.e. Φ_R includes the functions that may read from communicating streams and Φ_W the ones that may write to communicating streams). In other words, only the types of components that may appear in the system at any point are a priori fixed.

Using the above information, the control device can generate a new component and attach it to the communicating machine Z, through the operator GEN, destruct an existing component of Z and rearrange the communication of the other components appropriately, through the operator DES, and add or remove channels of communication between a component and a communicating machine due to some system reconfigurations, through the operators ATT and DET.

The communicating X-machine system provides a modelling tool, where a complex system can be decomposed in small components that can be modelled as simple X-machine models. The communication side of all these components can be specified separately in order to form the complete system as a communicating X-machine model. This implies a modular bottom-up approach and supports an iterative gradual development. It also facilitates the reusability of existing components, making the management of the whole project more flexible and efficient, achieving its completion with lower cost and less development time.

The communicating X-machine method supports a disciplined modular development, allowing the developers to decompose the system under development and model large scale systems. Since the communicating X-machine model is viewed as the composition of X-machine type components with their initial memory and initial state as well as with a set of input/output streams and associations of these streams to functions, the development of a general model of a complex system can be mapped into the following distinct actions: (a) Develop X-machine type components independently of the target system, or use existing models as they are. (b) Code the X-machine model into XMDL. With the use of tools that are built around the XMDL language it is possible to syntactically check the model and then automatically animate it [23]. Through this simulation it is possible for the developers to informally verify that the model corresponds to the actual system under development, and then also to demonstrate the model to the end-users aiding them to identify any misconceptions regarding the user requirements. (c) Use the formal verification technique (model checking) for X-machine models in order to increase the confidence that the proposed model has the desired characteristics. This technique enables the designer to verify the developed model against temporal logic formulas that express the properties that the system should have. (d) Test the implementation against the model. X-machines support not only static but also dynamic analysis. It is possible to use the formal testing strategy to test the implementation and prove its correctness with respect to the X-machine model. (e) Create X-machine instances of the original types and determine the way in which the independent instance models communicate. (f) Extend the model to a communicating system in order to provide additional functionality by defining the interaction between components. (g) Define appropriate meta-rules that describe the reconfiguration of the system.

With the continuous verification and testing from the early stages risks are reduced and the developer is confident of the correctness of the system under development throughout the whole process. It is worth noticing that components that have been verified and tested can be reused without any other quality check.

X-machine modelling is based on a mathematical notation, which, however, implies a certain degree of freedom, especially as far as the definition of functions are concerned. In order to make the approach practical and suitable for the development of tools around X-machines, a standard notation is devised and its semantics fully defined [19]. The aim is to use this notation, namely X-Machine Description Language (XMDL), as an interchange language between developers who could share models written in XMDL for different purposes. To avoid complex mathematical notation, the language symbols are completely defined in ASCII.

Briefly, an XMDL model is a list of definitions corresponding to the construct tuple of the X-machine definition. The language also provides syntax for (a) use of built-in types such as integers, Booleans, sets, sequences, bags, etc., (b) use of operations on these types, such as arithmetic, Boolean, set operations etc., (c) definition of new types, and (d) definition of functions and the conditions under which they are applicable. In Table 1 basic keywords used in XMDL to describe a stream X-machine are presented and briefly explained. In XMDL, the functions take two parameter tuples, i.e. an input symbol and a memory value, and return two new parameter tuples, i.e. an output and a new memory value. A function may be applicable under conditions (*if-then*) or unconditionally. Variables are denoted by a preceding ?. The informative **where** in combination with the operator <- is used to describe operations on memory values. A function has the following general syntax:

```
#fun <function name> ( <input tuple> , <memory tuple> ) =
if <condition expression> then
   ( <output tuple>, <memory tuple> )
where    <informative expression>.
```

Table 1. XMDL keywords

X-machine element	XMDL syntax	Informal semantics
$\mathcal{M}$	$\#model\ <modelname>$	Assigns a name to a model
Σ	$\#input\ <setofinputs>$	Describes the input set
Γ	$\#output\ <setofoutputs>$	Describes the output set
Q	$\#states\ <setofstates>$	Defines the set of states
M	$\#memory\ <memorytuple>$	Defines the memory tuple
q_0	$\#init\_state\ <state>$	Sets the initial state
m_0	$\#init\_memory\ <memory>$	Sets the initial memory
F	$\#transition\ (q, \phi) = q$	Defines each transition in F
Φ	$\#fun\ <functiondefinition>$	Defines a function in Φ

XMDL has also been extended (XMDL-c) in order to code communicating components. XMDL-c is used to define instances of models by providing a new initial state and a new initial memory instance:

```
#model <model_instance> instance_of <model_type>
with:
#init_state <initial_state>;
#init_memory <initial_memory>.
```

In addition, XMDL-c provides syntax that facilitates the definition of the communicating functions. The general syntax is the following:

```
#communication of function <function_name>:
#reads from <model instance>;
#writes <message tuple> to <model_instance>
    using <variable> from output <output tuple> and
    using <variable> from input <input tuple> and
    using <variable> from memory <memory tuple>
where    <informative expression>.
```

A function can either read or write or both from other components (model instances). It is not necessary to specify the incoming message because it is of the same type as the input defined in the original component. However, it is necessary specify the outgoing message as a tuple which may contain values that exist in either output or input tuples of the function or even in the memory tuple of the component. The informative expression is used to perform various operations on these values before they become part of the outgoing message tuple.

Based on XMDL and XMDL-c, various tools have been developed [18] such as translators to other notations or executable code (e.g. Z, Prolog), an animator that simulates the computation occurring in an X-machine or communicating X-machine system, a model checker for X-machines etc. It should be worthwhile to investigate towards expanding model-checking and testing techniques for the Communicating X-machine formalism though this should be attempted after formally establishing the theoretical framework.

4   Population P System Model

Membrane computing represents a new and rapidly growing research area which is part of the natural computing paradigm. Already a monograph has been dedicated to this subject [26] and some fairly recent results can be found in [27], [24]. Membrane computing has been introduced with the aim of defining a computing device, called *P system*, which abstracts from the structure and the functioning of living cells [25]. Membranes are among the main elements of the living cells which separate the cell from its environment and split the content of the cell into small compartments by means of internal membranes. Each compartment contains its own enzymes and their specialized molecules. Therefore, a membrane structure has been identified as the main characteristic of every P system that is defined as a hierarchical arrangement of different membranes embedded in a unique main membrane that identify several distinct regions inside the system. Each region contains a finite multiset of objects and a finite set of rules either modifying the objects or moving them from a place to another one. Formally we have the following:

Definition 1. *A P system is a construct*

$$\Pi = (V, \mu, w_1, w_2, \ldots, w_n, R_1, R_2, \ldots, R_m, i_O),$$

where:

1. *V is a finite set of symbols called objects;*
2. *μ is a membrane structure consisting of m membranes, with the membranes (and hence the regions) injectively labeled by $1, 2, .., m$;*
3. *for each $1 \leq i \leq n$, R_i is a finite set of evolution and communication rules; the evolution rules rewrite different objects with others and the objects of the result may stay in the same region or may go into another one; pure communication rules, called also symport/antiport rules exchange objects between two regions (for details see [26]);*
4. *$i_O \in \{1, 2, .., m\}$ is the label of an elementary membrane that identifies the output membrane.*

The basic feature of a P system is the membrane structure μ that consists of a hierarchical arrangement of m distinct membranes embedded in a unique main membrane called the skin membrane. This membrane structure is usually represented as a string of pairs of matching square brackets, which are labeled in an one-to-one manner by $1, 2, .., m$. Each pair of square brackets represents a membrane (membrane i) with its corresponding region (the region delimited by membrane i, or region i). Moreover, this representation makes possible to point out the relationships of inclusions among membranes and regions: we say a region i contains a membrane j if and only if, the pair of square brackets labeled by i embraces the pair of square brackets labeled by j.

Then, each region i contains a finite multiset of objects w_i, which defines the initial content of the region i, and a finite set of rules R_i.

As usual, by starting from the initial configuration, a computation is obtained by applying to the objects contained in the various regions the corresponding set of rules in a maximal parallel manner. A computation is said to be successful if it reaches a configuration where no more rules can be applied to the objects in the system.

A natural generalisation of the P system model can be obtained by considering P systems where its structure is defined as an arbitrary graph. Each node in the graph represents a membrane and contains a multiset of objects and a set of rules modifying these objects and communicating them between membrane components. The communication between two components is possible if they are connected by an edge of the graph [26]. These networks of communicating membranes are also known as *tissue P systems* because, from a biological point of view, they can be interpreted as an abstract model of multicellular organisms. If the components are regarded not only as simple cells surrounded by membranes but as more general bio-entities then this model may be considered for more complex organisms, or colonies of simple or more complex components.

These populations of individuals are usually far from being stable; mechanisms enabling new components to be added or removed, links between them to be dynamically updated, play a fundamental role in the evolution of a biological system as a population of interacting/cooperating elements.

We introduce here a notion of population P systems as a finite collection of different componets that are free of forming/removing bonds according to a finite set of bond making rules in a given environment.

Definition 2. *A population P system is a construct [3]*

$$\mathcal{P} = (V, \gamma, \alpha, w_E, C_1, C_2, \ldots, C_n, c_O)$$

where:

1. *V is a finite alphabet of symbols called objects;*
2. *$\gamma = (\{1, 2, \ldots n\}, E)$, with $E_n \subseteq \{\{i, j\} \mid 1 \leq i \neq j \leq n\}$, is a finite undirected graph;*
3. *α is a finite set of bond making rules $(i, x_1; x_2, j)$, with $x_1, x_2 \in V^*$, and $1 \leq i \neq j \leq n$;*
4. *$w_E \in V^*$ is a finite multiset of objects initially assigned to the environment;*
5. *$C_i = (w_i, S_i, R_i)$, for each $1 \leq i \leq n$, is a component of the system with:*
   (a) *$w_i \in V^*$ a finite multiset of objects,*
   (b) *S_i is a finite set of communication rules;*
   (c) *R_i is a finite set of transformation rules;*
6. *c_O is the output component.*

A population P system $\mathcal{P}$ is defined as a collection of n components where each component C_i corresponds in an one-to-one manner to a node i in a finite undirected graph γ, which defines the initial structure of the system. Components are allowed to communicate alongside the edges of the graph γ, which are unordered pairs of the form $\{i, j\}$, with $1 \leq i \neq j \leq n$. The components C_i, $1 \leq i \leq n$, are associated in an one-to-one manner with the set of nodes $\{1, 2, \ldots n\}$. For this reason, each component C_i will be subsequently identified by its label i from the aforementioned set.

Each component C_i contains a finite multiset of objects w_i, a finite set of communication rules S_i, and a finite set of transformation rules R_i.

Component capability of moving objects alongside the edges of the graph is then influenced by particular bond making rules in α that allow these components to form new bonds. In fact, a bond making rule $(i, x_1; x_2, j)$ specifies that, in the presence of a multiset x_1 in i and a multiset x_2 inside j, a new bond can be created between these two components. This means a new edge $\{i, j\}$ can be added to the graph that currently defines the structure of the system.

The model introduced will be further enriched with a concept of type which enables us to instantiate components. Each type component apart from objects and rules may also contain variables. The model enriched with these new features will be used from now on using a notation that is closer to a programming paradigm. An example of a component type is defined as follows:

```
component type a;
  element x, y, z; mult = 3;
  var t = 5, u = 10 : int;
  rule  x y --> x x z;  -- (r1)
  rule  z    --> z z;   -- (r2)
  rule  t    --> t+u;   -- (r3)
  end;
```

In this example a component type a is defined with object elements x, y, z, two variables t, u and three rewriting rules $r1, r2, r3$.

The objects x, y have one instance each, whereas z occurs in three copies. The integer variables t, u are introduced with initial values 5 and 10, respectively. The rules $r1$ and $r2$ rewrite xy and z, respectively, whereas $r3$ rewrites variable t with the sum of the values contained in t and u.

The rules may also be preceded by some Boolean conditions which allow the corresponding rules to be applied when these guards are true. Apart from rewriting rules, communication rules, division rules, and death rules are also provided. All the rules have an execution time associated with. By default this is 1, but may be greater than 1 as well and this means the rule needs more than 1 evolution steps in order to be performed.

From each component type various instances may be created. During the instantiation process the implicit values associated with various objects may be changed.

```
instance a1, a2: a;
  element x; mult 100;
instance a3: a;
```

In the example above two components $a1, a2$ are instantiated from a with 100 occurrences of x; y, z occur with the values mentioned in the definition of a. The component $a3$ has the same objects as a defined.

Apart from component types it is also possible to define the environment with objects of different types, but also bond making rules that create links between various components of the system.

5   Case Study: An Ant Colony

The first modelling approach will use an X-machine method. The ant is modelled so that it accepts a tuple (pos, stimuli) as input to its functions. The first element of the input tuple is a tuple representing the coordinates in which stimuli is perceived whereas the second element is the description of the stimuli. The latter can be *pheromone* or *space* describing the space denoted by the coordinates, a *hungry* or a *non-hungry* ant describing whether an ant that is perceived in the given coordinates carries food or not or, finally, a number greater than zero representing the quantity of food that is received by another ant that carries food. The memory of the ant holds (a) its current *position*, (b) the amount of *food* it carries, (c) a number denoting the *food quantity threshold* beneath which the ant becomes hungry, (d) the *food decay rate*, a number denoting the quantity of food that is consumed by the ant in each time unit and (e) the *food portion* that is to be given by an ant that is carrying food to another which is hungry. The behaviour of the systems is given by different functions processing input stimuli.

All these types are defined using XMDL declarations.

The *becomeHungry* function reduces the amount of food that the ant carries according to the food decay rate but is only applied when the updated value of the food quantity becomes less or equal to the hunger threshold $?ft$ in order to bring the ant to the *hungry* state.

```
#fun becomeHungry ((?p, ?in), (?pos, ?f, ?ft, ?fdr, ?mfp)) =
    if ?nf =< ?ft then
    ((gotHungry), (?pos, ?nf, ?ft, ?fdr, ?mfp))
    where ?nf <- ?f - ?fdr.
```

The *giveFood* function is applied when an ant gives $?mfp$ amount of food to the hungry ant it met. The updated food quantity that the ant will carry afterwards is reduced by the donated food portion $?mfp$ as well as by the food decay rate $?fdr$. All possible input is ignored by the ant which returns to the *inactive* state.

```
#fun giveFood ((?p, ?in), (?pos, ?f, ?ft, ?fdr, ?mfp)) =
    ((givingFood), (?pos, ?nf, ?ft, ?fdr, ?mfp))
    where ?food_reduction <- ?fdr + ?mfp
    and ?nf <- ?f - ?food_reduction.
```

The *die* function ignores all possible input and is only applied when the quantity of food in an ant's memory (the amount of food it is carrying) is equal to zero. It outputs a "dying" message and leaves the memory structure unaltered.

```
#fun die ((?p, ?in), (?pos, ?f, ?ft, ?fdr, ?mfp)) =
    if ?what_is_left =< 0 then
    ((dying), (?pos, 0, ?ft, ?fdr, ?mfp)).
    where ?what_is_left <- ?f - ?fdr.
```

To demonstrate how the reconfiguration operators are used we consider the case that after a food transaction, communication between the two ants needs to halt. The corresponding rule that will apply the detachment operator which will remove the communication channels between the two ant instances is:

$$(q_c, \ M_c, \ takeEnoughFood)_i \in SZ$$
$$\vee (q_c, \ M_c, \ takeNotEnoughFood)_i \in SZ$$
$$\rightarrow \textbf{DET} \ (i, \ Z)$$

Using the P system approach we may describe some of the rules applied to simulate the behaviour of the ant colony.

Each ant has a specific amount of found which will decrease as the time goes by. This is captured by the rule

```
foodL --> foodL-FoodDecayRate
```

where $foodL$ is a variable pointing to the current level of food; after applying this rule the updated value of this is obtained. When the level of food is under a threshold the ant will become hungry; this is shown by a rule

```
inactive and foodL < HungryLevel: inactive --> hungry
```

which will change *inactive* to *hungry* when the Boolean condition preceding the rule is true.

When an ant is hungry it is moving around looking for food. This is simulated by a communication rule which will put in the environment the current position and is getting a new position nearby.

```
Neighbour(pos,pos'): (out pos; in pos')
```

This rule will be read as "if the two positions *pos* and *pos'* are next to each other - predicate $Neighbour(pos, pos')$ is true, then the current position *pos* is sent out in the environment and a new position *pos'* from the environment enters the component".

When two ants are next to each other a bond making rule will create a link.

```
Neighbour(ant.pos, ant.pos'): <ant,ant>
```

In this case a bond will be created between the two ants if their positions are close enough.

A food transfer may take place between two ants that are linked.

```
transfer and foodL > HungryLevel:
(out FoodTransfer from foodL; outComponent ant) time=10
```

The ant that is not hungry and is in state transfer will provide $FoodTransfer$ units from its current amount of food. Correspondingly the ant that is at the other end of the link will receive the same $FoodTransfer$ that will be added to its amount of food. The transfer will take 10 units of simulation time.

When an ant cannot find food and its amount of food becomes 0 then it will die.

```
foodL <= 0:  (component_death)
```

6   Experiments

A variety of experiments were performed to examine how the Pharao's ant models behave [5]. Each worker ant logged a history of all food related actions it performed. These log files can then be analysed once the simulation has completed. The environment consisted of a nest with four entrances or exits, each of which was situated on a compass point (north, south, east, west). The colony consisted of 100 workers in a nest of 3cm by 3cm. The experiments show that the colony manages to distribute the food among the colony members before a mass forage occurs; the process has a cyclic nature and a smooth gradient.

In nature worker specialisation occurs. This is shown by a low proportion of worker ants focusing on feeding other colony members or foraging. The first case might be illustrated by some ants missing the forage cycle although no specific constraints were imposed in this respect and consequently a sort of emergent specialisation may be noticed. Although in our experiments in almost all the steps of the simulation there were ants missing the forage process is too early to identify a specialisation due to the reduced scale of the simulation time considered. It is likely that a more specific analysis of parameters involved in a long run simulation may lead to some conclusions regarding this phenomenon.

7   Conclusions

This work has been an attempt to model a simple biological system by using two different methods, namely population P systems and communicating X-machines. This simple case study shows the need to approach the dynamic structure and organisation of biological systems with models exhibiting such properties. Bond making rules in the context of P systems and operators **ATT**, **DET**, **GEN**, and **DES** in the case of communicating X-machines represent the key elements introduced in order to cope with the systems' dynamicity.

There are advantages to both methods, though at different modelling levels. The X-machine approach appears to be a natural model to express the internal behaviour of the components because they can naturally describe the internal states, transitions between them caused by stimuli and represent the data structures. However a communicating X-machine model cannot by itself manage the required reconfiguration, which is a prominent property of these biological systems. As a result, an external device, in the form of a meta-X-machine, is necessary; this device possesses global control over the structure of the overall system. Control is achieved through meta-operations which change the way that components interact or function. Population P systems, on the other hand, possess a natural trait for capturing the behaviour of a community of entities and how the structure of such a community may change over time. The new characteristics introduced in this paper, guards to rules, variables, arithmetic operations, improve the potential of this model to specify the internal behaviour of the componets.

Both methods have sound theoretical foundations and act as formal specification languages. Towards this end, the X-machine Description Language (XMDL) [19] has been defined offering the ability of formally describing X-machine models and acting as an interchange tool for software engineers. XMDL also serves as a common basis for the development of tools, such as the X-System [23], that allow the syntactical check and automatic animation of the models. In this paper the elements (component type, environment definition, component instantiation etc) of a specification language based on P systems were introduced for the first time.

In addition to this practical aspect, X-machines have further techniques supporting the modelling activity such as formal verification of desired system properties [8] and complete testing [14]. Towards practical modelling, appropriate XML notation in order to define population P systems is currently under development and soon expected to be made available. Formal properties of some classes of population P systems are also under investigation. Effort has been put into modelling a P system as a communicating X-machine [20]. Further investigations regarding possible transformations between communicating X-machine models and population P system models would be useful in order to support both a formal theoretical comparison as well as the modelling activity.

This case study shows not only the benefits of approaching systems with a dynamic structure by models exhibiting naturally these properties and the need to further develop these models, but it also suggests that this way of modelling may be reused in other contexts where multi-agent paradigm has to be considered. Communities of bacteria, cells in tissues, or more complex organisms composed of simpler components may be modelled in a similar way. In the next future we aim to use this approach in certain biological systems where to identify their emergent behaviour as well as potentially new computational paradigms inspired by these systems.

Acknowledgement. We are grateful to dr. George Eleftherakis who has helped us in developing the communicating X-machine methodology and to our students that have built various tools and experimented different case studies. We especially would like to thank James Clarke, Peter Langton, Liancheng Lu, Taihong Wu, Yang Yang who have built a tool helping experimenting with the X-machine model and Fei Lu and Ming-Hsin An who have worked on building a tool allowing to simulate P system specifications. The research of Marian Gheorghe was supported by the Engineering and Physical Science Research Council (EPSRC) of United Kingdom, Grant GR/R84221/01.

Bibliography

[1] Adleman, L.M. 1994. Molecular computation of solutions to combinatorial problems, *Science*, 226, 1021-1024.

[2] Banatre, J.P., Le Metayer, D. 1990. The gamma model and its discipline of programming, *Science of Computer Programming*, 15, 55-77.

[3] Bernardini, F., Gheorghe, M. 2004. Population P Systems, *Journal of Universal Computer Science*, 10, 509-539.

[4] Bianco, L., Fontana, F., Franco, G., Manca, V. 2004. P systems in Bio Systems. In Păun, Gh., ed. 2004. *Application of P systems*, submitted.

[5] Clarke, J., Langton, P., Lu, L., Wu, T., Yang, Y. 2002. Computational models of Pharao's ants using X-machines. Department of Computer Science, University of Sheffield, MSc final report.

[6] Dorigo, M., Maniezzo, V., Colorni, A. 1996. The Ant System: Optimisation by a colony of co-operating agents, *IEEE Transactions on Systems, Man and Cybernetics*, 26, 1-13.

[7] Eilenberg, S. 1974. Automata, Languages and Machines, Academic Press.

[8] Eleftherakis, G. 2003. *Formal Verification of X-Machine Models: Towards Formal Development of Computer-based Systems*, PhD Thesis, Department of Computer Science, University of Sheffield.

[9] Eleftherakis, G., Kefalas, P. 2000. Model Checking Safety Critical Systems specified as X-Machines, *Analele Universitatii Bucharest, Matematica-Informatica series*, 49, 59-70.

[10] Eleftherakis, G., Kefalas, P., Sotiriadou, A. 2003. Formal Modelling and Verification of Reactive Agents for Intelligent Control. In *Proceedings of the 12th Intelligent System Applications to Power Systems Conference* (ISAP).

[11] Gregson, A. M., Hart, A. G., Holcombe, M., Ratnieks, F. L. W. 2003. Partial nectar loads as a cause of multiple nectar transfer in the honey bee (Apis mellifera): a simulation model. *Journal of Theoretical Biology*, 222, 1-8.

[12] Holcombe, M. 1988. X-machines as a Basis for Dynamic System Configuration, *Software Engineering Journal*, 3, 69-76.

[13] Holcombe, M. 2001. Computational models of cells and tissues: Machines, agents and fungal infection, *Briefings in Bioinformatics*, 2, 271-278.

[14] Holcombe, M., Ipate, F. 1998. *Correct Systems: Building a Business Process Solution*, Springer-Verlag, London, 1998.

[15] Ipate, F., Holcombe, M. 1997. An Integration Testing Method that is proved to find all faults, *International Journal of Computer Mathematics*, 63, 159-178.

[16] Jennings, N.R. 2000. On agent-based software engineering, *Artificial Intelligence*, 117, 277-296.

[17] Kapeti, E., Kefalas, P. 2000. A Design Language and Tool for X-Machines Specification, In Fotiadis, D.I., Spyropoulos, S.D., eds. 2000. *Advances in Informatics*, World Scientific Publishing Company, 134-145.

[18] Kefalas P. 2000. Automatic translation from X-machines to Prolog. TR-CS01/00, Dept. of Computer Science, CITY Liberal Studies.

[19] Kefalas, P. 2000. XMDL user manual: version 1.6. TR-CS07/00, Dept. of Computer Science, CITY Liberal Studies.

[20] Kefalas, P., Eleftherakis, G., Holcombe, M., Gheorghe, M. 2003. Simulation and Verification of P Systems through Communicating X-Machines, *BioSystems*, 70, 135-148.

[21] Kefalas, P., Eleftherakis, G., Holcombe, M., Stamatopoulou, I. 2004. Formal Modelling of the Dynamic Behaviour of Biology-Inspired Agent-based Systems, In Gheorghe, M. ed. 2004. *Molecular Computational Models: Unconventional Approaches*, Idea Publishing, Inc, accepted.

[22] Kefalas, P., Eleftherakis, G., Kehris, E. 2003. Communicating X-Machines: A Practical Approach for Formal and Modular Specification of Large Systems, *Journal of Information and Software Technology*, 45, 269-280.

[23] Kefalas, P., Eleftherakis, G., Sotiriadou, A. 2003. Developing Tools for Formal Methods. *Proceedings of the 9th Panhellenic Conference in Informatics*. 625-639.

[24] Martin-Vide, C., Mauri, G., Păun, Gh., Rozenberg, G., Salomaa, A. (eds.) 2004. *Membrane Computing*. International Workshop, WMC 2003, Tarragona. Revised Papers in Lecture Notes in Computer Science 2933, Springer-Verlag, Berlin / Heidelberg / New York.

[25] Păun, G. 2000. Computing with membranes, *Journal of Computer and System Sciences*, 61, 1, 108-143.

[26] Păun, Gh. 2002. *Membrane Computing: An Introduction*, Springer-Verlag, Berlin.

[27] Păun, Gh., Rozenberg, G., Salomaa, A., Zandron, C.(eds.) 2002. *Membrane Computing*. International Workshop, WMC-CdeA 02, Curtea de Arges, Romania. Revised Papers in Lecture Notes in Computer Science 2597, Springer-Verlag, Berlin / Heidelberg / New York.

P Systems: Some Recent Results
and Research Problems*

Oscar H. Ibarra

Department of Computer Science, University of California,
Santa Barbara, CA 93106, USA
ibarra@cs.ucsb.edu

Abstract. Let $R = \{r_1, ..., r_k\}$ be the set of labeled rules in a P system. We look at the computing power of the system under three semantics of parallelism. For a positive integer $n \leq k$, define:

n-**Max-Parallel:** At each step, nondeterministically select a maximal subset of at most n rules in R to apply.

$\leq n$-**Parallel:** At each step, nondeterministically select any subset of at most n rules in R to apply.

n-**Parallel:** At each step, nondeterministically select any subset of exactly n rules in R to apply.

Note that in all three cases, at most one instance of any rule can be included in the selected subset. Moreover, if any rule in the subset selected is not applicable, then the whole subset is not applicable. When $n = 1$, the three semantics reduce to the **Sequential** mode.

For two models of P systems that have been studied in the literature, catalytic systems and communicating P systems, we show that n-**Max-Parallel** mode is strictly more powerful than any of the following three modes: **Sequential**, $\leq n$-**Parallel**, or n-**Parallel**. For example, it follows from a previous result that a 3-**Max Parallel** communicating P system is universal. However, under the three limited modes of parallelism, the system is equivalent to a vector addition system, which is known to only define a recursive set. This shows that "maximal parallelism" (in the sense of n-**Max-Parallel**) is key for the model to be universal.

We also summarize our recent results concerning membrane hierarchy, determinism versus nondeterminism, and computational complexity of P systems. Finally, we propose some problems for future research.

Some of the results presented here were obtained in collaboration with Zhe Dang and Hsu-Chun Yen.

Keywords: P system, maximally parallel, sequential, limited parallelism, vector addition system, semilinear set, membrane hierarchy, determinism versus nondeterminism, computational complexity.

* This research was supported in part by NSF Grants IIS-0101134, CCR-0208595, and CCF-0430945.

J.-P. Banâtre et al. (Eds.): UPP 2004, LNCS 3566, pp. 225–237, 2005.

1   Introduction

There has been a flurry of research activities in the area of membrane computing (a branch of molecular computing) initiated five years ago by Gheorghe Paun [20]. Membrane computing identifies an unconventional computing model, namely a P system, from natural phenomena of cell evolutions and chemical reactions. Due to the built-in nature of maximal parallelism inherent in the model, P systems have a great potential for implementing massively concurrent systems in an efficient way that would allow us to solve currently intractable problems (in much the same way as the promise of quantum and DNA computing) once future bio-technology (or silicon-technology) gives way to a practical bio-realization (or chip-realization).

The Institute for Scientific Information (ISI) has recently selected membrane computing as a fast "Emerging Research Front" in Computer Science. A P system is a computing model, which abstracts from the way the living cells process chemical compounds in their compartmental structure. Thus, regions defined by a membrane structure contain objects that evolve according to given rules. The objects can be described by symbols or by strings of symbols, in such a way that multisets of objects are placed in regions of the membrane structure. The membranes themselves are organized as a Venn diagram or a tree structure where one membrane may contain other membranes. By using the rules in a nondeterministic, maximally parallel manner, transitions between the system configurations can be obtained. A sequence of transitions shows how the system is evolving. Various ways of controlling the transfer of objects from a region to another and applying the rules, as well as possibilities to dissolve, divide or create membranes have been studied. P systems were introduced with the goal to abstract a new computing model from the structure and the functioning of the living cell (as a branch of the general effort of Natural Computing – to explore new models, ideas, paradigms from the way nature computes). Membrane computing has been quite successful: many models have been introduced, most of them Turing complete and/or able to solve computationally intractable problems (NP-complete, PSPACE-complete) in a feasible time (polynomial), by trading space for time. (See the P system website at http://psystems.disco.unimb/it for a large collection of papers in the area, and in particular the monograph [21].)

In the standard semantics of P systems [20, 21, 23], each evolution step of a system G is a result of applying all the rules in G in a maximally parallel manner. More precisely, starting from the initial configuration, w, the system goes through a sequence of configurations, where each configuration is derived from the directly preceding configuration in one step by the application of a multi-set of rules, which are chosen nondeterministically. For example, a catalytic rule $Ca \to Cv$ in membrane q is applicable if there is a catalyst C and an object (symbol) a in the preceding configuration in membrane q. The result of applying this rule is the evolution of v from a. If there is another occurrence of C and another occurrence of a, then the same rule or another rule with Ca on the left hand side can be applied. Thus, in general, the number of times a particular rule is applied at anyone step can be unbounded. We require that the application of the rules is maximal: all objects, from all membranes, which *can be* the subject of local evolution rules *have to* evolve simultaneously. Configuration z is reachable (from the starting configuration) if it appears in some execution sequence; z is halting if no rule is applicable on z.

In this paper, we study a different definition of maximal parallelism. Let $R = \{r_1, ..., r_k\}$ be the set of labeled rules in a P system. (Note that r_i uniquely specifies the membrane the rule belongs to.) At each step of the computation, a maximal subset of R is applied, and at most one instance of any rule is used at every step (thus at most k rules are applicable at any step). For example, if r_i is a catalytic rule $Ca \rightarrow Cv$ in membrane q and the current configuration has two C's and three a's in membrane q, then only one a can evolve into v using rule r_i. Of course, if there is another rule r_j ($i \neq j$), $Ca \rightarrow Cv'$, in membrane q, then the other a also evolves into v'. It is not necessary that v' be different from v. Thus, two different labels r_i and r_j ($i \neq j$) can specify the same evolution rule, e.g., rules r_1, r_2, r_3 can all be $Ca \rightarrow Cv$. Our definition is equivalent to one which requires that at every step, a maximal multiset of rules (i.e., a rule can be used more than once) that is applied is of size at most k. This is because we can give each evolution rule k distinct labels.

We investigate the computational power of two models of P systems – catalytic systems [20] and and communicating P systems [26] – under the following three semantics of parallelism: n-**Max-Parallel**, $\leq n$-**Parallel**, and n-**Parallel**. When $n = 1$, the three semantics reduce to the **Sequential** mode (i.e., zero parallelism).

We also summarize our recent results (that resolved some open problems in the field) concerning the existence of an infinite hierarchy with respect to the number of membranes in a natural (nonuniversal) model of P systems [13], determinism versus nondeterminism in P systems [15], and computational complexity of P systems [14]. Finally, we propose some problems for future research.

Some of the results presented in Sections 2 and 3 were obtained in collaboration with Zhe Dang and Hsu-Chun Yen in [4, 16]. No proofs are given in this paper. They can be found in the cited references.

2   Catalytic System (CS)

We recall the definition of a multi-membrane catalytic system (CS) as defined in [20]. The membranes (regions) are organized in a hierarchical (tree) structure and are labeled 1, 2, .., m for some m, with the outermost membrane (the skin membrane) labeled 1. At the start of the computation, there is a distribution of *catalysts* and *noncatalysts* in the membranes (the distribution represents the initial configuration of the system). Each membrane may contain a finite set of catalytic rules of the form $Ca \rightarrow Cv$, where C is a catalyst, a is a noncatalyst, and v is a (possibly null) string of noncatalysts. When this rule is applied, the catalyst remains in the membrane the rule is in, symbol a is deleted from the membrane, and the symbols comprising v (if nonnull) are transported to other membranes in the following manner. Each symbol b in v has a designation or target, i.e., it is written b_x, where x can be *here*, *out*, or in_j. The designation *here* means that the object b remains in the membrane containing it (we usually omit this target, when it is understood). The designation *out* means that the object is transported to the membrane directly enclosing the membrane that contains the object; however, we do not allow any object to be transported out of the skin membrane. The designation in_j means that the object is moved into a membrane, labeled j, that is directly enclosed by the membrane that contains the object.

It is important to note that our definition of catalytic system is different from what is usually called catalytic system in the literature. Here, we do not allow rules without catalysts, i.e., rules of the form $a \rightarrow v$. Thus our systems use only purely catalytic rules.

Suppose S is a CS with m membranes. Let $\{a_1, ..., a_n\}$ be the set of noncatalyst symbols (objects) that can occur in the configurations of S. Let $w = (w_1, ..., w_m)$ be the initial configuration, where w_i represents the catalysts and noncatalysts in membrane i. (Note that w_i can be null.) Each reachable configuration of S is an nm-tuple $(v_1, ..., v_m)$, where v_i is an n-tuple representing the multiplicities of the symbols $a_1, ..., a_n$ in membrane i. Note that we do not include the catalysts in considering the configuration as they are not changed (i.e., they remain in the membranes containing them, and their numbers remain the same during the computation). Hence the set of all reachable configurations of S, denoted by $R(S)$ is a subset of $\mathbf{N}^{mn}$. The set of all halting reachable configurations is denoted by $R_h(S)$.

It is known that for any set $Q \subseteq \mathbf{N}^n$ that can be accepted by a Turing machine, we can construct a 1-membrane CS G with only purely catalytic rules such that $R_h(G) = Q$ [26, 27]. Actually, the constructions in [26, 27] use non-catalytic of the form $a \rightarrow v$, but these rules can be simulated by purely catalytic rules. A recent result in [7] shows that for a purely catalytic system, three distinct catalysts (where each catalyst appears exactly once in the initial configuration) are already sufficient for universality. (The three catalysts can be reduced to two if rules of the form $a \rightarrow v$ are allowed.) Thus, in general, a 3-**Max-Parallel** 1-membrane CS can define a nonrecursive reachability set.

2.1   Sequential CS (Zero Parallelism)

In a sequential CS, each step of the computation consists of an application of a single nondeterministically chosen rule, i.e., the membrane and rule within the membrane to apply are chosen nondeterministically. Thus, the computation of the CS has no parallelism at all. It turns out that sequential CS's are much weaker. They define exactly the semilinear sets.

We need the definition of a vector addition system. An n-dimensional *vector addition system* (VAS) is a pair $G = \langle x, W \rangle$, where $x \in \mathbf{N}^n$ is called the *start point* (or *start vector*) and W is a finite set of vectors in $\mathbf{Z}^n$, where $\mathbf{Z}$ is the set of all integers (positive, negative, zero). The *reachability set* of the VAS $\langle x, W \rangle$ is the set $R(G) = \{z \mid$ for some $j, z = x + v_1 + ... + v_j$, where for all $1 \le i \le j$, each $v_i \in W$ and $x + v_1 + ... + v_i \ge 0\}$. The *halting reachability set* $R_h(G) = \{z \mid z \in R(G), z + v \not\ge 0$ for every v in $W\}$.

A VAS $G = \langle x, W \rangle$, where each vector in W is in $\mathbf{N}^n$ (i.e., has nonnegative components) generates a *linear set*. Any finite union of linear sets is called a *semilinear set*.

An n-dimensional *vector addition system with states* (VASS) is a VAS $\langle x, W \rangle$ together with a finite set T of transitions of the form $p \rightarrow (q, v)$, where q and p are states and v is in W. The meaning is that such a transition can be applied at point y in state p and yields the point $y + v$ in state q, provided that $y + v \ge 0$. The VASS is specified by $G = \langle x, T, p_0 \rangle$, where p_0 is the starting state. The *reachability set* is $R(G) = \{z \mid$ for some $j, z = x + v_1 + ... + v_j$, where for all $1 \le i \le j$, $p_{i-1} \rightarrow (p_i, v_i) \in T$, and $x + v_1 + ... + v_i \ge 0\}$. The *reachability problem* for a VASS (respectively, VAS) G is to determine, given a vector y, whether y is in $R(G)$. The *equivalence problem* is to determine given two VASS (respectively, VAS) G and G', whether $R(G) = R(G')$. Similarly, one can define the reachability problem and equivalence problem for halting configurations.

The following summarizes the known results concerning VAS and VASS [29, 10, 1, 11, 18]:

Theorem 1. *1. Let G be an n-dimensional VASS. We can effectively construct an $(n+3)$-dimensional VAS G' that simulates G.*

2. If G is a 2-dimensional VASS G, then $R(G)$ is an effectively computable semilinear set.

3. There is a 3-dimensional VASS G such that $R(G)$ is not semilinear.

4. If G is a 5-dimensional VAS G, then $R(G)$ is an effectively computable semilinear set.

5. There is a 6-dimensional VAS G such that $R(G)$ is not semilinear.

6. The reachability problem for VASS (and hence also for VAS) is decidable.

7. The equivalence problem for VAS (and hence also for VASS) is undecidable.

Clearly, it follows from part 6 of the theorem above that the halting reachability problem for VASS (respectively, VAS) is decidable.

A *communication-free VAS* is a VAS where in every transition, at most one component is negative, and if negative, its value is -1. They are equivalent to communication-free Petri nets, which are also equivalent to commutative context-free grammars [5, 12]. It is known that they have effectively computable semilinear reachability sets [5].

Our first result shows that a sequential CS is weaker than a maximally parallel CS.

Theorem 2. *The following are equivalent: communication-free VAS, sequential multi-membrane CS, sequential 1-membrane CS.*

Corollary 1. *1. If S is a sequential multi-membrane CS, then $R(S)$ and $R_h(S)$ are effectively computable semilinear sets.*

2. The reachability problem (whether a given configuration is reachable) for sequential multi-membrane CS is NP-complete.

2.2   CS Under Limited Parallelism

Here we look at the computing power of the CS under three semantics of parallelism. Let $R = \{r_1, ..., r_k\}$ be the set of rules of the CS. For a positive integer $n \leq k$, define:

1. n-**Max-Parallel:** At each step, nonderministically select a maximal subset of at most n rules in R to apply.
2. $\leq n$-**Parallel:** At each step, nondeterministically select any subset of at most n rules in R to apply.
3. n-**Parallel:** At each step, nondeterministically select any subset of exactly n rules in R to apply.

In all three cases above, if any rule in the set selected is not applicable, then the whole set is not applicable. Note that when $n = 1$, the three semantics reduce to the **Sequential** mode.

Theorem 3. *For* $n = 3$, *a 1-membrane CS operating under the* n-**Max-Parallel** *mode can define any recursively enumerable set. For any* n, *a multi-membrane CS operating under* $\leq n$-**Parallel** *mode or* n-**Parallel** *mode can be simulated by a VASS* (= *VAS*).

2.3   Simple Cooperative 1-Membrane System

Now consider the case when the 1-membrane CS has only one catalyst C with initial configuration $C^k x$ for some k and string x of noncatalysts. Thus, there are k copies of the same catalyst in the initial configuration. The rules allowed are of the form $Ca \rightarrow v$ or of the form $Caa \rightarrow Cv$, i.e., C catalyzes one or two copies of an object. This system is equivalent to a special form of cooperative P system [20, 21]. A simple cooperative system (SCS) is a P system where the rules allowed are of the form $a \rightarrow v$ or of the form $aa \rightarrow v$. Moreover, there is some fixed integer k such that the system operates in maximally parallel mode, but uses no more that k rules in any step. Clearly, the two systems are equivalent.

Theorem 4. *A 1-membrane SCS operating in* k-*maximally parallel mode can simulate a Turing machine when* k *is at least 9.*

3   Communicating P System (CPS)

A communication P System (CPS) has rules of the form (see [26]):

1. $a \rightarrow a_x$
2. $ab \rightarrow a_x b_y$
3. $ab \rightarrow a_x b_y c_{come}$

where x, y can be *here*, *out*, or in_j. As before, *here* means that the object remains in the membrane containing it, *out* means that the object is transported to the membrane directly enclosing the membrane that contains the object (or to the environment if the object is in the skin membrane), and *come* can only occur within the outermost region (i.e., skin membrane), and it means import the object from the environment. The designation in_j means that the object is moved into a membrane, labeled j, that is directly enclosed by the membrane that contains the object.

3.1   Sequential 1-Membrane CPS

First we consider the case when there is only one membrane (the skin membrane). The computation is *sequential* in that at each step there is only one application of a rule (to one instance). So, e.g., if nondeterministically a rule like $ab \rightarrow a_{here} b_{out} c_{come}$ is chosen, then there must be at least one a and one b in the membrane. After the step, a remains in the membrane, b is thrown out of the membrane, and c comes into the membrane. There may be several a's and b's, but only one application of the rule is applied. Thus, there is *no* parallelism involved. The computation halts when there is no applicable rule. Again, we are only interested in the multiplicities of the objects when the system halts.

We shall see below that a 1-membrane CPS can be simulated by a VASS (= VAS). However, the converse is not true:

Theorem 5. *The set of (halting) reachable configurations of a sequential 1-membrane CPS is a semilinear set.*

3.2   Sequential 1-Membrane Extended CPS (ECPS)

Interestingly, if we generalize the rules of a 1-membrane CPS slightly, the extended system becomes equivalent to a VASS. Define an extended CPS (ECPS) by allowing rules of the form:

1. $a \to a_x$
2. $ab \to a_x b_y$
3. $ab \to a_x b_y c_{come}$
4. $ab \to a_x b_y c_{come} d_{come}$

(i.e., by adding rules of type 4).

Theorem 6. *Sequential 1-membrane ECPS and VASS are equivalent.*

We can generalize rules of an ECPS further as follows:

1. $a_{i_1}...a_{i_h} \to a_{i_1 x_1}...a_{i_h x_h}$
2. $a_{i_1}...a_{i_h} \to a_{i_1 x_1}...a_{i_h x_h} c_{j_{1come}}...c_{j_{lcome}}$

where $h, l \geq 1$, and $x_m \in \{here, out\}$ for $1 \leq m \leq h$, and the a's and c's are symbols. Call this system ECPS+. ECPS+ is still equivalent to a VASS. Thus, we have:

Corollary 2. *The following systems are equivalent: Sequential 1-membrane ECPS, sequential 1-membrane ECPS+, and VASS.*

3.3   Sequential 2-Membrane CPS

In Section 3.1, we saw that a sequential 1-membrane CPS can only define a semilinear set. However, if the system has two membranes, we can show:

Theorem 7. *Sequential 2-membrane CPS and VASS are equivalent.*

3.4   Sequential Multi-membrane ECPS

In Theorem 6, we saw that a sequential 1-membrane ECPS can be simulated by a VASS. This result generalizes to:

Theorem 8. *The following are equivalent: VASS, sequential 2-membrane CPS, sequential 1-membrane ECPS, sequential multi-membrane ECPS, and sequential multi-membrane ECPS+.*

We can also prove:

Theorem 9. *For any n, a multi-membrane ECPS+ operating under $\leq n$-**Parallel** mode or n-**Parallel** mode is equivalent to a VASS.*

4   Membrane Hierarchy

The question of whether there exists a model of P systems where the number of membranes induces an infinite hierarchy in its computational power had been open since the beginning of membrane computing five years ago. Our recent paper [13] provided a positive answer to this problem.

Consider a restricted model of a communicating P system, called RCPS, whose environment does not contain any object initially. The system can expel objects into the environment but only expelled objects can be retrieved from the environment. Such a system is initially given an input $a_1^{i_1}...a_n^{i_n}$ (with each i_j representing the multiplicity of distinguished object a_i, $1 \leq i \leq n$) and is used as an acceptor. We showed the following results in [13]:

Theorem 10.   *1. RCPS's are equivalent to two-way multihead finite automata over bounded languages (i.e., subsets of $a_1^*...a_n^*$, for some distinct symbols $a_1, ..., a_n$).*
   2. For every r, there is an $s > r$ and a unary language L accepted by an RCPS with s membranes that cannot be accepted by an RCPS with r membranes.

We note that the proof of the infinite hierarchy above reduces the problem (in an intricate way) to the known hierarchy of nondeterministic two-way multihead finite automata over a unary input alphabet. An interesting problem for further investigation is whether the hierarchy can be made tighter, i.e., whether the result holds for $s = r+1$.

We also considered in [13] variants/generalizations of RCPS's, e.g, acceptors of languages; models that allow a "polynomial bounded" supply of objects in the environment initially; models with tentacles, etc. We showed that they also form an infinite hierarchy with respect to the number of membranes (or tentacles). The proof techniques can be used to obtain similar results for other restricted models of P systems, like symport/antiport systems [19]. These systems, which are similar to communicating P systems, use rules of the form (u, out), (u, in), and $(u, out; v, in)$ where u, v are (possibly null) strings of symbols (representing multisets of objects). A rule of the form (u, out) in membrane i sends the elements of u from membrane i out to the membrane (directly) containing i. A rule of the form (u, in) in membrane i transports the elements of u into membrane i from the membrane enclosing i. Hence this rule can only be used when the elements of u exist in the outer membrane. A rule of the form $(u, out; v, in)$ simultaneously sends u out of the membrane i while transporting v into membrane i. Hence this rule cannot be applied unless membrane i contains the elements in u and the membrane surrounding i contains the elements in v.

5   Determinism Versus Nondeterminism

An interesting class of P systems with symport/antiport rules was studied in [9] – each system is *deterministic* in the sense that the computation path of the system is unique, i.e., at each step of the computation, the maximal multiset of rules that is applicable is unique. It was shown in [9] that any recursively enumerable unary language $L \subseteq o^*$ can be accepted by a deterministic 1-membrane symport/antiport system. Thus, for symport/antiport systems, the deterministic and nondeterministic versions are equivalent. It also follows from the construction in [26] that for communicating P systems, the deterministic and nondeterministic versions are equivalent as both can accept any unary recursively enumerable language. The deterministic-versus-nondeterministic question was left open in [9] for the class of catalytic systems, where the proofs of universality involve a high degree of parallelism [26, 7]. In particular, it was an open problem [2] whether there is a class of (universal or nonuniversal) P systems where the nondeterministic (maximally parallel) version is strictly more powerful than the deterministic version.

In a recent paper [15], we looked at two classes of nonuniversal models of P systems. For one class, we showed that the deterministic and nondeterministic versions are equivalent if and only if deterministic and nondeterministic linear bounded automata (LBA) are equivalent. The latter problem is a long-standing open question in complexity theory. While it is known that a nondeterministic LBA (which is equivalent to a nondeterministic n space-bounded Turing machine) can be simulated by a deterministic n^2 space-bounded Turing machine [24], it is open whether this result is optimal. Thus, for this class of P systems, the question of whether or not the deterministic version is strictly weaker than the nondeterministic version reduces to an unresolved fundamental problem in computational complexity. For another class of P systems, we can actually showed that the deterministic version is strictly weaker than the nondeterministic version. We describe the models below.

The First Model. The first model is the RCPS defined in the previous section. A nondeterministic (respectively, deterministic) RCPS is one in which there may be more than one (respectively, at most one) maximally parallel multiset of rules that is applicable at each step. Thus, in the deterministic version, the maximally parallel multiset of rules applicable at each step of the computation is unique.

We showed in [15] that a unary language L is accepted by a deterministic (respectively, nondeterministic) RCPS if and only if it can be accepted by a deterministic (respectively, nondeterministic) two-way multihead finite automaton. Combining this with a result in [25] that nondeterministic and deterministic two-way multihead finite automata over a unary input alphabet are equivalent if and only if nondeterministic and deterministic linear bounded automata (over an arbitrary input alphabet) are equivalent, we get the following:

Theorem 11. *Every unary language accepted by a nondeterministic RCPS can be accepted by a deterministic RCPS if and only if every language (over an arbitrary input alphabet) accepted by a nondeterministic linear bounded automaton can be accepted by a deterministic linear bounded automaton.*

The Second Model. We define another restricted model of a CPS, called SCPA. An SCPA is a language acceptor over an input alphabet Σ containing a distinguished symbol $ (the right end marker for the input). The system uses other (noninput) symbols. An input to the SCPA is a string $a_1...a_n$, where $a_1, ..., a_{n-1}$ are in $\Sigma - \{$\}$ and $a_n = $. We impose the following conditions on the system:

1. No symbol in Σ appears in the initial configuration.
2. No symbols are expelled into the environment.

3. The rules (similar to those of a CPS) are of the form:
   (a) $a \rightarrow a_x$
   (b) $ab \rightarrow a_x b_y$
   (c) $ab \rightarrow a_x b_y c_{come}$

   The restrictions are the following:

   As before, a rule of type (c) (called a read-rule) can only appear in membrane 1. This brings in c if the next symbol in the input string $w = a_1...a_n$ that has not yet been processed (read) is c; otherwise, the rule is not applicable. Also, there are no rules in membrane 1 with c_{out} on the right-hand side of the rule for any symbol c (i.e., no symbol can be expelled from membrane 1 into the environment). It follows that the at any time after reading the j-th symbol of the input string but before reading the $j + 1$-st symbol, the system will have exactly j symbols from Σ.
   (d) Maximal parallelism in the application of the rules is assumed as usual. In particular, if in one step, $j \geq 1$ symbols are imported from the skin membrane, then the j symbols must be consistent with the next j symbols of the input string that have not yet been processed (by the semantics of the read-rule described in the preceding paragraph).
   (e) The input string $w = a_1...a_n$ (note that a_n is the right end marker $\$$) is accepted if, after reading all the input symbols, the SCPA eventually halts.

The language accepted by G is $L(G) = \{a_1...a_{n-1} \mid a_1...a_n$ is accepted by $G\}$ (we do not include the end marker).

We have two versions of the system described above: deterministic SCPA and nondeterministic SCPA. Again, in the deterministic case, the maximally parallel multiset of rules applicable at each step of the computation is unique. We showed the following result in [15]:

Theorem 12. *There is a language that can be accepted by a nondeterministic SCPA that cannot be accepted by any deterministic SCPA.*

6   Computational Complexity of P Systems

In [14], we showed how techniques in machine-based complexity can be used to analyze the complexity of membrane computing systems. The focus was on catalytic systems, communicating P systems, and systems with only symport/antiport rules, but the techniques are applicable to other P systems that are universal. We defined space and time complexity measures and showed hierarchies of complexity classes similar to well known results concerning Turing machines and counter machines. We also showed that the deterministic communicating P system simulating a deterministic counter machine in [26, 28] can be constructed to have a fixed number of membranes, answering positively an open question in [26, 28]. We proved that reachability of extended configurations for symport/antiport systems (as well as for catalytic systems and communicating P systems) can be decided in nondeterministic $log\ n$ space and, hence, in deterministic $log^2 n$ space or in polynomial time, improving the main result in [22]. We also proposed two equivalent systems that define languages (instead of multisets of objects): the first is a catalytic system language generator and the other is a communicating P system acceptor (or a symport/antiport system acceptor). These devices are universal and therefore can also be analyzed with respect to space and time complexity. Finally, we gave a characterization of semilinear languages in terms of a restricted form of catalytic system language generator.

7   Some Problems for Future Research

Limited parallelism in other P systems: We believe the results in Sections 2 and 3 can be shown to hold for other more general P systems (including those where membranes can be dissolved), provided the rules are not prioritized. For example, the results should apply to systems with symport/antiport rules. We plan to look at this problem.

Characterizations: We propose to investigate various classes of nonuniversal P systems and characterize their computing power in terms of well-known models of sequential and parallel computation. We plan to investigate language-theoretic properties of families of languages defined by P systems that are not universal (e.g., closure and decidable properties), find P system models that correspond to the Chomsky hierarchy, and in particular, characterize the "parallel" computing power of P systems in terms of well-known models like alternating Turing machines, circuit models, cellular automata, parallel random access machines. We will also study models of P systems that are not universal for which we can develop useful and efficient algorithms for their decision problems.

Reachability problem in cell simulation: Another important research area that has great potential applications in biology is the use of P systems for the modeling and simulation of cells. While previous work on modeling and simulation use continuous mathematics (differential equations), P systems will allow us to use discrete mathematics and algorithms. As a P system models the computation that occurs in a living cell, an important problem is to develop tools for determining reachability between configurations, i.e., how the system evolves over time. Specifically, given a P system and two configurations α and β (a configuration is the number and distribution of the different types of objects in the various membranes in the system), is β reachable from α? Unfortunately, unrestricted P systems are universal (i.e., can simulate a Turing machine), hence all nontrivial decision problems (including reachability) are undecidable. Therefore, it is important to identify special P systems that are decidable for reachability.

8   Conclusion

We showed in this paper that P systems that operate under limited parallelism are strictly weaker than systems that operate in "maximal parallelism" for two classes of systems: multi-membrane catalytic systems and multi-membrane communicating P systems. Our results on multi-membrane communicating P systems should also hold for symport/antiport systems [8, 17, 19]. We also summarized our recent results concerning membrane hierarchy, determinism versus nondeterminism, and computational complexity of P systems. Finally, we proposed some problems for future research.

There has been some related work on P systems operating in sequential mode. For example, sequential variants of P systems have been studied, in a different framework, in [6]. There, generalized P systems (GP-systems) were considered and were shown to be able to simulate graph controlled grammars. A comparison between parallel and sequential modes of computation in a restricted model of a P automaton was also recently investigated in [3], where it was shown that the parallel version is equivalent to a linear space-bounded nondeterministic Turing machine (NTM) and the sequential version is equivalent to a simple type of a one-way $log\ n$ space-bounded NTM.

References

1. H. G. Baker. Rabin's proof of the undecidability of the reachability set inclusion problem for vector addition systems. In *C.S.C. Memo 79, Project MAC, MIT*, 1973.
2. C. S. Calude and Gh. Paun. Computing with cells and atoms: after five years. (New text added to Russian edition of the book with the same title first published by Taylor and Francis Publishers, London, 2001). To be published by Pushchino Publishing House, 2004.
3. E. Csuhaj-Varju, O. H. Ibarra, and G. Vaszil. On the computational complexity of P automata. In *Proc. DNA 10* (C. Ferretti, G. Mauri, C. Zandron, eds.), Univ. Milano-Bicocca, 97–106,2004.
4. Z. Dang and O. H. Ibarra. On P systems operating in sequential mode. In *Pre-Proc. 6th Workshop on Descriptional Complexity of Formal Systems*, 2004.
5. J. Esparza. Petri nets, commutative context-free grammars, and basic parallel processes. In *Proc. Fundamentals of Computer Theory*, volume 965 of *Lecture Notes in Computer Science*, pages 221–232. Springer, 1995.
6. R. Freund. Sequential P-systems. Available at *http://psystems.disco.unimib.it*, 2000.
7. R. Freund, L. Kari, M. Oswald, and P. Sosik. Computationally universal P systems without priorities: two catalysts are sufficient. *Theoretical Computer Science*, 330(2): 251–266, 2005.
8. R. Freund and A. Paun. Membrane systems with symport/antiport rules: universality results. In *Proc. WMC-CdeA2002*, volume 2597 of *Lecture Notes in Computer Science*, pages 270–287. Springer, 2003.
9. R. Freund and Gh. Paun. On deterministic P systems. See *http://psystems.disco.unimib.it*, 2003.
10. M. H. Hack. The equality problem for vector addition systems is undecidable. In *C.S.C. Memo 121, Project MAC, MIT*, 1975.
11. J. Hopcroft and J.-J. Pansiot. On the reachability problem for 5-dimensional vector addition systems. *Theoretical Computer Science*, 8(2):135–159, 1979.
12. D.T. Huynh. Commutative grammars: The complexity of uniform word problems. *Information and Control*, 57:21–39, 1983.
13. O. H. Ibarra. The number of membranes matters. In *Proc. 4th Workshop on Membrane Computing*, Lecture Notes in Computer Science 2933, Springer-Verlag, 218-231, 2004.
14. O. H. Ibarra. On the computational complexity of membrane systems. *Theoretical Computer Science*, pages 89–109, 2004
15. O. H. Ibarra. On determinism versus nondeterminism in P systems. To appear in *Theoretical Computer Science*, 2005.
16. O. H. Ibarra, H. Yen, and Z. Dang. The power of maximal parallelism in P systems. In *Proc. 8th Int. Conf. on Developments in Language Theory*, pages 212-224, 2004.

17. C. Martin-Vide, A. Paun, and Gh. Paun. On the power of P systems with symport rules. *Journal of Universal Computer Science*, pages 317–331, 2002.

18. E. Mayr. Persistence of vector replacement systems is decidable. *Acta Informatica*, 15:309–318, 1981.

19. A. Paun and Gh. Paun. The power of communication: P systems with symport/antiport. *New Generation Computing*, pages 295–306, 2002.

20. Gh. Paun. Computing with membranes. *Journal of Computer and System Sciences*, 61(1):108–143, 2000.

21. Gh. Paun. *Membrane Computing: An Introduction*. Springer-Verlag, 2002.

22. Gh. Paun, M. Perez-Jimenez, and F. Sancho-Caparrini. On the reachability problem for P systems with symport/antiport. *Submitted*, 2002.

23. Gh. Paun and G. Rozenberg. A guide to membrane computing. *Theoretical Computer Science*, 287(1):73–100, 2002.

24. W. Savitch. Relationships between nondeterministic and deterministic tape complexities. *J. Comput. Syst. Sci.*, pages 177–192, 1970.

25. W. Savitch. A note on multihead automata and context-sensitive languages. *Acta Informatica*, pages 249–252, 1973.

26. P. Sosik. P systems versus register machines: two universality proofs. In *Pre-Proceedings of Workshop on Membrane Computing (WMC-CdeA2002), Curtea de Arges, Romania*, pages 371–382, 2002.

27. P. Sosik and R. Freund. P systems without priorities are computationally universal. In *Proceedings of Workshop on Membrane Computing (WMC-CdeA2002), Lecture Notes in Computer Science*, pages 400–409, 2003.

28. P. Sosik and J. Matysek. Membrane computing: when communication is enough. *Unconventional Models of Computation 2002, Lecture Notes in Computer Science*, pages 264–275, 2002.

29. J. van Leeuwen. A partial solution to the reachability problem for vector addition systems. In *Proceedings of STOC'74*, pages 303–309.

Outlining an Unconventional, Adaptive, and Particle-Based Reconfigurable Computer Architecture

Christof Teuscher

University of California, San Diego (UCSD), Department of Cognitive Science,
9500 Gilman Drive, La Jolla, CA 92093-0515, USA
christof@teuscher.ch
www.teuscher.ch/christof

Abstract. The quest for novel and unconventional computing machines is mainly motivated by the man-machine dichotomy and by the belief that dealing with new physical computing substrates, new environments, and new applications will require new paradigms to organize, train, program, and to interact with them. The goal of this contribution is to delineate a possible way to address the general scientific challenge of seeking for further progress and new metaphors in computer science by means of unconventional approaches. Here we outline an amalgamation of (1) a particle-based, randomly interconnected, and reconfigurable substrate, (2) membrane systems, and (3) artificial chemistries in combination with (4) an unconventional adaptation paradigm.

1 Introduction and Motivation

Biologically-inspired computing (see for example [28, 18] for a general introduction), also commonly called *natural computing*, is an interdisciplinary area of research which is heavily relied on the fields of biology, computer science, and mathematics. It is the study of computational systems that use ideas and draw inspiration from natural organisms to build large, adaptive, complex, and dynamical systems. The principal goal of biologically-inspired computing is to make machines more lifelike and to endow them with properties that traditional machines typically do not posses, such as for example adaptation, learning, evolution, growth, development, and fault-tolerance.

It is evident that biological organisms operate on completely different principles from those of computer science (i.e., the man-machine dichotomy). Whereas life itself might be defined as a chemical system capable of self-reproduction and of evolution, computers constitute a fundamentally different environment where such processes are not naturally occurring. This and our still poor understanding of nature in many aspects makes it particularly difficult to copy it. Further difficulty often resides in the way how information in computers is represented and processed. Mimicking biological information processing on computing devices, for example, which usually process information serially, is highly inefficient because of the massively parallel character of biological systems. Also, whereas

J.-P. Banâtre et al. (Eds.): UPP 2004, LNCS 3566, pp. 238–253, 2005.

the concepts of *computability* and *universal computation* are undoubtedly central to theoretical computer science, their importance might be questioned with regards to biological organisms and biologically-inspired computing machines. The well known concept of computation (as defined for example by a Turing machine) can in most cases not straightforwardly be applied to biological components or entire organisms and there is no evidence that such a system can compute universally, on the contrary, nature usually prefers highly specialized units. For example, it is much debated among neuroscientists, cognitive scientists, computer scientists, and philosophers whether the metaphor of the brain or mind as a digital computer is reasonable. However, although we have experienced in the past that biological organisms are generally difficult to describe by algorithmic processes, there is little reason to believe that they compute beyond the algorithmic horizon [33], since, at the bottom, one might reason, it is all just physical stuff doing what it "must." Yet another debate is focused on what cognitive paradigms should be used in order to obtain "intelligent" agents. This seems to somehow become an eternal and useless discussion since—as in many other fields—there is no best model. Different models are better for different things in different contexts.

The quest for novel computing machines and concepts is mainly motivated by the observation that fundamental progress in machine intelligence and artificial life seem to stagnate [3]. For example, one of the keys to machine intelligence is computers that learn in an open and unrestricted way, and we are still just scratching the surface of this problem. Connectionist models have been unable to faithfully model the nervous systems of even the simplest living things and parallel programming has failed to produce general methods for programming massively parallel systems. Our abilities to program complex systems are simply not keeping up with the desire to solve complex problems. But is "programming"—by means of a high-level language for example—really the best solution for this kind of challenge? I do have more hope in self-organization and learning when it comes to the creation of highly complex and massively parallel systems. But this opens numerous additional problems, such as the general lack of systematic and formal approaches which would allow to gradually create hierarchical and complex systems that scale-up well, for example.

Tomorrow's grand challenges for computer science are not likely to be bound to any specific real-world application, but one would rather like to have general mechanisms—at least in a first step—that would allow to gradually and automatically create complex systems. Typical issues often mentioned are robustness towards failures, scalability, adaptation towards an ever-changing environment, and more complex machines in general. Also, tomorrow's computers are likely to be ubiquitous and invisible, which requires a paradigm shift in how we organize, train, program, and interact with them. We believe that these challenges are best approached by unconventional paradigms instead of "straying" around the well-known concepts, changing the model's parameters, and putting hope in increasing computing power. Using Brooks' words, we rather believe in "[. . .] something fundamental and currently unimagined in our models" [3] than in all other possibilities, although they might play a role as well. We need new tools and new concepts that move seamlessly between brain, cognition, and computation—a finding that has also been made in a 2002 NSF/DOC-sponsored report [27].

The general goal of this contribution—presented in the form of a outline—is to illustrate *one* possible way to address the general scientific challenge of seeking for further progress and new metaphors in computer science by means of unconventional methods. The presented ideas should be seen as a fully integrative approach for an unconventional computing machine, which includes everything from the underlying hardware to its organizational principles. The work is ongoing and further develops some of the ideas first presented in [32]. Please also note that the goal of this contribution is to give an overview and it is therefore not self-contained and does not address all the details.

The remainder of the paper is as following: Section 2 gives an overview on the architecture and mentions some relevant related work. Section 3 illustrates the programmable reactor multitude and its communication structure. The implementation of cells and hierarchical structures is outlined in Section 4 and Section 5 explains the basics of chemical blending. Finally, Section 6 concludes the paper and delineates future work.

2   Architectural Overview

Different areas in computer science on different levels are facing the same fundamental problems. For example, an ideal mobile phone communication network is self-organized, robust, self-healing, and scalable, which might simply be translated into the capacity to adapt to a complex, uncertain, and ever-changing environment. The same generally applies to distributed sensor networks, mesh networks, the internet, collective robotics, amorphous computers, molecular electronics, and many other fields. All these applications are typically characterized by decentralized control, asynchronous operation, and by the fact that failures may occur at any time. However, they differ significantly in several aspects, such as for example power consumption, resources available, agent density, and communication infrastructure.

The specific goal of this work was to propose a novel reconfigurable computer architecture that is based on an amalgamation of (1) a particle-based and randomly interconnected substrate, (2) membrane systems, and (3) artificial chemistries in combination with (4) an unconventional adaptation paradigm. An overview of the architecture is given in Figure 1.

In order to obtain a fault-tolerant system, the proposed architecture relies on a simple, irregular, inhomogeneous, locally interconnected, asynchronously operating, and imperfect particle-based substrate (see Section 3), not unlike an amorphous computer. Currently, the only possibility to build a perfect machine out of imperfect components is to make use of redundancy at some level, such as spare components, which clearly favors a particle-based implementation. Scalability is assured by avoiding central control and by using local interactions only. We will also make extensive use of artificial chemistries, which represent—if appro-

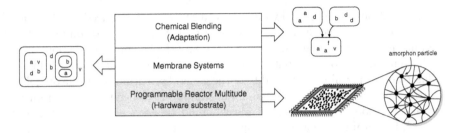

Fig. 1. Overview of the different levels of the proposed reconfigurable computer architecture: (1) particle substrate, (2) membrane systems used to build hierarchical levels, and (3) an unconventional method to search for "good" membrane systems. Artificial chemistries are used on all levels

priately used—an ideal means to compute in uncertain environments. Further, they have also been identified as potentially very promising for the perpetual creation of novelty [11], a feature that shall be later used to support adaptation. In order to be able to create hierarchical organizations, we will make use of cells and membranes throughout the system (see Section 4). Thereby, membrane systems will serve as a main source of inspiration. Finally, adaptation is achieved by a method inspired by *conceptual blending* [7,6], a framework of cognitive science that tries to explain how we think and deal with mental concepts. However, instead of dealing with concepts, we will use artificial chemistries in combination with membrane systems (see Section 5).

A number of completed and ongoing projects in the computer science research community are dealing with alternative computer architectures. We shall briefly focus on some relevant representatives. One of the most prominent projects in the field is certainly MIT's *amorphous computing project*[1] [1, 19]. Amorphous computing is the development of organizational principles and programming languages for obtaining coherent global behavior from the local cooperation of myriads of unreliable parts that all contain the same program and that are interconnected in unknown, irregular, and time-varying ways. In biology, this question has been recognized as fundamental in the context of animals (such as ants, bees, etc.) that cooperate and form organizations. Amorphous computing brings the question "down" to computing science and engineering. Using the metaphor of biology, the cells cooperate to form a multicellular organism (also called *programmable multitude*) under the direction of a genetic program shared by the members of the colony.

Blob Computing[2] [15, 14] is an ongoing project that is based on a coupled language-machine approach. The goal is to present an alternative to the well-established von Neumann paradigm in order to tackle the major limitations of current computer architectures. The model is designed to exploit "space" and is based on a massively parallel and asynchronous computational architecture

---

[1] Website:http://www.swiss.ai.mit.edu/projects/amorphous

[2] Website: http://blob.lri.fr

that offers a good scalability combined with a language that allows to fully exploit the underlying hardware. The programming language relies on a virtual machine called *graph machine*, which is a self-modifying and self-developing net of automaton. This basics of the language date back to Gruau's work on cellular encoding (see for example [12, 13]). Each node (i.e., automaton) of the graph can locally modify the graph and can apply cell division instructions in order to develop the graph. A cell can for example simulate a simplified artificial neuron, thus a cellular code can develop and simulate an artificial neural network. Mapping, a central challenge of parallel programming, is the problem of determining which processor will simulate which cell of the graph. Naturally, a good placement reduces the distance between the nodes that communicate. Gruau *et al.* use physical forces for optimizing the shape and the location of a blob and thus solve the mapping problem in an elegant way. As a proof of concept, they illustrate several interesting examples and experiments in [14], such as QuickSort, building neural networks, and matrix multiplication.

Both, the amorphous computing and the Blob computing project are based on an irregular, randomly arranged, and locally interconnected underlying hardware structure. Examples of unconventional reconfigurable hardware architectures based on a regular arrangement of the basic components are the *Embryonics* [17], the *POEtic* project [31,35], and the *CellMatrix* architecture [16], which all resemble traditional *Field Programmable Gate Arrays* (FPGAs) [34]. Finally, on a totally different level, but with very similar goals (i.e., robustness, self-healing and repair, adaptation), IBM has launched the *autonomic computing*[3] initiative some time ago.

3   The Programmable Reactor Multitude

At the bottom of our reconfigurable architecture (see Figure 1) lies the *Programmable Reactor Multitude* (PRM), which shall be briefly described in the next two sections. The programmable reactor multitude (i.e., the hardware) is made up of a set of interconnected particles, each of which contains as a main element a chemical reactor.

3.1   Communication Structure

MIT's amorphous computer communication model assumes that all processors have a circular broadcast of approximately the same fixed radius (large compared to the size of the processor) and share a single communication channel. Since our goal was to propose a new reconfigurable computer architecture, we have chosen wire-based communication instead of wireless broadcast. The communication model is illustrated in Figure 2. Each processor i receives inputs from an average of K_{avg} randomly chosen neighbors that lie within a maximum radius of c_i. Self-connections are not allowed, but multiple connections are allowed. Further, all

---

[3] Website: http://www.research.ibm.com/autonomic

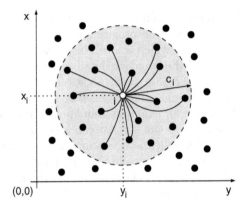

Fig. 2. Illustration of the inter-processor's communication model. Each randomly arranged processing element i (i.e., particle) receives inputs from an average of K_{avg} of its neighbors that lie within an maximum radius of c_i. Multiple connections to the same neighbors are allowed, self-connections are not allowed

communication channels are single and bidirectional. We also assume that the processors are randomly and densely distributed on a two-dimensional surface and that their physical position as well as their wiring are fixed, but that they might be unreliable. For applications such as reconfigurable silicon-based circuits, printable digital circuits, etc., this seems to be a reasonable constraint. The processors do not possess any information about their physical location and can only communicate with their immediate neighbors.

The main reason for choosing this alternative communication model was to facilitate circuit-based real-world implementations, where long-distance connections are generally costly in terms of resources used and where radio-broadcast is inadequate and unnecessary. It was further inspired by small-world graphs [30], which have short average interconnection lengths but high clustering coefficients. Although our connection graph does not exactly have small-world properties nor is it scale-free, it is a reasonably good approximation and easy to create. Obviously, a necessary condition for a correct operation is a connection graph without disconnected regions, as this would prevent communication among all particles. In order to provide a fault-tolerant communication structure, however, redundant links, i.e., multiple paths between two locations are necessary since it must be possible in such a case to re-route traffic via alternative routes.

The message routing protocol is very simple and is based on chemical gradients only. This makes the message handling easy in case of faulty connections and processors, in which case the messages simply choose an alternative route in the direction of the gradient. However, at the same time, the expected time to deliver a message is hard to estimate since its exact route is unknown. There are basically three types of communication primitives: (1) broadcast a message to all neighboring processors, (2) deliver a message to the source of a certain gradient, and (3) search for a processor that satisfies a specific condition. For more information, the interested reader is also referred to [32].

3.2   The Particle's Functionality

Several processor architectures have been proposed within the amorphous computing project at MIT. Here, we will focus on yet another version, which is mainly based on a chemical reactor paradigm, which helps to keep the overall design simple, uniform, and universal. The main part of the processor, also called *particle* or *amorphon* is essentially composed of a stochastic chemical reactor, which can host a limited number of molecules and reactions of an artificial chemistry. An *artificial chemistry* [5] is a man-made system defined by a set of reactions, a set of molecules, and by reaction dynamics which describe how the elements interact. Here, we use a rewriting-based chemistry with molecules such as for example $w = \{a, b, c\}$ and reactions such as $r = \{a \rightarrow c, b \rightarrow a\}$ (see also Section 4). In our case, the reaction dynamics are as following: the algorithm randomly draws a reaction and then checks whether it can be applied with the molecules currently present in the reactor. If yes, the rewriting takes place, otherwise a new reaction will be drawn.

Figure 3 shows a simplified view of a particle with its stochastic chemical reactor. All incoming messages containing molecules or reactions are fed into the reactor. Once in there, each chemical has a probability p_{leave} to leave the reactor and to be distributed to their interconnected neighbors according to the protocol they specify with their special symbols, which shall be described in the next section. We will see in Section 4 how the membranes will restrict the chemicals to float around on the entire substrate. The resulting system is a distributed reactor network with similar chemical concentrations in all reactors. The system is entirely reconfigurable since the contents of the reactors is not restricted.

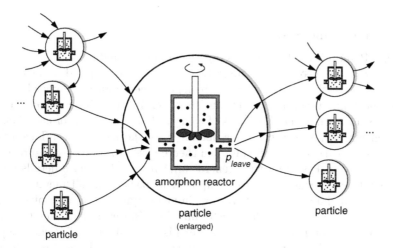

Fig. 3. Simplified view of a particle and its stochastic chemical reactor. Each chemical (i.e., molecule or reaction) has a probability of p_{leave} to leave the reactor. The particle is interconnected with its local neighbors as explained in the previous section

Note that this only gives a partial overview on the system. Each particle contains further components that deal for example with gradient information, that locally store their values, and that route messages. We shall not go into further details here as the chemical reactor represents the central element. Also, the issue on how the reactors are initialized is not addressed here and we simply assume a certain initial state of the entire programmable reactor multitude for the sake of simplicity.

In the next section we shall see how membrane systems can be built on top of a programmable reactor multitude.

4   Implementing Hierarchical Organizations with Membrane Systems

The biological cell is undoubtedly the structural and functional unit of all living organisms. Because of its importance, countless computational models with to goal to mimic or copy cells in nature have been proposed. In this section, we will draw inspiration from a particular cellular model in order to implement hierarchical membrane structures on top of a programmable reactor multitude. The main goal of this approach is to create hierarchical organizations, which will later be used by chemical blending (see Figure 1 and Section 5). Also, hierarchical composition is ubiquitous in any physical and biological system and offers many benefits. For example, it is a means to divide and "hide" complexity, to save resources since the building-blocks might be shared and re-used, and to create higher levels of abstraction. The formation of groups and hierarchies was also extensively addressed in the amorphous computing project. For more information, see for example [4, 20].

4.1   Membrane Systems

In 1998, Paun initiated *P systems* (or *membrane computing*) [22, 24] as a highly parallel, though theoretical computational model afar inspired by biochemistry and by some of the basic features of biological membranes. A typical P system (note that many variations exist) consists of cell-like membranes placed inside a unique "skin" membrane. Multisets of *symbol objects* and a set of *evolution rules* are then placed inside the regions delimited by the membranes. This artificial chemistry, which evolves over time, can then be used to compute. Figure 4 shows an example of a P system that generates $n^2, n \geq 1$. For more details see [22]. The fact that all rules have to be applied in parallel in all membranes adds resources and difficulties for hardware implementations because of the global control signals needed for the synchronization. However, it makes the system easier to create and to analyze. Despite this, Petreska and Teuscher [26] have recently proposed a first P system implementation on traditional reconfigurable circuits, which greatly speeds up their simulation. An additional problem is the fact that membrane systems are usually engineered by hand as no methodology exists so far on how to set up an artificial chemistry for a given task. Specifying

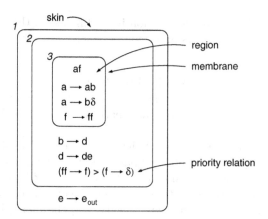

Fig. 4. A P system that generates $n^2, n \geq 1$, where n is the number of steps *before* the first application of the rule $a \rightarrow b\delta$. Redrawn from [23]

a non-trivial task algorithmically might of course by very hard, but if the problem is solvable by a machine, we know it can be done. Nevertheless, P systems are particularly interesting for our purposes since they allow to easily create hierarchies, which we consider a key issue for the creation of complex systems. Also, this will allow us to create compartments for constraining the unlimited spreading of the chemicals in the programmable reactor multitude network.

4.2   Membrane Systems on a Programmable Rector Multitude

In order to be able to efficiently and elegantly implement membrane systems on a programmable reactor multitude, we have modified classical P systems in several points. The following list provides an incomplete overview of the main points:

- The rules are no longer applied in parallel in each membrane, instead they are applied stochastically and asynchronously and there are no priority relations between the rules.
- Compared to classical P systems, where the rules do not usually change, our rules can be rewritten and created by rules as well. For instance, the rule $a(b \rightarrow c) \rightarrow d$ requires a molecule a and a rule $b \rightarrow c$ to be applied. The two elements would then be removed from the chemistry and replaced by d. This possibility allows to (self-) modify the reactor's "program," i.e., its rules, and offers more flexibility than a fixed set of rules.
- A set of special symbols defines additional actions for each rule: $r = (u, s, v) = (u \rightarrow sv)$, where u, v are multisets over the symbols of an alphabet V and the set R^* of all reactions r, and where s is a *special operator symbol* from a set S. The special symbols allow to send objects to different neighboring membranes, to dissolve and create membranes, and will later allow us to implement chemical blending, but overall, they offer simply a mechanism to attach a certain additional action of any kind to each rule. The implementation of the special symbols (i.e., the microsteps) is generally done outside the reactor.

– The inter-membrane communication is modified such that a membrane can not only send objects to its outer compartment, but also to a specific membrane in that compartment.

These modifications are less guided by theoretical than by practical considerations. Whether they make our membrane systems computationally more or less powerful than their classical counterparts remains to be investigated, but was not the focus on this work.

From an implementational point of view, every cell in a membrane system will be represented by a set of neighboring particles from the programmable reactor multitude. Chemicals of that cell can only leave this set of processors by means of special commands, otherwise they will move inside the cell only. Remember also that each reactor has a limited capacity, i.e., the more chemicals have to be stored, the more reactors are required to make up the cell. Also, the goal is to have a larger number of reactors available for each cell than it would be strictly necessary in order to obtain a fault-tolerant system. Ideally, there should be redundancy that allows to "lose" at least one particle out of one cell. In such a case, it is for instance possible to hold a concentration of chemicals (e.g, a) above a certain threshold by means of simple rules, even if the concentration is disturbed by removing or adding reactors. Figure 5 illustrates this with the following rules: $r_1 = a \rightarrow a^2$ and $r_2 = a^m \rightarrow a^n$, where $n < m$. Rule r_1 lets the concentration grow constantly but slowly, whereas rule r_2 reduces the number of molecules once it has reached a certain upper threshold m instantly by $m - n$

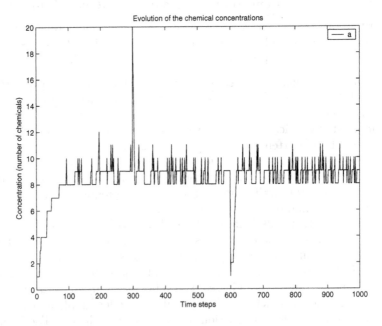

Fig. 5. Holding a concentration of chemicals a constant. The disturbances at time steps 300 and 600 do only briefly alter the concentration

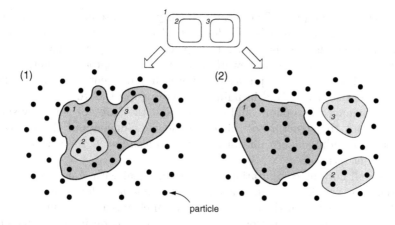

Fig. 6. Two possibilities of implementing hierarchical membrane systems on a programmable reactor multitude. See text for description

molecules. As one can see, the concentration shows a sawtooth-like behavior for $m = 10$ and $n = 8$, but proves to be very robust against unexpectedly external influences.

Let us now see how we can implement a membrane system, as shown in Figure 4, on a programmable reactor multitude. There are two principal ways: (1) respect the membrane's hierarchical organization or (2) lay the individual cells flat out. The two possibilities are illustrated in Figure 6. Possibility (1) seems more natural, but there is a major drawback when a new cell has to be added. In that case, existing cells would have to be enlarged in order to create room for the new cells, which represents a time-consuming and non trivial task—especially in the case of many hierarchical levels—given our simple processing elements. Possibility (2) avoids this drawback, but in that case the communication between the cells is more complicated. However, in most cases, this possibility seems to be more appropriate, since adding and removing cells is greatly simplified.

5   Chemical Blending

Conceptual blending (or *conceptual integration*) [7, 6] is a theory developed by Fauconnier and Turner about conceptual spaces and how they develop and proliferate as we talk and think. Conceptual spaces consist of elements and relations among them and are of course not directly instantiated in the brain, instead, they should be seen as a formalism invented by researchers to address and certain issues of their investigation. When two conceptual spaces are blended together, the new space contains parts of the original spaces, but it usually also contains emergent structure. Very simple examples are "houseboat" or "computer virus," a more complex blend would be "digging one own's grave." For most real-world situations that are more complex that a simple metaphor, blends develop in larger *conceptual integration networks*, which are networks of conceptual spaces and conceptual mappings. The blend's "quality" and "usefulness" is guided by a set of *optimality principles* (see [7] for more details), most of which use human judgment, which makes them hard to implement in computational frameworks. Since the entire blending framework lacks a formal approach, different people have worked on explicit computational approaches in recent years [36,8,9,25,10]. Also, conceptual spaces and blending are just a good tool to study meaning in natural language, metaphors, and concepts, but they are not generally suitable to talk about the structure of things [9]. Hence, Goguen and Harrell recently proposed a blending algorithm called *structural blending* [9,10], which also takes into account structure.

While all current computational approaches deal with concepts, we are interested in a very different approach here: we are looking for an unconventional adaptation paradigm in the context of artificial chemistries and membrane systems. Drawing inspiration from the constructing and optimality principles of blending seemed promising since blending creates emergent structure, i.e., novelty, and could therefore in principle be useful to discover new solutions. Also, as mentioned earlier, artificial chemistries have been identified as potentially very promising for the perpetual creation of novelty, which, together with a blending-inspired method, could lead to interesting properties. Finally, please note that the chemical blending approach is *not* intended to faithfully model blending, but only draws inspiration from it instead.

The following analogies were basically used: a mental space is replaced by a membrane system whereas objects and rules became molecules and reactions. Also, the three constructing principles of blending [7], namely (1) composition, (2) completion, and (3) elaboration can straightforwardly be replaced by composing, completing, and applying the rules of the membrane system. As the blending's optimality principles do basically only make sense for conceptual integration, we have completely replaced them in a first step by an alternative fitness-based measure as commonly used in evolutionary algorithms. The development of specialized optimality principles for artificial chemistries is envisaged for future work.

Figure 7 provides an overview on how a new cell is blended from two single-membrane input cells. We have implemented one possible method which shall now briefly be described. Let us assume two single-membrane systems (as shown in Figure 7) that contain a certain number of molecules and reactions. The goal is to create a new single-membrane system that contains "emergent content" from the two original cells. For the sake of simplicity and because the reactions represent the cell's "program," we will only focus on the chemical reactions and not on the molecules here. One of the first steps of blending consists in establishing a cross-space mapping between related elements. In order to do this, we introduce an *activity* and a *similarity measure*. The similarity measure considers the rule's symbols and structure and measures how related they are whereas the activity measure compares how often the rules are used. The idea is that rules with similar or opposite structure and activities should be more likely to be combined to form new rules than any other combination. The mapping is

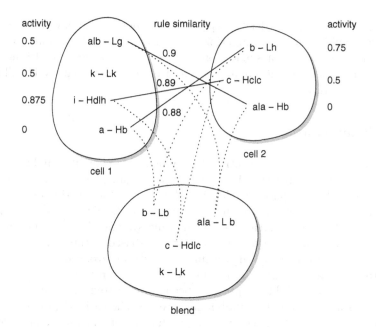

Fig. 7. Blending a new cell from two single-membrane input cells. See text for more details

established by merging the rules of the two cells together in one membrane and by letting them "float" around freely in the reactor network while they "look out" for suitable partners according to the similarity and the activity measure. Not all reactions need to be paired together with another reaction. After some time, the reaction pairs will be blended by randomly taking elements from one of the two reactions in order to form similar, yet new reactions. The resulting cell will therefore contain a mix of new reactions created on the basis of the old ones, but will also contain original elements as well. From an implementational point of view, all these steps are realized by means of special symbols in the reactions as described in Section 4.2. Note that the activity and similarity measure as well as the way the new rules are constructed depends on the application and on what information the objects and rules represent and work on. The above example should thus only be considered as a case study.

So far, we have have only seen how to blend a new cell from two input cells, but how can this mechanism be used for creating good new cells that would solve a certain problem? The basic idea is similar to the principles of evolutionary algorithms (EAs). Instead of using optimality principles, each cell becomes a fitness value assigned that expresses how good a given task is solved. As with EAs, one would then maintain a population of cells where the worst cells die out and the good ones survive. Instead of applying crossover and mutation operators, we simply apply the blending mechanism to create a daughter cell from to parent cells.

In [32], we have illustrated in a simple toy application that the above described blending method works for a simple pattern classification tasks. Extending the method in order to apply it to a robot's maze navigation task, for example, would be pretty straightforward. Also, we have so far only focused on a blending mechanism for single membrane systems. Blending multi-membrane systems and testing the gradual creation of more hierarchical levels will be addressed in future work.

6   Conclusion

We have outlined an unconventional reconfigurable computer architecture enhanced with an unconventional adaptation paradigm. The resulting architecture is completely decentralized, particle based, supports the creation of hierarchical membrane systems, and represents a support for chemical blending, which on its turn can be used to create new membrane systems. In combination with a population of membrane systems and a fitness-based optimality measure, this allowed us to implement an algorithm not unlike an evolutionary algorithm in order to create membrane systems able to solve a given task.

Most of the proposed concepts have been implemented and simulated in Matlab, but so far only on their individual level (as shown in Figure 1). Simulating the entire architecture, i.e., running chemical blending on the particles, was impractical and computationally too intensive in a first step. The simulations should be considered as a proof of concept only and we are certainly far away from solving any real world problems. Clearly, many questions remain open and further research will be necessary to investigate the properties, drawbacks, and strengths of that unconventional computing architecture.

Future work will be focused in particular on further developing and investigating variants of chemical blending in order to improve the performance and to be able to solve real-world problems, such as for example a robot navigation task. A further goal is to investigate the properties of chemical reactor networks as a function of their various parameters, such as their interconnection topology, their internal storage capacity, and the parameter p_{leave}. We also plan to propose a hardware implementation of the basic particle by means of a hardware description language such as VHDL.

Acknowledgments. The author was supported by the Swiss National Science Foundation under grant PBEL2-104420.

References

1. H. Abelson, D. Allen, D. Coore, C. Hanson, E. Rauch, G. J. Sussman, and R. Weiss. Amorphous computing. *Communications of the ACM*, 43(5):74–82, May 2000.
2. E. Bilotta, D. Gross, T. Smith, T. Lenaerts, S. Bullock, H. H. Lund, J. Bird, R. Watson, P. Pantano, L. Pagliarini, H. Abbass, R. Standish, and M. A. Bedau, editors. *Alife VIII-Workshops. Workshop Proceedings of the 8th International Conference on the Simulation and Synthesis of Living Systems.* University of New South Wales, Australia, December 2002.

3. R. Brooks. The relationship between matter and life. *Nature*, 409:409–411, January 18 2001.

4. D. Coore, R. Nagpal, and R. Weiss. Paradigms for structure in an amorphous computer. Technical Report AI Memo 1614, MIT Artificial Intelligence Laboratory, October 6 1997.

5. P. Dittrich, J. Ziegler, and W. Banzhaf. Artificial chemistries–a review. *Artificial Life*, 7(3):225–275, 2001.

6. G. Fauconnier and M. Turner. Conceptual integration networks. *Cognitive Science*, 22(2):133–187, April–June 1998.

7. G. Fauconnier and M. Turner. *The Way We Think: Conceptual Blending and the Mind's Hidden Complexities*. Basic Books, 2002.

8. J. Goguen. An introduction to algebraic semiotics, with applications to user interface design. In Nehaniv [21], pages 242–291.

9. J. Goguen and F. Harrell. Foundations for active multimedia narrative: Semiotic spaces and structural blending. *Interaction Studies: Social Behaviour and Communication in Biological and Artificial Systems*, 2004. (To appear).

10. J. Goguen and F. Harrell. Style as choice of blending principles. In *Proceedings of the Symposium on Style and Meaning in Language, Art, Music and Design, 2004 AAAI Fall Symposium*, Washington DC, Oct 21–24 2004.

11. D. Gross and McMullin B. The creation of novelty in artificial chemistries. In Standish et al. [29], pages 400–408.

12. F. Gruau. Cellular encoding of genetic neural networks. Technical Report 92-21, Ecole Normale Supérieure de Lyon, Institut IMAG, 1992.

13. F. Gruau. *Neural Network Synthesis Using Cellular Encoding and the Genetic Algorithm*. PhD thesis, Ecole Normale Supérieure de Lyon, 1994.

14. F. Gruau, Y. Lhuillier, P. Reitz, and O. Temam. BLOB computing. In S. Vassiliadis, J.-L. Gaudiot, and V. Piuri, editors, *Proceedings of the First Conference on Computing Frontiers*, pages 125–139, New York, NY, USA, 2004. ACM Press.

15. F. Gruau and P. Malbos. The Blob: A basic topological concept for hardware-free distributed computation. In C. Calude, M. J. Dinneen, and F. Peper, editors, *Unconventional Models of Computation*, volume 2509 of *Lecture Notes in Computer Science*, pages 151–163, Berlin, Heidelberg, 2002. Springer-Verlag.

16. N. J. Macias and L. J. K. Durbeck. Adaptive methods for growing electronic circuits on an imperfect synthetic matrix. *Biosystems*, 73(3):172–204, March 2004.

17. D. Mange, M. Sipper, A. Stauffer, and G. Tempesti. Toward robust integrated circuits: The embryonics approach. *Proceedings of the IEEE*, 88(4):516–540, April 2000.

18. D. Mange and M. Tomassini, editors. *Bio-Inspired Computing Machines: Towards Novel Computational Architectures*. Presses Polytechniques et Universitaires Romandes, Lausanne, Switzerland, 1998.

19. R. Nagpal. *Programmable Self-Assembly: Constructing Global Shape using Biologically-Inspired Local Interactions and Origami Mathematics*. PhD thesis, Massachusetts Institute of Technology, Department of Electrical Engineering and Computer Science, June 2001.

20. R. Nagpal and D. Coore. An algorithm for group formation in an amorphous computer. Technical Report AI Memo 1626, MIT Artificial Intelligence Laboratory, February 16 1998.

21. C. L. Nehaniv, editor. *Computation for Metaphor, Analogy and Agents*, volume 1562 of *Lecture Notes in Artificial Intelligence*. Springer-Verlag, Berlin, Heidelberg, 1999.

22. G. Paun. Computing with membranes. *Journal of Computer and System Sciences*, 61(1):108–143, 2000. First published in a TUCS Research Report, No 208, November 1998, http://www.tucs.fi.

23. G. Paun. *Membrane Computing*. Springer-Verlag, Berlin, Heidelberg, Germany, 2002.

24. G. Paun and G. Rozenberg. A guide to membrane computing. *Journal of Theoretical Computer Science*, 287(1):73–100, 2002.

25. F. C. Pereira and A. Cardoso. The horse-bird creature generation experiment. *The Interdisciplinary Journal of Artificial Intelligence and the Simulation of Behaviour*, 1(3):257–280, July 2003.

26. B. Petreska and C. Teuscher. A reconfigurable hardware membrane system. In C. Martin-Vide, G. Mauri, G. Paun, G. Rozenberg, and A. Salomaa, editors, *Membrane Computing*, volume 2933 of *Lecture Notes in Computer Science*, pages 269–285, Berlin, Heidelberg, 2004. Springer-Verlag.

27. M. C. Roco and W. S. Bainbridge, editors. *Converging Technologies for Improving Human Performance: Nanotechnology, Biotechnology, Information Technology and Cognitive Science*. World Technology Evaluation Center (WTEC), Arlington, Virginia, June 2002. NSF/DOC-sponsored report.

28. M. Sipper. *Machine Nature: The Coming Age of Bio-Inspired Computing*. McGraw-Hill, New York, 2002.

29. R. K. Standish, M. A. Bedau, and H. A. Abbass, editors. *Artificial Life VIII. Proceedings of the Eight International Conference on Artificial Life*. Complex Adaptive Systems Series. A Bradford Book, MIT Press, Cambridge, MA, 2003.

30. S. H. Strogatz. Exploring complex networks. *Nature*, 410:268–276, March 8 2001.

31. G. Tempesti, D. Roggen, E. Sanchez, Y. Thoma, R. Canham, A. Tyrrell, and J.-M. Moreno. A POEtic architecture for bio-inspired hardware. In Standish et al. [29].

32. C. Teuscher. *Amorphous Membrane Blending: From Regular to Irregular Cellular Computing Machines*. PhD thesis, Swiss Federal Institute of Technology (EPFL), Lausanne, Switzerland, 2004. Thesis No 2925.

33. C. Teuscher and M. Sipper. Hypercomputation: Hype or computation? *Communications of the ACM*, 45(8):23–24, August 2002.

34. S. M. Trimberger. *Field-Programmable Gate Array Technology*. Kluwer Academic Publishers, Boston, 1994.

35. A. Tyrrell, E. Sanchez, D. Floreano, G. Tempesti, D. Mange, J.-M. Moreno, J. Rosenberg, and Alessandro E. P. Villa. Poetic tissue: An integrated architecture for bio-inspired hardware. In A. M. Tyrrell, P. C. Haddow, and J. Torresen, editors, *Evolvable Systems: From Biology to Hardware. Proceedings of the 5th International Conference (ICES2003)*, volume 2606 of *Lecture Notes in Computer Science*, pages 129–140. Springer-Verlag, Berlin, Heidelberg, 2003.

36. T. Veale and D. O'Donoghue. Computation and blending. *Cognitive Linguistics*, 11(3–4):253–281, 2000.

Autonomic Computing

Autonomic Computing: An Overview*

Manish Parashar[1] and Salim Hariri[2]

[1] The Applied Software Systems Laboratory,
Rutgers University, Piscataway NJ, USA
[2] High Performance Distributed Computing Laboratory,
University of Arizona, Tucson AZ, USA
`parashar@caip.rutgers.edu`, `hariri@ece.arizona.edu`

Abstract. The increasing scale complexity, heterogeneity and dynamism of networks, systems and applications have made our computational and information infrastructure brittle, unmanageable and insecure. This has necessitated the investigation of an alternate paradigm for system and application design, which is based on strategies used by biological systems to deal with similar challenges – a vision that has been referred to as autonomic computing. The overarching goal of autonomic computing is to realize computer and software systems and applications that can manage themselves in accordance with high-level guidance from humans. Meeting the grand challenges of autonomic computing requires scientific and technological advances in a wide variety of fields, as well as new software and system architectures that support the effective integration of the constituent technologies. This paper presents an introduction to autonomic computing, its challenges, and opportunities.

1   Introduction

Advances in networking and computing technology and software tools have resulted in an explosive growth in networked applications and information services that cover all aspects of our life. These sophisticated applications and services are extremely complex, heterogeneous and dynamic. Further, the underlying information infrastructure (e.g., the Internet) globally aggregates large numbers of independent computing and communication resources, data stores and sensor networks, and is itself similarly large, heterogeneous, dynamic and complex. The combination has resulted in application development, configuration and management complexities that break current computing paradigms based on static requirements, behaviors, interactions and compositions. As a result, applications, programming environments and information infrastructures are rapidly becoming brittle, unmanageable and insecure. This has necessitated the investigation of an alternate paradigm for system and application design, which is based on strategies used by biological systems to deal with similar challenges of scale, complex-

---

* The research presented in this paper is supported in part by the National Science Foundation via grants numbers ACI 9984357, EIA 0103674, EIA 0120934, ANI 0335244, CNS 0305495, CNS 0426354 and IIS 0430826.

J.-P. Banâtre et al. (Eds.): UPP 2004, LNCS 3566, pp. 257–269, 2005.

ity, heterogeneity, and uncertainty – a vision that has been referred to as autonomic computing [5].

The *Autonomic Computing Paradigm* has been inspired by the human autonomic nervous system. Its overarching goal is to realize computer and software systems and applications that can manage themselves in accordance with high-level guidance from humans. Meeting the grand challenges of autonomic computing requires scientific and technological advances in a wide variety of fields, as well as new programming paradigm and software and system architectures that support the effective integration of the constituent technologies. This paper presents an introduction to autonomic computing, its challenges, and opportunities. In this paper, we first give an overview of the architecture of the nervous system and use it to motivate the autonomic computing paradigm. We then outline the key challenges of autonomic computing and present an overview of existing autonomic computing systems and applications.

2   The Autonomic Nervous System

The human nervous system is, to the best of our knowledge, the most sophisticated example of autonomic behavior existing in nature today. It is the body's master controller that monitors changes inside and outside the body, integrates sensory inputs, and effects appropriate response. In conjunction with the endocrine system, the nervous system is able to constantly regulate and maintain homeostasis. A homeostatic system (e.g., a large organization, an industrial firm, a cell) is an open system that maintains its structure and functions by means of a multiplicity of dynamic equilibriums that are rigorously controlled by interdependent regulation mechanisms. Such a system reacts to every change in the environment, or to every random disturbance, through a series of modifications that are equal in size and opposite in direction to those that created the disturbance. The goal of these modifications is to maintain internal balances.

The manifestation of the phenomenon of homeostasis is widespread in the human system. As an example, consider the mechanisms that maintain the concentration of glucose in the blood within limits - if the concentration should fall below about 0.06 percent, the tissues will be starved of their chief source of energy; if the concentration should rise above about 0.18 percent, other undesirable effects will occur. If the blood-glucose concentration falls below about 0.07 percent, the adrenal glands secrete adrenaline, which causes the liver to turn its stores of glycogen into glucose. This passes into the blood and the blood-glucose concentration drop is opposed. Further, a falling blood-glucose also stimulates appetite causing food intake, which after digestion provides glucose. On the other hand, if the blood-glucose concentration rises excessively, the secretion of insulin by the pancreas is increased, causing the liver to remove the excess glucose from the blood. Excess glucose is also removed by muscles and skin, and if the blood-glucose concentration exceeds 0.18 percent, the kidneys excrete excess glucose into the urine. Thus, there are five activities that counter harmful fluctuations in blood-glucose concentration [2].

The above example focuses on the maintenance of the blood-glucose concentration within safe or operational limits that have been 'predetermined' for the species. Similar control systems exist for other parameters such as systolic blood pressure, structural integrity of the medulla oblongata, severe pressure of heat on the skin, and so on. All these parameters have a bearing on the survivability of the organism, which in this case is the human body. However, all parameters are not uniform in their urgency or their relations to lethality. Parameters that are closely linked to survival and are closely linked to each other so that marked changes in one leads sooner or later to marked changes in the others, have been termed as essential variables by Ashby in his study of the design for a brain [2]. This is discussed below.

2.1   Ashby's Ultrastable System

Every real machine embodies no less than an infinite number of variables, and for our discussion we can safely think of the human system as represented by a similar sets of variables, of which we will consider a few. In order for an organism to survive, its essential variables must be kept within viable limits (see Figure 1). Otherwise the organism faces the possibility of disintegration and/or loss of identity (i.e., dissolution or death) [14].

The body's internal mechanisms continuously work together to maintain its essential variables within their limits. Ashby's definition of adaptive behavior as demonstrated by the human body follows from this observation. He states that a form of behavior is adaptive if it maintains the essential variables within physiological limits [2] that define the viability zone. Two important observations can be made:

1. The goal of the adaptive behavior is directly linked with the survivability of the system.
2. If the external or internal environment pushes the system outside its physiological equilibrium state the system will always work towards returning to the original equilibrium state.

Ashby observed that many organisms undergo two forms of disturbances: (1) frequent small impulses to the main variables and (2) occasional step changes to its parameters. Based on this observation, he devised the architecture of the Ultra-Stable system that consists of two closed loops (see Figure 2): one that controls small disturbances and a second that is responsible for longer disturbances.

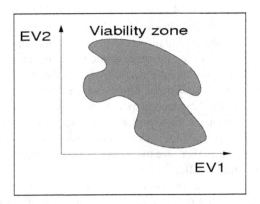

Fig. 1. Essential variables

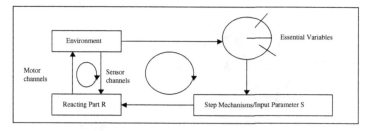

Fig. 2. The Ultra-Stable system architecture [2]

As shown in Figure 2, the ultrastable system consists of two sub-systems, the environment and the reacting part R. R represents a subsystem of the organism that is responsible for overt behavior or perception. It uses the sensor channels as part of its perception capability and motor channels to respond to the changes impacted by the environment. These set of sensors and motor channels constitute the primary feedback between R and the environment. We can think of R as a set of behaviors of the organism that gets triggered based on the changes affected by the environment. S represents the set of parameters that triggers changes in relevant features of this behavior set. Note that in Figure 2, S triggers changes only when the environment affects the essential variables in a way that causes them to go outside their physiological limits. As mentioned above, these variables need to be maintained within physiological limits for any adaptive system/organism to survive. Thus we can view this secondary feedback between the environment and R as responsible for triggering the adaptive behavior of the organism. When the changes impacted by the environment on the organism are large enough to throw the essential variables out of their physiological limits, the secondary feedback becomes active and changes the existing behavior sets of the organism to adapt to these new changes. Notice that any changes in the environment tend to push an otherwise stable system to an unstable state. The objective of the whole system is to maintain the subsystems (the environment and R) in a state of stable equilibrium. The primary feedback handles finer changes in the environment with the existing behavior sets to bring the whole system to stable equilibrium. The secondary feedback handles coarser and long-term changes in the environment by changing its existing behavior sets and eventually brings back the whole system to stable equilibrium state. Hence, in a nutshell, the environment and the organism always exist in a state of stable equilibrium and any activity of the organism is triggered to maintain this equilibrium.

2.2   The Nervous System as a Subsystem of Ashby's Ultrastable System

The human nervous system is adaptive in nature. In this section we apply the concepts underlying the Ashby's ultrastable system to the human nervous system. The nervous system is divided into the Peripheral Nervous System (PNS) and the Central Nervous System (CNS). The PNS consists of sensory neurons running from stimulus receptors that inform the CNS of the stimuli and motor neurons running from the CNS to the muscles and glands, called effectors, which take action. CNS is further divided into two parts: sensory-somatic nervous system and the autonomic nervous system. Figure 3 shows the architecture of the autonomic nervous system as an Ashby utrastable system.

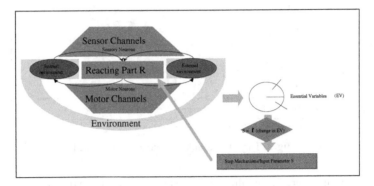

Fig. 3. Nervous system as part of an ultrastable system

As shown in Figure 3, the Sensory and Motor neurons constitute the Sensor and Motor channels of the ultrastable system. The triggering of essential variables, selection of the input parameter S and translation of these parameters to the reacting part R constitute the workings of the Nervous System. Revisiting the management of blood-glucose concentration within physiological limits discussed earlier, the five mechanisms that get triggered when the essential variable (i.e., concentration of glucose in blood) goes out of the physiological limits change the normal behavior of the system such that the reacting part R works to bring the essential variable back within limits. It uses its motor channels to effect changes so that the internal environment and the system (organism) come into the state of stable equilibrium. It should be noted that the environment here is divided into the internal environment and external environment. The internal environment represents changes impacted internally within the human system and the external environment represents changes impacted by the external world. However, the goal of the organism is to maintain the equilibrium of the entire system where all the sub-systems (the organism or system itself, and the internal and external environments) are in stable equilibrium.

3   The Autonomic Computing Paradigm

An autonomic computing paradigm, modeled after the autonomic nervous system, must have a mechanism whereby changes in its essential variables can trigger changes in the behavior of the computing system such that the system is brought back into equilibrium with respect to the environment. This state of stable equilibrium is a necessary condition for the survivability of the organism. In the case of an autonomic computing system, we can think of survivability as the system's ability to protect itself, recover from faults, reconfigure as required by changes in the environment, and always maintain its operations at a near optimal performance. Its equilibrium is impacted by both the internal environment (e.g., excessive memory/CPU utilization) and the external environment (e.g., protection from an external attack).

An autonomic computing system requires: (a) sensor channels to sense the changes in the internal and external environment, and (b) motor channels to react to and counter the effects of the changes in the environment by changing the system and maintaining equilibrium. The changes sensed by the sensor channels have to be analyzed to determine if any of the essential variables has gone out of their viability limits. If so, it has to trigger some kind of planning to determine what changes to inject into the current behavior of the system such that it returns to the equilibrium state within the new environment. This planning would require knowledge to select the right behavior from a large set of possible behaviors to counter the change. Finally, the motor neurons execute the selected change. 'Sensing', 'Analyzing', 'Planning', 'Knowledge' and 'Execution' are in fact the keywords used to identify an autonomic system [7, 3]. We use these concepts to present the architecture of an autonomic element and autonomic applications and systems.

3.1   Autonomic Computing – A Holistic View

As motivated above, the emerging complexity in computing systems, services and applications requires the system/software architectures to be adaptive in all its attributes and functionality (performance, security, fault tolerance, configurability, maintainability, etc.).

We have been successful in designing and implementing specialized computing systems and applications. However, the design of general purpose dynamically programmable computing systems and applications that can address the emerging needs and requirements remains a challenge. For example, distributed (and parallel) computing has evolved and matured to provide specialized solutions to satisfy very stringent requirements in isolation, such as security, dependability, reliability, availability, performance, throughput, efficiency, pervasive/amorphous, automation, reasoning, etc. However, in the case of emerging systems and applications, the specific requirements, objectives and choice of specific solutions (algorithms, behaviors, interactions, etc.) depend on runtime state, context, and content, and are not known a priori. The goal of autonomic computing is to use appropriate solutions based on current state/context/content and on specified policies.

The computer evolution have gone through many generations starting from single process single computer system to multiple processes running on multiple geographically dispersed heterogeneous computers that could span several continents (e.g., Grid). The approaches for designing the corresponding computing systems and applications have been evolutionary and ad hoc. Initially, the designers of such systems were mainly concerned about performance, and focused intensive research on parallel processing and high performance computer architectures and applications to address this requirement. As the scale and distribution of computer systems and applications evolved, the reliability and availability of the systems and applications became the major concern. This, in turn has led to separate research in fault tolerance and reliability, and to system and applications that were ultra reliable and resilient, but not high performance. In a similar way, ultra secure computing systems and applications have been developed to meet security requirement in isolation.

This ad hoc approach has resulted in the successful design and development of specialized computing systems and applications that can optimize a few of the attributes or functionalities of computing systems and applications. However, as we highlighted before, the emerging systems and applications and their contexts are dynamic. Consequently, their requirements will change during their lifetimes and may include high performance, fault tolerance, security, availability, configurability, etc. Consequently, what is needed is a new computing architecture and programming paradigm that takes a holistic approach to the design and development of computing systems and applications. Autonomic computing provides such an approach by enabling the design and development of systems/applications that can adapt themselves to meet requirements of performance, fault tolerance, reliability, security, etc., without manual intervention. Every element in an autonomic system or application consists of two main modules: the functional unit that performs the required services and functionality, and the management/control unit that monitors the state and context of the element, analyze its current requirements (performance, fault-tolerance, security, etc.) and adapts to satisfy the requirement(s).

3.2   Architecture of an Autonomic Element

An autonomic element (see Figure 4) is the smallest unit of an autonomic application or system. It is a self-contained software or system module with specified input/output interfaces and explicit context dependencies. It also has embedded mechanisms for self-management, which are responsible for implementing its functionalities, exporting constraints, managing its behavior in accordance with context and policies, and interacting with other elements. Autonomic systems and applications are constructed from autonomic elements as dynamic, opportunistic and/or ephemeral compositions. These compositions may be defined by policies and context, and may be negotiated. The key parts of an autonomic element are described below.

- **Managed Element:** This is the smallest functional unit of the application and contains the executable code (program, data structures) (e.g., numerical model of a physical process). It also exports its functional interfaces, its functional and behav-

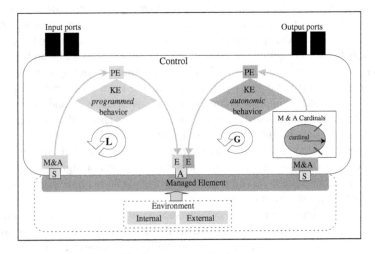

Fig. 4. An autonomic element

ioral attributes and constraints, and its control mechanisms. At runtime, the managed element can be affected in different ways, for example, it can encounter a failure, run out of resources, be externally attacked, or may hit a bottleneck impacting performance.

- **Environment:** The environment represents all the factors that can impact the managed element. The environment and the managed element can be viewed as two subsystems forming a stable system. Any change in the environment causes the whole system to go from a stable state to an unstable state. This change is then offset by reactive changes in the managed element causing the system to move back from the unstable state to a different stable state. Notice that the environment consists of two parts - internal and external. The internal environment consists of changes internal to the managed element, which reflects the state of the application/system. The external environment reflects the state of the execution environment.

- **Control:** Each autonomic element has its own manager that (1) accepts user-specified requirements (performance, fault tolerance, security, etc.), (2) interrogates the element and characterizes its state, (3) senses the state of the overall system/application, (4) determines state of the environment, and (5) uses this information to control the operation of the managed element in order to effectively achieve the specified behaviors. This control process repeats continuously throughout the lifetime of the autonomic element. As shown in Figure 4, the control part consists of two control loops - the local loop and the global loop.

The *local loop* can only handle known environment states and is based on knowledge that is embedded in the element. Its knowledge engine contains the mapping of environment states to behaviors. For example, when the load on the local system goes above the threshold value, the local control loop will work towards balancing the load by either controlling the local resources available to the managed element or by reducing the size of the problem handled by this element. This will work only if the local resources can handle the computational requirements. However, the local loop is blind to the overall behavior of the entire application or system and thus can not achieve the desired global objectives. In a scenario where the entire system is affected, the local loop will continue repeating local optimization that may lead to degradation in performance and result in sub-optimal or chaotic behavior. At some point, one of the essential variables of the system (in this case, a performance cardinal) may overshoot their limits. This is when the global loop comes into action.

The global loop can handle unknown environment states and may involve machine learning, artificial intelligence and/or human intervention. It uses four cardinals for the monitoring and analysis of the managed elements. These are performance, configuration, protection and security. These cardinals are like the essential variables described in Ashby's ultrastable system. This control loop results in new knowledge being introduced into the managed element to enable it to adapt its existing behaviors to respond to the changes in the environment. For example, the desired load-balancing behavior of the managed element (as directed by the local loop) requires its local load to be within prescribed limits. However, the local loop might not be able to maintain the local load within these acceptable limits, which in turn might degrade the performance of the overall system. Consequently, this change in the overall performance cardinal triggers the global loop, which then selects an alternate behavior pattern that can address the new load conditions. The new plan is then introduced into the managed element and used to adapt its behavior.

3.3   Autonomic Computing Systems and Applications

Autonomic applications and systems are composed from autonomic elements, and are capable of managing their behaviors and their relationships with other systems/ applications in accordance with high-level policies. Autonomic systems/applications exhibit eight defining characteristics [7]:

- **Self Awareness:** An autonomic application/system "knows itself" and is aware of its state and its behaviors.
- **Self Configuring:** An autonomic application/system should be able configure and reconfigure itself under varying and unpredictable conditions.
- **Self Optimizing:** An autonomic application/system should be able to detect sub-optimal behaviors and optimize itself to improve its execution.
- **Self-Healing:** An autonomic application/system should be able to detect and re-cover from potential problems and continue to function smoothly.
- **Self Protecting:** An autonomic application/system should be capable of detecting and protecting its resources from both internal and external attack and maintaining overall system security and integrity.
- **Context Aware:** An autonomic application/system should be aware of its execution environment and be able to react to changes in the environment.
- **Open:** An autonomic application/system must function in an heterogeneous world and should be portable across multiple hardware and software architectures. Consequently it must be built on standard and open protocols and interfaces.
- **Anticipatory:** An autonomic application/system should be able to anticipate to the extent possible, its needs and behaviors and those of its context, and be able to manage itself proactively.

Sample self-managing system/application behaviors include installing software when it is detected that the software is missing (self-configuration), restarting a failed element (self-healing), adjusting current workload when an increase in capacity is observed (self-optimization) and taking resources offline if an intrusion attempt is detected (self-protecting). Each of the characteristics listed above represents an active research area. Generally, self-management is addressed in four primary system/application aspects, i.e., configuration, optimization, protection, and healing. Further, self-management solutions typically consists of the steps outlined above: (1) the application and underlying information infrastructure provide information to enable context and self awareness; (2) system/application events trigger analysis, deduction and planning using system knowledge; and (3) plans are executed using the adaptive capabilities of the application/system. An autonomic application or system implements self-managing attributes using the control loops described above to collect information, make decisions, and adapt, as necessary.

4   Autonomic Computing Research Issues and Challenges

Meeting the grand challenges of autonomic computing presents fundamental and significant research challenges that span all levels, from the conceptual level to architecture, middleware, and applications. Key research issues and challenges are presented below.

Conceptual Challenges: Conceptual research issues and challenges include (1) defining appropriate abstractions and models for specifying, understanding, controlling, and implementing autonomic behaviors; (2) adapting classical models and theories for machine learning, optimization and control to dynamic and multi agent system; (3) providing effective models for negotiation that autonomic elements can use to establish multilateral relationships among themselves; and (4) designing statistical models of large networked systems that will let autonomic elements or systems detect or predict overall problems from a stream of sensor data from individual devices.

Architecture Challenges: Autonomic applications and systems will be constructed from autonomic elements that manage their internal behavior and their relationships with other autonomic elements in accordance with policies that humans or other elements have established. As a result, system/application level self-managing behaviors will arise from the self-managing behaviors of constituent autonomic elements and their interactions. System and software architectures in which local as well as global autonomic behaviors can be specified, implemented and controlled in a robust and predictable manner remains a key research challenge.

Middleware Challenges: The primary middleware level research challenge is providing the core services required to realize autonomic behaviors in a robust, reliable and scalable manner, in spite of the dynamism and uncertainty of the system and the application. These include discovery, messaging, security, privacy, trust, etc. Autonomic systems/applications will require autonomic elements to identify themselves, discover and verify the identities of other entities of interest, dynamically establish relationships with these entities, and to interact in a secure manner. Further the middleware itself should be secure, reliable and robust against new and insidious forms of attack that use self-management based on high-level policies to their own advantage.

Application Challenges: The key challenges at the application level is the formulation and development of systems and applications that are capable of managing (i.e., configuring, adapting, optimizing, protecting, healing) themselves. This includes programming models, frameworks and middleware services that support the definition of autonomic elements, the development of autonomic applications as the dynamic and opportunistic composition of these autonomic elements, and the policy, content and context driven definition, execution and management of these applications.

5   The Autonomic Computing Landscape

There have been a number of research efforts in both academia and industry addressing autonomic computing concepts and investigating the issues outlined above. Existing

Table 1. Systems incorporating autonomic properties

System	Application area	Key autonomic issues addressed
OceanStore [4, 9]	Global, consistent, highly-available persistent data storage.	Self-healing, self-optimization, self-configuration, self-protection. Policy-based caching, routing substrate adaptation, autonomic replication, continuous monitoring, testing, and repairing.
Storage Tank [11]	Multi-platform, universally accessible storage management.	Self-optimization, self-healing. Policy-based storage and data management, server redirection and log-based recovery.
Oceano [20]	Cost effective scalable management of computing resources for software farms.	Self-optimization, self-awareness. Autonomic demands distribution, constant component monitoring.
SMART DB2 [10]	Reduction of human intervention & cost for DB2.	Self-optimization, self-configuration Autonomic index determination, disaster recovery, continuous monitoring of DB2's health and alerting the DBA.
AutoAdmin [13]	Reducing Total Cost of Ownership (TCO)	Self-tuning, self-administration. Usage tracking, index tuning and recommending based on workload.
Sabio [17]	Autonomically Classifies Large Number of documents	Self-organization, self-awareness. Group documents according to the word and phrase usage.
Q-Fabric [16]	System Support for Continuous Online Management.	Self-organization. Continuous online quality management through "customizability" of each application's QoS.

projects and products can be broadly classified as (1) systems that incorporate autonomic mechanisms for problem determination, monitoring, analysis, management, etc., into systems, and (2) systems that investigate models, programming paradigms and development environments to support the development of autonomic systems and applications. A sampling of systems belonging to these categories are summarized in Tables 1 and Table 2 respectively.

6   Summary and Conclusion

In this paper, we introduced the *autonomic computing paradigm*, which is inspired by biological systems such as the autonomic human nervous system, and enables the development of self-managing computing systems and applications. The systems/applications use autonomic strategies and algorithms to handle complexity and uncertainties with minimum human intervention. An autonomic application/system is a collection of autonomic elements, which implement intelligent control loops to

Table 2. Systems supporting development of autonomic applications and systems

System	Focus	Autonomic issues addressed
KX (Kinesthetics eXtreme) [8]	Retrofitting automicity.	Enabling autonomic properties in legacy systems.
Anthill [12]	P2P systems based on Ant colonies.	Complex adaptive behavior of P2P systems.
Astrolabe [18]	Distributed information management.	Self-configuration, monitoring and to control adaptation.
Gryphon [19]	Publish/subscribe middleware.	Large communication.
Smart Grid [21]	Autonomic principles applied to solve Grid problems.	Autonomic Grid computing.
Autonomia [6]	Model and infrastructure for enabling autonomic applications.	Autonomic applications.
AutoMate [1, 15]	Execution environment for autonomic applications.	Autonomic applications.

monitor, analyze, plan and execute using knowledge of the environment. Several research efforts focused on enabling the autonomic properties address four main areas: self-healing, self-protection, self-configuration, and self-optimization. Projects in both industry and academia, have addressed autonomic behaviors at all levels, from the hardware level to software systems and applications. At the hardware level, systems may be dynamically upgradable, while at the operating system level, active operating system code may be replaced dynamically. Efforts have also focused on autonomic middleware, programming systems and runtime. At the application level, self-optimizing databases and web servers dynamically reconfigure to adapt service performance. These efforts have demonstrated both the feasibility and promise of autonomic computing. However, achieving overall autonomic behaviors remains an open and significant challenge, which will be accomplished through a combination of process changes, skills evolution, new technologies and architecture, and open industry standards.

References

1. M. Agarwal, V. Bhat, Z. Li, H. Liu, V. Matossian, V. Putty, C. Schmidt, G. Zhang, M. Parashar, B. Khargharia, and S. Hariri. AutoMate: Enabling Autonomic Applications on the Grid. In *Proceedings of Autonomic Computing Workshop The Fifth Annual International Workshop on Active Middleware Services(AMS 2003) IEEE Computer Society Press*, pages 48–57, Seattle, WA, June 25 2003.
2. W. R. Ashby. *Design for a Brain*. Chapman & Hall Ltd, 1960.

3. IBM Corporation. An architectural blueprint for autonomic computing. April 2003.
4. UC Berkeley Computer Science Division. The OceanStore Project, Project Overview. http://oceanstore.cs.berkeley.edu/info/overview.html, July 8 2002. Project Page.
5. S. Hariri and M. Parashar. *Handbook of Bioinspired Algorithms and Applications*, chapter The Foundations of Autonomic Computing. CRC Press LLC, 2005.
6. S. Hariri, L. Xue, H. Chen, M. Zhang, S. Pavuluri, and S. Rao. Autonomia: an autonomic computing environment. In *Performance, Computing, and Communications Conference, 2003. Conference Proceedings of the 2003 IEEE International*, April 9-11 2003.
7. P. Horn. Autonomic Computing:IBM's perspective on the State of Information Technology. http://www.research.ibm.com/autonomic/, Oct 2001. IBM Corp.
8. G. Kaiser, P. Gross, G. Kc, J. Parekh, and G. Valetto. An Approach to Autonomizing Legacy Systems. In *Workshop on Self-Healing, Adaptive and Self-MANaged Systems, SHAMAN*, New York City, NY, June 23 2002.
9. J. Kubiatowicz. OceanStore: Global-Scale Persistent Storage. http://oceanstore.cs. berkeley.edu/publications/talks/StanfordOceanStore.pdf, Spring 2001. Stanford Seminar Series, Stanford University,.
10. G. M. Lohman and S. S. Lightstone. SMART: Making DB2 (More) Autonomic. In *VLDB 2002 28th International Conference on Very Large Data Bases* , Kowloon Shangri-La Hotel, Hong Kong, China, August 20-23 2002.
11. J. Menon, D. A. Pease, R. Rees, L. Duyanovich, and B. Hillsberg. IBM Storage Tank–A Heterogeneous Scalable SAN file system. *IBM Systems Journal*, 42(2):250–267, 2003.
12. A. Montresor. The Anthill Project Part II: The Anthill Framework. http://www.cs.unibo.it/projects/anthill/papers/anthill-4p.pdf, 2001. The Anthill Project Documentation.
13. V. Narasayya. AutoAdmin: Towards Self-Tuning Databases, November 13 2002. Guest Lecture at Stanford University.
14. University of Sussex. Adaptive system lectures. http://www.cogs.susx.ac.uk/users/ezequiel/AS/lectures/AdaptiveSystems3.ppt, 2003.
15. M. Parashar, Z. Li, H. Liu V. Matossian, and C. Schmidt. *Self-Star Properties in Complex Information Systems*, volume 3460 of *Lecture Notes in Computer Science*, chapter Enabling Autonomic Grid Applications: Requirements, Models and Infrastructures. Springer Verlag, 2005.
16. C. Poellabauer. Q-Fabric. http://www.cc.gatech.edu/systems/projects/ELinux/qfabric.html, 2002. Q-Fabric - System Support for Continuous Online Quality Management.
17. R. Pool. Natural selection. http://domino.watson.ibm.com/comm/wwwr_thinkresearch.nsf/-pages/selection200.html, 2002. A New Computer Program Classifies Documents Automatically.
18. R.V. Renesse, K.P. Birman, and W. Vogels. Astrolabe: A robust and scalable technology for distributed systems monitoring, management, and data mining. *ACM Transaction on Computer Systems*, 21(2):164–206, 2003.
19. IBM Research. The Gryphon Project. http://www.research.ibm.com/gryphon/gryphon.html. IBM Corp.
20. IBM Research. The Océano Project. http://www.research.ibm.com/oceanoproject/. IBM Corp.
21. Columbia University Smart Grid. Smart Grid Test Bed. http://www.ldeo.columbia.edu/res/pi/4d4/testbeds/.

Enabling Autonomic Grid Applications: Dynamic Composition, Coordination and Interaction*

Zhen Li and Manish Parashar

The Applied Software Systems Laboratory,
Rutgers University, Piscataway NJ 08904, USA
{zhljenny, parashar}@caip.rutgers.edu

Abstract. The increasing complexity, heterogeneity and dynamism of networks, systems and applications have made our computational and information infrastructure brittle, unmanageable and insecure. This has necessitated the investigation of an alternate paradigm for system and application design, which is based on strategies used by biological systems to deal with similar challenges of complexity, heterogeneity, and uncertainty, i.e. autonomic computing. Project AutoMate investigates conceptual models and implementation architectures to enable the development and execution of self-managing applications. It supports the definition of autonomic elements, the development of autonomic applications as the dynamic and opportunistic composition of these autonomic elements, and the policy, content and context driven execution and management of these applications. This paper introduces AutoMate architecture and describes the Rudder coordination framework and its use in enabling autonomic behaviors.

1 Introduction

The emergence of wide-area distributed and decentralized "Grid" environments, such as pervasive information systems, peer-to-peer systems, and distributed computational infrastructures, has enabled a new generation of applications that are based on seamless access, aggregation and interactions. Examples include pervasive applications that leverage the pervasive information Grid to continuously manage, adapt, and optimize our living context, crisis management applications that use pervasive conventional and unconventional information for crisis prevention and response, medical applications that use in-vivo and in-vitro sensors and actuators for patient management, scientific and engineering simulations of complex physical phenomena that symbiotically and opportunistically combine computations, experiments, observations, and real-time data to provide important insights into complex systems, and business applications that use anytime-anywhere information access to optimize profits.

However, these emerging Grid computing environments are inherently large, heterogeneous and dynamic, globally aggregating large numbers of independent computing and communication resources, data stores and sensor networks. Further, emerging

---

* The research presented in this paper is supported in part by the National Science Foundation via grants numbers ACI 9984357, EIA 0103674, EIA 0120934, ANI 0335244, CNS 0305495, CNS 0426354 and IIS 0430826.

J.-P. Banâtre et al. (Eds.): UPP 2004, LNCS 3566, pp. 270–285, 2005.

Grid applications are similarly large and highly dynamic in their behaviors and interactions. Together, these characteristics result in application development, configuration and management complexities and uncertainties that break current paradigms based on passive elements and static compositions and interactions. This has led researchers to consider alternative programming paradigms and management techniques that are based on strategies used by biological systems to deal with complexity, dynamism, heterogeneity and uncertainty. The approach, referred to as autonomic computing [8], aims at realizing computing systems and applications capable of managing themselves with minimal human intervention.

Enabling autonomic systems and applications presents many conceptual and implementation challenges, primarily due to the highly dynamic, context and content-dependent behaviors. A key challenge is supporting coordination in a robust and scalable manner. Coordination is the *management of runtime dependencies and interactions among the elements in the system.* In case of autonomic systems/applications, these dependencies and interactions can be complex and various (e.g. peer-to-peer, client-server, producer-consumer, collaborative, at-most/at-least/exactly, etc.), and both, the coordinated entities and the nature of the relationships and interactions between them can be ad hoc and opportunistic.

Project AutoMate investigates autonomic solutions to deal with the challenges of complexity, dynamism, heterogeneity and uncertainty in Grid environments. The overall goal of Project AutoMate is to develop conceptual models and implementation architectures that can enable the development and execution of such self-managing Grid applications. These include programming models, frameworks and middleware services that support definition of autonomic elements, the development of autonomic applications as the dynamic and opportunistic composition of these autonomic elements, and the policy, content and context driven execution and management of these applications. This paper introduces AutoMate and its key components. Specifically, this paper focuses on the design and implementation of the Rudder coordination framework. Rudder provides software agents that enable application/system self-managing behaviors, and a fully decentralized coordination middleware that enables flexible and scalable interaction and coordination among agents and autonomic elements. The operation of AutoMate and Rudder is illustrated using an autonomic oil reservoir optimization application that is enabled by the framework.

The rest of this paper is organized as follows. Section 2 outlines the challenges and requirements of pervasive Grid systems and applications. Section 3 introduces Project AutoMate, presents its overall architecture and describes its key components. Section 4 presents the describes the design, implementation and evaluation of the Rudder coordination framework, including the Rudder agent framework and the COMET coordination middleware. Section 5 presents the autonomic oil reservoir application enabled by AutoMate and Rudder. Section 6 presents a conclusion.

2   Enabling Grid Applications – Challenges and Requirements

The goal of the Grid concept is to enable a new generation of applications combining intellectual and physical resources that span many disciplines and organizations, providing vastly more effective solutions to important scientific, engineering, business and government problems. These new applications must be built on seamless and secure discovery, access to, and interactions among resources, services, and applications owned by many different organizations.

Attaining these goals requires implementation and conceptual models. Implementation models address the virtualization of organizations which leads to Grids, the creation and management of virtual organizations as goal-driven compositions of organizations, and the instantiation of virtual machines as the execution environment for an application. Conceptual models define abstract machines that support programming models and systems to enable application development. Grid software systems typically provide capabilities for: (i) creating a transient "virtual organization" or virtual resource configuration, (ii) creating virtual machines composed from the resource configuration of the virtual organization (iii) creating application programs to execute on the virtual machines, and (iv) executing and managing application execution. Most Grid software systems implicitly or explicitly incorporate a programming model, which in turn assumes an underlying abstract machine with specific execution behaviors including assumptions about reliability, failure modes, etc. As a result, failure to realize these assumptions by the implementation models will result in brittle applications. The stronger the assumptions made, the greater the requirements for the Grid infrastructure to realize these assumptions and consequently its resulting complexity. In this section we first highlight the characteristics and challenges of Grid environments, and outline key requirements for programming Grid applications. We then introduce self-managing Grid applications that can address these challenges and requirements.

2.1   Characteristics of Grid Execution Environments and Applications

Key characteristics of Grid execution environments and applications include:

Heterogeneity: Grid environments aggregate large numbers of independent and geographically distributed computational and information resources, including supercomputers, workstation-clusters, network elements, data-storages, sensors, services, and Internet networks. Similarly, applications typically combine multiple independent and distributed software elements such as components, services, real-time data, experiments and data sources.

Dynamism: The Grid computation, communication and information environment is continuously changing during the lifetime of an application. This includes the availability and state of resources, services and data. Applications similarly have dynamic runtime behaviors in that the organization and interactions of the components/services can change.

Uncertainty: Uncertainty in Grid environment is caused by multiple factors, including (1) dynamism, which introduces unpredictable and changing behaviors that can only be detected and resolved at runtime, (2) failures, which have an increasing probability of occurrence and frequencies as system/application scales increase; and (3) incomplete knowledge of global system state, which is intrinsic to large decentralized and asynchronous distributed environments.

Security: A key attribute of Grids is flexible and secure hardware/software resource sharing across organization boundaries, which makes security (authentication, authorization and access control) and trust critical challenges in these environments.

2.2 Requirements for Programming Systems and Middleware Services

The characteristics outlined above require that Grid programming systems and middleware services must be able to specify and support applications that can detect and dynamically respond to the changes in the runtime environment and application states. This requirement suggests that (1) Grid applications should be formulated from discrete composable elements, which incorporate separate specifications for all of functional, non-functional, and interaction and coordination behaviors; (2) The interface definitions of these elements should be separated from their implementations to enable heterogeneous elements to interact and to enable dynamic selection of elements; (3) Specifications of composition, coordination and interaction should be separated from computation behaviors, and may be dynamically specified and implemented.

Given these requirements, a Grid application requiring a given set of computational behaviors may be integrated with different interaction and coordination models or languages (and vice versa) and different specifications for non-functional behaviors such as fault recovery and QoS to address the dynamism and heterogeneity of the application and the underlying environments.

2.3 Self-managing Applications on the Grid

As outlined above, the inherent scale, complexity, heterogeneity, and dynamism of emerging Grid environments and applications result in significant programming and runtime management challenges, which break current approaches. This is primarily because the programming models and the abstract machine underlying these models make strong assumptions about common knowledge, static behaviors and system guarantees that cannot be realized by Grid virtual machines and, which are not true for Grid applications. Addressing these challenges requires redefining Grid programming frameworks and middleware services to address the separations outlined above. Specifically, it requires (1) static (defined at the time of instantiation) application requirements and system and application behaviors to be relaxed, (2) the behaviors of elements and applications to be sensitive to the dynamic state of the system and the changing requirements of the application and be able to adapt to these changes at runtime, (3) required common knowledge be expressed semantically (ontology and taxonomy) rather than in terms of names, addresses and identifiers, and (4) the core enabling middleware services (e.g., discovery, messaging) be driven by such a semantic knowledge. In the rest of this paper we describe Project AutoMate, which attempts to address these challenges by enabling autonomic self-managing Grid applications.

3 Project AutoMate: Enabling Self-managing Grid Applications

Project AutoMate [17, 16] investigates autonomic computing approaches to realize systems and applications that are capable of managing (i.e., configuring, adapting, optimiz-

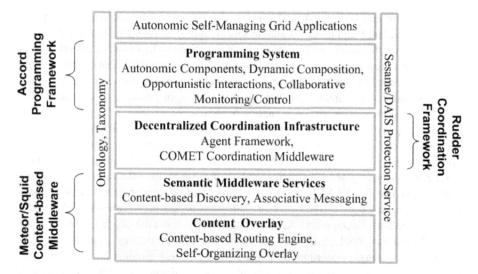

Fig. 1. A schematic overview of AutoMate

ing, protecting, healing) themselves. The overall goal is to investigate the conceptual models and implementation architectures that can enable the development and execution of such self-managing Grid applications. Specifically, it investigates programming frameworks and middleware services that support the development of autonomic applications as the dynamic and opportunistic composition of autonomic elements, and the execution and management of these applications.

A schematic overview of AutoMate is presented in Figure 1. Components of AutoMate include the Accord [10, 11] programming system, the Rudder [9] decentralized coordination framework and agent-based deductive engine, which is the focus of this paper, and the Meteor [7, 6] content-based middleware providing support for content-based routing, discovery and associative messaging. Project AutoMate additionally includes the Sesame [21] context-based access control infrastructure, the DAIS [20] cooperative-protection services and the Discover collaboratory [4, 12, 13] services for collaborative monitoring, interaction and control, which are not described here.

The Accord programming system [10, 11] extends existing programming systems to enable autonomic element definitions, self-managing Grid application formulation and development. Specifically it extends the entities and composition rules defined by the underlying programming model to enable computational and composition/interaction behaviors to be defined at runtime using high-level rules. *Autonomic Elements* in Accord extend programming elements (i.e., objects, components, services) to define a self-contained modular software unit with specified interfaces and explicit context dependencies. Additionally, an autonomic element encapsulates rules, constraints and mechanisms for self-management, and can dynamically interact with other elements and the system.

Each autonomic element is associated with an element manager (possibly embedded) that is delegated to manage its execution. The element manager monitors the state of the element and its context, and controls the execution of rules. Rules incorporate high-level guidance and practical human knowledge. *Behavioral rules* control the run-time functional behaviors of an autonomic element (e.g., the dynamic selection of algorithms, data representation, input/output format used by the element), while *Interaction rules* control the interactions between elements, between elements and their environment, and the coordination within an autonomic application (e.g., communication mechanism, composition and coordination of the elements).

Meteor [7, 6] is a scalable content-based middleware infrastructure that provides services for content routing, discovery, and associative interactions. The Meteor stack consists of 3 key components: (1) a self-organizing overlay, (2) a content-based routing engine and discovery service (Squid), and (3) the Associative Rendezvous Messaging Substrate (ARMS). The Meteor overlay is composed of Rendezvous Peer (RP) nodes, which may be any node on the Grid (e.g., gateways, access points, message relay nodes, servers or end-user computers). RP nodes can join or leave the overlay network at any time. The overlay topology is based on standard structured overlays. The content overlay provides a single operation, *lookup(identifier)*, which requires an exact identifier (e.g., name). Given an identifier, this operation locates the peer node where the content should be stored. Squid [18] is the Meteor content-based routing engine and decentralized information discovery service. It supports flexible content-based routing and complex queries containing partial keywords, wildcards, and ranges, and guarantees that all existing data elements that match a query will be found.

The ARMS layer [7] implements the Associative Rendezvous (AR) interaction paradigm. AR is a paradigm for content-based decoupled interactions with programmable reactive behaviors, and extends the conventional name/identifier-based rendezvous in two ways. First, it uses flexible combinations of keywords (i.e, keyword, partial keyword, wildcards and ranges) from a semantic information space, instead of opaque identifiers (names, addresses) that have to be globally known. Interactions are based on content described by these keywords. Second, it enables the reactive behaviors at the rendezvous points to be encapsulated within messages increasing flexibility and enabling multiple interaction semantics (e.g., broadcast multicast, notification, publisher/subscriber, mobility, etc.).

Rudder [9] is an agent-based decentralized coordination framework for enabling self-managing Grid applications, and provides the core capabilities for supporting autonomic compositions, adaptations, optimizations, and fault-tolerance. It enables composition, coordination and interaction behaviors to be separated from computational behaviors, and allows them to be semantically separately expressed and efficiently implemented. Rudder and its components are described in more detail in the following sections.

4   Rudder Coordination Framework

Rudder consists of two key components: an agent framework and the COMET coordination middleware. The agent framework provides protocols for coordination and cooperation to enable peer agents to individually and collectively achieve self-managing behaviors. COMET implements the coordination abstractions and mechanisms and provides a decentralized and associative shared coordination-space.

4.1   The Rudder Agent Framework

The Rudder agent framework is composed of a dynamic network of software agents existing at different levels, ranging from individual system/application elements to the overall system/application. These agents monitor the element states, manage the element behaviors and dependencies, coordinate element interactions, and cooperate to manage overall system application behaviors.

Agent Classification: The Rudder agent framework consists of three types of peer agents: Component Agent (CA), System Agent (SA), and Composition Agent (CSA). CAs and SAs are part of the system/application elements, while CSAs are transient and are generated to satisfy specific application requirements. CAs manage the computations performed locally within application elements and their interaction and communication behaviors and mechanisms. They are integrated with the Accord element managers. SAs are embedded within Grid resource units (e.g., compute resources, instrument, data store). CSAs enable dynamic composition of autonomic elements by defining and executing workflow-selection and element-selection rules. Workflow-selection rules are used to select appropriate composition plans to enact. Element-selection rules are used to semantically discover and select registered elements. CSAs negotiate to select interaction patterns for a specific application workflow, and coordinate with associated element agents to define and execute associated interaction rules at runtime. This enables autonomic applications to dynamically change flows, elements and element interactions to address application and system dynamics and uncertainty.

Agent Coordination Protocols: Rudder provides a set of common discovery and control protocols to all agents. Discovery protocols support the registering, unregistering, and discovery of system/application elements. Control protocols allow the agents to query element states, control their behaviors and orchestrate their interactions. These protocols include negotiation, notification, and mutual exclusion. The agent coordination protocols are scalably and robustly implemented in logically decentralized, physically distributed Grid environments using the abstractions provided by COMET, which are described below.

4.2   COMET Coordination Middleware

The overall goal of COMET is to enable scalable peer-to-peer content-based coordination in large-scale decentralized distributed environments. The COMET implements a global Linda-like shared-space [5], which is constructed from a globally known semantic multi-dimensional information space. The information space is defined by the ontology used by the coordinated entities, and is deterministically mapped, using a locality preserving mapping, to a dynamic set of peer nodes in the system. The resulting peer-to-peer information lookup system maintains content locality and guarantees that content-based information queries, using flexible content descriptors in the form of keywords, partial keywords and wildcards, are delivered with bounded costs.

The COMET Model. The COMET model consists of layered abstractions prompted by a fundamental separation of communication and coordination concerns.

The *communication abstraction* provides an associative communication service and guarantees that content-based information queries, specified using flexible content descriptors, are served with bounded costs. It supports content-based discovery, routing and messaging. This layer essentially maps the virtual information space in a deterministic way on to the dynamic set of currently available peer nodes in the system, while maintaining content locality. It thus manages system scale, heterogeneity and dynamism. The communication abstraction provides a single operator: **deliver** ($\mathcal{M}$). The message $\mathcal{M}$ consists of (1) a semantic selector that is flexibly defined using keywords from the information space, and specifies a region in this space, and (2) a payload consisting of the data and operation to be performed at the destination.

The *coordination abstraction* extends the traditional data-driven model with event-based reactivity to changes in system state and to data access operations. It defines a *reactive tuple*, which consists of 2 additional components: a *condition* that associates *reaction* to events, and a *guard* that specifies how and when the reaction will be executed (e.g., immediately, once). This abstraction provides the basic **Out**, **In**, and **Rd** primitives. These basic operations operate on regular as well as reactive tuples and retain the Linda semantics. The operations are directly implemented on the **deliver** operator provided by the communication abstraction.

Transient Spaces in COMET. Coordination middlewares based on the model outlined above are naturally suitable for context-transparent applications that are developed and executed without explicit knowledge of the system context. Furthermore, since the underlying implementation maintains content locality in the information space, it is both scalable and flexible. However, certain applications, e.g., mobile applications, require context locality to be maintained in addition to content locality, i.e., they impose requirements for context-awareness. The uniform operators provided by COMET do not distinguish between local and remote components of a space. While this is a convenient abstraction, it does not maintain context locality and may have a detrimental effect on system efficiency for these applications. To address this issue, COMET defines transient spaces that have a specific scope definition (e.g., within the same geographical region or the same physical subnet). The transient spaces have exactly the same structure and semantics as the original space, and can be dynamically created. An application can switch between spaces at runtime and can simultaneously use multiple spaces.

The COMET Design and Implementation. A schematic overview of the COMET system architecture is shown in Figure 2. The current prototype has been implemented on Project JXTA [2], a general-purpose peer-to-peer framework. The coordination space is provided as a JXTA peergroup service that can be concurrently exploited by multiple applications. The design and implementation of the COMET coordination and communication layers are described below.

Communication Layer: The communication layer of COMET is built on the Meteor messaging substrate[7], which provides scalable content-based routing and data delivery operations. Meteor consists of a structured self-organizing overlay and the Squid content-based routing engine.

Squid [18] provides a decentralized information discovery and associative messaging service. It uses a locality preserving and dimension reducing indexing scheme,

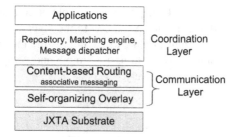

Fig. 2. A schematic overview of the COMET system architecture

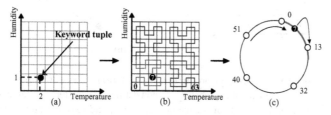

Fig. 3. Routing using a simple keyword tuple in Squid: (a) the simple keyword tuple (2, 1) is viewed as a point in a multi-dimensional space; (b) the keyword tuple is mapped to the index 7, using Hilbert SFC; (c) the data will be routed in the overlay (an overlay with 5 RP nodes and an identifier space from 0 to 2^6-1) at RP node 13, the successor of the index 7

based on the Hilbert Space Filling Curve (SFC), to effectively map a multi-dimensional information space to the peer identifier space and to the current peer nodes in the system. The peer nodes form a structured overlay. The resulting peer-to-peer information system supports flexible content-based routing and complex queries containing partial keywords, wildcards, and ranges, and guarantees that all existing data elements that match a query will be found. Keywords can be common words or values of globally defined attributes, and are defined by applications. In the case of COMET, these keywords are part of the common ontology used by the coordinating entities. The keywords form the multi-dimensional information space, i.e., keyword tuples represent points or regions in this space and the keywords are the coordinates. A *keyword tuple* in Squid is defined as a list of d keywords, wildcards and/or ranges, where d is the dimensionality of the keyword space. A keyword tuple only containing complete keywords is called *simple*, and a tuple containing partial keywords, wildcards and/or ranges is called *complex*.

Content-based routing in Squid is achieved as follows. SFCs are used to generate a 1-dimensional index space from the multi-dimensional keyword space. Further, using the SFC, a query consisting of a simple keyword tuple can be mapped to a point on the SFC. Similarly, any complex keyword tuple can be mapped to regions in the keyword space and to corresponding clusters (segments of the curve) in the SFC. The 1-dimensional index space generated from the entire information space is mapped onto the 1-dimensional identifier space used by the overlay network formed by the peer nodes. As a result, using the SFC mapping any simple or complex keyword tuple can be located. Squid provides a simple abstraction to the layer above consisting of a single operation: **post**(*keyword tuple, data*), where *data* is the message payload provided by the messaging layer above. The routing for simple and complex keyword tuples is illustrated in Figures 3 and 4 respectively.

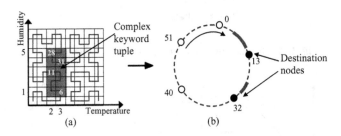

Fig. 4. Routing using a complex keyword tuple (2-3, 1-5): (a) the keyword tuple defines a rectangular region in the 2-dimensional keyword space consisting of 2 clusters (2 segments on the SFC curve); (b) the clusters (the solid part of the circle) correspond to destination RP nodes 13 and 32, which are routed to

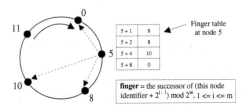

Fig. 5. Example of the Chord overlay network. Each node stores the keys that map to the segment of the curve between itself and the predecessor node

The Meteor content overlay is composed of peer nodes, which may be any node in the system (e.g., gateways, access points, message relay nodes, servers or end-user computers). The peer nodes can join or leave the network at any time. The overlay topology is based on standard structured overlays. The current implementation of Meteor uses the Chord [19] overlay network where peer nodes form a ring topology. Advantages of Chord include its guaranteed performance and logarithmic in number of messages. Every node in Chord is assigned a unique identifier and maintains a *finger table* for routing. The lookup algorithm in Chord enables the efficient data routing with O(log N) cost, where N is the number of nodes in the system. An example of a Chord overlay network with 5 nodes is shown in Figure 5. The Meteor overlay network layer provides a simple abstraction to the layers above, consisting of a single operation: **lookup**(*identifier*). Given an identifier, this operation locates the node that is responsible for it, i.e, the node with an identifier that is the closest identifier greater than or equal to the queried identifier.

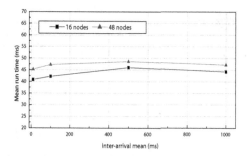

Fig. 6. Average round trip time for the *Out* operation for different mean inter-arrival time

Coordination Layer: The coordination layer implements the coordination abstraction and primitives. Its main components include a data repository for storing, pending requests, and retrieving tuples, a flexible matching engine, and a message dispatcher that interfaces with the communication layer to convert the coordination primitives to messaging operations and vice versa. Tuples and templates are represented as simple XML strings, as they provide small-sized flexible formats that are suitable for efficient information exchange in distributed heterogeneous environments.

The COMET **Out**, **Rd** and **In** operations are implemented using Squid routing. Using the tag and fields of a tuple, each tuple/template is associated with a sequence of keywords, which are then used to generate the *keyword tuple* required by the Squid *post* operator. It is assumed that all peer nodes agree on the structure and dimension of the information space used to define the keyword tuples.

Tuple distribution consists of the following steps: (1) Keywords are extracted from the tuple and used to create the keys for the Squid *post* operation. The payload of the message consists of the tuple and the coordination operation. (2) Squid uses the SFC mapping to identify the indices corresponding to the keyword tuple and the corresponding peer id(s). (3) The overlay *lookup* operator is used to route to the appropriate peer nodes. This operator maps the logical peer identifer to a JxtaId and sends the tuple using the JXTA Resolver Protocol. The *Out* operator only returns after receiving the *Resolver Query Response* from the destination to guarantee tuple delivery. In the case of *In* and *Rd* operations, the templates are routed in a similar manner. These two operations block until a matched tuple is returned by the destination in a peer-to-peer manner.

Experimental Evaluation of COMET. COMET has been deployed in a distributed network of 64 Linux-based computers in Rutgers University. Each node has an Intel(R) Pentium-4 1.70GHz CPU with 512MB RAM and is running Linux 2.4.20-8 (kernel version). Each machine serves as a peer node in COMET overlay. The experiments include measuring the average run time for each of the coordination primitives provided by COMET. For an *Out* operation, the measured time corresponds to the time interval between when the tuple is posted into the space and when the response from the destination is received. For a *In/Rd* operation, the measured time is the time interval between when the template is posted into the space and when the matched tuple is returned to the application assuming that a matched tuple exists in the space. This time includes the duration of template routing, repository matching and returning the matched tuple. The measurements use the native clocks of the peer nodes.

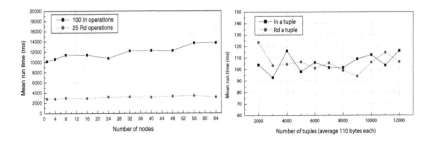

(a) Average time for 100 *In* and 25 *Rd* operations for increasing system sizes.

(b) Average time for *In* and *Rd* operations with increasing number of tuples. System size fixed at 4 nodes.

Fig. 7. Scalability and performance of *In* and *Rd* operations

Evaluation of the Out Operation. To evaluate the *Out* operation, regular XML tuples were used, which consist of randomly generated strings with fixed length. The average size of a tuple was 110 bytes. Furthermore, network traffic was modelled as poisson arrival *Out* operations with different inter-arrival mean time. Figure 6 shows the performance of the *Out* operations with inter-arrival mean time of 10ms, 100ms, 500ms, and 1000ms, and a system size of 16 and 48 peer nodes. The Y axis is the average run time. The figure shows that the *Out* operation is fairly independent of the traffic inter-arrival time and scales with system size at the order of O(logN) where N is the number of nodes in the system. The maximum average time of the 48 peer node system is approximately 47ms, which we believe is acceptable.

Evaluation of the In/Rd Operation. To study the behavior of the *In/Rd* operation, two experiments were conducted. The first experiment evaluated the average time required for data retrieval and extraction using *In* and *Rd* operations with different system sizes. The operation latency was measured for 25 *Rd* operations and 100 *In* operations. In this experiment we assumed that the tuples were previously stored into the space by *Out* operations. In the second experiment, the average time required for each single operation was measured for different numbers of tuples, with a fixed system size of 4 nodes. The lengths of the tuples are fixed at 110 bytes. The tuples were generated with random strings. The results are shown in Figure 7. The plots show that the *In/Rd* operations scale well with the number of nodes and their performance is largely independent of the number of tuples in the system. The average latency for *Rd/In* operations is approximately 105ms for experiments with numbers of tuples ranging from 2000 to 12000.

5   An Illustrative Example: Autonomic Oil Reservoir Optimization

One of the fundamental problems in oil reservoir production is determining the optimal locations of the oil production and injection wells. However, the selection of appropriate optimization algorithms, the runtime configuration and invocation of these

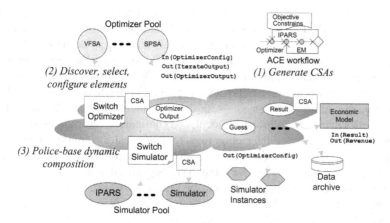

Fig. 8. Autonomic Oil Reservoir Optimization

algorithms and the dynamic optimization of the reservoir remain challenging problems. In this example we use AutoMate to support the autonomic compositions, interactions and adaptations to enable an autonomic self-optimizing reservoir application. The application consists of the following elements: (1) sophisticated reservoir simulation components (e.g. IPARS [1] factory) that encapsulate complex mathematical models of the physical interactions in the subsurface; (2) distributed data archives that store historical, experimental, and observed data; (3) sensors embedded in the instrumented oilfield providing real-time data about the current state of the oil field; (4) optimization services based on the Very Fast Simulated Annealing (VFSA) [14] and Simultaneous Perturbation Stochastic Approximation (SPSA) [15]; (5) the economic modeling service.

These elements need to dynamically discover one another and interact as peers to achieve the overall application objectives. First, the simulation components should dynamically obtain necessary resources, detect current resource state, and negotiate required qualities of service. Next, the simulation components must interact with one another, and with archived history and real-time sensor data, to enable a better characterization of the reservoir. Further, the reservoir simulation components interact with optimization services and with the data to optimize well configuration and operation, with weather services to control production, and with economic modelling service to detect current and predicted future oil prices so as to maximize the revenue from the production.

The operation of this application using AutoMate, and specially Rudder, is illustrated in Figure 8. The overall process is achieved by (1) generating composition agents based on application workflows, (2) agents discovering and composing the involved components to enable the oil reservoir management process, which includes monitoring oil production behaviors and detecting needs for optimization, and (3) agents using high-level policies to orchestrate interactions to optimize well operation and oil production.

First, the AutoMate composition engine (ACE) [3] generates the following workflows to satisfy the application objectives: (i) the optimization service provides the

IPARS reservoir simulator with an initial guess of well parameters based on the configuration of the oil field; (ii) IPARS uses the well parameters along with current market parameters to periodically compute the current revenue using an Economic Model (EM) service; and (iii) IPARS iteratively interacts with the optimization service to optimize well parameters for maximum profit. Based on above workflows, three CSAs are instantiated for the EM, Optimizer, and IPARS respectively. The CSAs dynamically discover the appropriate autonomic elements with desired functionality and cost/performance characteristics using the discovery protocol, and configure the workflows using interaction rules. The CAs use the interaction rules to dynamically establish interaction relationships among the elements and using appropriate communication mechanisms. The CSAs then coordinate with the CAs using the decentralized tuple-space.

Application self-management and self-optimization behaviors are achieved via the police-based autonomic behaviors of the agents. Each CA monitors and manages the execution of its element, while the CSAs discover and compose elements and resources to satisfy current application objectives. For example, the choice of optimization algorithm depends on the size and nature of the reservoir. In case of reservoirs with many randomly distributed maxima and minima, the VFSA algorithm can be employed during the initial optimization phase. Once convergence slows down, VFSA can be replaced by SPSA, which is suited for larger reservoirs with relatively smooth characteristics. Using these policies, the Optimizer CSA selects the appropriate optimization service, and configures it to optimize the application according to the current objectives of the application. Similarly, the SAs monitor and manage the runtime utilization of the resource and dynamically balance workload.

6   Conclusion

In this paper, we introduced Project AutoMate and described Rudder, its coordination framework. Project AutoMate investigates solutions that are based on the strategies used by biological systems to deal with challenges of complexity, dynamism, heterogeneity and uncertainty. This approach, referred to as autonomic computing, aims at realizing systems and applications that are capable of managing (i.e., configuring, adapting, optimizing, protecting, healing) themselves. The overall goal of Project AutoMate is to investigate conceptual models and implementation architectures that can enable the development and execution of such self-managing Grid applications. Specifically, it investigates programming models, frameworks and middleware services that support the definition of autonomic elements, the development of autonomic applications. The Rudder coordination framework consists of an agent framework and the COMET coordination middleware and enables dynamic discovery, composition and the policy, content and context driven definition, execution and management of these applications. The design, implementation and evaluation of Rudder was presented. The operation of AutoMate and Rudder was illustrated using an autonomic self-optimization oil reservoir application.

References

1. IPARS: Integrated Parallel Reservoir Simulator, The University of Texas at Austin, http://www.ices.utexas.edu/CSM.
2. "Project JXTA", http://www.jxta.org.
3. M. Agarwal and M. Parashar, "Enabling Autonomic Compositions in Grid Environments," in *Proceedings of 4th International Workshop on Grid Computing (Grid 2003)*, IEEE Computer Society Press 2003, 34 - 41.
4. V. Bhat and M. Parashar, "Discover Middleware Substrate for Integrating Services on the Grid," in *Proceedings of 10th International Conference on High Performance Computing (HiPC 2003)*, Springer-Verlag, December 2003, 373-382.
5. D. Gelernter, "Generative communication in Linda", *ACM Trans. Program. Lang. System*, ACM Press, 7(1) 1985, 80–112.
6. N. Jiang and M. Parashar, "Enabling Applications in Sensor-Based Pervasive Environments," in *Proceedings of BROADNETS 2004: Workshop on Broadband Advanced Sensor Networks (BaseNets 2004)*, San Jose, CA, USA October 25, 2004.
7. N. Jiang, C. Schmidt, V. Matossian and M. Parashar, "Content-based Middleware for Decoupled Interactions in Pervasive Environments", Rutgers University, Wireless Information Network Laboratory (WINLAB), Piscataway, NJ, USA, 2004.
8. J. Kephart, M. Parashar, V. Sunderam and R. Das, eds., *Proceedings of the First International Conference on Autonomic Computing*, IEEE Computer Society Press, 2004.
9. Z. Li and M. Parashar, "Rudder: A Rule-based Multi-agent Infrastructure for Supporting Autonomic Grid Applications," in *Proceedings of 1st IEEE International Conference on Autonomic Computing (ICAC-04)*, May 2004, 10 -17.
10. H. Liu and M. Parashar, "Accord: A Programming Framework for Autonomic Applications," *IEEE Transactions on Systems, Man and Cybernetics, Special Issue on Engineering Autonomic Systems*, Editors: R. Sterritt and T. Bapty, IEEE Press, to appear.
11. H. Liu, M. Parashar and S. Hariri, "A Component-based Programming Framework for Autonomic Applications," in *Proceedings of 1st IEEE International Conference on Autonomic Computing (ICAC-04)*, IEEE Computer Society Press 2004, 278 - 279.
12. V. Mann, V. Matossian, R. Muralidhar and M. Parashar, "DISCOVER: An Environment for Web-based Interaction and Steering of High-Performance Scientific Applications", *Concurrency and Computation: Practice and Experience*, 13(8-9), 2001, 737-754.
13. V. Mann and M. Parashar, "Engineering an Interoperable Computational Collaboratory on the Grid", *Concurrency and Computation: Practice and Experience, Special Issue on Grid Computing Environments*, 14(13-15), 2002, 1569-1593.
14. V. Matossian, V. Bhat, M. Parashar, M. Peszynska, M. Sen, P. Stoffa and M. F. Wheeler, "Autonomic Oil Reservoir Optimization on the Grid", *Concurrency and Computation: Practice and Experience, John Wiley and Sons*, John Wiley and Sons, Vol. 17, Issue 1, pp. 1 - 26, 2005.
15. V. Matossian, M. Parashar, W. Bangerth, H. Klie and M. F. Wheeler, "An Autonomic Reservoir Framework for the Stochastic Optimization of Well Placement", *Cluster Computing: The Journal of Networks, Software Tools, and Applications, Special Issue on Autonomic Computing, Kluwer Academic Press*, March 2004.
16. M. Parashar, Z. Li, H. Liu, C. Schmidt, V. Matossian and N. Jiang, "Enabling Autonomic Applications: Models and Infrastructure," in *Proceedings of European Commission - US National Science Foundation Strategic Research Workshop on Unconventional Programming Paradigms: Challenges, Visions and Research Issues for New Programming Paradigms*, Spring Verlag 2004.

17. M. Parashar, H. Liu, Z. Li, V. Matossian, C. Schmidt, G. Zhang and S. Hariri, "AutoMate: Enabling Autonomic Grid Applications," *Cluster Computing: The Journal of Networks, Software Tools, and Applications, Special Issue on Autonomic Computing*, Kluwer Academic Publishers, November 2003.

18. C. Schmidt and M. Parashar, "Enabling Flexible Queries with Guarantees in P2P Systems", *IEEE Internet Computing*, 8(3), May-June 2004, 19 - 26.

19. I. Stoica, R. Morris, D. Karger, F. Kaashoek and H. Balakrishnan, "Chord: A Scalable Peer-to-Peer Lookup Service for Internet Applications," in *Proceedings of ACM SIGCOMM*, August 2001.

20. G. Zhang and M. Parashar, "Cooperative Defense against Network Attacks,", in *Proceedings of the 3rd International Workshop on Security In Information Systems (WOSIS 2005), 7th International Conference on Enterprise Information Systems (ICEIS 2005)*, Miami, FL, USA, May 2005.

21. G. Zhang and M. Parashar, "Dynamic Context-aware Access Control for Grid Applications," in *Proceedings of 4th International Workshop on Grid Computing (Grid 2003)*, IEEE Computer Society Press 2003, 101 - 108.

Grassroots Approach to Self-management in Large-Scale Distributed Systems⋆

Ozalp Babaoglu, Márk Jelasity⋆⋆, and Alberto Montresor

Department of Computer Science, University of Bologna, Italy
{babaoglu, jelasity, montreso}@cs.unibo.it

Abstract. Traditionally, autonomic computing is envisioned as replacing the human factor in the deployment, administration and maintenance of computer systems that are ever more complex. Partly to ensure a smooth transition, the design philosophy of autonomic computing systems remains essentially the same as traditional ones, only autonomic components are added to implement functions such as monitoring, error detection, repair, etc. In this position paper we outline an alternative approach which we call "grassroots self-management". While this approach is by no means a solution to all problems, we argue that recent results from fields such as agent-based computing, the theory of complex systems and complex networks can be efficiently applied to achieve important autonomic computing goals, especially in very large and dynamic environments. Unlike traditional compositional design, in the grassroots approach, desired properties like self-healing and self-organization are not programmed explicitly but rather "emerge" from the local interactions among the system components. Such solutions are potentially more robust to failures, are more scalable and are extremely simple to implement. We discuss the practicality of grassroots autonomic computing through the examples of data aggregation, topology management and load balancing in large dynamic networks.

1 Introduction

The desire to build fault-tolerant computer systems with an intuitive and simple user interface has always been part of the computer science research agenda. Yet, the current scale and complexity of computer systems is becoming alarming, especially because our everyday life has come to depend on such systems to an increasing degree. There is a general feeling in the research community that coping with this new situation—which emerged as a result of Moore's Law, the widespread adoption of the Internet and computing becoming pervasive in

⋆ This work was partially supported by the Future & Emerging Technologies unit of the European Commission through Projects BISON (IST-2001-38923) and DELIS (IST-001907).
⋆⋆ Also with RGAI, MTA SZTE, Szeged, Hungary.

J.-P. Banâtre et al. (Eds.): UPP 2004, LNCS 3566, pp. 286–296, 2005.
© Springer-Verlag Berlin Heidelberg 2005

general—calls for radically new approaches to achieve seamless and efficient functioning of computer systems.

Accordingly, significant effort is being devoted to tackle the problem of self-management. One of the most influential and widely publicized approaches is IBM's *autonomic computing* initiative, launched in 2001 [11]. The term "autonomic" is a biological analogy referring to the autonomic nervous system. The function of this system in our body is to control "routine" tasks such as blood pressure, hormone levels, heart rate, breathing rate, etc. allowing our conscious mind to focus on higher level tasks like planning and problem solving. The idea is that autonomic computing is just that: computer systems should take care of routine tasks themselves while system administrators and users can focus on the actual task instead of spending most of their time troubleshooting and tweaking their systems.

Since the original initiative, the term has been adopted by the wider research community [3, 1] although it is still strongly associated with IBM and, more importantly, IBM's specific approach to autonomic computing. This is somewhat unfortunate because the term *autonomic* would allow for a much deeper and more far-reaching interpretation, as we explain soon. In short, we should not only consider *what* the autonomic nervous system does but also *how* it does it. We believe that the remarkably successful self-management of the autonomic nervous system, and biological organisms in general, lies exactly in the *way* they achieve this functionality. Ignoring the exact mechanisms and stopping at the shallow analogy at the level of functional description misses some important possibilities and lessons that can be learned by computer science.

1.1   The Meaning of "Self"

The traditional approach to autonomic computing is to replace human system administrators with software or hardware components that continuously monitor some subsystem assigned to them, forming so-called *control loops* [11] which involve monitoring, knowledge based planning and execution (see Figure 1). Biological systems, however, achieve self-management and control through entirely different, often fully distributed and *emergent* ways of processing information. In other words, the usual biological interpretation of self-management involves no managing and managed entities. There is often no subsystem responsible for self-healing or self-optimization; instead, these properties simply arise from some simple local behavior of the components typically in a highly nontrivial way. The term "self" is meant truly in a grassroots sense, and we believe that this fact might well be the reason for many desirable properties such as extreme robustness and adaptivity, despite very simple implementations.

1.2   Trust

There are a few practical obstacles in the deployment of grassroots self-management. One of them is due to the entirely different and somewhat unnatural thinking that self-organization and emergence require and the relative lack of our understanding of the principles behind them [14]. Accordingly, *trust*

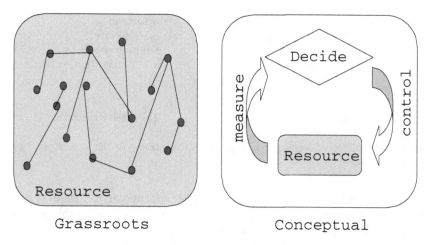

Fig. 1. Models of self-management

delegation represents a problem: psychologically it is more comforting to have a single point of control, an explicit controlling entity. In the case of the autonomic nervous system we cannot do anything else but trust it, although probably many people would prefer to have more control, especially when things go wrong. Indeed, the tendency in engineering is to try to isolate and create central units that are responsible for a function. A good example is the car industry that uses computers in increasing numbers in our cars to explictly control the different functions, thereby replacing old-and-proven mechanisms that were often based on self-optimizing mechanism (like the carburetor). To some extent, this results in sacrificing the self-healing and robustness features for these functions.

1.3   Modularity

To exploit the power and simplicity of emergent behavior and yet ensure that these mechanisms can be trusted and be incorporated in systems in an informed manner, we believe that a *modular paradigm* is required. The idea is to identify a collection of simple and predictable services as *building blocks* and combine them in arbitrarily complex functions and protocols. Such a modular approach presents several attractive features. Developers will be allowed to plug different components implementing a desired function into existing or new applications, being certain that the function will be performed in a predictable and dependable manner. Research may be focused on the development of simple and well-understood building blocks, with a particular emphasis on important properties like robustness, scalability, self-organization and self-management.

The goal of this position paper is to promote this idea by describing some of our preliminary experiences. Our recent work has resulted in a collection of simple and robust building blocks, which include *data aggregation* [9,13], *membership management* [8], *topology construction* [6,12] and *load balancing* [10]. Our building blocks are typically no more complicated than a cellular automaton or

do forever	do forever
wait(T time units)	$s_p \leftarrow$ receive(*)
$p \leftarrow$ GETPEER()	send s to sender(s_p)
send s to p	$s \leftarrow$ UPDATE(s, s_p)
$s_p \leftarrow$ receive(p)	
$s \leftarrow$ UPDATE(s, s_p)	
(a) active thread	(b) passive thread

Fig. 2. The skeleton of a gossip-based protocol. Notation: s is the local state, s_p is the state of the peer p

a swarm model which makes them ideal objects for research. Practical applications based on them can also benefit from a potentially more stable foundation and predictability, a key concern in fully distributed systems. Most importantly, they are naturally self-managing, without dedicated system components. In the rest of the paper, we briefly describe these components.

2   A Collection of Building Blocks

In the context of the BISON project [2], our recent activity has focused on the identification and development of protocols for several simple basic functions. The components produced so far can be informally subdivided into two broad categories: *overlay protocols* and *functional protocols*. An overlay protocol is aimed at maintaining application-layer, connected communication topologies over a set of distributed nodes. These topologies may constitute the basis for functional protocols, whose task is to compute specific functions over the data maintained at nodes.

Our current bag of protocols includes: (i) protocols for organizing and managing structured topologies such as super-peer based networks (SG-1 [12], grids and tori (T-MAN [6]); (ii) protocols for building unstructured networks based on the random topology (NEWSCAST [8]); (iii) protocols for the computation of a large set of aggregate functions, including maximum and minimum, average, sum, product, geometric mean, variance, etc [13, 9]; and (iv) protocols for load balancing [10].

The relationships between overlay and functional protocols may assume several different forms. Topologies may be explicitly designed to optimize the performance of a specific functional protocol (this is the case of NEWSCAST [8] used to maintain a random topology for aggregation protocols). Or, a functional protocol may be needed to implement a specific overlay protocol (in superpeer networks, aggregation can be used to identify the set of superpeers).

All the protocols we have developed so far are based on the gossip-based paradigm [4, 5]. Gossip-style protocols are attractive since they are extremely robust to both computation and communication failures. They are also extremely responsive and can adapt rapidly to changes in the underlying communication structure without any additional measures.

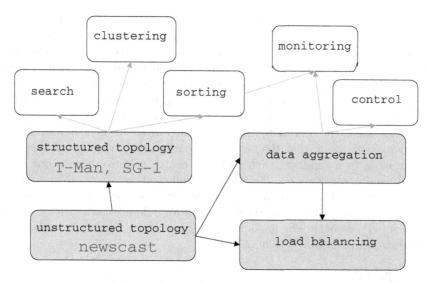

Fig. 3. Dependence relations between components

The skeleton of a generic gossip-based protocol is shown in Figure 2. Each node possesses a local state and executes two different threads. The *active* one periodically initiates an *information exchange* with a peer node selected randomly, by sending a message containing the local state and waits for a response from the selected node. The *passive* thread waits for messages sent by an initiator and replies with its local state.

Method UPDATE builds a new local state based on the previous local state and the state received during the information exchange. The output of UPDATE depends on the specific function implemented by the protocol. The local states at the two peers after an information exchange are not necessarily the same, since UPDATE may be non-deterministic or may produce different outputs depending on which node is the initiator.

Even though our system is not synchronous, it is convenient to talk about *cycles* of the protocol, which are simply consecutive wall clock intervals during which every node has its chance of performing an actively initiated information exchange.

In the following we describe the components. Figure 3 illustrates the dependence relations between them as will be described.

2.1   Newscast

In NEWSCAST [8], the state of a node is given by a *partial view*, which is a set of peer descriptors with a fixed size c. A *peer descriptor* contains the address of the peer, along with a *timestamp* corresponding to the time when the descriptor was created.

Method GETPEER returns an address selected randomly among those in the current partial view. Method UPDATE merges the partial views of the two nodes involved in an exchange and keeps the c freshest descriptors, thereby creating a new partial view. New information enters the system when a node sends its partial view to a peer. In this step, the node always inserts its own, newly created descriptor into the partial view. Old information is gradually and automatically removed from the system and gets replaced by newer information. This feature allows the protocol to "repair" the overlay topology by forgetting dead links, which by definition do not get updated because their owner is no longer active.

In NEWSCAST, the overlay topology is defined by the content of partial views. We have shown in [8] that the resulting topology has a very low diameter and is very close to a random graph with out-degree c. According to our experimental results, choosing $c = 20$ is already sufficient for very stable and robust connectivity. We have also shown that, within a single cycle, the number of exchanges per node can be modeled through a random variable with the distribution $1 + \mathrm{Poisson}(1)$. The implication of this property is that no node is more important (or overloaded) than others.

2.2   T-Man

Another component of our collection is T-MAN [6], a protocol for creating a large class of topologies. The idea behind the protocol is very similar to that of NEWSCAST. The difference is that instead of using the creation date (freshness) of descriptors, T-MAN applies a ranking function that ranks any set of nodes according to increasing distance from a base node. Method GETPEER returns neighbors with a bias towards closer ones, and, similarly, UPDATE keeps peers that are closer, according to the ranking.

Figure 4 illustrates the protocol, as it constructs a torus topology. In [6] it was shown that the protocol converges in logarithmic time even for networks of 10^6 nodes and for other topologies including rings and binary trees. With the appropriate ranking function, T-MAN can also be used to sort a set of numbers.

T-MAN relies on another component for generating an initial random topology which is later evolved into the desired one. In our case this service is provided by NEWSCAST.

2.3   SG-1

SG-1 [12] is yet another component based on NEWSCAST, whose task is to self-organize a *superpeer-based* network. This special kind of topology is organized through a two-level hierarchy, as illustrated in Figure 5: nodes that are faster and/or more reliable than "normal" nodes take on server-like responsibilities and provide services to a set of clients. The superpeer paradigm allows decentralized networks to run more efficiently by exploiting heterogeneity and distributing load to machines that can handle them. On the other hand, it avoids the flaws of the client-server model since no bottleneck or single point of failure exist.

In our model, each node is characterized by a *capacity* parameter, that defines the maximum number of clients that can be served by the node. The task of SG-1 is to form a network where the role of superpeers is played by the nodes with highest capacity. All other nodes become clients of one or more superpeers. The

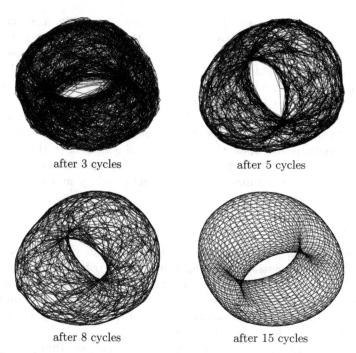

after 3 cycles   after 5 cycles

after 8 cycles   after 15 cycles

Fig. 4. Illustrative example of T-MAN constructing a torus over $50 \times 50 = 2500$ nodes, starting from a uniform random topology with $c = 20$. For clarity, only the nearest 4 neighbors (out of 20) of each node are displayed

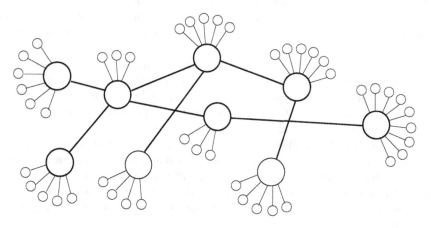

Fig. 5. A superpeer topology. Superpeers (thick circles) are connected together through a random network, while clients (thin circles) are associated to a single superpeer

goal is to identify the minimal set of superpeers that are able to provide the desired quality of service, based on their capacity.

In SG-1, NEWSCAST is used in two ways. First, it provides a robust underlying topology that guarantees connectivity of the network in spite of superpeer failures. Second, NEWSCAST is used to maintain, at each node, a partial view containing a random sample of superpeers that are currently *underloaded* with respect to their capacity. At each cycle, each superpeer s tries to identify a superpeer t that (i) has more capacity than s, and (ii) is underloaded. If such superpeer exist and can be contacted, s transfers the responsibility of parts of its clients to t. If the set of clients of s becomes empty, s becomes a client of t.

Experimental results show that this protocol converges to the target superpeer topology in logarithmic time for network sizes as large as 10^6 nodes, producing very good approximations of the target topology in a constant number of cycles.

2.4   Gossip-Based Aggregation

In the case of gossip-based aggregation [9, 13], the state of a node is a numeric value. In a practical setting, this value can be any attribute of the environment, such as the load or the storage capacity. The task of the protocol is to calculate an aggregate value over the set of all numbers stored at nodes. Although several aggregate functions may be computed by our protocol, in this paper we provide only the details for the average function.

In order to work, this protocol needs an overlay protocol that provides an implementation of method GETPEER. Here, we assume that this service is provided by NEWSCAST, but any other overlay could be used.

To compute the average, method UPDATE(a, b) must return $(a + b)/2$. After one state exchange, the sum of the values maintained by the two nodes does not change, since they have just balanced their values. So the operation does not change the global average either; it only decreases the variance over all the estimates in the system.

In [9] it was shown that if the communication topology is not only connected but also sufficiently random, at each cycle the empirical variance computed over the set of values maintained by nodes is reduced by a factor whose expected value is $2\sqrt{e}$. Most importantly, this result is independent of the network size, confirming the extreme scalability of the protocol.

In addition to being fast, our aggregation protocol is also very robust. Node failures may perturb the final result, as the values stored in crashed nodes are lost; but both analytical and empirical studies have shown that this effect is generally marginal [13]. As long as the overlay network remains connected, link failures do not modify the final value, they only slow down the aggregation process.

2.5   A Load-Balancing Protocol

To a certain extent, the problem of load balancing is similar to the problem of aggregation. Each node has a certain amount of load and the nodes are allowed to transfer portions of their load between themselves. The goal is to reach a state where each node has the same amount of load. To this end, nodes can make decisions for sending or receiving load based only on locally available information. Unlike aggregation, however, the amount of load that can be transfered in a given cycle is bounded: the transfer of a unit of load may be an expensive operation. In our present discussion, we use the term *quota* to identify this bound and we denote it by Q. Furthermore, we assume that the quota is the same at each node.

A simple, yet far from optimal idea for a completely decentralized algorithm could be based on the aggregation mechanism illustrated above. Periodically, each node contacts a random node among its neighbors. The loads of the two nodes are compared; if they differ, a quantity q of load units is transfered from the node with more load to the node with less load. q is clearly bounded by the quota Q and the amount of load units needed to balance the nodes.

If the network is connected, this mechanism will eventually balance the load among all nodes. In fact, in a connected network a path exist between any pair of overloaded and underloaded nodes, allowing a flow of load between them. Nevertheless, it fails to be optimal with respect to load transfers. The reason is simple: if the loads of two nodes are both higher than the average load, transferring load units from one to the other is useless. Instead, they should contact nodes whose load is smaller than the average, and perform the transfer with them.

Our load-balancing algorithm is based exactly on this intuition. The nodes obtain an estimate of the current average load through the aggregation protocol described above. This estimate is the target load; based on its value, a node may decide if it is overloaded, underloaded, or balanced. Overloaded nodes contact their underloaded neighbors in order to transfer their excess load and underloaded nodes contact their overloaded neighbors to perform the opposite operation. Nodes that have reached the target load stop participating in the protocol. Although this was a simplified description, it is easy to see that this protocol is optimal with respect to load transfer, because each node transfers exactly the amount of load needed to reach its target load. As we show in [10], the protocol is also optimal with respect to speed under some conditions on the initial load distribution.

3   Notes on Combining the Building Blocks

The combination of the building blocks is done in the traditional way: a building block has a local interface (within one node) towards the other components, and it has a protocol and an implementation associated with it. The implementation can differ over different nodes, just like the local interface. For this reason, we have focused on protocols in the above discussion. Nodes using the same protocol (for example, aggregation) form a "layer" in the system. This, however, is not a layer in the usual sense: we allow for arbitrary dependency relations between the building blocks. In general, the directed graph that describes the dependencies (such as the example shown in Figure 3) will not contain cycles, however, this is not strictly required. Two "layers" can mutually depend on each other's services; for instance, in a bootstrapping phase when they can catalyze each other's performance.

Having said that, we need to mention one exception. There is a "lowest layer" in our framework, which in a sense represents the group abstraction: the set of nodes that form the domain of the other components. This layer is the random network component, which provides the *peer sampling service* (see Section 2.1 and [7]). The main requirement for this service is that it must return all nodes with equal probability, in particular, no nodes are to be excluded forever. The peer sampling service is used to support and bootstrap other services like aggregation or structured topologies.

Finally, the aspect of *time-scale* should also be noted. While all of the protocols are based on the scheme given in Figure 2, the waiting time T can be different for different building blocks. This degree of freedom allows for certain architectures that otherwise would not be possible. For example, if an up-to-date aggregate value is needed "instantly" according to the timescale of a relatively slow layer, like load balancing, then we can simply apply aggregation at a relatively faster timescale.

4   Conclusions

We have presented examples of simple protocols that exhibit self-managing properties without any explicit management component or control loops; in other words, without increased complexity. We argued that a modular approach might be the way towards efficient deployment of such protocols in large distributed systems. To validate our ideas, we have briefly presented gossip-based protocols as possible building blocks: topology and membership management (T-MAN, SG-1 and NEWSCAST), aggregation, and load balancing.

References

1. M. Agarwal, V. Bhat, Z. Li, H. Liu, B. Khargharia, V. Matossian, V. Putty, C. Schmidt, G. Zhang, S. Hariri, and M. Parashar. AutoMate: Enabling Autonomic Applications on the Grid. In *Proceedings of the Autonomic Computing Workshop, 5th Annual International Active Middleware Services Workshop (AMS2003)*, pages 48–57, Seattle, WA, USA, June 2003.
2. The Bison Project. http://www.cs.unibo.it/bison.
3. A. Brown and D. Patterson. Embracing Failure: A Case for Recovery-Oriented Computing (ROC). In *2001 High Performance Transaction Processing Symposium*, Asilomar, CA, USA, October 2001.
4. Alan Demers, Dan Greene, Carl Hauser, Wes Irish, John Larson, Scott Shenker, Howard Sturgis, Dan Swinehart, and Doug Terry. Epidemic algorithms for replicated database management. In *Proceedings of the 6th Annual ACM Symposium on Principles of Distributed Computing (PODC'87)*, pages 1–12, Vancouver, August 1987. ACM.
5. Patrick Th. Eugster, Rachid Guerraoui, Anne-Marie Kermarrec, and Laurent Massoulié. Epidemic information dissemination in distributed systems. *IEEE Computer*, 37(5):60–67, May 2004.

6. Márk Jelasity and Ozalp Babaoglu. T-Man: Fast gossip-based construction of large-scale overlay topologies. Technical Report UBLCS-2004-7, University of Bologna, Department of Computer Science, Bologna, Italy, May 2004. http://www.cs.unibo.it/techreports/2004/2004-07.pdf.
7. Márk Jelasity, Rachid Guerraoui, Anne-Marie Kermarrec, and Maarten van Steen. The peer sampling service: Experimental evaluation of unstructured gossip-based implementations. In Hans-Arno Jacobsen, editor, *Middleware 2004*, volume 3231 of *Lecture Notes in Computer Science*. Springer-Verlag, 2004.
8. Márk Jelasity, Wojtek Kowalczyk, and Maarten van Steen. Newscast computing. Technical Report IR-CS-006, Vrije Universiteit Amsterdam, Department of Computer Science, Amsterdam, The Netherlands, November 2003.
9. Márk Jelasity and Alberto Montresor. Epidemic-style proactive aggregation in large overlay networks. In *Proceedings of The 24th International Conference on Distributed Computing Systems (ICDCS 2004)*, pages 102–109, Tokyo, Japan, 2004. IEEE Computer Society.
10. Márk Jelasity, Alberto Montresor, and Ozalp Babaoglu. A modular paradigm for building self-organizing peer-to-peer applications. In Giovanna Di Marzo Serugendo, Anthony Karageorgos, Omer F. Rana, and Franco Zambonelli, editors, *Engineering Self-Organising Systems*, volume 2977 of *Lecture Notes in Artificial Intelligence*, pages 265–282. Springer, 2004. invited paper.
11. Jeffrey O. Kephart and David M. Chess. The vision of autonomic computing. *IEEE Computer*, 36(1):41–50, January 2003.
12. Alberto Montresor. A robust protocol for building superpeer overlay topologies. In *Proceedings of the 4th IEEE International Conference on Peer-to-Peer Computing (P2P'04)*, pages 202–209, Zurich, Switzerland, August 2004. IEEE Computer Society.
13. Alberto Montresor, Márk Jelasity, and Ozalp Babaoglu. Robust aggregation protocols for large-scale overlay networks. In *Proceedings of The 2004 International Conference on Dependable Systems and Networks (DSN)*, pages 19–28, Florence, Italy, 2004. IEEE Computer Society.
14. Julio M. Ottino. Engineering complex systems. *Nature*, 427:399, January 2004.

Autonomic Runtime System for Large Scale Parallel and Distributed Applications

Jingmei Yang[1], Huoping Chen[1], Byoung uk Kim[1], Salim Hariri[1], and Manish Parashar[2]

[1] University of Arizona
{jm_yang, hpchen, hariri}@ece.arizona.edu
[2] Rutgers, The State University of New Jersey
parashar@caip.rutgers.edu

Abstract. The development of efficient parallel algorithms for large scale wildfire simulations is a challenging research problem because the factors that determine wildfire behavior are complex; they include fuel characteristics and configurations, chemical reactions, balances between different modes of heat transfer, topography, and fire/atmosphere interactions. These factors make static parallel algorithms inefficient, especially when large number of processors are used because we cannot predict accurately the propagation of the fire and its computational requirements at runtime. In this paper, we present an Autonomic Runtime Manager (ARM) to dynamically exploit the physics properties of the fire simulation and use them as the basis of our self-optimization algorithm. At each step of the wildfire simulation, the ARM decomposes the computational domain into several natural regions (e.g., burning, unburned, burned) where each region has the same temporal and special characteristics. The number of burning, unburned and burned cells determines the current state of the fire simulation and can then be used to accurately predict the computational power required for each region. By regularly monitoring the state of the simulation and analyzing it, and use that to drive the runtime optimization, we can achieve significant performance gains because we can efficiently balance the computational load on each processor. Our experimental results show that the performance of the fire simulation has been improved by 45% when compared with a static portioning algorithm that does not take into considerations the state of the computations.

1 Introduction

For over fifty years, attempts have been made to understand and predict the behavior (intensity, propagation speed and direction, and modes of spread) of wildfires. However, the factors that determine wildfire behavior are complex; as a result, the computational loads associated with regions in the domain vary greatly, both in time and space. Furthermore, partitioning, load balancing and efficient parallel execution of these simulations on large numbers of processors present significant challenges. Clearly, there is a need for a fundamental change in how these applications are programmed, developed and managed. This has led researchers to consider

J.-P. Banâtre et al. (Eds.): UPP 2004, LNCS 3566, pp. 297–311, 2005.

alternative programming paradigms and management techniques that are based on the strategies used by biological systems to deal with complexity, dynamism, heterogeneity and uncertainty. The approach, referred to as autonomic computing aims at realizing computing systems and applications capable of managing themselves with minimum human intervention [27]. This approach has been inspired by the human autonomic nervous system that has the ability to self-configure, self-tune and even repair itself without any conscious human involvement.

An autonomic computing system can be viewed as a collection of autonomic components, which can manage their internal behaviors and relationships with others in accordance to high-level policies. The principles that govern all such systems have been summarized as following [27]:

- *Self-Configuring:* an autonomic system must have the ability to dynamically adjust its resources based on its state and the state of its execution environment.
- *Self-Optimizing:* an autonomic system should be able to detect sub-optimal behaviors and able to intelligently perform self-optimization functions.
- *Self-Protecting:* an autonomic system is equally prone to attacks and hence it should be capable of detecting and protecting its resources from both internal and external attack and maintaining overall system security and integrity.
- *Self-Healing:* an autonomic system must be aware of potential problems and should have the ability to reconfigure itself to continue to function smoothly.

Optimizing the performance of parallel applications though load balancing is well studied and it can be classified as either static or dynamic. The compile-time static approaches [8], [9], [10], [11] assign work to processors before the computation starts and can be efficient if we know how the computations will progress a priori. On the other hand, if the workload cannot be estimated beforehand, dynamic load balancing strategies have to be used [13][14][15]. For example, the diffusion-based methods [14][15] divide the processor pool into small and overlapping neighborhoods. Some global schemes [16][17][18] predict future performance based on past information or based on some prediction tools, such as Network Weather Service (NWS)[19]. In [18], the authors use the predicted CPU information provided by NWS to guide scheduling decisions. Dome [17] remaps the computation based on the time each processor spends on computing during the last computational phase. Other optimization techniques are based on application-level scheduling [20][21][22]. AppLeS in [20][21] assumes the application performance model is static and provided by users and GHS system [22] assumes the total computation load of applications is a constant.

There are few techniques that assume adaptive applications [23][24][25]. The wild fire simulation is a continuously changing application and requires adaptive and efficient runtime optimization techniques. In this paper, we present an Autonomic Runtime Manager (ARM) that is continuously monitoring the computing requirements of the application, analyzing the current state of the application as well as the computing and networking resources and then making the appropriate planning and scheduling actions at runtime. The ARM control and management activities are overlapped with the application execution to minimize the overhead incurred using the ARM self-optimization algorithm.

The reminder of this paper is organized as follows: Section 2 presents our Autonomic Computing Framework, Autonomia that is used to implement the fire autonomic runtime manager (ARM). Section 3 gives a brief overview of the ARM system and a detailed analysis of the wild fire simulation. Results from the experimental evaluation of the ARM self-optimization algorithm are presented in Section 4. We also compare the performance of the wild fire simulation with and without the self-optimization algorithm. A conclusion and outline of future research directions are presented in Section 5.

2 Autonomia – An Autonomic Computing Framework

We have proposed and implemented an Autonomic Computing Framework, *Autonomia* [6], which includes the following main modules (see Figure 1): Application Management Editor (AME), Autonomic Runtime System (ARS) and Distributed Computing Environment (DCE).

2.1 Application Management Editor (AME)

User and/or application developer can specify the characteristics and requirements of their applications using an Application Management Editor (AME). It consists of policy console and policy translation.

Policy console allows creating an application as a set of components expressed in a workflow model. The attributes associated with each node in the workflow graph specify the policies needed to maintain the self-healing, self-protecting and self-optimizing behaviors.

Policy translation maps high level policies into low level policies and stores them into the Application Information Knowledge (AIK) repository.

2.2 Autonomic Runtime System (ARS)

The ARS can be viewed as an application-based operating system that provides applications with all the services and tools required to achieve the desired autonomic behaviors (self-configuring, self-healing, self-optimizing, and self-protection). The primary modules of ARS are the following:

Application Information and Knowledge (AIK) Repository: The AIK repository stores the application requirements, user specified self-management policies, the application information status, and knowledge about configuration strategies for both applications and system resources that have proven to be successful and effective. In addition, AIK contains the *Component Repository (CR)* that stores the components that are currently available for the users to compose their applications.

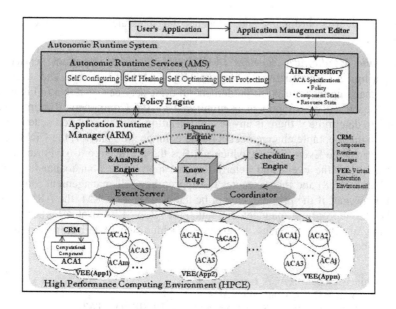

Fig. 1. Autonomia Architecture

Event Server: The Event server receives events from the component runtime managers (CRMs) that monitor components and systems and then notifies the corresponding engines subscribed to these events.

Autonomic Runtime Services *(Self-Configuring, Self-Optimizing, Self-healing, and Self-Protecting):* These runtime services maintain the autonomic properties of applications and system resources at runtime. To simplify the control and management tasks, we dedicate one runtime service for each desired attribute or functionality such as self-healing, self-optimizing, self-protection, etc. The event server notifies the appropriate runtime service whenever the events it subscribed become true.

Monitoring Service: There are two kinds of monitoring services: *Resource Monitoring Service* and *Component Monitoring Service. Resource Monitoring Service (RMS)* monitors the workload information and performance metrics associated with resources such as: CPU/memory information, disk I/O information, and network information. *Component Monitoring Service (CMS)* defines a general interface for autonomic components such that each component can expose its status data associated with execution time and current operating state.

Application Runtime Manager (ARM): The ARM performs online monitoring to collect the status and state information using the component sensors. It analyzes component behaviors and when detecting any anomalies or drastic state changes (for example, degradation in performance, component failure), the ARM takes the appropriate control and management actions as specified in its control policy.

Coordinator: It coordinates and allocates the scheduled tasks to the appropriate resources.

Autonomic Middleware Services (AMS) provides four important services: Self-configuring, Self-optimizing; Self-protecting; and Self-healing. The overall self-management algorithm used to implement all these services is shown in Figure 2. The state of each active component is monitored by the Component Runtime Manager (CRM) to determine if there is any severe deviation from the desired state (steps 1-3). When an unacceptable change occurs in the component behavior, the CRM generates an event into the Event Server, which notifies the ARM (step 4-6). Furthermore, the CRM analyzes the event and determines the appropriate plan to handle that event (step 7 and step 8) and then executes the appropriate self-management routines (steps 9-10). However, if the problem cannot be handled by the CRM, the ARM is invoked to take the appropriate management functions (steps 12-13) at a higher granularity (e.g., migrate the components to another machine due to failure or degradation in performance).

```
1 While (Component ACAᵢ is running) do
2       State = CRMᵢ Monitoring (ACAᵢ)
3       State_Deviation = State_Compare(State, DESIRED_STATE)
4       If (state_deviation == TRUE)
5               CRMi Send_Event(State)
6               Event Server Notify ARM
7               Event_Type = CRM_Analysis (State)
8               If (CRMᵢ ABLE) Then
9                       Actions = CRM_Planning(State, Event_Type)
10                      Autonomic_Service ASᵢ ∈ {ASconfig,ASheal,ASoptimization,ASsecurity}
11                      Execute ASᵢ (Actions)
12              Else
13                      Actions = ARM_Analysis (State, Event_Type)
14                      Execute Asᵢ (Actions)
15              EndIf
16      EndIf
17 EndWhile
```

Fig. 2. Self-Management Algorithm

2.3 High Performance Computing Environment (HPCE)

In our environment, we define HPCE as the environment that controls and runs a collection of autonomic distributed applications, where each application is expressed as a workflow graph of autonomous components. The autonomous components are developed based on an Autonomic Component Architecture (ACA) [7, 26]. In effect, each ACA component is a standalone entity that can manage itself locally.

ACA Component
An autonomic component is the fundamental building block for autonomic applications in our Autonomic Computing Framework (see Figure 1). An autonomic

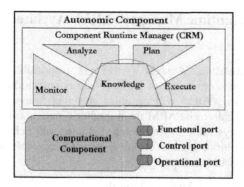

Fig. 3. Autonomic Computing Architecture (ACA)

component is a simple computational component with encapsulated rules, constraints and mechanisms for self-management and dynamic interactions with other components. It extends traditional component architecture to support autonomic operations. The structure of an autonomic component is shown in Figure 3.

The ACA implements three different ports (functional, control and operational ports) for importing/exporting the functionalities of the component, sensing and changing the runtime state of component and for managing the performance of the component.

Functional port (Γ) defines a set of functionalities provided and used by the autonomic component. $\gamma \in \Omega \times \Lambda$, where Ω is the set of inputs and Λ is the set of outputs of the components, and γ defines a valid input-output set.

Control port (Σ) is the set of tuples (σ, ξ), where σ is a set of sensors and actuators exported by the component, and ξ is the constraint set that controls access to the sensors/actuators. Sensors are interfaces that provide information about the component while actuators are interfaces for modifying the state of the component. Constraints are based on state, context and/or high-level access polices, and can control who invokes the interface, when and how they are invoked.

Operational port (Θ) defines the interfaces to formulate, inject and manage rules, and encapsulates a set of rules that are used to manage the runtime behaviors of the autonomic component. Rules incorporate high-level guidance and practical human knowledge in the form of conditional if-then expressions.

Behavior rules control the runtime functional behaviors of autonomic components and applications.

Interaction rules control the interactions between components, between components and their environments, and the coordination within an autonomic application.

Component Runtime Manager (CRM)

Each autonomic component has its own manager that is delegated to manage its execution. It is the local control subsystem that also consists of online monitoring, online analyzing, online planning and online executing functionality.

3 Autonomic Runtime Manager (ARM) Architecture for Fire Simulation

The Autonomic Runtime Manager (ARM) is responsible for controlling and managing the execution environment for large-scale applications at runtime. Once the application is running, ARM will optimize the application execution to improve performance dynamically. The ARM main modules include (see Figure 4): 1) Online Monitoring and Analysis and 2) Autonomic Planning and Scheduling. In this paper, we will use the wildfire simulation as a running example to explain the main operations of the ARM modules.

1) Online Monitoring and Analysis Module
The ARM uses online monitoring and analysis module interfaces with different sensors for collecting the states of applications and underlying resources and partitions the application domain into Natural Regions (*NRs*), where each region has the same temporal and spatial characteristics (e.g., burned region (*NR1*), burning (*NR2*), and unburned regions (*NR3*)).

2) Autonomic Planning and Scheduling
Planning engine uses the resource capability models as well as performance models associated with the computations, and the knowledge repository to select the appropriate models and partitions for each region (empirical-based, physics-based) and then decompose the computational workloads for each natural region into schedulable Virtual Computational Units (*VCUs*).

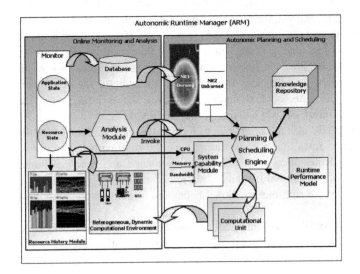

Fig. 4. Autonomic Runtime Manager (ARM) architecture

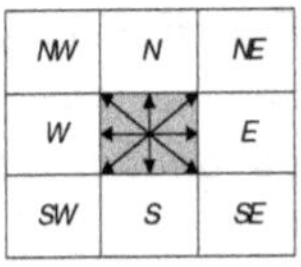

Fig. 5. Fire direction after ignition

3.1 An Illustrative Example – Wild Fire Simulation

In the wildfire simulation model, the entire area is represented as a 2-D cell-space composed of cells of dimensions l x b (l: length, b: breadth). For each cell, there are eight major wind directions N, NE, NW, S, SE, SW, E, W as shown in Figure 5. A cell interacts with its neighbors along all the eight directions.

When a cell is ignited, its state will change from "unburned" to "burning". During its "burning" phase, the fire will propagate to its eight neighbors. The direction and the value of the maximum fire spread rate within the burning cell can be computed using Rothermel's fire spread model [3]. When the simulation time advances to the ignition times of neighbors, the neighbor cells will ignite and their states will change from "unburned" to "burning". In a similar way, the fire would propagate to the neighbors of these cells. With different terrain, vegetation and weather conditions, the fire propagation could form very different spread patterns within the entire region.

Our wild fire simulation model is based on fireLib [1], which is a C function library for predicting the spread rate and intensity of free-burning wildfires. We parallelized the sequential version of the fire simulation using MPI [5]. This parallelized fire simulation divides the entire cell space among multiple processors such that each processor works on its own portion and exchanges the necessary data with each other after each simulation time step. The parallel wild fire simulation is a loosely synchronous iterative application. Each processor performs the computation on part of the whole space, maintains the ignition map which is the ignition times of all cells, and proceeds to next ignition cell as the simulation advances. At each time step,

- each processor computes the ignition times of the 8 neighbors of the current ignited cell, and updates the ignition time of the neighbors in the ignition map if the new ignition time is less than the current ignition time.
- at the end of each time step, the ignition map changes are exchanged between processors to enable them to have a whole view of ignition times for the next time step.

In our current implementation, a cell coordinator processor gathers the changes in the ignition map from each working processor and then broadcasts all the changes to all processors. Since there are only a few cells whose ignition times are changed at each time step, we believe the communication overhead with the coordinator is low. Based on this implementation, the estimated execution time for processor P_i can be defined as follows:

$$T_i(t) = T_{comp}(P_i, t) + T_{comm}(P_i, t) \tag{1}$$

where $T_{comp}(P_i, t)$ is the computation time at time step t on processor P_i, $T_{comm}(P_i, t)$ is the communication time at time step t on processor P_i, where $i = 0, P-1$ (P denotes the total number of processors). The computing time of burning cells is much larger than that of unburned cells and that contributes significantly to the imbalance conditions at runtime. Hence, the application computational workload (ACW) of the simulation is heavily dependent on the number of burning cells in each region, that is

$$ACW(t) = N_B(t)T_B + N_U(t)T_U \tag{2}$$

where $N_B(t)$ is the number of burning cells at time t, $N_U(t)$ is the number of unburned cells at time t. Let α_i be the fraction of the workload assigned to processor P_i, it will be given an $\alpha_i \times ACW(t)$ of the total workload, where $\alpha_i > 0$ and $\sum_{i=0}^{P-1} \alpha_i = 1$. Therefore, the expected execution time for processor P_i can be defined as follows:

$$
\begin{aligned}
T_{comp}(P_i, t) &= \alpha_i(N_B(t)T_B + N_U(t)T_U) \\
&= N_B(P_i, t)T_B + N_U(P_i, t)T_U
\end{aligned}
\tag{3}
$$

where $N_B(P_i, t)$ and $N_U(P_i, t)$ are number of burning cells and unburned cells assigned to processor P_i at time step t, T_B and T_U are the estimated computation times of each burning cell and unburned cell, respectively. $T_B > T_U$ because burning cells are more compute intensive than unburned cells. We use a burning-to-unburned factor f_{B-U} to quantify the computational load difference between burning cells and unburned cells:

$$f_{B-U} = \frac{T_B}{T_U} \tag{4}$$

The communication cost $T_{comm}(P_i, t)$ includes the time required for data gathering, synchronization and broadcasting, which can be defined as follows:

$$T_{comm}(P_i, t) = T_{gather}(P_i, t) + T_{sync}(P_i, t) + T_{bcast}(t) \tag{5}$$

Data gathering operation can be started once the computation is finished and it depends on the number of bytes that needed to send to the coordinate processor. The data gathering time of processor P_i at time step t is given by:

$$T_{gather}(P_i, t) = m T_{Byte} N_c(P_i, t) \tag{6}$$

where m is the message size in bytes sent by one cell, $N_c(P_i, t)$ is the number of cells assigned to processor P_i whose ignition times are changed during the time step t, T_{Byte} is the data transmission time per byte. It is important to notice that, broadcast operation can only start after the coordinator processor receives the data from all processors. Consequently, the data broadcasting time can be defined as:

$$T_{bcast}(t) = m T_{Byte} \sum_{i=0}^{P-1} N_c(P_i, t) \tag{7}$$

Then, the estimated execution time of the wild fire simulation can be computed as:

$$T_{total} = \sum_{t=1}^{N_t} T_{step}(t) \tag{8}$$

Where N_t is the number of time steps performed by the wild fire simulation.

In the next subsections, we show how these estimates can be used by the ARM modules to significantly reduce the imbalance conditions and thus dynamically improve the overall application performance.

3.2 Online Monitoring and Analysis

The online monitoring module collects the information about the wild fire simulation state, such as the number and the location of burning cells and unburned cells, and the actual computation time for the last time step. Based on the fire simulation state, online module partitions the whole wildfire simulation domain into two Natural Regions (*NRs*): burning region and unburned regions. At the same time, this module monitors the states of the resources involved in the execution of the fire simulation, such as the CPU load, available memory, network load etc. The runtime state information is stored in the backend database. The online analysis module analyzes the imbalance conditions of the wild fire simulation and then determines whether or not the current allocation of workload needs to be changed.

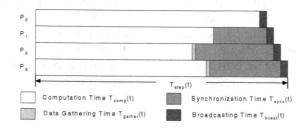

Fig. 6. The breakdown of the processor execution time at time step t

For example, Figure 6 shows the breakdown of the execution time and type of activities performed by four processors. Processor P_0 and P_1 do not need to broadcast any information because their part of ignition map has not been changed. Processor P_0 has the longest computation time because it is handling a large number of burning cells. Consequently, all the other three processors have to wait until processor P_0 finishes its computation and then the data broadcasting can be started. Recall that during each time step there are only a few cells whose ignition times are changed. Thus the broadcasting time is negligible compared to the computation time. To balance at runtime the simulation workload, the online analysis module should quickly detect large imbalance conditions and invoke the repartitioning operation.

To quantify the imbalance conditions, we introduce a metric, Imbalance Ratio (IR) that can be computed as:

$$IR(t) = \frac{Max_{i=0}^{P-1}(T_{comp}(P_i,t)) - Min_{i=0}^{P-1}(T_{comp}(P_i,t))}{Min_{i=0}^{P-1}(T_{comp}(P_i,t))} \times 100\% \tag{9}$$

We use a predefined threshold $IR_{threshold}$ to measure how severe the imbalance condition is. If $IR(t) > IR_{threshold}$, the imbalance conditions are considered severe and repartitioning is required. Then the automatic planning and scheduling module will be invoked to carry the appropriate actions to repartition the simulation workload.

The selection of the threshold $IR_{threshold}$ can significantly impact the effectiveness of the self-optimization approach. If the threshold chosen is too low, too many load repartitioning will be triggered and the high overhead produced outweighs the expected performance gains. On the other hand, when the threshold is high, the imbalance conditions cannot be detected quickly such that the performance improvement will be reduced. In the experimental results subsection, we show how we can experimentally choose this threshold value.

3.3 Autonomic Planning and Scheduling

The autonomic planning and scheduling module partitions the whole fire simulation domain into several natural regions based on its current state and then assigns them to processors by taking into consideration the states of the processors involved in the fire simulation execution.   To reduce the rescheduling overhead, we use a dedicated processor to run the ARM self-optimizing algorithm and overlap that with the worker processors that compute their assigned workloads. Once the new partition assignments are finalized, a message is sent to all the worker processors to read the new assignments once they are done with the current computations. Consequently, the ARM self-optimization activities are completely overlapped with the application computation and the overhead is very minimum less than 4% as will be discussed later.

4   Experimental Results

In this section, we evaluate the performance of our approach on the Beowulf clusters at the University of Arizona and Rutgers University. In our experiments, all processors are dedicated to the fire simulation. The experiments were performed on two problem sizes for the fire simulation. The first problem size is a 256*256 cell space with 65536 cells. The other one is a 512*512 cell domain with 262144 cells. To introduce a heterogeneous fire patterns, the fire is started in the southwest region of the domain and then propagates northeast along the wind direction until it reaches the edge of the domain. In order to make the evaluation for different problem sizes accurate, we maintain the same ratio of burning cells to 17%; the total number of burning cells when the simulation terminates is about 17% of the total cells for both problem sizes.

4.1   Sensitivity Analysis of the Threshold Value

To better understand how $IR_{threshold}$ affects the performance of the fire simulation, we ran the fire simulation with a problem size of 262144 on 16 processors and varied the $IR_{threshold}$ values to determine the best value that minimizes the execution time. The results of this experiment are shown in Figure 7. The execution times are taken as the average for three runs. We observed that the best execution time, 700 seconds, was achieved when the $IR_{threshold}$ is equal to 30%.

Figure 8 shows how the imbalance ratios increase linearly as the simulation progresses using static partitioning algorithm and compare that with our self-

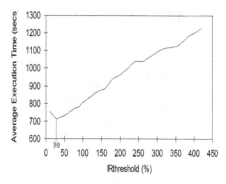

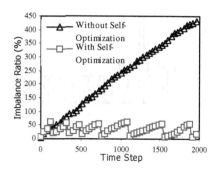

Fig. 7. The sensitivity of the fire simulation to the $IR_{threshold}$ value

Fig. 8. Imbalance ratios for 2000 time steps of the fire simulation, problem size = 65536, number of processors = 16, $IR_{threshold}$ = 50%

optimization algorithm. For example, at 2000 time steps of the simulation, the imbalance ratio in the static parallel algorithm is about 450% while it is around 25% in our approach. In fact, using our approach, the imbalance ratio is kept bound within a small range. This occurs because the self-optimization algorithm uses heuristic techniques to estimate the computation times on each processor.

4.2 Performance Results

Figure 9 shows the computation time for each processor at time steps 1, 300 and 600 with and without the ARM self-optimization. For example, at time step 1, the computation load is well balanced among most processors for both static partitioning and self-optimization. However, as shown in Figure 9(a), at time step 300, processor P_0 and P_1 experience longer computation times while other processors keep the same computation time as before. This is caused by having many burning cells assigned to these two processors P_0 and P_1. At time step 600, more and more cells on processor P_0 and P_1 are burning and the maximum computation time of 0.24 seconds is observed for P_1. However, if we apply the ARM self-optimization algorithm, all processors finish their computations around the same time for all the simulation time steps (see Figure 9 (b)). For example, the maximum execution time of 0.1 seconds is observed for processor P_2 at time step 600, which is 58% reduction in execution time when compared to the 0.24 seconds observed for the static portioning algorithm.

Tables 1 and 2 summarize the comparison of the execution time of the fire simulation with and without our self-optimization algorithm.

Our experimental results show that the self-optimization approach improves the performance by up to 45% for a problem size of 262144 cells on 16 processors. We expect to get even better performance as the problem size increases because it will need more simulation time and will have more burning cells than smaller problem sizes.

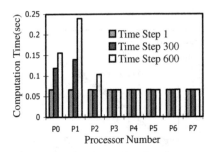
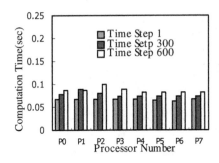

(a)   (b)

Fig. 9. Computation times of different time steps on 8 processors. Each group of adjacent bars shows the computation time of time step 1, 300 and 600, respectively. (a) Without self-optimization (b) With self-optimization

Table 1. Performance comparison for the fire simulation with and without self-optimization for different number of processors, problem size = 65536, and $IR_{threshold}$ = 30%

Number of Processors	Execution Time without Self-Optimization (sec)	Execution Time with Self-Optimization (sec)	Performance Improvement
8	2232.11	1265.94	43.29%
16	1238.87	713.17	42.43%

Table 2. Performance comparison for the fire simulation with and without self-optimization for different number of processors, problem Size = 262144, and $IR_{threshold}$ = 30%

Number of Processors	Execution Time without Self-Optimization (sec)	Execution Time with Self-Optimization (sec)	Performance Improvement
16	17276.02	9486.3	45.09%
32	9370.96	5558.55	40.68%

4.3 Overhead Analysis

In our implementation approach, one processor is dedicated to the autonomic planning and scheduling operations while all the worker processors are running the simulation loads assigned to them. Consequently, our self-optimization algorithm will not have high overhead impact on the performance of the fire simulation. The only overhead incurred in our approach is the time spent by the fire simulation to write its current state information to ARM sensors and the time spent in reading the new assigned simulation loads to the worker processors. To quantify the overhead on the whole system, we conducted experiments to measure the overhead introduced by our algorithm. Based on our experiments, we observed that the overhead cost is less than 4% of the total execution time for both problem sizes of the fire simulation and it is negligible compared to the 45% of performance gain.

5 Conclusions and Future Work

In this paper, we described a novel architecture for an autonomic runtime manager that can self-optimize the parallel execution of large scale applications at runtime by continuously monitoring and analyzing the state of the computations and the underlying resources, and efficiently exploit the physics of the problem being optimized. In our approach, the physics of the problem and its current state are the main criterion used to in our self-optimization algorithm. The Autonomic Runtime Manager (ARM) main modules include online monitoring and analysis and autonomic planning and scheduling modules. The activities of the ARM modules are overlapped with the algorithm being self-optimized to reduce the overhead. We show that the overhead of our self-optimization algorithm is less than 4%. We have also evaluated the ARM performance on a large wildfire simulation for different problem sizes and different number of processors. The experimental results show that using the ARM self-optimization, the performance of the wild fire simulation can be improved by up to 45% when compared to the static parallel partitioning algorithm.

References

[1] <http://www.fire.org>
[2] P. L. Andrews, "BEHAVE: Fire Behavior Prediction and Fuel Modeling System - BURN Subsystem", Part 1. General Technical Report INT-194. Ogden, UT: U.S. Department of Agriculture, Forest Service, Intermountain Research Station; 1986. 130 p.
[3] R. C. Rothermel, "A Mathematical Model for Predicting Fire Spread in Wildland Fuels", Research Paper INT-115. Ogden, UT: U.S. Department of Agriculture, Forest Service, Intermountain Forest and Range Experiment Station; 1972. 40 p.
[4] H. E. Anderson, "Predicting Wind-Driven Wildland Fire Size and Shape", Research Paper INT-305. Ogden, UT: U.S. Department of Agriculture, Forest Service, Intermountain Forest and Range Experiment Station; 1983. 26 p.
[5] M. Snir, S. Otto, S. Huss-Lederman, and D. Walker, "MPI the Complete Reference", MIT Press, 1996
[6] Hariri, S., Lizhi Xue, Huoping Chen etc., "AUTONOMIA: an autonomic computing environment", Conference Proc. of the 2003 IEEE IPCCC
[7] Salim Hariri, Bithika Khargharia, Huoping Chen, Yeliang Zhang, Byoung Kim, Hua Liu and Manish Parashar; "The Autonomic Programming Paradigm", Submitted to IEEE computer 2004.
[8] P.E. Crandall, and M. J. Quinn, "Block Data Decomposition for Data-parallel Programming on a Heterogeneous Workstation Network", 2nd IEEE HPDC, pp. 42-49, 1993
[9] Y. F. Hu, and R. J. Blake, "Load Balancing for Unstructured Mesh Applications", Parallel and Distributed Computing Practices, vol. 2, no. 3, 1999

[10] S. Ichikawa, and S. Yamashita, "Static Load Balancing of Parallel PDE Solver for Distributed Computing Environment", Proc. 13th Int'l Conf. Parallel and Distributed Computing Systems, pp. 399-405, 2000

[11] M. Cierniak, M. J. Zaki, and W. Li, "Compile-Time Scheduling Algorithms for Heterogeneous Network of Workstations", Computer J., vol. 40, no. 6, pp. 256-372, 1997

[12] M. Willebeek-LeMair, and A.P. Reeves, "Strategies for Dynamic Load Balancing on Highly Parallel Computers", IEEE Trans. Parallel and Distributed Systems, vol.4, no. 9, pp. 979-993, Sept. 1993.

[13] F. C. H. Lin, and R. M. Keller, "The Gradient Model Load Balancing Method", IEEE Trans. on Software Engineering, vol. 13, no. 1, pp. 32-38, Jan. 1987

[14] G. Cybenko, "Dynamic Load Balancing for Distributed Memory Multiprocessors", J. Parallel and Distributed Computing, vol. 7, no.2, pp. 279-301, 1989

[15] G. Horton, "A Multi-Level Diffusion Method for Dynamic Load Balancing", Parallel Computing, vol.19, pp. 209-229, 1993

[16] N. Nedeljkovic, and M. J. Quinn, "Data-Parallel Programming on a Network of Heterogeneous Workstations", 1st IEEE HPDC, pp. 152-160, Sep. 1992

[17] J. Arabe, A. Beguelin, B. Lowekamp, E. Seligman, M. Starkey, and P. Stephan, " Dome: Parallel Programming in a Heterogeneous Multi-User Environment," Proc. 10th Int'l Parallel Processing Symp., pp. 218-224, 1996.

[18] C. Liu, L. Yang, I. Foster, and D. Angulo, "Design and Evaluation of a Resource Selection Framework for Grid Applications", 11th IEEE HPDC. Edinburgh. Scotland, 2002

[19] R. Wolski, N. Spring, and J. Hayes, "The Network Weather Service: A Distributed Resource Performance Forecasting Service for Metacomputing", Journal of Future Generation Computing Systems (1998), pp. 757-768

[20] F. Berman, R. Wolski, S. Figueria, J. Schopf, and G. Shao, "Application-Level Scheduling on Distributed Heterogeneous Networks", Supercomputing'96, 1996

[21] F. Berman, R. Wolski, H. Casanova, W. Cirne, H. Dail, M. Faerman, S. Figueira, J. Hayes, G. Obertelli, J. Schopf, G. Shao, S. Smallen, N. Spring, A. Su, and D. Zagorodnov, "Adaptive Computing on the Grid Using AppLeS", IEEE Trans. on Parallel and Distributed Systems, Volume 14, Number 4, pp 369--382, April, 2003

[22] X.-H. Sun and M. Wu, "Grid Harvest Service: A System for Long-Term, Application-Level Task Scheduling," Proc. of 2003 IEEE International Parallel and Distributed Processing Symposium (IPDPS 2003), Nice, France, April, 2003.

[23] L. Oliker, and R. Biswas, "Plum: Parallel Load Balancing for Adaptive Unstructured Meshes", J. Parallel and Distributed Computing, vol. 52, no. 2, pp. 150-177, 1998

[24] C. Walshaw, M. Cross, and M. Everett, "Parallel Dynamic Graph Partitioning for Adaptive Unstructured Meshes", J. Parallel and Distributed Computing, vol. 47, pp. 102-108, 1997

[25] Y. Zhang, J. Yang, S. Chandra, S. Hariri and M. Parashar, "Autonomic Proactive Runtime Partitioning Strategies for SAMR Applications", Proceedings of the NSF Next Generation Systems Program Workshop, IEEE/ACM 18th International Parallel and Distributed Processing Symposium, Santa Fe, NM, USA, 8 pages. April 2004

[26] H. Liu, M. Parashar and S. Hariri, "A Component-based Programming Framework for Autonomic Applications," Proceedings of the 1st IEEE International Conference on Autonomic Computing (ICAC-04), IEEE Computer Society Press, New York, NY, USA, pp. 278 - 279, May 2004.

[27] J. O. Kephart and D.M. Chess. "The Vision of Autonomic Computing". IEEE Computer, 36(1), pages 41-50, January 2003.

Generative Programming

Towards Generative Programming

Pierre Cointe

OBASCO group, EMN-INRIA, LINA (CNRS FRE 2729),
École des Mines de Nantes, 4 rue Alfred Kastler, La Chantrerie,
44307 Nantes Cedex 3, France
cointe@emn.fr

Abstract. Generative Programming (GP) is an attempt to manufacture software components in an automated way by developing programs that synthesize other programs. Our purpose is to introduce the *what* and the *how* of the GP approach from a programming language point of view. For the *what* we discuss the lessons learned from object-oriented languages seen as general purpose languages to develop software factories. For the *how* we compare a variety of approaches and techniques based on program transformation and generation. On the one hand, we present the evolution of open-ended languages from metalevel programming to aspect-oriented programming. On the other hand, we introduce domain-specific languages as a way to bridge the gap between conceptual models and programming languages.

1 Automating Software Components

"The transition to automated manufacturing in software requires two steps. First, we need to move our focus from engineering single systems to engineering families of systems - this will allow us to come up with the "right" implementation components. Second, we need to automate the assembly of the implementation components using generators" [15].

Generative Programming (GP) is an attempt to provide a variety of approaches and techniques to manufacture software components in an automated way by developing programs that synthesize other programs [GPCE]. According to Czarnecki & Eisenecker's book, the two main steps to industrialize software manufacturing are i) the modeling and the engineering of a program family and ii) the use of generators to automate the assembly of components. From a software engineering perspective one challenge is to bridge the gap between modeling and programming languages. On the one hand, we need to improve the level of abstraction by hiding the implementation concerns and make them independent from the target platform. On the other hand, we have to design new programming languages (and associated tools) well suited to deal with software ubiquity and adaptability. These languages must support the incremental introduction of non anticipated concerns [24].

J.-P. Banâtre et al. (Eds.): UPP 2004, LNCS 3566, pp. 315–325, 2005.

1.1   Lessons from Object-Oriented Languages

More than twenty years of industrial practices have clearly enlightened the contributions but also the limitations of object-oriented technologies when dealing with software complexity [24]. Obviously, OO languages have contributed to significant improvements in the field of software engineering and open middleware [39]. Today every general purpose language provides an object model either *ex nihilo* either as a library. Nevertheless, programming the network as advocated by Java, made clear that the object model[1], even extended with the design of reusable micro-architectures such as patterns or frameworks, is not well suited to deal with critical issues such as scalability, reusability, adaptability and composability of software components [7, 24, 20].

When programming in the large, a major source of problems is the lack of mechanisms to modularize crosscutting concerns and then to minimize code tangling and code scattering [40]. Another source of problems is the difficulty of representing micro-architectures based only upon classes and their methods. A last source of problems is the need of mechanisms to incrementally modify the structure or the behavior of a program. Considering object-oriented programming as the sole technology to solve these issues has some well known drawbacks [12, 24] :

1. Classes schizophrenia : as already quoted by Borning in 1986, classes play too many roles and there is some confusion around the concerns of a class as an object generator, a class as a method dispatcher and an (abstract) class as a part of the inheritance graph [28]. One source of the complexity surrounding classes in Smalltalk is the interaction of message lookup with the role of classes as the generators of new objects, which gives rise to the need for metaclasses [10].

2. Granularity of behavioral factoring : when expressing behavioral concerns there is no intermediate level of granularity between a method and a class. For instance, there is no way in Java to factorize and then manipulate a set of methods as a whole. Similarly, a Java package - seen as a group of related classes - has not direct tangible representation at the code level. Then, there is a real need for stateless groups of methods *à la* trait to implement and compose reusable modules [35].

3. Class inheritance and transversal concerns : inheritance is not the solution for reusing crosscutting non-functional behaviors such as security or display that are by essence non hierarchical. For instance in Java, even very elementary state-less concerns such as being colorable, traceable, memoizable, movable, paintable, clonable, runnable, serializable, . . . must be expressed by interfaces to be reused. Unfortunately, these interfaces do not provide any method implementations but only method specifications, limiting drastically code reusability.

---

[1] As defined by its related concepts of encapsulation, message sending, and class inheritance [42].

4. Design patterns traceability : patterns provide reusable micro-architectures based on explicit collaborations between a group of classes [23]. Unfortunately they have no direct representation (reification) at the programming language level raising traceability and understandability issues [38, 22].

5. Framework extensibility : frameworks are also micro-architectures but adaptable and built to organize libraries dedicated to a specif application domain. Unfortunately the adaptation process is closely related to the understanding of the inheritance and instantiation relationships used to organize the classes involved in the framework [1].

6. Bridging the gap between programming and modeling languages : some UML concepts such as aggregation, association and composition are rather ambiguously defined at the modeling level without the corresponding mechanisms at the programming level [26]. Obviously, this lack of correspondence complicates the transformation process advocated by the Model Driven approach [MDA].

Nevertheless, these "cons" put together with the simplicity and the generality of the object model have challenged new open research ideas in the field of conventional programming languages design and contributed to the (re)emergence of paradigms such as feature modeling [15], domain specific languages [14, 25], and aspect-oriented programming [20, 40, 18]. A common objective of these paradigms is to provide new protocols, new translators and new generators to modularize crosscutting concerns (items 1,2,3), to automate design patterns and frameworks applications (items 4,5), and to make executable modeling languages (item 6).

1.2   Reflective Architectures and Meta-object Protocols

"Reflection: An entity's integral ability to represent, operate on, and otherwise deal with itself in the same way that it represents, operates or and deals with its primary subject matter"[36].

Metalevel architectures have clearly illustrated the potential of reflection to deal with self description and adaptative behavior [30, 43]. They are good candidates to solve some of the *self* issues* discussed in the field of autonomic computing [5] or to develop self-organizing functionality as required by amorphous computing [2].

The reflective approach makes the assumption that it is possible to separate in a given application, its *why* expressed at the base level, from its *how* expressed at the metalevel. In the case of a reflective object-oriented language *à la* Smalltalk and *à la* CLOS, the principle is to reify at the metalevel its structural representation, *e.g.*, its classes, their methods and the error-messages but also its computational behavior, *e.g.*, the message sending, the object allocation and the class inheritance. Depending on which part of the representation is accessed, reflection is said to be structural or behavioral. Meta-objects protocols (MOPs) are specific protocols describing at the meta-level the behavior of the reified entities. Specializing a given MOP by inheritance, is the standard way [11, 19] to extend and to open the base language with new mechanisms such as explicit metaclasses [28], multiple-inheritance [8], concurrency & distribution [31, 32] and aspects [9].

The design of metaobject protocols such as ObjVlisp/ClassTalk and CLOS contributed to the development of techniques to introspect and intercess with program structures and behaviors [10, 7, 34, 8]. They also influenced the Meta-Object Facility (*MOF*) developped for UML by the OMG [UML]. The minimal ObjVlisp model was built upon two classes : Object the root of inheritance tree, Class the first metaclass and as such the root of the instantiation link, plus MethodDescription, the reification of objet methods. Then object creation (structural reflection) and message sending (behavioral reflection) can be expressed as two compositions of primitive operations defined in one of these three classes[2] :

- Class.allocate 0 Object.initialize
- Class.lookup 0 MethodDescription.apply

As developed in [28], modifying one of this primitive was the way to model and implement alternative class model. The Java model looks very similar to the ObjVlisp one, the main difference being that Class - its sole metaclass - is **final** making Class and then the associated Java class model non extensible [10]. Resulting from a compromise between an open-ended and a secure architecture, the Java reflective API (as defined by its java.lang.reflect package) provides a MOP principally dedicated to self-description and introspection [13].

In the case of an open middleware [29], the main usage of behavioral reflection is to control message sending by interposing a metaobject in charge of adding extra behaviors/services (such as transaction, caching, distribution) to its base object. Nevertheless, the introduction of such *interceptors/wrappers* metaobjects requires to instrument the base level with some *hooks* in charge of causally connecting the base object with its metaobject. Those metaobjects prefigured the introduction of AspectJ *crosscuts*, *e.g.*, the specification of execution points where extra actions or *advice* should be woven in the base program [21, 17].

1.3   Aspect-Oriented Languages

Aspect-oriented programming as well as aspect-oriented modeling go beyond the (meta)object model by providing mechanisms to express *crosscutting concerns*. These new units of independent behaviors called aspects, support the identification, the encapsulation and then the manipulation of a set of (non functional) properties describing a specific concern such as graphic user interfaces (GUI), transaction policies, errors handling .... These aspects must allow adaptation of program units across module boundaries [40]. While beeing added to a legacy application and in accordance with the modularity principle, they should not

---

[2] The dot notation Class.allocate meaning the allocate method defined in the Class class.

pollute the base application. Consequently, aspects have to be specified as independent units and then woven with the associated base program in a non invasive way.

Technically, the main intuition behind AOP is to introduce *join points* raising events every time an interesting point is reached during the execution of a program. The idea is to propose a *pointcut language* to select specific *join points* and an *advice language* to express the extra code to be woven at those pointcuts. Today AOP is a very dynamic field of research where some groups prototype new languages focusing on the pointcut and advice models while other groups develop formal techniques based on program transformation and analysis [AOSD].

AspectJ: An Archetype of AOL. *"A characteristic of aspect-oriented programming, as embodied in AspectJ, is the use of advice to incrementally modify the behavior of a program. An advice declaration specifies an action to be taken whenever some condition arises during the execution of the program. The condition is specified by a formula called a pointcut designator. The events during execution at which advice may be triggered are called joint points. In this model of aspect-oriented programming, join points are dynamic in that they refer to events during the execution of the program [41]."*

AspectJ is a general purpose language built as a super set of Java. For a first introduction see [AspectJ, 27] and chapter 6 of [18]. The idea is to introduce a new unit called an *aspect* in charge of modularizing crosscutted concerns. This unit looks like a class definition but supports the declarations of pointcuts and advice. These pointcuts are used by a specific compiler to weave the advice with regular Java code. From an industrial perspective, AspectJ is the first largely spread language used to develop or reengineer relevant applications according to aspect-oriented design [18, AOSD]. From an academic point ov view, AspectJ is the aspect-oriented pioneer and as such the natural candidate to expose the relationships between objects, metaobjects and aspects and then to answer some issues raised by post-object-oriented programming.

The Pointcut and Advice Models. In the case of AspectJ both the pointcut language and the advice language are extensions of Java. Revisiting [20] we propose the following definitions :

- Join point : a well defined point in the execution of a program. As an extension of Java, AspectJ proposes about ten different kinds of those points related to object-oriented execution; method call, method execution, field reference (get and set), constructor call, (static) initializer execution, constructor execution, object (pre) initialization, exception handler execution [27].
- Pointcut (*when*) : an expression designating a set of join points that optionally expose some of the values in the associated execution context. These pointcuts can be either user-defined or primitives. These pointcuts can be composed (like predicates) according to three logical operators : logical and (&& operator), logical or (|| operator) and logical negation (! operator).

- Advice (*how/what*) : a declaration of what an aspect computes at intercepted join points. In fact a method like mechanism used to declare that certain code should execute when a given pointcut matched. The associated code can be told to run before the actual method starts runing, after the actual method body has run, and instead/around the actual method body.
- Inter-type declaration (introductions) : declarations of members that cut across multiple classes or declarations of change in the inheritance relationship between classes. In a reflective way, those declarations are used to open a class by statically introducing new members or by changing its super class or super interfaces.
- Aspect : a unit of modular crosscutting implementation, composed of pointcuts and advice, plus ordinary Java member declarations. An AspectJ aspect declaration has a form similar to that of a Java class declaration.

A Flavor of AspectJ. [13] develops a guided tour of AspectJ demonstrating by examples how to define aspects tracing or memoizing methods. In this same volume, [1] introduces a Logging and a RepaintProtocol aspect crosscutting a Clock class. To go a step forward in the adaptation of the AWT framework as discussed by S. Chiba, we introduce the RunnableAspect.

The idea is to address the recurrent question of how to make objects active? Java idioms suggest to use a Runnable interface in charge of adapting a class to the Java concurrency model. The AspectJ alternative is to replace the standard execution of a method by the launching of a new private Thread dedicated to its execution :

```
public aspect RunnableAspect {
  // a pointcut declaration
  pointcut executeMain() : execution(static void Clock.main(String[])) {
  // an advice definition
  void around() : executeMain() {
    new Thread(){
      public void run() {
        System.out.println("Started in another thread");
        proceed();
      }
    }.start();
  }
}
```

The executionMain *pointcut* is associated to the execution of the static Clock.main method[3]. The associated *around advice* starts the execution of this method in a new Thread. The *proceed* construction allows to execute the regular Clock.main body.

---

[3] The wild card operator "*" authorizes to capture all the defined main methods :
```
pointcut executionAllMain : execution(static void *.main(String[]))
```

1.4   Renewal of Domain Specific Languages

A DSL is a high-level language providing constructs appropriate to a particular family of problems. Contrarily to a general purpose language (GPL), a DSL is readable for domain experts and usually declarative [14]. The use of such a language simplifies programming, because solutions can be expressed in a way that is close to the domain and because low-level optimizations and domain expertise are captured in the language implementation rather than being coded explicitly by the programmer. The avoidance of low-level source code in itself improves program robustness. More importantly, the use of domain-specific constructs facilitates precise, domain-specific verifications, that would be costly or impossible to apply to comparable code written in a general-purpose language [33].

The advantages of DSLs have drawn the attention of rapidly evolving markets where there is a need for building families of similar software, by introducing product lines [DSL, 25, 3, 4]. DSL are also good candidates for markets where reactivity or software certification are critical : Internet, cellular phones, smart cards, electronic commerce, bank ATM, telephony services ...

Coupling Domain Specific Languages and Aspects

DSL languages as MDA models offer high-level constructs dedicated to a domain. They require high-level compilers able to target a general purpose language (GPL) by providing the *ad hoc* mapping between the DSL and the GPL constructs. A real challenge is to improve DSL compilers to optimize the generation and/or compilation of executable programs [16]. In that perspective the AOP techniques of pointcuts and advice could provide a better modularization of DSL compilers themselves. AOD can be also used as a separation of concern methodology to reengineer legacy software by instrumenting an application with pointcut statements generation and then by inferfacing the associated set of events with a DSL [6]. Finally, mirroring Architecture, a DSL could be used as an ASL to provide the good level of abstraction when defining a specific aspect. Obviously, building a weaver able to compose a GPL application with aspects expressed via specific languages seems a very long term challenge!

2   Open and Challenging Issues

This section is a short summary of the workshop discussion related to generative programming. The guest speakers have a strong background in (meta)object, aspect and component oriented programming and they were asked to discuss the *what and the* how of the GP approach.

1. When opening the track, Pierre Cointe pointed out that GP is really an attempt to solve industrial problems such as adaptability, scalability and reusability by improving current modeling and programming technologies. When considering the automation (generation, composition and transformation) of software components, he suggested going behind object-oriented languages by still looking at the physical world as a source of inspiration. A

promising step in the direction of unconventional programming paradigms is the aspect-oriented programming approach seen as a way to provide unplanned and none invasive adaptability by incrementally modifying the behavior of a program. As for reflection, metalevel architectures and open systems, the challenge is to have a precise description and control of computation either at the structural or at the behavioral levels. Considering Architecture as a second source of inspiration, another challenge is to consider DSLs as a formalism to express complex aspects such as security, concurrency, GUI, ..., and then to define weavers to superimpose aspect-specific languages with legacy applications.

2. Krzysztof Czarnecki gave an *overview of generative software development* focusing on software reuse and development processes. He suggested a paradigm shift towards modeling and programming system families by first discussing the issues around the mapping between the problem space (the what) and the solution space (the why). Then, he related in detail the feature-oriented approach and emphasized the use of DSLs at the modeling level [3].

3. Shigeru Chiba introduced *generative programming from a post object-oriented programming view point* by sketching an application for automating the use of the AWT framework. This talk was the opportunity to introduce Javassist, a Java byte code translator, and to discuss how to use it as a programmable program translator. It was also the occasion to present Javassist first as a load-time metaobject protocol, then as a basic kernel to implement AOP languages *à la* AspectJ [1].

4. Mira Mezini developed *a comparison of program generation with aspect-oriented programming*. She argued that general purpose programming languages should be augmented with abstraction mechanisms to encode and superimpose different crosscutting models instead of using program generation techniques to encode domain-specific knowledge. She introduced Caesar - her general purpose language - to demonstrate how to encode such domain specific models by developing the notion of pointcuts and advice languages. In these proceedings, she also sketches the ALPHA prototype designed to provide more expressive pointcuts at the levels of the control flows graph, the abstract syntax tree, the object graph, ... [4].

5. Charles Consel presented *generative programming from a DSL viewpoint* and discussed how to compile DSL programs into GPL programs. He mentionned how to drive generative tools by using declarations and annotations and pointed out how to benefit from metaprogramming technology.

Acknowledgments

This work is part of the new AOSD network of excellence and its language laboratory (see http://www.aosd-europe.net).

References

[AspectJ] AspectJ site. : See http://eclipse.org/aspectj.

[AOSD] AOSD conference site. : See http://aosd.net.

[DSL] See http://lab.msdn.microsoft.com/teamsystem/Workshop/DSLTools/.

[GPCE] Batory, D., Czarnecki, K., Eisenecker, U., Smaragdakis., Y., Szti-panivits J.: Generative Programming and Component Engineering. See http://www.cs.rice.edu/taha/gpce/.

[MDA] Model Driven Architecture (MDA) site. : See http://www.omg.org.

[UML] See http://www.uml.org.

1. Chiba, Shigeru.: Generative Programming from a Post Object-Oriented Programming ViewPoint. Same volume.

2. Coore, D.: Introduction to Amorphous Computing. Same volume.

3. Czarnecki, K.: Overview of Generative Software Development. Same volume.

4. Mezini, M., Ostermann, K.: A Comparison of Programm Generation with Aspect-Oriented Programming. Same volume.

5. Parashar, M., Hairi, S.: Autonomic Computing: An Overview. Same volume.

6. Aberg, R. A., Lawall, J., Sudholt, M., Muller, G., Lemeur, A.-F.: On the automatic evolution of an OS kernel using temporal logic and AOP. 18th IEEE International Conference on Automated Software Engineering, ASE 2003, Montreal, Canada, October 2003.

7. Aksit, M., Black, A., Cardelli, L., Cointe. P., Guerraoui, R. (editor), and al.: Strategic Research Directions in Object Oriented Programming, ACM Computing Surveys, volume 8, number 4, page 691-700, 1996.

8. Bouraqadi-Sadani, M.N. , Ledoux, T., Rivard F.: Safe Metaclass Programming. Proceedings of OOPSLA 1998. Editor Craig Chambers,ACM-Sigplan, pages 84-96, volume 33, number 10, Vancouver, British Columbia, Canada, October 1998.

9. Bouraqadi-Sadani, M.N. , Ledoux, T.: Supporting AOP Using Reflection. Chapter 12 of [18], pages 261-282, 2005.

10. Cointe, P.: Metaclasses are First Class: The ObjVlisp Model. Proceedings of the second ACM SIGPLAN conference on Object-Oriented Programming, Systems, Languages, and Applications (OOPSLA 1987). Editor Jerry L. Archibald, ACM SIGPLAN Notices, pages 156-167, volume 22, number 12, Orlando, Florida, USA, October 1987.

11. Cointe, P.: CLOS and Smalltalk : a Comparison. Chapter 9, pages 215-250 of [34]. The MIT Press, 1993.

12. Cointe, P., Noyé, J., Douence, R., Ledoux, T., Menaud, J.M., Muller, G., Südholt, M.: Programmation post-objets. Des langages d'aspect aux langages de composants. RSTI série L'objet. volume 10, number 4, pages 119-143, 2004. See also http://www.lip6.fr/colloque-JFP.

13. Cointe, P., Albin Amiot, Denier, S.: From (meta) objects to aspects : from Java to AspectJ. Third International Symposium on Formal Methods for Components and Objects, FCMO 04, Leiden, The Netherlands, November 2004. To appear as a LNCS volume. 2005.

14. Consel, C.: From A Program Family To a Domain-Specific Language. Pages 19-29 of LNCS 3016, Springer Verlag. State-of-theArt Survey in Domain-Specific Program Generation. International Seminar, Dagstuhl Castle, 2004.

15. Czarnecki, K., Eisenecker, U.W.: Generative Programming. Methods, Tools, and Applications. Addison-Wesley, 2000.

16. Dmitriev, S.: Language Oriented Programming : The Next Programming Paradigm. onBoard, www.onboard.jetbrains.com, November 2004.
17. Douence, R., Motelet, O., Sudholt, M.: A formal definition of crosscuts. Proceedings of the 3rd International Conference on Reflection 2001, LNCS volume 2192, pages 170-186, 2001.
18. Filman, E. R., Elrad, T., Clarke, S., Aksit, M.: Aspect-Oriented Software Development. Addison-Wesley, 2005.
19. Kiczales, G., Ashley, J., Rodriguez, L., Vahdat, A., Bobrow, D.: Metaobject Protocols Why We Want Them and What Else They Can Do. Chapter 4, pages 101-118 of [34]. The MIT Press, 1993.
20. Kiczales, G., Lamping, J., Mendhekar, A., Maeda, C., Lopes, C, Loingtier, J.-M., Irwin, J.: Aspect-Oriented Programming. 11th European Conference on Object-Oriented Programming, ECOOP 1997, LNCS volume 1241, pages 220-242, 1997.
21. Kiczales, G., Hilsdale, E., Hugunin, J., Kersten, M., Palm, J., Griswold, W.: An Overview of AspectJ 15th European Conference on Object-Oriented Programming, ECOOP 2001, LNCS volume 2072, pages 327-354, 2001.
22. Hannemann, J., Kiczales, G.: Design Pattern Implementation in Java and AspectJ. Pages 161-173 of the proceedings of OOPLSA 2002. Editor Ron Crocker and Guy L. Steele, Jr. 2002.
23. Gamma, E., Helm, R., Johnson. R., Vlissides, J.: Design Patterns. Elements of Reusable Object-Oriented Software. Addison-Wesley Professional Computing Series. 1995
24. Gabriel, R.: Objects Have Failed. See http://www/dreamsongs/com/Essays.html.
25. Greenfield, J., Short, K., Cook, S., Stuart, K.: Software Factories : Assembling Applications with Patterns, Models, Frameworks & Tools. John Wiley & Sons. See also www.softwarefactories.com, September 2004.
26. Guéhéneuc, Y., Albin Amiot, H.: Recovering Binary Class relationships: Putting Icing on the UML Cake. Pages 301-314 of the OOPSLA 2004 proceedings, ACM Sigplan, Vancouver, October 2004.
27. Kiselev, I.: Aspect-Oriented Progamming with AspectJ. Sams Publishing, 2003.
28. Ledoux, T., Cointe, P.: Explicit Metaclasses As a Tool for Improving the Design of Class Libraries. Pages 38-55 of the JSSST-JAIST ISOTAS 1996 proceedings, Springer Verlag, LNCS Volume 1049. Kanazawa, Japan, 1996.
29. Ledoux, T.: OpenCorba: A Reflective Open Broker. Pages 197-214 of the proceedings of the second international conference on Meta-Level Architectures and Reflection (Cointe, P. editor). Springer Verlag, LNCS Volume 1616, Saint-Malo, France, 1999.
30. Maes, P., Nardi, D. editors.: Meta-Level Architectures and Reflection. Selection of papers presented at the workshop on *Meta-Level Architectures and Reflection* held in Alghero during october 1986. North-Holland 1988.
31. McAffer, J.: Meta-level Programming with CodA. Proceedings of ECOOP 1995. Page 190-214, Springer LNCS Volume 952, Aarhus, Danemark, 1995
32. McAffer, J.: Engineering the Meta-Level. Proceedings of Reflection 96, pages 39-61, Edited by G. Kiczales. San Francisco, April 1996.
33. Muller, G., Consel, C., Marlet, R., Barreto, L.P., Mérillon, F., Réveillère, L.: Towards Robust OSes for Appliances: A New Approach Based on Domain-Specific Languages. Pages 19-24 of the Proceedings of the ACM SIGOPS European Workshop 2000 (EW2000), Kolding, Denmark, 2000
34. Pæpcke, A.: Object-Oriented Programming : The CLOS perspective. The MIT Press, 1993.

35. Scharli, N., Ducasse, S., Nierstrasz, O., Black, P.: Traits: Composable Units of Behaviour. 17th European Conference on Object-Oriented Programming, ECOOP 2003. Editor L. Cardelli. LNCS volume 2743, pages 248-274. 2003.
36. Smith, B.: What do you mean, meta? Proceedings of the First Workshop on Reflection and Metalevel Architectures in Object-Oriented Programming. OOPSLA-ECOOP'90, Ottawa, 1990.
37. Tanter, E., Noyé, J., Caromel, D., Cointe, P.: Partial Behavioral Reflection: Spatial and Temporal Selection of Reification. Proceedings of the 18th ACM SIGPLAN conference on Object-Oriented Programing, Systems, Languages, and Applications, OOPSLA 2003. Editor Ron Crocker and Guy L. Steele, Jr. ACM SIGPLAN Notices, volume 38, number 11, pages 27-46, 2003.
38. Tatsubori, M., Chiba, S.: Programming Support of Design Pattern with Compile-time Reflection. Proceedings of the OOPSLA 1998 workshop on Reflective Programming in C++ and Java. Availabla as at technical report of the Center for Computational Physics, Univcersity of Tsukuba. Vancouver, Canada, October 1998.
39. Thomas, D.: Reflective Software Engineering - From MOPS to AOSD. Journal Of Object Technology, volume 1, number 4, pages 17-26. October 2002.
40. Wand, M.: Understanding Aspects. Invited talk at the International Conference on Functional Programming, ICFP 2003. Available at www.ccs.neu.edu/home/wand/ICFP, 2003.
41. Wand, M., Kiczales, G., Dutchyn, C.: A semantics for Advice and Dynamic Joint Points in AOP. ACM Toplas Volume 26 Issue 5, 2004.
42. Wegner, P.: Dimensions of Object-Based Language Design. Proceedings of the second ACM SIGPLAN conference on Object-Oriented Programming, Systems, Languages, and Applications (OOPSLA 1987). Editor Jerry L. Archibald. ACM SIGPLAN Notices, pages 168-182, volume 22, number 12, Orlando, Florida, USA, October 1987.
43. Yonezawa, A., Smith, Brian, C., editors.: Reflection and Meta-Level Architectures. Proceedings of the IMSA workshop held in Tokyo during November 4-7 1992.

Overview of Generative Software Development

Krzysztof Czarnecki

University of Waterloo, Canada
czarnecki@acm.org

Abstract. System family engineering seeks to exploit the commonalities among systems from a given problem domain while managing the variabilities among them in a systematic way. In system family engineering, new system variants can be rapidly created based on a set of reusable assets (such as a common architecture, components, models, etc.). Generative software development aims at modeling and implementing system families in such a way that a given system can be automatically generated from a specification written in one or more textual or graphical domain-specific languages. This paper gives an overview of the basic concepts and ideas of generative software development including DSLs, domain and application engineering, generative domain models, networks of domains, and technology projections. The paper also discusses the relationship of generative software development to other emerging areas such as Model Driven Development and Aspect-Oriented Software Development.

1 Introduction

Object-orientation is recognized as an important advance in software technology, particularly in modeling complex phenomena more easily than its predecessors [1]. But the progress in reusability, maintainability, reliability, and even expressiveness has fallen short of expectations. As units of reuse, classes have proven too small. Frameworks are hard to compose, and their development remains an art. Components—as independently-deployable units of composition with contractually specified interfaces [2]—offer reuse, but the more functional the component, the larger and less reusable it becomes. And patterns, while intrinsically reusable, are not an implementation medium.

Current research and practical experience suggest that achieving significant progress with respect to software reuse requires a paradigm shift towards modeling and developing software system families rather than individual systems. *System-family engineering* (also known as *product-line engineering*) seeks to exploit the commonalities among systems from a given problem domain while managing the variabilities among them in a systematic way [3, 4,5]. In system-family engineering, new system variants can be rapidly created based on a set of reusable assets (such as a common architecture, components,

J.-P. Banâtre et al. (Eds.): UPP 2004, LNCS 3566, pp. 326–341, 2005.

models, etc.).[1] Frameworks and components are still useful as implementation technologies, but the scope and shape of reusable abstractions is determined and managed through a system-family approach.

Generative software development is a system-family approach, which focuses on automating the creation of system-family members: a given system can be automatically generated from a specification written in one or more textual or graphical *domain-specific languages* [6, 7, 3, 8, 9, 10, 11].

This paper gives an overview of the basic concepts and ideas of generative software development including DSLs, domain and application engineering, generative domain models, networks of domains, and technology projections. The paper closes by discussing the relationship of generative software development to other emerging areas such as Model Driven Development and Aspect-Oriented Software Development.

2 Domain-Specific Languages

A domain-specific language (DSL) is a language offering expressive power focused on a particular problem domain, such as a specific class of applications or application aspect. Whereas general-purpose programming languages such as Java or C++ were designed to be appropriate for virtually any kind of applications, DSLs simplify the development of applications in specialized domains at the cost of their generality.

DSLs are certainly not a new idea. In fact, before common programming abstractions were identified and packaged into general-purpose programming languages, many of the early computer languages were application-specific. For example, in his landmark paper "The Next 700 Hundred Programming Languages", Landin [12] cites a 1965 Prospectus of the American Mathematical Association: "... today... 1,700 special programming languages used to 'communicate' in over 700 application areas." Although many DSLs have been developed over the years, the systematic study of DSLs is more recent, e.g., [6, 13, 14, 15].

The domain specificity of a language is a matter of degree. While any language has a certain scope of applicability, some languages are more focused than others. Programming languages such as Fortran or Cobol, although designed with some application focus in mind, are still fairly general. For example, Fortran was designed to target mathematical applications, but it can be used to program anything from databases to user interfaces. When referring to DSLs, we consider much more focused languages, such as HTML or SQL. In fact, a great share of existing DSLs are not even programming languages [16].

Narrowing the application scope of a language allows us to provide better support for solving problems within the scope compared to what a general purpose

---

[1] System-family engineering is mainly concerned with building systems from common assets, whereas product-line engineering additionally considers scoping and managing common product characteristics from the market perspective. In order to be more general, this paper adheres to system-family terminology.

programming language could offer. A DSL can offer several important advantages over a general-purpose language:

- *Domain-specific abstractions*: a DSL provides pre-defined abstractions to directly represent concepts from the application domain.
- *Domain-specific concrete syntax*: a DSL offers a natural notation for a given domain and avoids syntactic clutter that often results when using a general-purpose language.
- *Domain-specific error checking*: a DSL enables building static analyzers that can find more errors than similar analyzers for a general-purpose language and that can report the errors in a language familiar to the domain expert.
- *Domain-specific optimizations*: a DSL creates opportunities for generating optimized code based on domain-specific knowledge, which is usually not available to a compiler for a general-purpose language.
- *Domain-specific tool support*: a DSL creates opportunities to improve any tooling aspect of a development environment, including, editors, debuggers, version control, etc.; the domain-specific knowledge that is explicitly captured by a DSL can be used to provide more intelligent tool support for developers.

The traditional approach to providing domain-specific abstractions in programming languages is through libraries of user-defined functions, classes, and data structures. We consider the application programming interfaces (APIs) exposed by such libraries as a possible implementation form for DSLs. User-defined abstractions is a way to extend a language with domain-specific vocabulary, and library and API design is a form of language design. Of course, open-ended language design is more challenging than API design, which is constrained and guided by the host language. At the same time, while satisfying the first benefit in the list above, traditional libraries and APIs usually come short on the other items, such as domain-specific notation (beyond operator overloading, which may be available in the host language), error checking, and optimizations. Achieving the latter goals usually requires some form of metaprogramming.

DSLs come in a wide variety of forms, e.g., textual languages (stand-alone or embedded in a general-purpose programming language), diagrammatic languages, form-based languages, grid-based languages, etc. Section 6 lists different DSLs implementation technologies.

3   Domain Engineering and Application Engineering

System family engineering distinguishes between at least two kinds of development processes: *domain engineering* and *application engineering* (see Figure 1). Typically, there is also a third process, *management*, but this paper focuses on the two development processes (for more information on process issues see [4,3]). Generative software development, as a system-family approach, subscribes to the process model in Figure 1, too.

Domain engineering (also known as *product-line development* or *core asset development*) is "development for reuse". It is concerned with the development

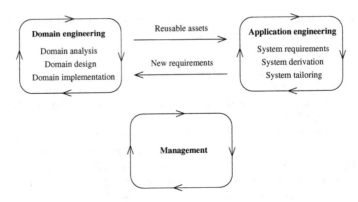

Fig. 1. Main processes in system-family engineering

of reusable assets such as components, generators, DSLs, analysis and design models, user documentation, etc. Similar to single-system engineering, domain engineering also includes analysis, design, and implementation activities. However, these are focused on a class of systems rather than just a single system.[2] *Domain analysis* involves determining the scope of the family to be built, identifying the common and variable features among the family members, and creating structural and behavioral specifications of the family. *Domain design* covers the development of a common architecture for all the members of the system family and a plan of how individual systems will be created based on the reusable assets. Finally, *domain implementation* involves implementing reusable assets such as components, generators, and DSLs.

Application engineering (also referred to as *product development*) is "development with reuse", where concrete applications are built using the reusable assets. Just as traditional system engineering, it starts with requirements elicitation, analysis, and specification; however, the requirements are specified as a delta from or configuration of some generic system requirements produced in domain engineering. The requirements specification is the main input for *system derivation*, which is the manual or automated construction of the system from the reusable assets.

Both processes feed on each other: domain-engineering supplies application engineering with the reusable assets, whereas application engineering feeds back new requirements to domain engineering. This is so because application engineers identify the requirements for each given system to be built and may be faced with requirements that are not covered by the existing reusable assets. Therefore, some amount of application-specific development or *tailoring* is often required in order to quickly respond to the customer's needs. However, the new requirements

---

[2] Both terms "system family" and "domain" imply a class of systems; however, whereas the former denotes the actual set of systems, the latter refers more to the related area of knowledge. The use of the one or the other in compounds such as "domain engineering" is mostly historical.

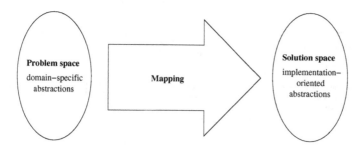

Fig. 2. Mapping between problem space and solution space

should be fed back into domain engineering in order to keep the reusable assets in sync with the product needs. Different models for setting up these processes in an organization, e.g., separate or joint product-development and domain-engineering teams, are discussed in [17].

Domain engineering can be applied at different levels of maturity. At minimum, domain analysis activities can be used to establish a common terminology among different product-development teams. The next level is to introduce a common architecture for a set of systems. Further advancement is to provide a set of components covering parts or all of the systems in the system family. Finally, the assembly of these components can be partially or fully automated using generators and/or configurators. The last level represents the focus of generative software development. In general, the generated products may also contain non-software artifacts, such as test plans, manuals, tutorials, maintenance guidelines, etc.

4   Mapping Between Problem Space and Solution Space

A key concept in generative software development is that of a mapping between *problem space* and *solution space* (see Figure 2), which is also referred to as a *generative domain model*. Problem space is a set of domain-specific abstractions that can be used to specify the desired system-family member. By "domain-specific" we mean that these abstractions are specialized to allow application engineers to express their needs in a way that is natural for their domain. For example, we might want to be able to specify payment methods for an electronic commerce system or matrix shapes in matrix calculations. The solution space, on the other hand, consists of implementation-oriented abstractions, which can be instantiated to create implementations of the specifications expressed using the domain-specific abstractions from the problem space. For example, payment methods can be implemented as calls to appropriate web services, and different matrix shapes may be realized using different data structures. The mapping between the spaces takes a specification and returns the corresponding implementation.

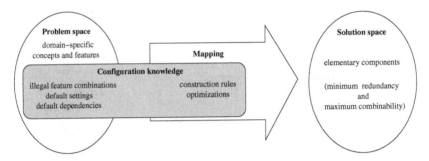

Fig. 3. Configuration view on the mapping between problem space and solution space

4.1   Configuration and Transformation

There are at least two different views at the mapping between problem space and solution space in generative software development: *configuration* view and *transformational* view.

In the configuration view, the problem space consists of domain-specific concepts and their features (see Figure 3). The specification of a given system requires the selection of features that the desired system should have. The problem space also defines illegal feature combinations, default settings, and default dependencies (some defaults may be computed based on some other features). The solution space consists of a set of implementation components, which can be composed to create system implementations. A system-family architecture sets out the rules how the components can be composed. In the configuration view, an application programmer creates a configuration of features by selecting the desired ones, which then is mapped to a configuration of components. The mapping between both spaces is defined by construction rules (certain configurations of features translate into certain configurations of implementation components) and optimizations (some component configurations may have better non-functional properties then others). The mapping plus the illegal feature combinations, default settings, and default dependencies collectively constitute *configuration knowledge*. Observe that the separation between problem and solution space affords us the freedom to structure abstractions in both spaces differently. In particular, we can focus on optimally supporting application programmers in the problem space, while achieving reuse and flexibility in the solution space.

In the transformational view, a problem space is represented by a domain-specific language, whereas the solution space is represented by an implementation language (see Figure 4). The mapping between the spaces is a transformation that takes a program in a domain-specific language and yields its implementation in the implementation language. A domain-specific language is a language specialized for a given class of problems. Of course, the implementation language may be a domain-specific language exposed by another domain. The

Fig. 4. Transformational view on the mapping between problem space and solution space

transformational view directly corresponds to the Draco model of domains and software generation [6].

Despite the superficial differences, there is a close correspondence between both views. The problem space with its common and variable features and constraints in the configuration view defines a domain-specific language, and the components in the solution space can also be viewed as an implementation language. For example, in the case of generic components, we can specify this target language as a GenVoca grammar with additional well-formedness constraints [18, 8]. Thus, the configuration view can also be interpreted as a mapping between languages.

The two views relate and integrate several powerful concepts from software engineering, such as domain-specific languages, system families, feature modeling, generators, components, and software architecture. Furthermore, the translation view provides a theoretical foundation for generative software development by connecting it to a large body of existing knowledge on language theory and language translation.

4.2   Network of Domains

Observe that Figure 2 can be viewed recursively, i.e., someone's problem space may be someone else's solution space. Thus, we can have chaining of mappings (see Figure 5 a). Furthermore, a mapping could take two or more specifications and map them to one (or more) solution space (see Figure 5 b). This is common when different aspects of a system are represented using different DSLs. A mapping can also implement a problem space in terms of two or more solution spaces (see Figure 5 c). Finally, different alternative DSLs (e.g., one for beginners and one for expert users) can be mapped to the same solution space (see Figure 5 d), and the same DSL can have alternative implementations by mappings to different solution spaces (e.g., alternative implementation platforms; see Figure 5e).

In general, spaces and mappings may form a hypergraph, which can even contain cycles. This graph corresponds to the idea of a *network of domains* by Jim Neighbors [6], where each implementation of a domain exposes a DSL,

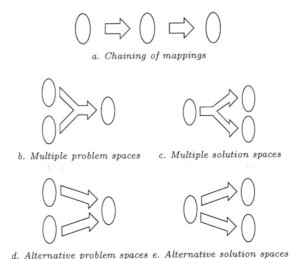

a. Chaining of mappings

b. Multiple problem spaces   c. Multiple solution spaces

d. Alternative problem spaces e. Alternative solution spaces

Fig. 5. Different arrangements of mappings between problem and solution spaces

which may be implemented by transformations to DSLs exposed by other domain implementations.

5   Feature Modeling and Feature-Oriented Approach

Feature modeling is a method and notation to elicit and represent common and variable features of the systems in a system family. Feature modeling was first proposed by Kang et al in [19] and since then has been extended with several concepts, e.g., feature and group cardinalities, attributes, and diagram references [20].

An example of a feature model is shown in Figure 6. The model expresses that an electronic commerce system supports one or more different payment methods; it provides tax calculation taking into account either the street-level address, or

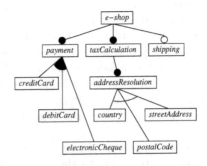

Fig. 6. Example of a feature diagram

postal code, or just the country; and it may or may not support shipment of physical goods. A feature diagram such as in Figure 6 may be supplemented with additional information including constraints (selecting a certain feature may require or exclude the selection of another feature), binding times (features may be intended to be selected at certain points in time), default attribute values and default features, stakeholders interested in a given feature, priorities, and more. Features may or may not correspond to concrete software modules. In general, we distinguish the following four cases:

- *Concrete* features such as data storage or sorting may be realized as individual components.
- *Aspectual* features such as logging, synchronization, or persistency may affect a number of components and can be modularized using aspect technologies.
- *Abstract* features such as performance requirements usually map to some configuration of components and/or aspects.
- *Grouping* features may represent a variation point and map to a common interface of plug-compatible components, or they may have a purely organizational purpose with no requirements implied.

Feature modeling gives rise to a feature-oriented approach to generative software developement [8]. In the early stages of software family development, feature models provide the basis for scoping a system family by recording and assessing information such as which features are important to enter a new market or remain in an existing market, which features incur a technological risk, what is the projected development cost of each feature, and so forth [21]. Subsequently, feature models created in domain analysis are the starting point in the development of both system-family architecture and DSLs (see Figure 7). Architecture development takes a solution-space perspective at the feature models: it concentrates on the concrete and aspectual features that need to be implemented as components and aspects. Familiar architectural patterns, such as in [22,23], can be applied, but with the special consideration that the variation points expressed in the feature models need to be realized in the architecture. During subsequent DSL development, a problem-space perspective concentrating on features that should be exposed to application developers determines the required DSL scope, possibly requiring additional abstract features.

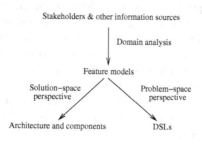

Fig. 7. Feature-oriented approach

6   Technology Projections and Structure of DSLs

Each of the elements of a generative domain model can be implemented using different technologies, which gives rise to different *technology projections*:

- DSLs can be implemented as new textual languages (using traditional compiler building tools), embedded in a programming language (e.g., template metaprogramming in C++ or Template Haskell [24], OpenC++ [25], Open-Java [26], Metaborg [27]), graphical languages (e.g., UML profiles [28], GME [29], MetaEdit+ [30], or Microsoft's DSL Technology in VisualStudio), wizards and interactive GUIs (e.g., feature-based configurators such as Feature-ModelingPlugin [31], Pure::Consul [32], or CaptainFeature [33]), or some combination of the previous. The appropriate structure of a DSL and the implementation technology depend on the range of variation that needs to be supported (see Figure 8). The spectrum ranges from routine configuration using wizards to programming using graphical or textual graph-like languages.

- Mappings can be realized using product configurators (e.g., Pure::Consul) or generators. The latter can be implemented using template and frame processors (e.g., TL [9], XVCL [34], or ANGIE [35]), transformation systems (e.g., DMS [36], StrategoXT [37], or TXL [38]), multi-staged programming [39], program specialization [40, 41, 42], or built-in metaprogramming capabilities of a language (e.g., template metaprogramming in C++ or Template Haskell).

- Components can be implemented using simply functions or classes, generic components (such as in the C++ Standard Template Library), component models (e.g., JavaBeans, ActiveX, or CORBA), or aspect-oriented programming approaches (e.g., AspectJ [43], HyperJ [44], or Caesar [45]).

While some technologies cover all elements of a generative domain model in one piece (e.g., OpenJava or template metaprogramming in C++), a more flexible approach is to use an intermediate program representation to allow using different DSL renderings (e.g., textual or graphical) with different generator back-ends (e.g., TL or StrategoXT).

The choice of a specific technology depends on its technical suitability for a given problem domain and target users. For example, in the case of DSLs, concise textual languages may be best appropriate for expert users, but wizards may be better suited for novices and infrequent users. In the case of generator technologies, the need for complex, algebraic transformations may require using a transformation system instead of a template processor. Furthermore, there may be non-technical selection criteria such as mandated programming languages, existing infrastructure, familiarity of the developers with the technology, political and other considerations.

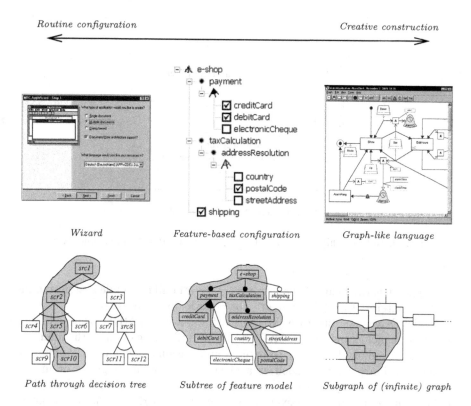

Routine configuration   *Creative construction*

Wizard   Feature-based configuration   Graph-like language

Path through decision tree   Subtree of feature model   Subgraph of (infinite) graph

Fig. 8. Spectrum of DSL structures

7   Model Driven Development

Perhaps the closest related area to generative software development is model-driven development (MDD), which aims at capturing every important aspect of a software system through appropriate models. A model is an abstract representation of a system and the portion of the world that interacts with it. Models allow answering questions about the software system and its world portion that are of interest to the stakeholders. They are better than the implementing code for answering these questions because they capture the intentions of the stakeholders more directly, are freer from accidental implementation details, and are more amenable to analysis. In MDD, models are not just auxiliary documentation artifacts; rather, models can be compiled directly into executable code that can be deployed at the customer's site.

There has been a trend in MDD towards representing models using appropriate DSLs, which makes MDD and generative software development closely related. Perhaps the main difference between MDD and generative software

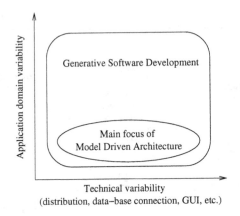

Fig. 9. Relationship between generative software development and MDA

development is the focus of the latter on system families. While system families can be of interest to MDD, they are not regarded as a necessity.

Model-Driven Architecture (MDA) is a framework for MDD proposed by the Object Management Group (OMG) [46]. While still being defined, the main goal of MDA is to allow developers to express applications independently of specific implementation platforms (such as a given programming language or middleware). In MDA, an application is represented as a Platform Independent Model (PIM) that later gets successively transformed into series of Platform Specific Models (PSMs), finally arriving at the executable code for a given platform. The models are expressed using UML and the framework uses other related OMG standards such as MOF, CWM, XMI, etc. A standard for model transformations is work in progress in response to the Request for Proposals "MOF 2.0 Query/Views/Transformations" issued by OMG.

MDA concepts can be mapped directly onto concepts from generative software development: a mapping from PIM to PSM corresponds to a mapping from problem space to solution space. Beyond the similarities, there are interesting synergies. On the one hand, benefits of MDA include a set of standards for defining and manipulating modeling languages and the popularization of generative concepts in practice. Thanks to MDA, current UML modeling tools are likely to evolve towards low-cost DSL construction tools. On the other hand, the MDA efforts until now have been focusing on achieving platform independence, i.e., system families with respect to technology variation. However, generative software development addresses both technical and application-domain variability, and it may provide valuable contributions to MDA in this respect (see Figure 9). Often asked questions in the MDA context are (1) what UML profiles or DSLs should be used to represent PIMs and (2) what is a platform in a given context. Domain analysis and domain scoping can help us to address these questions.

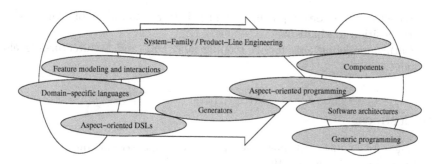

Fig. 10. Relationship between generative software development and other fields (from [47])

8   Other Related Fields

Figure 10 classifies a number of related fields by casting them against the elements of a generative domain model. Components, architectures, and generic programming are primarily related to the solution space. Aspect-oriented programming provides more powerful localization and encapsulation mechanisms than traditional component technologies. In particular, it allows us to replace many "little, scattered components" (such as those needed for logging or synchronization) and the configuration knowledge related to these components by well encapsulated aspectual modules. However, we still need to configure aspects and other components to implement abstract features such as performance properties. Therefore, aspect-oriented programming technologies such as AspectJ cover the solution space and only a part of the configuration knowledge. But aspects can also be found in the problem space, esp. in the context of DSLs used to described different aspects of a single system. Areas such as DSLs, feature modeling, and feature interactions address the problem space and the front part of the configuration knowledge. Finally, system-family and product-line engineering span across the entire generative domain model because they provide the overall structure of the development process (including domain and application engineering).

9   Concluding Remarks

Generative software development builds upon and exploits the synergies among several key concepts:

1. Software system families are the key to achieving systematic software reuse.
2. Domain-specific languages are about providing optimal support for application developers.
3. Mappings enable design knowledge capture.

4. Aspect-oriented development provides better separation of concerns and composition mechanisms.
5. Feature modeling aids family scoping, and DSL and architecture development.

References

1. Meyer, B.: Object-Oriented Software Construction. Second edn. Prentice Hall, Upper Saddle River, NJ (1997)
2. Szyperski, C.: Component Software—Beyond Object-Oriented Programming. Second edn. Addison-Wesley / ACM Press, Boston, MA (2002)
3. Weiss, D.M., Lai, C.T.R.: Software Product-Line Engineering: A Family-Based Software Development Process. Addison-Wesley (1999)
4. Clements, P., Northrop, L., eds.: Software Product Lines: Practices and Patterns. International Series in Computer Science. Addison-Wesley (2001)
5. Parnas, D.: On the design and development of program families. IEEE Transactions on Software Engineering **SE-2** (1976) 1–9
6. Neighbors, J.M.: Software Construction using Components. PhD thesis, Department of Information and Computer Science, University of California, Irvine (1980) Technical Report UCI-ICS-TR160. Available from `http://www.bayfronttechnologies.com/thesis.pdf`.
7. Cleaveland, J.C.: Building application generators. IEEE Software **9** (1988) 25–33
8. Czarnecki, K., Eisenecker, U.W.: Generative Programming: Methods, Tools, and Applications. Addison-Wesley (2000)
9. Cleaveland, C.: Program Generators with XML and Java. Prentice-Hall (2001)
10. Batory, D., Johnson, C., MacDonald, B., von Heeder, D.: Achieving extensibility through product-lines and domain-specific languages: A case study. ACM Transactions on Software Engineering and Methodology (TOSEM) **11** (2002) 191–214
11. Greenfield, J., Short, K.: Software Factories: Assembling Applications with Patterns, Models, Frameworks, and Tools. Wiley, Indianapolis, IN (2004)
12. Landin, P.J.: The next 700 programming languages. Commun. ACM **9** (1966) 157–166
13. Bentley, J.L.: Little languages. Communications og the ACM **29** (1986) 711–721
14. van Deursen, A., Klint, P., Visser, J.: Domain-specific languages: an annotated bibliography. SIGPLAN Not. **35** (2000) 26–36
15. Mernik, M., Heering, J., Sloane, A.M.: When and how to develop domain-specific languages. Technical Report SEN-E0309, CWI, Amsterdam (2003) Available from `http://www.cwi.nl/ftp/CWIreports/SEN/SEN-E0309.pdf`.
16. Wile, D.S.: Supporting the dsl spectrum. CIT Journal of Computing and Information Technology **9** (2001) 263–287
17. Bosch, J.: Software product lines: Organizational alternatives. In: Proceedings of the 23rd International Conference on Software Engineering (ICSE). (2001)
18. Batory, D., O'Malley, S.: The design and implementation of hierarchical software systems with reusable components. ACM Transactions on Software Engineering and Methodology **1** (1992) 355–398
19. Kang, K., Cohen, S., Hess, J., Nowak, W., Peterson, S.: Feature-oriented domain analysis (FODA) feasibility study. Technical Report CMU/SEI-90TR-21, Software Engineering Institute, Carnegie Mellon University, Pittsburgh, PA (1990)

20. Czarnecki, K., Helsen, S., Eisenecker, U.: Staged configuration using feature models. In Nord, R.L., ed.: Software Product Lines: Third International Conference, SPLC 2004, Boston, MA, USA, August 30-September 2, 2004. Proceedings. Volume 3154 of Lecture Notes in Computer Science., Springer-Verlag (2004) 266–283

21. DeBaud, J.M., Schmid, K.: A systematic approach to derive the scope of software product lines. In: Proceedings of the 21st International Conference on Software Engineering (ICSE), IEEE Computer Society Press (1999) 34–43

22. Buschmann, F., Jkel, C., Meunier, R., Rohnert, H., Stahl, M., eds.: Pattern-Oriented Software Architecture – A System of Patterns. International Series in Computer Science. John Wiley & Sons (1996)

23. Bosch, J.: Design and Use of Software Architecture: Adopting and evolving a product-line approach. Addison-Wesley (2000)

24. Czarnecki, K., O'Donnel, J., Striegnitz, J., Taha, W.: Dsl implementation in metaocaml, template haskell, and c++. [48] 50–71

25. Sigeru Chiba: OpenC++ (2004) Available at http://opencxx.sourceforge.net/index.shtml.

26. M. Tatsubori: OpenJava: An extensible Java (2004) Available at http://sourceforge.net/projects/openjava/.

27. Bravenboer, M., Visser, E.: Concrete syntax for objects. domain-specific language embedding and assimilation without restrictions. In C.Schmidt, D., ed.: Proceedings of the 19th ACM SIGPLAN conference on Object-Oriented Programing, Systems, Languages, and Applications (OOPSLA'04). Vancouver, Canada. October 2004, ACM SIGPLAN (2004)

28. Jeff Grey et al.: OOPSLA'02 Workshop on Domain-Specific Visual Languages (2002) Online proceedings at http://www.cis.uab.edu/info/OOPSLA-DSVL2/.

29. Lédeczi, Á., Árpád Bakay, Maróti, M., Völgyesi, P., Nordstrom, G., Sprinkle, J., Karsai, G.: Composing domain-specific design environments. IEEE Computer 34 (2001) 44–51

30. MetaCase, Jyväskylä, Finland: MetaEdit+ User Manual. (2004) Available from http://www.metacase.com.

31. Antkiewicz, M., Czarnecki, K.: FeaturePlugin: Feature modeling plug-in for Eclipse. In: OOPSLA'04 Eclipse Technology eXchange (ETX) Workshop. (2004) Paper available from http://www.swen.uwaterloo.ca/~kczarnec/etx04.pdf. Software available from gp.uwaterloo.ca/fmp.

32. pure-systems GmbH: Variant management with pure::consul. Technical White Paper. Available from http://web.pure-systems.com (2003)

33. Bednasch, T., Endler, C., Lang, M.: CaptainFeature (2002-2004) Tool available on SourceForge at https://sourceforge.net/projects/captainfeature/.

34. Wong, T., Jarzabek, S., Swe, S.M., Shen, R., Zhang, H.: Xml implementation of frame processor. In: Proceedings of the ACM Symposium on Software Reusability (SSR'01), Toronto, Canada, May 2001. (2001) 164–172 http://fxvcl.sourceforge.net/.

35. Delta Software Technology GmbH: ANGIE - A New Generator Engine (2004) Available at http://www.delta-software-technology.com/GP/gptop.htm.

36. Baxter, I., Pidgeon, P., Mehlich, M.: Dms: Program transformations for practical scalable software evolution. In: Proceedings of the International Conference on Software Engineering (ICSE'04), IEEE Press (2004)

37. Visser, E.: Program transformation with stratego/xt: Rules, strategies, tools, and systems. [48]

38. Cordy, J., Dean, T., Malton, A., Schneider, K.: Source transformation in software engineering using the txl transformation system. Information and Software Technology **44** (2002)
39. Taha, W.: A gentle introduction to multi-stage programming. [48]
40. Jones, N., Gomard, C., , Sestoft, P., eds.: Partial Evaluation and Automatic Program Generation. International Series in Computer Science. Prentice-Hall (1993)
41. Consel, C., Danvy, O.: Tutorial notes on partial evaluation. In: Conference Record of the Twentieth Annual ACM SIGPLAN-SIGACT Symposium on Principles Of Programming Languages, Charleston, SC, USA, ACM Press (1993) 493–501
42. Consel, C.: From a program family to a domain-specific language. [48] 19–29
43. Kiczales, G., Hilsdale, E., Hugunin, J., Kersten, M., Palm, J., Griswold, W.G.: An overview of aspectj. In: Proceedings of ECOOP'01. Lecture Notes in Computer Science, Springer-Verlag (2001)
44. Tarr, P., Ossher, H., Harrison, W., , Sutton, S.M.: N degrees of separation: Multidimensional separation of concerns. In: Proceedings International Conference on Software Engineering (ICSE) '99, ACM Press (1999) 107–119
45. Mezini, M., Ostermann, K.: Variability management with feature-oriented programming and aspects. In: Foundations of Software Engineering (FSE-12), ACM SIGSOFT (2004)
46. Object Management Group: Model-Driven Architecture (2004) www.omg.com/mda.
47. Barth, B., Butler, G., Czarnecki, K., Eisenecker, U.: Report on the ecoop'2001 workshop on generative programming. In: ECOOP 2001 Workshops, Panels and Posters (Budapest, Hungary, June 18-22, 2001). Volume 2323 of Lecture Notes in Computer Science., Springer-Verlag (2001)
48. Christian Lengauer, D.B., Consel, C., Odersky, M., eds.: Domain-Specific Program Generation, International Seminar, Dagstuhl Castle, Germany, March 23-28, 2003, Revised Papers. Volume 3016 of Lecture Notes in Computer Science. Springer-Verlag (2004)

A Comparison of Program Generation with Aspect-Oriented Programming

Mira Mezini and Klaus Ostermann

Darmstadt University of Technology, Germany
{mezini, ostermann}@informatik.tu-darmstadt.de

Abstract. Program generation and transformation techniques have gained considerable attention in the context of domain-specific languages (DSLs) and model-driven architecture (MDA). In this paper we compare domain-specific program generators with general-purpose aspect-oriented languages. We argue that program generation techniques have severe disadvantages with respect to composability, scalability, understandability, and other important software engineering issues. Finally, we advocate general-purpose aspect-oriented languages as an alternative for the implementation of domain-specific languages.

1 Introduction

Today's software has become very complex – besides the part of the program responsible for the so-called *business logic* many other concerns such as networking, security, platform, user interface etc. have to be considered as well. If all these concerns have to be kept in mind while programming, programming obviously becomes painful, with well-known disadvantages for understandability, reusability, etc.

This is the reason why recent trends in software engineering and programming languages try to provide technology with which these concerns can be treated more or less isolated from other concerns. For example, the business domain expert should be able to concentrate on programming the business logic of the application without worrying about persistence management or security.

In this paper, we compare two of these technologies. One of these technologies, *program generation*, is frequently proposed in the context of model-driven architecture[1] and domain-specific languages. The idea behind program generation is that the business logic of the application is expressed in a domain-specific language. The code for other concerns is latter added by a program generator or program transformator, which translates the domain-specific program into a program in a general-purpose language, whereby the generated program contains the code for all concerns.

Aspect-oriented languages [8], on the other hand, are general-purpose languages that try to address the same problem by providing mechanisms to lo-

---

[1] www.omg.org/mda

J.-P. Banâtre et al. (Eds.): UPP 2004, LNCS 3566, pp. 342–354, 2005.

calize and modularize crosscutting concerns, e.g., pointcuts and advice and introductions in AspectJ [1]. In contrast to program generation, however, these mechanisms are *inside* the language itself.

Technically, there is no real difference between the notions of program generation, program transformation, and compilation. Whether a program in some language is interpreted on-the-fly, compiled to some intermediate language, pre- or post-compiled by some tool, or directly translated to machine code, does not make a big difference from a software engineering perspective. The main difference between these two technologies is that the generation- or compilation step is specific to a particular DSL in the first case, whereas this step is a general-purpose translation in the AOP case.

The reminder of this paper is organized as follows. In Sec. 2 we state our perspective why conventional programming languages are insufficient to deal with the problems addressed by domain-specific program generation and AOP. In Sec. 3 we investigate the usage of program generation to deal with this problem and argue that this approach is very powerful and expressive but also implies a number of principal disadvantages of this technology. In Sec. 4 we position aspect-oriented languages as an alternative to domain-specific program generation techniques. In Sec. 5 we discuss the result of the comparison and conclude.

2   Conventional Languages and the Problem of Non-hierarchical Modularity

Let us at first discuss, why conventional languages like Java or C# are insufficient to build domain-specific languages. Each of these languages has mechanisms to define new names (procedures, classes, etc.) and give meaning to them. Hence, programming languages do not have a fixed vocabulary but are inherently extensible because we can define new names (e.g., a procedure) in terms of the vocabulary defined so far (e.g., implementation of a procedure).

Since a procedure definition also acts as an abstraction boundary (we can use a procedure as black-box), the conventional notion of a domain-specific library of functions, data structures, etc., seems to be an ideal solution to our problem outlined in the introduction: Procedure- and data-type implementations hide the concerns that are not interesting from the perspective of the respective domain; the programmer can just use the domain-specific abstractions defined in the library.

However, this approach does not work if the concerns encapsulated in the library do not fit to the modular structure of the respective domain: Conventional abstraction mechanisms (like functional, procedural, or class-based abstraction) are very good at creating a *hierarchy* of abstraction layers. At every layer boundary, we can hide the details of a particular concern to the users of the layer. The problem with this approach is that some concerns cannot be modularized in terms of the modular structure provided by a lower-level abstraction layer: A concern has to fit into the modular structure of the lower-level abstraction [9].

We can also view the problem from the following perspective: It is well-known that the criteria which we choose to decompose software systems into modules has significant impact on the software engineering properties of the software. In [13] Parnas observed that a data-centric decomposition eases changes in the representation of data structures and algorithms operating on them. Following on Parnas work, Garlan et al. [5] argue that function-centric decomposition on the other side better supports adding new features to the system, a change which they show to be difficult with the data-centric decomposition.

Conventional software decomposition techniques, including object-oriented decomposition, are weak at supporting multi-view decomposition, i.e., the ability to simultaneously breakdown the system into inter-related units, whereby each breakdown is guided by independent criteria. What current decomposition technology enables is to view a system at different abstraction levels, resulting in several *hierarchical* models of it, with each model be a refined version of its predecessor in the abstraction levels.

By multi-view decomposition, we mean support for simultaneous *crosscutting* rather than *hierarchical* models. Our perception of the world depends heavily on the perspective from which we look at it: Every software system can be conceived from multiple different perspectives, resulting in different decompositions of it into different "domain-specific" types and notations. In general, these view-specific decompositions are equally reasonable, none of them being a subordinate of the others, and the overall definition of the system results from a superimposition of them.

Models resulting from simultaneous decomposition of the system according to different criteria are in general "crosscutting" with respect to the execution of the system resulting from their composition. With the conceptual framework used so far, *crosscutting* can be defined as a relation between two models with respect to the execution of the software described by the models. This relation if defined via *projections* of models (hierarchies).

A projection of a model M on the execution space of a program is a partition of the execution space into subsets $o_1, \ldots, o_n$ such that each subset o_i corresponds to a leaf in the model. Now, two models, M and M', are said to be crosscutting, if there exist at least two sets o and o' from their respective projections, such that, $o \cap o'$, and neither $o \subseteq o'$, nor $o' \subseteq o1$. On the contrary, a model M is a *hierarchical refinement* of a model M' if their projections $o_1, \ldots, o_n$ and $o'_1, \ldots, o'_m$ are in a subset relation to each other as follows: there is a mapping $p : \{1, \ldots, n\} \to \{1, \ldots, m\}$ such that $\forall i \in \{1, \ldots, n\} : o_i \subseteq o'_{p(i)}$.

The motivating observation for both the aspect-oriented paradigm and for program generation techniques is that a programming technique that does not support simultaneous decomposition of systems along different criteria suffers from what we call *arbitrariness of the decomposition hierarchy* problem, which manifests itself as tangling and scattering of code in the resulting software, with known impacts on maintainability and extendibility. With a "single-minded" decomposition technique that supports only hierarchical models, we have to choose one fixed classification sequence. However, the problem is that with a fixed classification sequence, only one concern is expressed concisely in terms of its inherent concepts whereas all other concerns are tangled in the resulting hierarchical structure. Crosscutting models are themselves not the problem, since they are inherent in the domains we model. The problem is that our languages and decomposition techniques do not (properly) support crosscutting modularity.

In the case of program generation, domain-specific languages are not realized by means of libraries but by means of specifying a generator that transforms a program written in a DSL to some general-purpose language. The code for crosscutting models is added at the appropriate places in the generation or transformation step.

In the case of AOP, domain-specific languages are realized by domain-specific libraries defined and used in a general-purpose language. The code for crosscutting models is combined with the code of the library and its client by means of crosscutting mechanisms. The term *domain-specific embedded language* (DSEL) is sometimes used to describe this approach to domain-specific languages [6].

3   Program Generation (Pros and Cons)

Let us now consider the usage of program generation techniques to cope with the identified problem. The most comon program generation techniques for domain-specific languages are as follows [15]:

- In *API-based approaches*, programs are generated in a classic meta-programming fashion: The programs to be generated have a first-class representation in the generator language (e.g., a first-class representation of the AST or the byte-code) that can be manipulated arbitrarily.
- In *template-based approaches*, code is generated by instantiating some kind of code template with some parameters (the domain-specific program). The advantage of template-based approaches over conventional procedural abstraction is that it is more flexible with respect to the kinds of parameters – with procedural abstraction, we can only abstract over first-class values, whereas with template parameters, we can abstract over all kinds of entities (e.g., procedure names, types, etc.)
- In *meta-model-based approaches*, the generation process is structured by mapping the entities in the domain-specific program to entities defined in a meta-model. For example, the domain-specific concept "Person" may be mapped to the meta-model concept "persistent object". The advantage over the template-based approach lies in the separation of the code generation logic and the implementation of the meta-model concepts, which can varied independently (to some degree).
- In *attribute-based approaches*, the domain-specific parts of the language are encoded in the form of attributes – arbitrary information that can be associated with procedures, methods, or classes. The remainder of the code is written in a general-purpose language. For example, a class can be marked as

"session bean" in an attribute of the class. This enables the code generator to transform program entities based on their attributes.

These techniques differ in the expressiveness of the transformation and in the degree of structure provided for programming transformation. API-based approaches are the most general, in a sense, because any transformation semantics whatsoever can be exressed. On the other hand, this approach does not imply any structure for the transformation, hence it is hard to write and understand such transformers. Template-based approaches can be understood more easily, because they are based on the intuitive metaphor of instantiating a template. On the other hand, the expressiveness is limited because not every transformation can be expressed in terms of template instantiation. Meta-model based approaches are closely associated to the notion of overlapping crosscutting models, because the domain model is mapped to a (crosscutting) meta-model. Attribute-based approaches are special in that languages like Java or C# have special support for attributes (called *annotations* in Java) - a language extension is thus not needed to introduce a new kind of attribute. From a pragmatic point of view, this approach has several advantages because existing tools for the base language (e.g., IDEs and parsers) can be reused. From a conceptual point of view, attribute-based DSLs are equivalent to having dedicated DSLs separate from the base language. They can be implemented by using any of the first four approaches.

Hence, any transformation semantics whatsoever can easily be encoded using one of these approaches. Another advantage is that it is easy to incorporate artefacts from several different programming language or non-programming artefacts such as documentation.

However, domain-specific code generation also has some severe disadvantages, which we want to outline in the following:

- **Understandability of the programming model:** Program generation is hard to understand: Instead of encoding the intention of the programmer directly, one has to think about the semantics of a program in terms of the program it generates. This additional "indirection" is a tremendous burden for both the DSL programmer and the programmer of the code generator. The situation becomes worse if the concerns to be added by the generator cannot be mapped directly to locations in the source code (dynamic crosscutting). For example, the applicability of a generated statement may depend on dynamic conditions like the control flow or the history of the execution. In this case, complicated conditional logic further obfuscates both the code of the generator and the generated code.
- **Scalability:** Today's programs range tremendously in their size. This is the reason why any abstraction mechanism that works only on one abstraction level and cannot be re-applied recursively does not scale – there are too many orders of magnitude w.r.t. the size of applications in order to have different abstraction mechanisms for different program sizes. In the context of program generation, recursive application of this abstraction mechanism

would mean that program generators would generate code that is the input to a lower-level code generator. However, each of these layers would introduce an additional layer of "meta"-indirection: In order to understand code in the base language, one has to think about every transformation step. Such a hierarchy of code generators would be very hard to understand and maintain, which is probably the reason why it is hardly used in practice (to the best knowledge of the authors).

- **Composability:** In general, the features added by code generators cannot be organized hierarchically. Hence, in order to make code generators reusable, a separation of concerns for code generators would be desirable as well, meaning that every code generator concentrates only on one concern. However, for this mechanism to work, code generators would have to be composable. However, in general it is unclear how two domain-specific languages and their generators can be composed, hence the semantics of a composition cannot be computed automatically but has to be implemented by hand for every single case of composition.
- **Traceability of errors:** If the program contains errors, traceability of errors becomes an important issue: What is the location and cause of the error? This is frequently a problem in the context of program generation because errors frequently show up only in the context of the target language and need to be mapped to their meaning in the source language. For example, the static type system of the target language may indicate an error in generated code. Tools like debuggers typically work only for general-purpose languages - if dynamic errors should be investigated, the programmer suddenly has to deal with generated code and has to map the generated code back to his original code.
- **Preplanning and insufficiency:** Basically all features that are added by the program generator have to be known in advance, before writing the program generator. Writing a highly-configurable program generator makes the required effort even bigger. Hence, one either has the problem that one needs either perfect preplanning, or that the DSL and its generator may be insufficient for some purposes.
- **Redundancy:** To support a new domain-specific model requires to write a new program generator. A scalable domain-specific language needs features similar to those already available in conventional languages (e.g., functional abstraction, control structures, type-checking). This means that these features have to be re-invented and re-implemented or are simply missing in DSLs.

4   Aspect-Oriented Languages

Let us now consider aspect-oriented languages as an alternative to domain-specific program generation techniques. It is our conviction that we should strive for new general-purpose abstraction mechanisms for domain-specific models that render the need for isolated DSLs and domain-specific program generators superfluous. Our position is that general-purpose languages (GPLs) with built-in support for expressing the interaction (superimposition) of independent partial models in accordance with the principles of abstraction and information hiding are needed.

In a model of software construction as a superimposition of different partial crosscutting models, the key questions are how to express this superimposition in a modular way and what abstractions are needed for the interface between crosscutting models. Fig. 1 is an attempt to illustrate the issue schematically. The figure illustrates the case when there are two overlapping models of the same system. The tricky part is to describe how these two models interact with each other in the execution space without exposing too much of the implementation details of the models. This is illustrated by the black box with lollipops on top of the lower model: We need a kind of *interface* to a crosscutting model that hides its implementation details equivalent to the well-known black-box abstraction.

We distinguish between mechanisms for *structural (concept) mapping* between partial models and mechanisms for *behavioral (control/data flow) mapping*. These two mechanisms are illustrated in Fig. 2, by a mapping of two object-oriented crosscutting models. In order to express how these two independent models interact in creating a whole, we need both to express how their concepts map to each other, illustrated by the arrows in the upper part of the figure, as well as how there control flows interact, illustrated by the lower part of Fig. 2.

We view aspect-oriented languages, especially AspectJ [7], as an excellent starting point for the new generation of GPLs that we envisage. However, we observe that more powerful abstraction mechanisms are needed than currently supported by these languages. In [10, 11] we outline the deficiencies of AspectJ

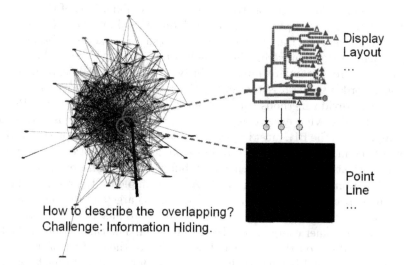

Fig. 1. Information hiding and crosscutting models

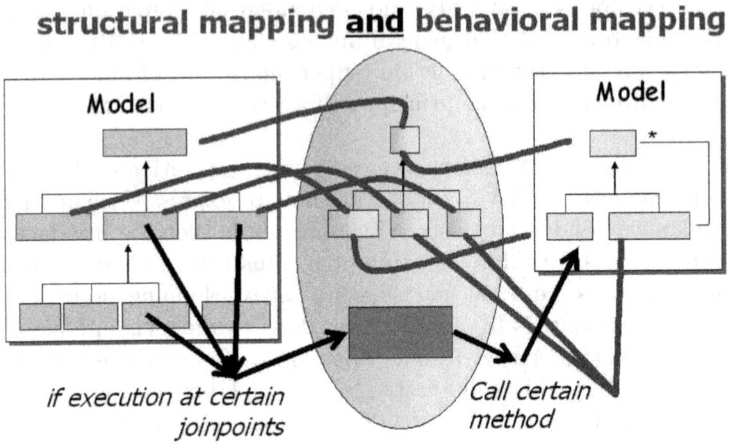

structural mapping and behavioral mapping

Fig. 2. Superimposing crosscutting models

with respect to the first facet of expressing model superimposition. In [11], we argue that AspectJ is lacking a layer module concept as powerful as the one supported in feature-oriented approaches and discuss how the aspect-oriented language Caesar [10] solves these problems. In the following, we will briefly summarize how Caesar [10] advances AspectJ with respect to structural mapping. Subsequently, we outline the problems with current mechanisms for behavioral mapping as well as ideas about how to solve these problems.

4.1   Combining Domain-Specific Models

Caesar enables to encode domain specific models in their own model and ontology and provides language constructs to express combinations of these different models. A central concept is the notion of bidirectional interfaces (BI for short). A BI serves to specify the abstractions that together make up a feature/aspect independent of the context in which the feature/aspect will be deployed.

BIs differ from standard interfaces in two ways. First, BIs exploit interface nesting in order to express the abstractions of an aspect and their interplay. Second, BIs divide methods into provided and expected contracts. Provided methods describe what every component that is described in terms of this model (i.e., implements the BI), must implement. Expected methods represent variation points of the model that are used to integrate features into a concrete system.

For illustration, the BI Pricing that bundles the definition of the generic pricing functionality is shown in Fig. 3. As an example for the reification of provided and expected contracts, consider Customer.charge and Product.basicPrice in Fig. 3. The ability to charge a customer for a product is at the core of pricing; hence, Customer.charge is marked as provided. The calculation of the basic price of a product, on the other hand, is specific to the context of usage which determines what will be the products to charge for; hence, Product.basicPrice is marked as expected.

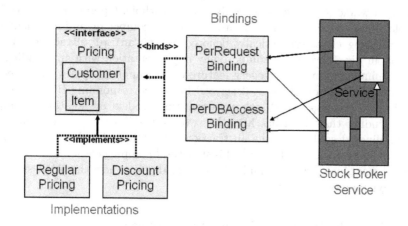

Fig. 3. Overview of Caesar concepts

Different components can be implemented in terms of this domain model. Later on, such a model can be superimposed on an existing system by means of a so-called *binding*, which defines both a structural and a behavioral mapping in order to coordinate both worlds. The categorization of the operations into expected and provided comes with a new model of what it means to implement a BI: We explicitly distinguish between implementing a BI's provided contract and binding the same BI's expected contract. Two different keywords are used for this purpose, implements, respectively binds. In the following, we refer to classes that are declared with the keyword implements, respectively binds, as aspect implementations, respectively aspect bindings.

An implementation must (a) implement all provided methods of the BI and (b) provide an implementation class for each of the BI's nested interfaces. In doing so, it is free to use respective expected methods. Furthermore, an implementation may or may not add methods and state to the BI's abstractions it implements. In Fig. 3, two possible implementations of the `Pricing` BI are shown, implementing two different pricing strategies, a regular pricing schema in `RegularPricing` and a discount pricing in `DiscountPricing`.

An aspect binding must provide zero or more nested binding classes (declared via binds clauses) for each of the BI's nested interfaces (we may have multiple bindings of the same interface). In these binding classes, all expected methods have to be implemented. Just as implementation classes can use their respective expected facets, the implementation of the expected methods of a BI and its nested interfaces can call methods declared in the respective provided facets. In Fig. 3, two possible bindings of the `Pricing` BI are shown, implementing two different pricing modes, one in which we charge per request (`PerRequestBinding`) and another one in which we charge per database resources used (`PerDBAccess-Binding`).

Implementation and binding classes are in their own not operational, i.e., cannot be instantiated; the respective contracts implemented by them are only parts of a whole and make sense only within a whole. Operational classes that completely implement an interface are created by composing an implementation and a binding class, syntactically denoted as aBI<anImpl,aBinding>. In the example in Fig. 3, we could compose any implementation with any binding.

To summarize, in Caesar every feature can be implemented with respect to its own model and ontology as described by the corresponding BI. This model can then be composed with other crosscutting models by creating an appropriate binding that describes how the two models interact which each other. The bindings describe how the abstractions of the models relate to each other structurally by creating adapters. This structural mapping is then used in the behavioral mapping (pointcuts and advice) that describe how the models interact in the dynamic control flow.

4.2   Towards Expressive Pointcuts Languages

In [11], we argue that AspectJ is superior to feature-oriented approaches (FOAs for short) [14, 3, 2] for its sophisticated and powerful pointcut model that allows to express the behavioral mapping in a more precise and abstract way as it is possible with FOA. In contrast to the FOA solution, no shadowing is necessary in order to trigger the functionality of a feature in the base application.

Pointcuts enable us to abstract over control flows. With more advanced mechanisms such as wildcards, field get/set, cflow, etc., a pointcut definition also becomes more stable with respect to changes in the base structure than the corresponding set of overridden methods in FOA. The use of pointcuts instead of shadowing parts of an inherited base structure avoids the scalability problem mentioned in the FOA discussion.

The key point is that with pointcuts we can abstract over details in the control flow that are irrelevant to the feature integration. Equivalent abstraction mechanisms are missing in FOAs. In its current instantiation, Caesar has adopted the pointcut language of AspectJ. However, this language has its limitations both with regard to the abstraction mechanisms as well as the richness of the underlying model of program execution.

AspectJ-like languages come with a set of predefined pointcut designators, e.g., call or get, and the standard set operations for combining them. What is, however, missing is an abstraction mechanism equivalent to the well-known functional abstraction that would allow to pass the result of a pointcut as a parameter to another pointcut. Furthermore, the underlying model of program execution is not reach enough.

To convey an intuition of what we mean, let us consider identifying all setter join points were the value of a variable is changed that is read in the control flow of a certain method, m, the goal being that we would like to recall m, at any such point. Assuming a hypothetical AspectJ compiler that employs some static analysis techniques to predict control flows, one can write a pointcut p1 that selects all getters in the predicted control flow of m. However, it is not possible to combine p1 with another pointcut p2 which takes the result of p1 as a parameter, retrieves the names of the variables read in the join points selected

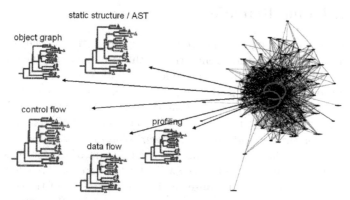

Fig. 4. Crosscutting models of program semantics

by p1, and than selects the set of setter join points where one of these variables is changed. What we need is the ability to reason about p1 and p2.

Furthermore, various models of program semantics are needed to enable reasoning about program execution. For example, the abstract syntax tree (AST) alone is not a very good basis for quantifying over dynamics of program execution because it is a very indirect representation of the program execution semantics that makes it intractable to specify dynamic properties.

Our vision is that it should be possible to reason about a pointcut, and especially to define new pointcuts by reasoning about other pointcuts. We envision an AOP model in which pointcuts are sets of nodes in some representation of the program's semantics. Such sets are selected by queries on node attributes written in a query language and can be passed around to other query functions as parameters. These semantic models can be as diverse as abstract syntax trees, control flow graphs, data flow graphs, object graphs or profiling models; Fig. 4) schematically illustrates pointcuts as queries over multiple rich models of program semantics.

We have some initial very encouraging results with a prototype implementation of the sketched approach in the interpreter for the aspect-oriented language ALPHA [12]. ALPHA's interpreter supports 4 models of programs: The AST, the type assignment of the static type checker, the dynamic execution trace, and the dynamic object graph. These models are represented as logic facts; pointcuts in ALPHA are logic queries over the logic databases produced by the interpreter. In [12], we also discuss a technique for an efficient implementation of the approach that uses abstract interpretation of pointcuts to calculate join point shadows off-line prior to program execution. Facts are produced at runtime and queries are evaluated only at these points.

5   Concluding Remarks

Since aspect-oriented languages are general-purpose languages, they do not suffer from the problems of program generation outlined in Sec. 3: Concerning *understandability*, there is no indirection - code can be understood by reasoning only about the program and not something that is generated. Crosscutting that depends on dynamic conditions can be (based on the expressiveness of the pointcut language) encoded inside of declarative pointcuts instead of complicated conditional logic. Concerning *scalability* and *composability*, aspects can usually refer and reason about other aspects, and the combination of aspects has a defined meaning (although it may not necessarily be the intended meaning). *Errors* can be traced more directly, because the intermediate step of translating into a general-purpose language is missing. *Preplanning* and *insufficiency* are not such a big problem because crosscutting models can be added or extended by writing new aspects in the language itself. Since there is only one compiler/generator, redundancy is also not a problem.

However, aspect-oriented languages are also not without problems. Conventional aspect-oriented languages do not provide any structure to combine independently developed crosscutting models (addressed by meta-model approaches in the case of program generation). This is where we hope that the model binding mechanism of Caesar will prove useful. Also, the pointcut languages of today's AOP languages are limited in their expressiveness; a problem that we try to address in our ALPHA language [12]. With program generation techniques, it is easy to combine multiple different artefacts such as source files from different languages, descriptors, etc. This is not possible with current AOP languages. In [4] we describe a pointcut language that can be used to combine information from different artefacts by providing a common representation of all artefacts in XML and using the query language XQuery as pointcut language. Finally, program generation techniques make it easy to generate source files in a specific format, e.g., in order to interoperate with some legacy or 3rd party application. This is a technical problem that cannot be solved offhand with a general-purpose aspect-oriented language.

To summarize: Both program generation and aspect-oriented programming are powerful techniques to reduce the complexity of software. We have argued that aspect-oriented programming is an interesting alternative to using domain-specific program generators. Although AOP has still some limitations, we are confident that future AOP languages can subsume most applications of program generation today.

References

1. AspectJ homepage, 2005. http://aspectj.org.
2. D. Batory, J. N. Sarvela, and A. Rauschmayer. Scaling step-wise refinement. *International Conference on Software Engineering (ICSE '03)*, 2003.
3. D. Batory, V. Singhal, J. Thomas, S. Dasari, B. Geraci, and M. Sirkin. The genvoca model of software-system generators. *IEEE Software*, 11(5), 1994.

4. M. Eichberg, M. Mezini, K. Ostermann, and T. Schäfer. Xirc: A kernel for cross-artifact information engineering in software development environments. In B. Werner, editor, *Eleventh Working Conference on Reverse Engineering*, pages 182–191, Delft, Netherlands, November 2004. IEEE Computer Society.

5. D. Garlan, G. E. Kaiser, and D. Notkin. Using tool abstraction to compose systems. *Computer*, 25(6):30–38, 1992.

6. P. Hudak. Building domain-specific embedded languages. *ACM Comput. Surv.*, 28(4es):196, 1996.

7. G. Kiczales, E. Hilsdale, J. Hugunin, M. Kersten, J. Palm, and W. G. Griswold. An overview of AspectJ. In *Proceedings of ECOOP '01*, 2001.

8. G. Kiczales, J. Lamping, A. Mendhekar, C. Maeda, C. Lopes, J.-M. Loingtier, and J. Irwin. Aspect-oriented programming. In M. Aksit and S. Matsuoka, editors, *Proceedings ECOOP'97*, LNCS 1241, pages 220–242, Jyvaskyla, Finland, 1997. Springer-Verlag.

9. M. Mezini and K. Ostermann. Integrating independent components with on-demand remodularization. In *Proceedings of OOPSLA '02, Seattle, USA*, 2002.

10. M. Mezini and K. Ostermann. Conquering aspects with Caesar. In *Proc. International Conference on Aspect-Oriented Software Development (AOSD '03), Boston, USA*, 2003.

11. M. Mezini and K. Ostermann. Variability management with feature-oriented programming and aspects. In *Proceedings of FSE '04 (to appear)*, 2004.

12. K. Ostermann, M. Mezini, and C. Bockisch. Expressive pointcuts for increased modularity. *European Conference on Object-Oriented Programming (ECOOP'05), to appear*, 2005.

13. D. L. Parnas. On the criteria to be used in decomposing systems into modules. *Communications of the ACM*, 15(12):1053–1058, 1972.

14. Y. Smaragdakis and D. Batory. Implementing layered designs with mixin-layers. In *Proceedings of ECOOP '98*, pages 550–570, 1998.

15. M. Völter. A collection of patterns for program generation. In *Proceedings Euro-PLoP '03*, 2003.

Generative Programming from a Post Object-Oriented Programming Viewpoint

Shigeru Chiba

Dept. of Mathematical and Computing Sciences,
Tokyo Institute of Technology
chiba@is.titech.ac.jp

Abstract. This paper presents an application of generative programming to reduce the complications of the protocol for using an application framework written in an object-oriented language. It proposes that a programmable program translator could allow framework users to write a simple program, which is automatically translated by the translator into a program that fits the framework protocol. Then it mentions the author's experience with Javassist, which is a translator toolkit for Java, and discusses a research issue for applying this idea to real-world software development.

1 Introduction

Object-oriented programming languages have enabled us to develop component libraries that are often called *application frameworks*. They are sets of related classes that can be specialized or instantiated to implement a new application. A well-known simple example of such libraries is a graphical user interface (GUI) library. Since application frameworks provide a large portion of the functionality that application software has to implement, they can significantly reduce the development costs of application software.

However, application frameworks involve hidden costs. The developers who want to build their own application software with an application framework must first learn how to use the framework. Then they must write their programs to follow the complex protocol provided by the framework. The complexity of the protocol often originates from the use of design patterns [6] in the framework. Design patterns are recurring solutions to design problems frequently found in object-oriented programming, such as how software should be decomposed into objects and how objects should interact with each other. Although the design patterns themselves are useful, the use of them in the implementation of the framework often makes it difficult for the framework users to understand the framework protocol since the use of the design patterns is usually invisible from the framework users.

The costs due to following the framework protocol are considerably large if the framework provides relatively complex functionality. For example, to implement GUI with a typical GUI library (i.e. framework), the developers must learn the

J.-P. Banâtre et al. (Eds.): UPP 2004, LNCS 3566, pp. 355–366, 2005.

basic GUI architecture and a few concepts such as a callback and a listener. Then they must carefully write their programs to implement such a callback method and listener. To implement a web application on top of the J2EE framework, the developers must first take a tutorial course about J2EE programming and then write a program to follow the complicated J2EE protocol. For example, they must define two interfaces whenever they define one component class.

In this paper, we present an idea for reducing the hidden costs involved in application frameworks written in object-oriented languages. Our idea is to use a *programmable* program translator/generator, which automatically generates glue code for making the program written by a developer match the protocol supplied by an application framework. Thus the developer do not have to learn or follow the protocol given by the framework. Note that the program translator is not a fully-automated system. It is driven by a control program that is written by the framework developer. This is why the program translator used in our proposal is called programmable. In our idea, the framework must be supplied with the control program for customizing a program translator for that framework.

A research issue on this idea is how to design a language used to write a control program of the program translators/generator. We have developed a Java bytecode translator toolkit, named *Javassist* [3], and built several systems on top of that toolkit. Our experience in this study revealed that a programmable translator such as Javassist can be used to implement our idea. However, control programs for Javassist are still somewhat complicated and thus writing such a control program is not a simple task for framework developers. Studying a language for writing control programs is one of the future work.

2   Object-Oriented Application Framework

Object-oriented programming languages enable a number of programming techniques, some of which are known as the design patterns [6]. These techniques play a crucial role in constructing a modern application framework. In some sense, they are always required to construct an application framework that provides complex functionality, in particular, non-functional concerns such as persistence, distribution, and user interface. The application framework that provides such functionality would be difficult to have simple API (Application Programming Interface) if object-oriented programming techniques are not used.

On the other hand, the users of such an application framework written in an object-oriented language must learn the protocol for using that framework. They must understand how design patterns have been applied to the framework, or they must know at least which methods should be overridden to obtain desirable effects and so on. These efforts are often major obstacles to use the application framework. A larger application framework tends to require a longer training period to the users of that framework.

The complications of such a framework protocol mainly come from the use of object-oriented programming techniques. For example, we below show a (pseudo) Java program written with the standard GUI framework (Java AWT/Swing framework). It is a program for showing a clock. If this program does not have GUI, then it would be something like the following simple and straightforward one:

```
class Clock {
  static void main(String[] args) {
    while (true) {
      System.out.println(new Date());
      Thread.sleep(60000L /* milliseconds */);
    }
  }
}
```

This program only prints the current time on the console every one minute. "new Date()" constructs an object representing the current time.

We can use the standard GUI library (Java AWT/Swing framework) to extend this program to have better look. To do that, we must read some tutorial book of the Java AWT/Swing framework and edit the program above to fit the protocol that the book tells us. First, we would find that the Clock class must extend Panel. Also, the Clock class must prepare a paint method for drawing a picture of clock on the screen. Thus you would define the paint method and modify the main method. The main method must call not the paint method but the *auxiliary* repaint method, which the tutorial book tells us to call when the picture is updated. The following is the resulting program (again, it is pseudo code. it cannot run without further modification to fit the real protocol of the framework):

```
class Clock extends Panel {
  void paint(Graphics g) {
    // draw a clock on the screen.
  }
  static void main(String[] args) {
    Clock c = new Clock();
    while (true) {
      c.repaint();
      Thread.sleep(60000L /* milliseconds */);
    }
  }
}
```

Note that the structure of the program is far different from that of the original program. It is never simple or straightforward. For example, why do we have to define the paint method, which dedicates only to drawing a picture? Why does the main method have to call not the paint method but the repaint method, which indirectly calls the paint method? To answer these questions, we have to understand the underlying architecture of the framework provided by the GUI library. Since this architecture is built with a number of programming techniques, such as inheritance, callback handlers, and multi threading, and most of tutorial books do not describe such details, understanding the underlying architecture is often difficult for "average" developers who do not have the background of GUI programming.

Despite this problem, a number of application frameworks have been developed and design patterns are really popular in software industry. An obviously better approach would be to develop a *domain-specific language* instead of an application framework for that domain. Domain-specific languages provide specialized syntax and semantics for a particular application domain. In the research community, even domain-specific languages for helping to program with the design patterns in [6] have been developed [13, 1].

However, industrial developers prefer to using a standard general-purpose language that comes with comprehensive tool supports. They are often reluctant to learn and use a new language, for which only poor tool supports would be available. In fact, a domain-specific language with poor tool supports would not improve the productivity of developers compared to a general-purpose language with powerful tool supports. On the other hand, developing a domain-specific language with powerful tool supports is considerably expensive. Therefore, a number of application frameworks have been developed instead of domain-specific languages. They can be regarded as domain-specific programming systems that are less powerful but less expensive to develop than domain-specific languages. Also, they allow developers to use their preferred standard language and poweful development tools.

3   Protocol-Less Framework and Programmable Program Translator

To overcome the problem mentioned in the previous section, we propose an idea of using a *programmable* program translator. The users of an application framework should not be concerned about "the protocol" of a framework when writing their application programs. They should be able to write simple and intuitively understandable programs, which should be automatically translated into programs that fit the protocol for using the framework. I think that reducing the awareness about a framework protocol due to object-orientation is a key feature of post object-oriented programming.

Ideally, the transformation from the original Clock class into the GUI-based Clock class shown in the previous section should be performed automatically by a program translator instead of a human being. At least, the following modification for making the original program fit the protocol of the framework should be performed by a program translator:

- The Clock class must extend the Panel class. User classes of an application framework must often extend a class provided by the framework or implement an interface provided by the framework. Such class hierarchy should be automatically maintained by a program translator.
- The Clock class must declare the paint method. User classes of an application framework must often override some specific methods. Such overriding should be implicit. If necessary, the method drawing a picture should be able to have some other name than paint. If paint is not declared in user classes,

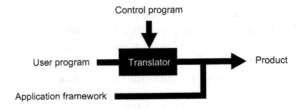

Fig. 1. Programmable program translator

the default method declaration of paint should be automatically added by a program translator.

For example, the program manually written by a human being should look like the following:

```
@GUI class Clock {
  @drawer void drawClock(Graphics g) {
    // draw a clock on the screen.
  }
  static void main(String[] args) {
    Clock c = new Clock();
    while (true) {
      c.drawClock();
      Thread.sleep(60000L /* milliseconds */);
    }
  }
}
```

Here, @GUI and @drawer are annotations (meta tags) for describing the developer's intention. The program translator should recognize these annotations and automatically translate the program above into one that really fits the framework protocol.

Executing the automatic program transformation presented above is not realistic if any hints are not given. In our idea, this transformation is executed by a program translator controlled by a control program written by the developer of the application framework (Figure 1). Thus the program translator must be *programmable*. Since the framework developer knows the underlying architecture of that framework, writing such a control program should be fairly easy for her. Application frameworks should be distributed together with program translators and control programs of them.

The programmable program translator proposed here can be regarded as a compiler toolkit for *domain-specific languages*. Here, a domain means the target domain of an application framework. Although the programmable program translator does not provide new syntax designed for a particular application domain, it provides programming supports specialized for that domain within confines of the original syntax of the base language. Specialized syntax for a particular domain often makes programming easier but it is not an all-around solution. Thus it would not be a serious problem that the programmable program translator cannot provide new syntax. Furthermore, designing appropriate syntax for a given domain is not a simple task and badly designed syntax rather decreases productivity of developers.

4   Javassist

A challenge is to develop a good language for describing a control program given to the program translator in Figure 1. Toward this goal, we have been developing a Java bytecode translator toolkit named *Javassist* [3]. It is a Java class library for transforming a compiled Java program at the bytecode level (the bytecode is assembly code in Java).

A unique feature of Javassist is that it provides source-level abstraction for the developers who want to write a program for transforming Java bytecode. There are several similar Java libraries that allow editing a class file (a compiled Java binary file). These libraries help the users read a class file, parse it, and produce objects that directly represent the internal data structures included in the class file. The users can modify the contents of the class file through these objects. However, since these objects directly correspond to the data structures in a class file, the users must learn the specifications of such internal data structures so that they can use these objects for modifying the contents of a class file. For example, they have to learn what the constant pool is and what the code attribute is. The former is a symbol table and the latter is a code block representing a method body.

Since Javassist provides source-level abstraction, the users of Javassist do not have to learn the specifications of the Java class file. Javassist translates the internal data structures in a class file into objects that represent the concepts familiar to Java developers (Figure 2), such as a class and a method. The users of Javassist can parse a class file and obtain objects representing a class, fields, methods, and constructors derived from the original class file. If the users change attributes of those objects, then the changes are reflected on the class file. For example, if the setName method is called on an object representing a class, Javassist changes the name of the class that the original class file represents. If the users give Javassist a String object representing the source code of a method, Javassist compiles it and adds that new method to an existing class file.

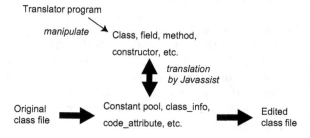

Fig. 2. Javassist translates bytecode-level concepts into source-level concepts

4.1   Metaobject Protocol (MOP)

The design of Javassist is based on the idea of *metaobject protocol* [7], also known as *reflection* [11, 10]. The objects into which Javassist translates the internal data structure of a class file are similar to the objects provided by the Java reflection API. They represent a class, field, or method. However, unlike the objects of the Java reflection API, which provide only limited ability for reflection, the objects of Javassist are modifiable; the state of these objects can be changed and the changes are reflected onto the original class file. In other words, Javassist enables advanced macro processing through a metaobject protocol instead of abstract syntax trees reproduced from a class file.

The original idea of metaobject protocols and reflection is to produce objects representing the meta entities of a program. These objects are often called *metaobjects* for distinction from normal objects. Examples of the meta entities are classes, source programs, runtime environments, compilers, virtual machines, and so on. They are entities used for program execution but not the data directly processed by that program. The data processed by a program, or the values computed in a program, are base-level entities while the structures for processing data are meta-level entities.

Metaobject protocols have two significant operations, *reify* and *reflect*, although these operations are often implicit. The reify operation is to produce a metaobject representing some meta entity in a program. The reflect operation is to apply the changes of the state of the metaobject back to the original meta entity. Suppose that a Clock class is a meta entity. The reify operation produces a class metaobject representing Clock. If the program calls the setSuperclass method on that metaobject, the internal state of the metaobject will be changed but the original definition of the Clock class will not be changed until the reflect operation is applied to the metaobject.

Early metaobject protocols (and ones currently called *runtime* metaobjects) allow a program to perform the reify and reflect operations on that running program itself. This means that the program can modify itself during the run time. Implementing this meta circularity with reasonable efficiency has been a significant research topic in this research area. Note that metaobjects are not identical to the meta entities represented by those metaobjects. The metaobjects are objects that can be dealt with as other normal objects while they are associated with the corresponding meta entities by the runtime system, that is to say, they are *causally connected* to the meta entities.

The metaobjects of Javassist does not represent the meta entities of a running program itself; it represents the meta entities of a class file, which is a program that has not been loaded yet. Hence the metaobject protocol of Javassist is categorized into *compile-time* metaobject protocols [2] (or load-time metaobject protocol). The compile-time metaobject protocols allow the reify and reflect operations only at compile time while it keeps the well-designed abstraction of the programming interface of runtime metaobject protocols. However, that limitation of compile-time metaobject protocols is paid off since the runtime overheads due to metaobject protocols are zero (or negligible). Furthermore, that limitation is not a serious problem in most of practical scenarios.

4.2   Aspect-Oriented Programming (AOP)

The design of Javassist also borrowed ideas from aspect-oriented programming [8]. Aspect-oriented programming allows developers to modularize a *crosscutting concern*, which is a concern that cannot be implemented as a separate independent module or component with normal programming paradigms, in particular, object-oriented programming. Although the implementation of a crosscutting concern in object-oriented programming is spread over (or cuts across) classes of other concerns, aspect-oriented programming provides a mechanism for separating the implementation of such a crosscutting concern from other unrelated modules such as classes.

Example: A typical example of crosscutting concerns is a logging or tracing concern. The main body of the implementation of logging concern can be modularized into a single class, for example, in Java:

```
class Logging {
  PrintStream output = System.out;
  static void setStream(PrintStream out) {
    output = out;
  }
  static void print(String m) {
    output.println(m);
  }
}
```

However, method calls to the print method in Logging class must be embedded in other classes that want to print a logging message. Suppose that we want to print a logging message when the paint method in the Clock class in Section 2 is executed. We must edit the paint method as following:

```
class Clock extends Panel {
  void paint(Graphics g) {
    Logging.print("** call paint method");    // change!
    // draw a clock on the screen.
  }
  static void main(String[] args) { .. }
}
```

Although this is a very typical Java program, the logging concern is a crosscutting concern since it cuts across Clock class. The logging concern invades the definition of the Clock class. Thus, it is impossible to reuse the Clock class without the Logging class unless the definition of Clock is edited to remove a method call expression to paint. The Clock class and the Logging class are not separated from each other but they are tangled with each other.

AspectJ: Aspect-oriented programming solves this problem. For example, in AspectJ, the Logging concern can be implemented as a single independent module called an *aspect*. AspectJ is an aspect-oriented extension to Java [9]. See the following program:

```
aspect Logging {
  PrintStream output = System.out;
  static void setStream(PrintStream out) {
    output = out;
  }
  static void print(String m) {
    output.println(m);
  }

  // before advice
  before(): call(void Clock.paint(Graphics)) {
    print("** call paint method");
  }
}
```

The original definition of the Clock class does not have to be edited to call the paint method. Thus, the Logging concern is not a crosscutting one in AspectJ.

The advice declaration in the Logging aspect:

```
before(): call(void Clock.paint(Graphics)) {
  print("** call paint method");
}
```

means that the print method must be called just before the paint method in Clock is called. The compiler automatically modifies the definition of the Clock class to implement this behavior.

The key concepts of aspect-oriented programming is joinpoints, pointcuts, and advice. In this programming paradigm, program execution is modeled as a sequence of fine-grained events, such as method calls, field accesses, object creation, and so on. These events are called *joinpoints. pointcuts* are filters of joinpoints. They select interesting joinpoints during program execution. Then, if a joinpoint selected by some pointcut occurs, the *advice* associated to that pointcut is executed. In the case of the example above,

```
call(void Clock.paint(Graphics))
```

is a pointcut. The advice is the declaration beginning with before and ending with a block {..}.

A crosscutting concern is implemented as a set of advice in an aspect. The connection between the aspect and other classes is described by pointcuts. Joinpoints can be regarded as execution points at which an aspect and a class are connected to each other.

Separating the Repaint Protocol: AspectJ allows us to separately implement the repaint protocol shown in the Clock example of Section 3. The repaint protocol can be implemented as a separate module, that is, an aspect. Although the module implementing the repaint protocol must be manually written in AspectJ, this separation of concern is a significant step toward enabling the protocol-less application framework. As we have seen above, Java does not enable clear separation of the repaint protocol; since the repaint protocol was a crosscutting concern, it was embedded in the application framework and the Clock class and thus the definition of the Clock class was difficult to understand.

If AspectJ is used, the definition of the Clock class can be quite straightforward and ideal:

```
public class Clock {
  public void drawClock(Graphics g) {
    // draw a clock on the screen.
  }
  public static void main(String[] args) {
    Clock c = new Clock();
    while (true) {
      c.drawClock(null);
      Thread.sleep(60000L /* milliseconds */);
    }
  }
}
```

The repaint protocol can be implemented as the following aspect:

```
aspect RepaintProtocol {
  declare parents: Clock extends Panel;
  public void Clock.paint(Graphics g) {
    drawClock(g);
  }

  // around advice
  void around(Clock c, Graphics g):
      call(void Clock.drawClock(Graphics)) && target(c)
      && args(g) && if(g == null) {
    c.repaint();
  }
}
```

This aspect uses AspectJ's mechanism called *intertype declaration*. It first declares that the Clock class extends the Panel class. Then it declares the paint method in the Clock class. paint is a method that only calls the drawClock method. Note that drawClock is a method for drawing a clock although the repaint protocol requires that the name of that method is paint. The Repaint-Protocol aspect fills this gap. Finally, this aspect defines an around advice, which substitutes the call to the repaint method in Panel for the call to the drawClock method. Note that the repaint protocol requires that the repaint method is called for redrawing a clock. This around advice is executed instead of the drawClock method when the drawClock method is called with the null argument. If the around advice is executed, the repaint method in Panel is called.

Javassist and AOP: One of the reasons of the complicated protocols of application frameworks is that application frameworks include a number of crosscutting concerns and hence they must complicate protocols to deal with those concerns. Such crosscutting concerns include repainting, concurrency, mobility, and security. Since the code implementing a crosscutting concern is tangled with the code implementing other concerns, the interface between them cannot be simple or easy to understand and thus the protocol related to that interface is made complicated. Aspect-oriented programming can untangle crosscutting concerns so that the protocol can be simple and easy to understand.

Javassist provides a basic mechanism for aspect-oriented programming. Although Javassist is not a programming language but a class library, the users of Javassist can emulate aspect-oriented programming in Java through the programming interface of Javassist. They can use this mechanism to untangle the implementations of application frameworks so that the interface among the components of the frameworks will be simple and clean. This enables the frameworks to provide simpler protocols for the framework users. Javassist (and other systems based on compile/load-time metaobject protocols) can be also used as a platform for implementing an aspect-oriented language [4, 12].

5   Concluding Remarks

Our experiences with Javassist for several years revealed that developing a programmable program translator mentioned in Section 3 is a realistic idea. However, to actually use this idea for real-world software development, we need further study.

One of the open issues is a programming language for describing program transformation, that is, describing a control program in Figure 1. The source-level abstraction by Javassist has made it easier to write such a control program but making such a program sufficiently generic still needs further study. At least, one control program must be able to translate a number of user programs to fit the protocol of the application framework that the control program was written for. To do that, however, a control program must be able to recognize differences among user programs and find which parts of the code must be edited. For example, in the case of the Clock example shown above, the control program must find which class must extend the Panel class and which method is for drawing a picture on the screen.

As we showed in Section 3, the users might have to give some hints to the control program. Since Java has recently supported annotations (meta data), this approach is now widely being investigated. With annotations, developers can annotate for a class, a method, and a field to describe their roles. However, if they must specify a large amount of annotations, the resulting application framework would be as difficult to use as today's frameworks coming with a complicated protocol.

Another approach is the model driven architecture (MDA) [5]. This allows developers to first draw a platform-independent model of the software in UML. This model is automatically transformed by a model compiler into a model depending on a specific platform and then, if needed, it is further transformed into a (skeleton of) source program written in some concrete language like Java. Since MDA is not a magic architecture, the algorithm of the transformation from a platform-independent model to a specific platform-dependent model must be given to the model compiler in the form of program written by MDA experts.

The language describing this transformation algorithm would be applicable to the program translator proposed in this paper. MDA and the program translator is similar to each other except that MDA is a top-down architecture (from the modeling phase to the implementation phase) whereas the program translator proposed in this paper is a bottom-up, source-code centric architecture. However, today's MDA compilers still require developers to annotate in a platform-independent model so that the MDA compilers can recognize the roles of entities in that platform-independent model. They cannot execute transformation without such annotations. For this reason, MDA has a similar problem mentioned above for Java annotations.

References

1. Bryant, A., Catton, A., Volder, K.D., Murphy, G.: Explicit programming. In: Proc. of 1st Int'l Conf. on Aspect-Oriented Software Development (AOSD 2002), ACM Press (2002) 10–18
2. Chiba, S.: A metaobject protocol for C++. In: Proc. of ACM Conf. on Object-Oriented Programming Systems, Languages, and Applications. Number 10 in SIG-PLAN Notices vol. 30, ACM (1995) 285–299
3. Chiba, S.: Load-time structural reflection in Java. In: ECOOP 2000. LNCS 1850, Springer-Verlag (2000) 313–336
4. Chiba, S., Nakagawa, K.: Josh: an open AspectJ-like language. In: Int'l Conf. on Aspect Oriented Software Development (AOSD'04). (2004) 102–111
5. Frankel, D.S.: Model Driven Architecture: Applying MDA to Enterprise Computing. John Wiley & Sons Inc. (2003)
6. Gamma, E., Helm, R., Johnson, R., Vlissides, J.: Design Patterns. Addison-Wesley (1994)
7. Kiczales, G., des Rivières, J., Bobrow, D.G.: The Art of the Metaobject Protocol. The MIT Press (1991)
8. Kiczales, G., Lamping, J., Mendhekar, A., Maeda, C., Lopes, C., Loingtier, J., Irwin, J.: Aspect-oriented programming. In: ECOOP'97 – Object-Oriented Programming. LNCS 1241, Springer (1997) 220–242
9. Kiczales, G., Hilsdale, E., Hugunin, J., Kersten, M., Palm, J., Griswold, W.G.: An overview of AspectJ. In: ECOOP 2001 – Object-Oriented Programming. LNCS 2072, Springer (2001) 327–353
10. Maes, P.: Concepts and experiments in computational reflection. In: Proc. of ACM Conf. on Object-Oriented Programming Systems, Languages, and Applications. (1987) 147–155
11. Smith, B.C.: Reflection and semantics in Lisp. In: Proc. of ACM Symp. on Principles of Programming Languages. (1984) 23–35
12. Tanter, E.: From Metaobject Protocols to Versatile Kernels for Aspect-Oriented Programming. PhD thesis, Université de Nantes, France and Universidad de Chile, Chile (2004)
13. Tatsubori, M., Chiba, S.: Programming support of design patterns with compile-time reflection. In: Proc. of OOPSLA'98 Workshop on Reflective Programming in C++ and Java. (1998) 56–60

Author Index

Lecture Notes in Computer Science

For information about Vols. 1–3492

please contact your bookseller or Springer

Vol. 3540: H. Kalviainen, J. Parkkinen, A. Kaarna (Eds.), Image Analysis. XXII, 1270 pages. 2005.

Vol. 3537: A. Apostolico, M. Crochemore, K. Park (Eds.), Combinatorial Pattern Matching. XI, 444 pages. 2005.

Vol. 3536: G. Ciardo, P. Darondeau (Eds.), Applications and Theory of Petri Nets 2005. XI, 470 pages. 2005.

Vol. 3535: M. Steffen, G. Zavattaro (Eds.), Formal Methods for Open Object-Based Distributed Systems. X, 323 pages. 2005.

Vol. 3533: M. Ali, F. Esposito (Eds.), Innovations in Applied Artificial Intelligence. XX, 858 pages. 2005. (Subseries LNAI).

Vol. 3532: A. Gómez-Pérez, J. Euzenat (Eds.), The Semantic Web: Research and Applications. XV, 728 pages. 2005.

Vol. 3531: J. Ioannidis, A. Keromytis, M. Yung (Eds.), Applied Cryptography and Network Security. XI, 530 pages. 2005.

Vol. 3530: A. Prinz, R. Reed, J. Reed (Eds.), SDL 2005: Model Driven. XI, 361 pages. 2005.

Vol. 3528: P.S. Szczepaniak, J. Kacprzyk, A. Niewiadomski (Eds.), Advances in Web Intelligence. XVII, 513 pages. 2005. (Subseries LNAI).

Vol. 3527: R. Morrison, F. Oquendo (Eds.), Software Architecture. XII, 263 pages. 2005.

Vol. 3526: S.B. Cooper, B. Löwe, L. Torenvliet (Eds.), New Computational Paradigms. XVII, 574 pages. 2005.

Vol. 3525: A.E. Abdallah, C.B. Jones, J.W. Sanders (Eds.), Communicating Sequential Processes. XIV, 321 pages. 2005.

Vol. 3524: R. Barták, M. Milano (Eds.), Integration of AI and OR Techniques in Constraint Programming for Combinatorial Optimization Problems. XI, 320 pages. 2005.

Vol. 3523: J.S. Marques, N. Pérez de la Blanca, P. Pina (Eds.), Pattern Recognition and Image Analysis, Part II. XXVI, 733 pages. 2005.

Vol. 3522: J.S. Marques, N. Pérez de la Blanca, P. Pina (Eds.), Pattern Recognition and Image Analysis, Part I. XXVI, 703 pages. 2005.

Vol. 3521: N. Megiddo, Y. Xu, B. Zhu (Eds.), Algorithmic Applications in Management. XIII, 484 pages. 2005.

Vol. 3520: O. Pastor, J. Falcão e Cunha (Eds.), Advanced Information Systems Engineering. XVI, 584 pages. 2005.

Vol. 3519: H. Li, P. J. Olver, G. Sommer (Eds.), Computer Algebra and Geometric Algebra with Applications. IX, 449 pages. 2005.

Vol. 3518: T.B. Ho, D. Cheung, H. Liu (Eds.), Advances in Knowledge Discovery and Data Mining. XXI, 864 pages. 2005. (Subseries LNAI).

Vol. 3517: H.S. Baird, D.P. Lopresti (Eds.), Human Interactive Proofs. IX, 143 pages. 2005.

Vol. 3516: V.S. Sunderam, G.D.v. Albada, P.M.A. Sloot, J.J. Dongarra (Eds.), Computational Science – ICCS 2005, Part III. LXIII, 1143 pages. 2005.

Vol. 3515: V.S. Sunderam, G.D.v. Albada, P.M.A. Sloot, J.J. Dongarra (Eds.), Computational Science – ICCS 2005, Part II. LXIII, 1101 pages. 2005.

Vol. 3514: V.S. Sunderam, G.D.v. Albada, P.M.A. Sloot, J.J. Dongarra (Eds.), Computational Science – ICCS 2005, Part I. LXIII, 1089 pages. 2005.

Vol. 3513: A. Montoyo, R. Muñoz, E. Métais (Eds.), Natural Language Processing and Information Systems. XII, 408 pages. 2005.

Vol. 3512: J. Cabestany, A. Prieto, F. Sandoval (Eds.), Computational Intelligence and Bioinspired Systems. XXV, 1260 pages. 2005.

Vol. 3511: U.K. Wiil (Ed.), Metainformatics. VIII, 221 pages. 2005.

Vol. 3510: T. Braun, G. Carle, Y. Koucheryavy, V. Tsaousidis (Eds.), Wired/Wireless Internet Communications. XIV, 366 pages. 2005.

Vol. 3509: M. Jünger, V. Kaibel (Eds.), Integer Programming and Combinatorial Optimization. XI, 484 pages. 2005.

Vol. 3508: P. Bresciani, P. Giorgini, B. Henderson-Sellers, G. Low, M. Winikoff (Eds.), Agent-Oriented Information Systems II. X, 227 pages. 2005. (Subseries LNAI).

Vol. 3507: F. Crestani, I. Ruthven (Eds.), Information Context: Nature, Impact, and Role. XIII, 253 pages. 2005.

Vol. 3506: C. Park, S. Chee (Eds.), Information Security and Cryptology – ICISC 2004. XIV, 490 pages. 2005.

Vol. 3505: V. Gorodetsky, J. Liu, V. A. Skormin (Eds.), Autonomous Intelligent Systems: Agents and Data Mining. XIII, 303 pages. 2005. (Subseries LNAI).

Vol. 3504: A.F. Frangi, P.I. Radeva, A. Santos, M. Hernandez (Eds.), Functional Imaging and Modeling of the Heart. XV, 489 pages. 2005.

Vol. 3503: S.E. Nikoletseas (Ed.), Experimental and Efficient Algorithms. XV, 624 pages. 2005.

Vol. 3502: F. Khendek, R. Dssouli (Eds.), Testing of Communicating Systems. X, 381 pages. 2005.

Vol. 3501: B. Kégl, G. Lapalme (Eds.), Advances in Artificial Intelligence. XV, 458 pages. 2005. (Subseries LNAI).

Vol. 3500: S. Miyano, J. Mesirov, S. Kasif, S. Istrail, P. Pevzner, M. Waterman (Eds.), Research in Computational Molecular Biology. XVII, 632 pages. 2005. (Subseries LNBI).

Vol. 3499: A. Pelc, M. Raynal (Eds.), Structural Information and Communication Complexity. X, 323 pages. 2005.

Vol. 3498: J. Wang, X. Liao, Z. Yi (Eds.), Advances in Neural Networks – ISNN 2005, Part III. XLIX, 1077 pages. 2005.

Vol. 3497: J. Wang, X. Liao, Z. Yi (Eds.), Advances in Neural Networks – ISNN 2005, Part II. XLIX, 947 pages. 2005.

Vol. 3496: J. Wang, X. Liao, Z. Yi (Eds.), Advances in Neural Networks – ISNN 2005, Part II. L, 1055 pages. 2005.

Vol. 3495: P. Kantor, G. Muresan, F. Roberts, D.D. Zeng, F.-Y. Wang, H. Chen, R.C. Merkle (Eds.), Intelligence and Security Informatics. XVIII, 674 pages. 2005.

Vol. 3494: R. Cramer (Ed.), Advances in Cryptology – EUROCRYPT 2005. XIV, 576 pages. 2005.

Vol. 3493: N. Fuhr, M. Lalmas, S. Malik, Z. Szlávik (Eds.), Advances in XML Information Retrieval. XI, 438 pages. 2005.